Stories in Red and Black

Stories in Red

and Black

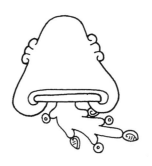

Pictorial Histories of the

Aztecs and Mixtecs

Elizabeth Hill Boone

University of Texas Press, Austin

First edition, 2000

Requests for permission to reproduce material from this work
should be sent to Permissions, University of Texas Press, Box 7819,
Austin, TX 78713-7819.

♾ The paper used in this book meets the minimum requirements of
ANSI/NISO Z39.48-1992 (R1997) (Permanence of Paper).

Library of Congress Cataloging-in-Publication Data

Boone, Elizabeth Hill.
Stories in red and black : pictorial histories of the Aztecs and Mixtecs
/ Elizabeth Hill Boone. — 1st ed.
    p. cm.
Includes bibliographical references and index.
ISBN 0-292-70876-9 (hardcover : alk. paper)
1. Manuscripts, Nahuatl.   2. Aztec painting.   3. Nahuatl lan-
guage—Writing. 4. Manuscripts, Mixtec. 5. Mixtec art. 6. Mixtec
language—Writing. I. Title.
F1219.54.A98 B66 2000
972'.01—ddc21   99-6214

Publication of this book has been aided by a grant from the Millard
Meiss Publication Fund of the College Art Association.

In tlili in tlapalli, the black, the red,
these are
the writings, the paintings, the books, knowledge.

Nahuatl metaphor, adapted from Sahagún, bk. 10, ch. 29

Contents

Illustrations

Figures

Tables

Preface

The study of Mesoamerican manuscript painting has come into its own as a field of investigation in recent years. More scholars than ever before are focusing on the Mexican codices: they are reanalyzing and reinterpreting already published works, editing and publishing other pictorials in facsimile for the first time, and seeking out manuscripts that still have remained beyond scholarly attention. The *Guide to Ethnohistorical Sources of the Handbook of Middle American Indians* (vols. 12–15) has given us basic bibliographic control of the corpus (at least up to 1970). Art historians, anthropologists, historians, and linguists are bringing their special perspectives to bear on the codices, which are increasingly being contextualized and linked back to the concerns of the individuals and communities that created them. These scholars, more and more, are tying their manuscript studies to other concerns in the humanities and social sciences, so manuscript studies are having an impact on such issues as kingship and rule, writing and cross-cultural communication, syncretism and acculturation, native agency and resistance, just to name a few. It is a good time to be a Mexican manuscript specialist.

Still, the field of manuscript studies has been a hard one for the nonspecialist to enter. The greatest need has been for an overview of the Mesoamerican manuscript tradition, one that clearly outlines the structure and explains the nature of this corpus. The present study is intended to help fill this lacuna by providing an overview of the pictorial histories of central and southern Mexico. It grew out of a larger project to review the entire tradition when it became clear that the larger project was best undertaken in stages.

This work has benefited from fellowships in residence at the Institute for Advanced Study in Princeton in 1986–1987 and at the Center for Advanced Study in the Visual Arts in 1993–1994. I am grateful to these institutions for the opportunity to concentrate on the pictorial codices without interruptions, and to Dumbarton Oaks for the research leaves that made these periods of concentration possible. Irving Lavin, Marilyn Lavin, and John Elliott at the Institute for Advanced Study, Henry Millon and Teresa May at the CASVA, and Angeliki Laiou and Henry McGuire at Dumbarton Oaks provided good counsel and criticism.

This study began while I was at Dumbarton Oaks and came with me to Tulane University. A roundtable entitled "Art and Writing: Recording Knowledge in Pre-Columbian America" at Dumbarton Oaks in 1991 culminated a year's thought and discussion about the way pre-Columbian societies recorded and preserved information. That roundtable culminated in an edited volume with Walter Mignolo, *Writing without Words: Alternative Literacies in Mesoamerica and the Andes* (1994), where I outlined my general approach to Mexican pictography and the pictorial histories. At Tulane University, seminars on Mesoamerican manuscript painting challenged me in other ways and drew in the probing questions and comments of a dynamic cohort of graduate students, including William Barnes, Lori Boornazian Diel, Nicholas Johnson, Bryan Just, Christopher Nichols, Susan Spitler, Dan Stauber, and Alison Stern. Among the many colleagues who helped shape this study by their insight-inducing conversations and questionings, I want to thank Anthony Aveni, Bruce Byland, Davíd Carrasco, Susan Evans, Jill Furst, Robert Haskett, Frances Hayashida, Cecelia Klein, Viola König, Joyce Marcus, Walter Mignolo, John Monaghan, Barbara Mundy, John Pohl, Jeanette Sherbondy, Barbara Tedlock, Dennis Tedlock, Emily Umberger, Gary Urton, and Stephanie Wood. I am particularly grateful to Victoria Bricker, Stephen Houston, Nicholas Johnson, Dana Leibsohn, Ross Parmenter, and Mary Elizabeth Smith, who read and commented on all or part of the present work. Although I did not always follow their good advice, this book has benefited greatly from their suggestions.

Librarians and curators in Mexico, Europe, and the United States have generously allowed me access to the original codices they keep and have facilitated photographic requests. I want to thank Barbara Conklin formerly of the American Museum of Natural History, Laura Gutierrez-Witt and Michael Hironymous of the Benson Latin American Collection of the University of Texas at Austin, Consuelo Méndez Tamargo of the Biblioteca del Museo Nacional de Antropología in Mexico, Monique Cohen of the Bibliothèque Nationale in Paris, Bruce Barker-Benfield and Mary Clapinson of the Bodleian Library, Elisabeth Carmichael formerly of the British Museum, Diana Fane of the Brooklyn Museum, Marie Gaida of the Museum für Völkerkunde in Berlin, Angela Raljic and Arni Brownstone of the Royal Ontario Museum, and Guillermo Nañez of the Latin American Library of Tulane University. In 1983 Carmen Aguilera generously helped me acquire a number of study photographs from the Biblioteca del Museo Nacional de Antropología in Mexico. Funds from the Martha and Donald Robertson Chair in Latin American Art, the Roger Thayer Stone Center for Latin American Studies, the Graduate School, and the Art History Discretionary Fund at Tulane helped with expenses for research, the illustrations, and the index. For the index itself, my thanks go to Bryan Just. At the University of Texas Press, I am grateful for Theresa May's early and ongoing enthusiasm for the book, for Carolyn Wylie's and Alison Tartt's fine editorial sense, and for Heidi Haeuser's good design. A grant from the Millard Meiss Publication Fund of the College Art Association helped defray the production costs of the illustrations.

Mary Elizabeth Smith, by the example of her fine scholarship and her selflessness in the pursuit of knowledge and fun fiction, has been a continued support. John Verano, by virtue of his different scholarly tract and exquisite wit, added the counterweights that kept the project in balance.

Elizabeth Hill Boone

Stories in Red and Black

Configuring the Past

In December 1539, Don Baltasar, hereditary lord of indigenous Culhuacan, found himself under investigation by the Holy Office of the Inquisition; the charge was idolatry. The Inquisition was not old in Mexico; Bishop Juan de Zumárraga had instituted the Holy Office only two and a half years earlier, but the bishop was determined to root out the remaining pockets of native religious practice and to hunt down any idols that had not yet been found and destroyed. From the beginning, Zumárraga had been tracking the principal cult statues removed from the Templo Mayor in Tenochtitlan just before the Spaniards burned the temple in 1520, but he had had little success in actually finding the statues. Now he had information that these very idols had been brought there to Culhuacan in the southern lake area. This drew him to the ancient and venerated city of Culhuacan, where the distinguished royal bloodline ran fully back to the Toltecs.

A local manuscript painter had accused the lord Baltasar of hiding the statues in caves years before. The painter testified that he had once painted a history and genealogy of Don Baltasar's family that showed the cave from which the ruler's ancestors and the community's gods had emerged; he said the idols had been hidden in that cave. Thus confronted, Don Baltasar, already baptized as a Christian and fearful of the Inquisi-

tion's judgment, confessed that the son of the emperor Moctezuma had brought the statues to Culhuacan sixteen years earlier (in 1523) and had personally overseen their sequestering. By denying any active involvement, Don Baltasar thus distanced himself, to the extent that he could, from the act of hiding the idols, and he further offered information on other caves and sacrificial sites. No other charges were leveled against the Culhua ruler, and the matter seems then to have been dropped (Procesos 1912: 177–184; Robertson 1959: 35; Greenleaf 1962: 64).

This little story, no more than a vignette, brings us to the heart of my enterprise. It locates us in Central Mexico a generation after the "Spanish conquest" of 1519–1521. The conquest—a Spanish invasion that touched off an indigenous revolution—has destroyed the Triple Alliance empire of the Aztecs and has shifted control of most of Mexico from Aztec to Spanish hands. Some indigenous lords, especially those who had allied themselves with Hernán Cortés against their overlords in Tenochtitlan, still continue to rule their community kingdoms, but their tribute and service now go to the Spaniards. Spanish laws and Spanish administrators govern at the top. The conquered people are Christians by this time and thus have officially discarded their painted religious books, but they still keep their painted histories. The histories have remained crucial records of the past, valuable locally for preserving the towns' and rulers' stories and important even in Spanish courts when documentation about the past is needed.

The painted history referred to in the accusation against Don Baltasar has not survived. Others have, however, and from them we can infer some of its characteristics. As a painting that showed the emergence of the town deities and ancestors from a cave, it most likely belonged to the genre of migration history. It would thus have traced the story of the community kingdom from its beginnings when the gods and first lords emerged from Chicomoztoc (Seven Caves), the legendary place of origin for many Aztecs. Then it would have traced the people's migration to Culhuacan and presented the establishment and territorial consolidation of the polity. It may have been visually organized as an annals history like the Codex Mexicanus (Figs. 142–143), or a map-based cartographic history like Cuauhtinchan Map 2 (Fig. 111), or a mixed genre like the Selden Roll (Fig. 88), all of which tell similar stories about their polities. The lost Culhuacan document also included a genealogy that carried the ruling family up to the present time and certified that the line of hereditary succession was unbroken.

The manuscript was just one of many indigenous histories painted on the edges of the conquest, executed in the traditional graphic style and, if painted after the Spaniards had arrived, perhaps also incorporating European elements and postconquest events and people. Indigenous leaders who commissioned and relied on these pictorial histories considered them just as valid and truthful after the conquest as before; and the Spanish authorities were quick to recognize the native histories as admissible evidence. Don Baltasar's painted history became an item in the accusation against him, but nowhere in the proceedings was he or the painter faulted for having commissioned or painted it.

This was not the only kind of history that existed. Different patrons and situations called for different stories. The archives of community kingdoms held a variety: some perhaps stressing supernatural origins, others focusing on long migrations, and others detailing events that affected the polity after it was established. Some focused more on the polity than on the family of the ruling dynasty, whereas others were predominantly genealogical. They came, too, in different shapes and made of various materials.

Every one of them was created for a reason or set of reasons, but they were undoubtedly then called up, read, and interpreted at various times over the years for other purposes. The events they recorded and the stories they contained came to figure in other stories. The origin history painted for Don Baltasar, for example, served Culhuacan as a deep well from which community memory and solidarity could be drawn. Perhaps it was painted on the occasion of Don Baltasar's father's death when royal succession and the family's right to rule may have been an issue, and then later it functioned cartographically to point the way to sacred caves where idols might have been hidden. Like so many painted histories from Aztec Mexico, it never had just one purpose or a single situational context.

The story about Don Baltasar, Bishop Zumárraga, the painter, and his painting also embodies broader lessons about history and about art. Much of what it tells us about sixteenth-century Mexican histories is true for all histories. They exist in multiples: they tell different stories, from multiple points of view, and for a range of purposes. As the time and location, and thus the context, of their reading change, so do the messages they give. They may preserve a particular view, which was held by an individual at the one moment the history was painted or written (and it may later be possible to recover most of that view), but they equally hold other views, ones given them, read into them, drawn out of them by later interpreters. We should recognize that these later views are no less valid and may become even more important than that first one. Elements in the stories, or even the stories in their entirety, intersect with other stories. Cumulatively, all the histories join in an intricate and dense network of stories about the past, so that, ultimately, none of the histories can be fully cut from the others.

The place of Don Baltasar's painting in the history of art and in studies of visual communication is at that point where stories are told pictorially. At this juncture, studies of narrative, questions of graphic notation, and visual language coincide. Static works of visual art easily present things (places, persons, objects), but they do not so easily present movement or the passage of time. All stories have a temporal mode, however, and it is incumbent on a history painter to overcome the difficulties of representing action and time. The Mexican painters, trained in the art for centuries, show us how they accomplished this; we see it in their pictorial histories, those that were not lost or destroyed.

My concerns in this present study are these: What are the stories? How are they told? To this pair of questions should be added the most difficult: Why is this so? Hundreds of pictorial histories, painted in the native tradition, have come down to us from pre-Columbian and early colonial Mexico. In this book I focus on the narrative content of the histories (the kinds of stories they tell) and on how the painters have structured these stories (the manner of the telling), not that these two parts of the investigation can easily be pulled apart from each other. Fundamental to any explanation of the different genres of stories and the ways they are structured is an explanation of the reasons these stories were recorded in the first place and by whom, and then the reasons they were presented in the ways they were.

This approach to the pictorial histories, of course, means that other approaches are forgone. Although most of the manuscripts under discussion date from the colonial period, they are considered here as indigenous documents rather than as particularly colonial products; my focus is on the native tradition of history painting and its continuation after the conquest rather than on the place of these histories in a distinctly colonial discourse. Too, painting style is little treated. It is not that questions of pre-Columbian painting styles and their early colonial hybrids are unimportant; the contrary is true. Much has already been written about the stylistic aspects of Mexican manuscript painting both before and after the conquest,[1] and much more remains to be said. It is only that a single volume cannot treat everything fully. All histories, and this one is no exception, have their own purpose and point of view; all highlight and omit. This volume looks broadly at Don Baltasar's and other painted histories in order to understand the nature of history painting in indigenous Mexico before and after the Spanish conquest.

People with History, People with Writing

A fundamental concern, explored in Chapter 2, is with native understandings of history and the uses to which histories were put by leaders, families, and communities in Mexico. This also includes an explanation of the status and role of the historian and scribe, who were often (but not always) the same individual. In Chapter 3, I take up the issue of Mexican pictography to explain the vocabulary and grammar of the pictorial writing system they used. In these respects, my study participates in long-standing and ongoing discussions about Mesoamerican historiography and writing.

There have always been those—historians and anthropologists alike—who deny historicity to pre-Columbian cultures, who have argued that the painted records are not history in the "proper" or "true" sense. As early as the sixteenth century, such arguments were surrounded by and integrated into the larger debates about the intelligence and humanity of the Mexicans and other American peoples—whether the Amerindians were rational and civilized. A historical consciousness, exemplified by a historiographic tradition, was an important element in this discussion. Writing was another crucial element, one so closely related to the issue of history that writing and history became conceptually braided together by those who understood history to be written history.

Some of the first Europeans to write about Amerindian peoples mention, with some sense of excitement, that the people had books. Peter Martyr, the Italian humanist and friend of the Spanish crown who from 1493 to 1525 published a running account of Spain's adventures in America, tells in 1516 of a Panamanian native who jumped for joy to see a Spaniard reading a book and who wondered how it was that the Spaniards also had books and writing. Peter Martyr's point was that the Americans had books just as the Spanish did,[2] even though Mexico, with its strong tradition of manuscript painting, had not yet come to Spanish attention. When it did, the Mexican codices were immediately a focus of interest. Cortés and other conquering soldiers spoke highly of the secular pictorials they encountered, remarking on the reliability of indigenous maps and the accuracy of other documents.

Cortés even sent two codices back to Charles V, after which they were circulated through Europe. The Franciscan friar Motolinía (1951: 74) immediately recognized the pictorials as books. Writing to his Spanish patron in 1541, he listed the different genres of Aztec books and said he prized their books of history because they recounted the truth. Diego Durán, Bernardino de Sahagún, and other mendicant friars in Mexico who were actively interested in recording the Aztec past knew the Aztecs to have books, because they themselves collected them when possible and relied on them in writing their own histories.

At this same time, however, there were others who denied the Aztecs history because they denied the Aztecs writing. Pedro de Gante, one of the first Franciscan missionaries in Mexico (he arrived in 1524), wrote to Philip II in 1558 that the Aztecs were a "people without writing, without letters, without written characters and without any kind of enlightenment."[3] Juan Ginés de Sepúlveda, who sought to justify the enslavement of the Amerindians by denying them intelligence, said that the Mexicans not only lacked culture but "do not even know how to write" (Hanke 1974: 85; Root 1988: 209). In this view, writing was as much a necessity for civilization as it was for history. Juan de Torquemada clearly tied history to alphabetic writing, and, seeing the Aztecs lacking in one, he proclaimed them lacking in the other. In his *Monarquía indiana* he indicated that "just as the inhabitants did not have letters, or were even familiar with them, so they neither left records of their history."[4] José de Acosta, too, found it difficult to believe that history could be produced without alphabetic writing. In the debate over Amerindian intellectual consciousness, he argued strongly for the intelligence and rationality of the Mexicans, but as he wrote his kinsman Juan de Tovar, he still did not understand how the Mexicans could have histories if they did not have writing.[5]

This denial of a Mexican historiographical tradition was seated in the deep conviction that history could not be written without alphabetic writing, which the Mexicans clearly lacked. As Walter Mignolo has persuasively argued, the denial of history was grounded in Renaissance ideas about letters and about history.[6] European intellectuals and men of letters understood writing to have reached its evolutionary pinnacle in the alphabet, and they believed (alphabetic) writing to have

been a major factor in what they saw as the political and social supremacy of the West: writing was a complement and agent of advanced civilization. Accompanying this was the understanding, rooted in the legacy of Greek and Roman historians who set down their narratives alphabetically, that alphabetic writing was the only means by which memory could be preserved accurately. As Mignolo (1995b: 96) has pointed out, these views resulted in "a powerful complicity between the power of the letter and the authority of history," which together conspired to deny history to the Mexicans.

With respect particularly to the Aztecs and their neighbors, the view that they lacked writing continues today. Students of writing and literacy, from Isaac Taylor (1899), Ignace Gelb (1963), and David Diringer (1962) to Walter Ong (1967, 1982) and Jack Goody (1982, 1986, 1987), expound the view—which has now become common—that writing exists to record speech and that it has been developing over thousands of years in a trajectory of progress that culminates in alphabetic script. Not one of these specialists in writing or literacy would consider the Aztecs to have had writing in what has been defined as its fullest sense. Instead, the Mexican pictorial systems either lie at the beginning of the sequence or they fall outside of it, but they are not equivalent to alphabetic systems.

Among Americanists, the views about writing have been divided, and the separation often depends largely on whether the scholar works on the Aztec and Mixtec cultures or on the ancient Maya. The Mayanists, who study people who had a logographic, language-based system of discrete hieroglyphic texts, tend to define writing as recorded language; they include Maya hieroglyphic writing within their definitions of writing, but they generally exclude the Aztec and Mixtec systems (e.g., Lounsbury 1989: 203; Coe 1992: 13). Central Mexican specialists, as might be expected, draw the line around "writing" somewhat wider so that they can include the Mexican pictorial texts. But we have still tied the definition, if tenuously, to language (Dibble 1971; Smith 1973a: 7; Marcus 1992: 17, 61). Recently I have argued for a broader, expanded definition of writing that would include not only the pictorials of Mexico but the knotted cords of Peru and Bolivia (Boone 1994b), and I take up this issue again in Chapter 3.

The sixteenth-century European view that Mexicans lacked true history also continues to this day. Eighteenth-century writers such as the Comte de Buffon and Cornelius de Pauw, followed by late-nineteenth-century historians such as Lewis Morgan and Adolph Bandelier, debased pre-Columbian cultural achievements in Mexico, denying the Aztecs a high level of social and political organization, among other features of so-called civilized societies (Keen 1971: 249–251, 260–268, 380–398). Early students of Aztec pictorial codices, such as Paul Radin (1920: 132), argued for the authenticity of the painted histories and the historiographical corpus precisely in response to such attacks.

These responses were only partially successful, however. To most people, history remains alphabetically written history, and people who lack letters are "prehistoric" or "a-historic." One sees this distinction in the traditional separation between the disciplines of anthropology and history, whereby anthropologists study unlettered people, primitives without history, while historians study lettered people with history. This distinction is reflected in Eric Wolf's masterful study that unifies humankind and human history during the Renaissance. Under the title *Europe and the People without History,* he brings "the populations anthropologists have called 'primitives,'" including the Aztecs, into the stream of European history. He recognizes that the process set in motion by the expansion of Europe during the Renaissance was part of their histories as well (Wolf 1982: 3–4, 385). Thus, the history he writes for "the so-called primitives, people 'without history,'" begins after these people were touched by Europe and embraced by the expanding horizon of European discourse. Efforts to link Aztec history and European history after the conquest have almost always subsumed the Aztecs to Europe.

Two books on the conquest of Mexico, by Tzvetan Todorov and Hugh Thomas, exemplify the suppression of indigenous Aztec historiography in different ways. They both circumvent the Aztec pictorial sources. Todorov, in *The Conquest of America* (1984), constructs the Aztecs as an exotic and savage Other, which failed to recognize the difference that made itself felt in Mexico as conquering Europe. Although he purports to represent the Aztecs' point of view, Todorov (1984: 80–81) denies the Aztecs writing and history

and draws on the pictorials only for decontextualized illustrations for his text. He sees the Aztecs as having been defeated by signs, by the superior rhetorical and symbolic systems of their conquerors. In wrapping the Aztecs in the mantle of "otherness," Todorov defines them according to their cultural and symbolic inadequacy vis-à-vis the Europeans. Thus his book stands as another discursive conquest of Mexico. In contrast, Hugh Thomas's *Conquest* (1995) stands fully in the tradition of Prescott as a narrative of the battles and personal intrigues between Cortés, Moctezuma, and their followers, drawn largely from Spanish sources. Although Thomas uses a range of indigenous sources as well, he subsumes the Aztec story to the Spanish one. These books both function to silence the Aztecs. Not only are the Aztec pictorial histories absent from these presentations of the conquest, but the alphabetic texts in Nahuatl, with their Aztec voices, are either missing or overwhelmed by the Spanish documentation.[7] By privileging European texts and perspectives, they belong to the historical and critical literature that helps form modern (and postmodern) Western discourse about Others.

The Pictorials in Colonial Discourse

On the other side of the discursive divide (and, in most cases, on the other side of the Atlantic as well) are those scholars whose life's work has been precisely to recover the Aztec voice, as it was heard both before and after the conquest. Based in a philological tradition that began with the early Franciscans—Andrés de Olmos, Motolinía, Alonso de Molina, Bernardino de Sahagún, and their colleagues—Nahuatlatos have worked with the alphabetically recorded Nahuatl texts to capture Aztec history and understanding. One focus, represented by Miguel León-Portilla and his mentor, Father Angel María Garibay, as well as by Alfredo López Austin, has been on the major songs, poems, and histories of the Aztec elite, with the purpose of recovering Aztec philosophy, religion, and literature. Another focus, represented by James Lockhart and his students, has concentrated not on the religious and historical texts of the metropolis but on mundane texts from smaller polities in order to understand the everyday business of colonial Aztec life. These two foci remain separate, but distinctions between the pre-Columbian and postconquest Aztecs are beginning to blur, largely because both groups of Nahuatlatos are working with colonial documents. Too, both groups are beginning to participate in, or are finding themselves pulled into, wider discussions of colonial culture and colonial discourse.

Somehow, however, the pictorial documents have not been a significant part of these discussions. This may be due to the tendency among Nahuatl specialists to see the pictorials as mnemonic devices that trigger oral recitations of learned texts (Klor de Alva 1989: 150), and if one has the Nahuatl texts, one might argue that one does not need the pictorial trigger. Language, and in this case it is alphabetically written language, is seen as the fundamental, telling cultural element. Additionally, when Aztec writing is discussed, it tends to be in terms of name- and place-glyphs (Dibble 1971; Nicholson 1973; Marcus 1992: 46–57; Lockhart 1992: 326–373). Of the pre- and postconquest Aztec scholars, León-Portilla and López Austin perhaps move the most freely between alphabetic and pictorial worlds.

It is natural and sensible for historians to rely principally on alphabetic texts for their histories, but it does leave some telling gaps. I was struck, for example, by the shifts in the narrative of Enrique Florescano's *Memory, Myth, and Time in Mexico,* an important and insightful discussion of historical thought in Mexico from the Aztecs to Independence. Florescano relied on the pictorial codices when he discussed pre-Columbian history, but with the arrival of the Spaniards he shifted entirely to Spanish texts and Sahagún for the conquest and colonization. When he returned later to the Nahuatl perspective, his points of reference were the Nahuatl-language primordial titles and painted Techialoyan codices in the late seventeenth and eighteenth centuries. He bypassed the sixteenth- and seventeenth-century mestizo historians because he rightly saw them as writing within the Spanish historiographic tradition (Florescano 1994: 120), and he was silent on the colonial pictorials. For Florescano, as for most of us, the pictorial histories have not existed conceptually as colonial records; they have not been part of colonial historiography.

Some of us—in a line that runs from Joseph M. A. Aubin in the nineteenth century to Paul Rabin (1920), H. B. Nicholson (1971), Joyce Marcus (1992), and me

(Boone 1994a)—have analyzed the pictorials as histories, but we have held them to a pre-Columbian frame. Until very recently, no one except Donald Robertson (1959), who stressed painting style, has looked at the colonial nature of most of the Aztec pictorials. This is changing and will, I hope, continue to change. The last half dozen years have seen a growing interest in the pictorials as colonial products. Walter Mignolo, in particular, has focused on the pictorial tradition in Mexico as an alternative semiotic system that confronted and ultimately succumbed to the book and the letter of the West.[8] Dana Leibsohn (1993, 1994, 1995, 1996) has analyzed pictorial/alphabetic juxtaposition in painted manuscripts from Cuauhtinchan to explain how these documents continued successfully in the colonial era to configure Cuauhtinchan identity. Barbara Mundy (1996) has concentrated on the differential blending of European and indigenous traditions in the *Relación geográfica* maps. Focusing not on the Aztecs but on the Mixtecs, Mary Elizabeth Smith (1963, 1966, 1973a, 1994, 1998; Smith and Parmenter 1991) has long considered the colonial nature of extant Mixtec screenfolds and lienzos, in studies that adroitly reveal the evidence for their use and importance in colonial Mixtec society. More studies like these are needed to introduce the pictorials into the salon of colonial discourse.

Meanwhile, those specialists who concentrate on translating and using Nahuatl (alphabetic) texts are finding themselves under fire from those who argue that these "authentic voices" are distorted by colonial transcription. Enrique Florescano, Jorge Klor de Alva, and Walter Mignolo have all argued that the act of transcribing the oral speeches and the painted manuscripts was an inherently colonial act.[9] It denied the viability of Aztec historiography—their long-held habits of writing and speaking about the past—and replaced it with a history that belonged to the European historiographic tradition. It separated the original, painted text from its oral interpretation, a process that robbed the text of its multiple significance and interpretive richness (Florescano 1994: 122). It reduced the multivalency of the images to a single interpretation, which, as the sole reading, became the only authentic one. As Florescano (1994: 123) puts it, "This conversion of the ancient Indian ideograms into written letters signals,

then, a crucial moment in the history of the acculturation and domination of the American peoples. Before
these ideograms were transferred to the European alphabet, their reading was another, indigenous; but as
soon as they were transferred to the new alphabet and
transformed into texts with a univocal meaning and explanation, they acquired the categories and values of
western culture. This fact demonstrates another poorly
studied phase of the drama of the Conquest: not only
is the history of the conquered written by the conqueror, but the conquered's own historical tradition is
first suppressed and then expropriated by the conqueror, who converts it into a reading that only the victor can carry out."

The message of Florescano, Klor de Alva, and Mignolo is that all alphabetic texts are at least one step removed from the indigenous act of speaking or painting. They may also have within them European devices
and structures that must be noticed and taken into consideration, but that is an additional issue. The point
these scholars make is that even the "purest" Nahuatl
text is radically transformed by becoming alphabetic.

León-Portilla as been one of the first to respond to
this challenge. From his position as a translator of ancient Nahuatl, in a 1992 article he presents the evidence
we have for Mesoamerican historiographic traditions
and then compares several extant versions (alphabetic
and pictorial both) of an indigenous text to show how
"an authentic thread of the Mesoamerican cultural
weaving" can be reached (León-Portilla 1992b). His
judgment is that, rigorously done, the ancient indigenous word *can* be reached through the alphabetic texts.

In his comparison of Nahuatl texts, León-Portilla
introduces a pictorial codex, which represents the
paintings, or the kinds of paintings, that gave rise to
the Nahuatl readings. My sense is that we should be
doing much more of this. Our appreciation of Mexican
historiography would be much richer if we were to
look more directly at the existing pictorial histories.
Equally, our understanding of Aztec life after the arrival of the Spanish would be truer if we were to draw
the pictorials more fully into our approaches to colonial history and colonial discourse. In the sixteenth
century, while all the debates raged about the intelligence, rationality, and historicity of the Amerindians,
Aztecs (individuals and towns) continued to have their
histories painted. These histories had not yet been read

that one final time and hardened into an alphabetic
transcription; they were still flexible and amendable.
And they still represented and documented the past for
those who needed such records.

Foundations for Understanding the Painted Histories

We have been moving closer to an understanding of
the Mexican pictorial histories at least since the mid-
nineteenth century, when scholars and intellectuals on
both sides of the Atlantic began to recognize the value
of the codices as historical sources and to publish
them.[10] Nine painted histories were among the codices
reproduced as color lithographs in the first three vol-
umes of Lord Kingsborough's massive *Antiquities of
Mexico*. Although Kingsborough did not comment on
them extensively or explain their nature, his 1831–1848
publication directed international attention to the
Mexican pictorials. Its excessively lavish production
may also have sharpened the interest of the French
Mexicanist Joseph M. A. Aubin, who began in 1849 to
publish serious studies of pictorials he had collected in
Mexico. Aubin's were the first scholarly attempts to
interpret the Mexican historical codices, followed by
those of his Mexican colleague José Fernando Ramírez
(Glass 1975b: 23; Cline 1973: 374–377). The Columbian
Quatrocentennial of 1892 then provided an impetus
for Mexico to publish two groups of facsimiles. As the
nineteenth century closed and the twentieth opened,
facsimiles of a half dozen other histories appeared
with commentaries by Alfredo Chavero, Franz Ehrle,
Ernest T. Hamy, Zelia Nuttall, Francisco del Paso y
Troncoso, and Antonio Peñafiel.[11] The turn of the century was a time of intense study and publication of
Mexican histories.

As the twentieth century progressed, scholars continued to publish more historical codices. William
Gates issued large-scale line drawings of several cartographic histories. Ernst Mengin, Konrad Preus, Walter
Lehmann, and James Cooper Clark published important commentaries of major pictorial histories, accompanied now by photographic facsimiles. At the middle
of the century and later, much of the work on the
painted histories came from three individuals: Alfonso

Caso, Robert Barlow, and Charles Dibble. Caso's commentaries on many of the Mixtec screenfolds and lienzos made him the father of Mixtec manuscript studies. Barlow and Dibble brought equal erudition to the Central Mexican histories, with commentaries that have not been surpassed.[12]

The second half of the century saw a surge in the number of photographic facsimiles and commentaries. Notable among these are José Corona Núñez's four-volume reissue of Kingsborough's *Antiquities of Mexico* (1964–1967), the three Mixtec screenfolds published in facsimile by the Sociedad Mexicana de Antropología with commentaries by Alfonso Caso, and the series of facsimiles published by the Akademische Druck- und Verlagsanstalt. It is hard to overestimate the importance of the Akademische series, with its superb color photography and physical replication of the codices; although the facsimiles are accompanied not by commentaries but by brief discussions of the manuscripts' history and physical properties, they allow one to understand the codex as an object and to see the details of its production. In addition to these, about two dozen other reproductions were published between 1970 and 2000. A new series of facsimiles begun in 1992 as a joint venture between the Akademische Druck- und Verlagsanstalt and the Fondo de Cultura Económica has made the codices both more accessible and affordable. The result of all this productivity, this century and a half of scholarly work on the pictorial histories, is that most of the principal manuscripts are published, some exceedingly well or in multiple editions. A great many of the lesser histories have also been individually reproduced and discussed. Together they create a dense foundation for studying the corpus of pictorial histories. In the present study, I have relied largely on photographs and published facsimiles, although I have also consulted or made detailed studies of many originals, especially those from the Aztec realm.

Predecessors in Synthesizing the Histories

Paul Radin, in 1920, was the first to take up the task of categorizing and assessing the veracity of the Central Mexican pictorial histories. Responding to the charge that the Aztecs were "primitive" peoples who lacked "a highly developed historical sense," Radin (1920: 4) reviewed the major Aztec pictorial histories to prove that the Aztecs did indeed possess authentic histories. In so doing, he offered a still-useful model for understanding the pictorials. Radin distinguished, first, between primary sources (pictorials painted in the native tradition), primary sources preserved only as alphabetic readings (such as the Historia de los Mexicanos por sus Pinturas), and secondary sources (chronicles written either by Spaniards or mestizos that relied on older pictorials). Then among the primary sources he further distinguished between accounts of the Aztec migration period, accounts of the postmigration or imperial period, and those that covered both. His is a neat, extremely helpful classification based on the fundamentally pictorial or alphabetic nature of the sources and then on their general content.

It was not history but painting style that principally concerned Donald Robertson when he looked at the pictorial histories in 1959. His pioneering study of early colonial manuscript painting from the Valley of Mexico considered the many genres of manuscripts, from cadastrals to calendar wheels, and assessed them in a traditionally art historical way as products of distinct schools of painting and patronage. His focus was thus on the manuscripts' geographic provenance, on the styles of painting, and on the relative adoption of European influence. In his discussion of codices from Mexico City, however, he took up the question of pictorial histories and grouped them not according to their content but according to their organizational principles, which he called "styles" (Robertson 1959: 62–65). He divided the histories into three types: "time-oriented" histories like annals, where "history is a series of events ordered according to time"; "place-oriented" histories organized around geography; and "event-oriented" histories, in which the narrative moves from event to event as in the Mixtec screenfolds.

Robertson saw these styles as representing a developmental sequence, in which the stream-of-time form was the oldest, from which the "place-oriented" and "event-oriented" histories developed. Although I find no support for Robertson's developmental sequence, I believe his basic typology has much to offer as a classificatory tool, and I have since followed it in a general way in my own analyses of the pictorial histories

(Boone 1992, 1994b). John Glass (1975b: 32), surveying the Mesoamerican pictorial manuscripts for the *Handbook of Middle American Indians,* also used it to categorize the historical codices.

H. B. Nicholson cast a bigger net when he considered the pictorial histories in a 1971 article that stemmed from a symposium on Mexican history. In an impressively detailed and exampled essay on the pre-Columbian historiographic tradition of Central Mexico, Nicholson covered archaeological monuments and the records of oral transmissions as well as the painted books. He did not draw the Mixtec screenfolds into his discussion. Like Radin, Nicholson wanted to ensure that the Aztec historical tradition was recognized in broader discussions of historiography. Toward this aim, he proposed the first typology that considered the full range of Central Mexican pictorial histories, supported by listings of most of the relevant examples. Combining criteria of format and content, Nicholson recognized five kinds of histories: continuous year-count annals, sporadically dated or undated annals, cartographic histories, genealogies, and dynastic lists. Robertson (1971), Edward Calnek (1978: 243), and I (1992) have subsequently suggested modifications to this typology, but we all recognize Nicholson's essay as the most detailed and comprehensive assessment of the kinds of pictorial histories to date. Used in conjunction with the Guide to Ethnohistorical Sources in the *Handbook of Middle American Indians* (vols. 13–15), it remains a fundamental point of entry into the historical documents (both pictorial and alphabetic) of Central Mexico.

Seldom have the Mixtec genealogical/historical screenfolds been brought into the discussion of Mexican historiography, for the larger project has usually been seen as an Aztec one, and the Mixtec material has been thought to be too distant geographically and culturally. Too, Mixtec codex specialists in the last half century have wanted little to do with Aztec perspectives and terminology (e.g., Smith 1973a: 3–4, Troike 1978, Jansen 1990), and justifiably so. For years the Mixtec codices were misunderstood as Aztec, until Alfonso Caso, in a pivotal study of the *Relación geográfica* map of Teozacoalco (1949), established that the Mixtec codices recorded the dynastic history of the Mixtec rulers. Consequently studies of Mixtec pictorial histories have followed their own road, proceeding according to their own rhythms and foci.

Because the corpus of Mixtec pictorials is relatively small compared to the Central Mexican corpus, scholars have worried less about organizing the manuscripts typologically. They have focused instead on reconstructing the dynastic and cosmogonic histories recorded in the codices, identifying the place signs geographically, and establishing the absolute chronology of events. These tasks have been more difficult for the Mixtec codices than for the Aztec ones because the Mixtec codices often lack explanatory glosses (that so many of the Aztec ones have), and there are so relatively few ethnohistorical sources for the Mixtecs. Thus Mixtec scholars, perhaps more so than Aztec scholars, build their histories from the full range of extant pictorial documents and move readily between the sources. The scarcity of alphabetic texts pertaining to pre-Columbian and early colonial Mixtecs also has meant that the pictorials are the greatest resource for recovering the outlines of Mixtec history. Thus scholars have focused particularly on interpreting their content.

Those who have looked at the Mixtec codices broadly as painted manuscripts have done so within the Mixtec corpus, and usually as a prelude or adjunct to another topic. Such is Mary Elizabeth Smith's (1973a: 3–35) brief but unsurpassed overview, which introduces her analysis of Mixtec place signs and maps; there she organizes the histories according to their painting styles and explains the conventions for their reading. Later, as an appendix to her and Ross Parmenter's commentary to the Codex Tulane (1991), she offers a valuable bibliographic essay on the manuscripts and archaeology of the Mixteca Baja region of northwestern Oaxaca and southern Puebla. Alfonso Caso's posthumous *Reyes y reinos de las mixteca* (1977, 1979), which culminates and synthesizes his thinking on the Mixtec pictorials, also opens with a discussion of the nature of the codices and lienzos—their historical content, language affiliation, and briefly how to read them—and has sections on families of manuscripts, such as those from the Coixtlahuaca Valley. The purpose of his study, however, is not to organize the pictorial codices but to fuse them to achieve a synthetic history of the Mixtec dynasties. In the same spirit, Bruce Byland and John Pohl's (1994) analysis of Mixtec history and archaeology draws on the codices to explain the archaeological record, and vise versa.

Joyce Marcus's study, *Mesoamerican Writing Systems* (1992), stands out because it looks equally at historical records in four Mesoamerican cultures: Aztec, Mixtec, Zapotec, and Maya. Her focus is on the role of hieroglyphic writing in these cultures rather than on painted histories themselves. Drawing examples from manuscripts, stone monuments, and ceramics, she compares how each culture presents, through its texts and images, its calendars, people, and places, as well as its ideas about divine ancestors, royal marriages and accessions, territory, and warfare.

The Mexican Painted Histories

My own approach, developed in two earlier articles (Boone 1992, 1994b) and presented here, follows in the tradition of Radin, Robertson, and Nicholson. Like them, I organize the more than 160 extant documents according to the way manuscript painters structured their stories, and then I look at the kind of stories they recorded. Typologies such as this create roads leading into the corpus at different points and allow one to focus on and understand one kind of manuscript or narrative within the context of the whole, and they are most useful when they follow intentionally significant differences in the existing codices. We must still recognize, however, that all organizational schema are artificial to some extent; they follow our trains of thought and represent our intentions and our perspectives on the codices. These schema are our own armatures on which we construct the history of the pictorial histories. This volume is no exception.

In Chapter 2, I look broadly at different conceptions of history and then focus on the ancient Mexicans' understanding of the past and the role of the painted histories. This chapter explains who the historians and painters were, where they learned their discipline and art, and how their painted histories fit within the social context of their societies. It also considers the physicality of the pictorials, explaining how the manuscripts were created and what forms they took.

Chapter 3 analyzes Mexican pictography as a system of writing and lays out its pictorial conventions and general laws of reading. It treats both the glyphic and figural components of the system, explaining how the painters recorded time, persons, places, and events. It provides the background that allows one to interpret the historical codices of the Aztec and Mixtec worlds.

Building on this foundation, I then explore in Chapter 4 the several ways stories can be structurally organized and presented graphically. I compare ancient Mexican examples with solutions reached by European and U.S. artists in the eighteenth through twentieth centuries in order to show that pictorial histories are not simply a curious feature of Mesoamerican culture but are all around us. I show, too, that graphically presented histories usually occur as one of several types. The Mexicans, like graphic historians elsewhere, structured the past as annals or a time line, as a series of linked events or *res gestae,* and as a cartographic presentation, although they also blended these structures to achieve specific balances.

The major groups of Mexican histories are presented in Chapters 5 through 8. Chapter 5 reviews the *res gestae* genealogical histories painted as screenfolds by the Mixtecs of southern Mexico. It focuses on the origin stories, the genealogies, and the life of Lord 8 Deer, one of the principal Mixtec rulers who brought much of the Mixteca under his control. The life of Lady 6 Monkey, one of 8 Deer's great rivals, is recounted in Chapter 4, based on the record in the Codex Selden. Chapters 6 and 7 present the cartographic histories and the *res gestae*/cartographic blends. The lienzos and tiras of Oaxaca and southern Puebla (including the Coixtlahuaca Valley manuscripts) belong to the Mixtec sphere of influence and are analyzed in Chapter 6. The map-based stories that participate in the Aztec world are then treated in Chapter 7. These Aztec documents are largely migration stories or narratives that concern the early histories of *altepetl,* including the map-based histories from Texcoco in the Valley of Mexico and from Cuauhtinchan near Cholula in western Puebla. Chapter 8 explains the annals histories of the Aztecs, codices that organize the past around an ongoing time line. Often these annals histories continue through the conquest and into the colonial period to reveal how the Aztecs themselves viewed the Spanish invasion and conquest and the new social order. One sees in Chapters 5 through 8 that similar themes run through the Mexican histories, despite their Mixtec or Aztec origin. Chapter 9 draws together some of these themes and demonstrates that the stories being told in the histories are often tied to the structure of their telling. This final chapter also looks at the social function of the pictorials, recognizing them as documents specifically created to bolster the positions and aspirations of the leaders and families that created them.

The geographic and cultural range of this study is broad. Although not every history is covered, I include the range of histories that are primarily pictorial, where the figures and images themselves compose the texts. This embraces both the Aztec and Mixtec worlds. As an Aztec specialist, I recognize that I seem to be going against the argument that Mixtec histories and Mixtec culture must be seen in terms of the Mixtec language and not Nahuatl. My intent, however, is not to focus an Aztec lense on the Mixtec codices or to ignore the languages of the historians. Instead, my purpose is to offer a complementary approach to the more linguistically based studies and to analyze all the manuscripts primarily as pictorial expressions of a widespread visual language. I have also come to see the value of comparing the different subtraditions of manuscript painting. After years of working on the Aztec codices, it was only after I had come to understand the Mixtec ones and saw how different the two were that I understood some of the special features of the Aztec ones. The reverse also proves true. The Mixtec and Aztec histories are like overlapping sets, having some differences and some similarities, the most important of which is that they share a predominantly pictorial means of writing.

I used the term "Aztec" to refer generally to the Nahua-speaking peoples of Central Mexico who shared a common political system, religion, and iconography. Most were united under the Triple Alliance empire, although they individually identified themselves as being people of their *altepetl* or community kingdom. Thus, the people of Tenochtitlan, Texcoco, and Chalco understood themselves to be Tenochca, Texcoca, and Chalca. Aztec is our modern term, derived from their origins in Aztlan. The Tenochca also referred to themselves as the Mexica, the people of Mexico-Tenochtitlan, and I use "Mexica" to specify the Aztecs of Tenochtitlan.

Maya manuscripts are not part of this study because they belong to a fundamentally different painting tradition, one that juxtaposes pictorial images with hieroglyphic texts. Their glyphic texts read in a fixed order and preserve the spoken word, yielding phrases and sentences and being inextricably tied to language. Their pictorial components have a complementary and separate function, but they do not carry the burden of meaning in the same way that the Mexican images do. Also, of the four surviving Maya codices, all are ritual and divinatory manuscripts, and although some have history woven into them, they are not primarily historical in nature.

Throughout this study, I privilege the pictorial images over any alphabetic glosses or texts that might accompany them. Sometimes these glosses do clearly explain the images (as in the Codex Mendoza), but sometimes they represent an entirely different presentation (as in the Codex Colombino). Glosses on most manuscripts fall in between—often they explain the images correctly, but occasionally they do not or they slant the presentation. This can be a real danger for investigators who rely (as many do) on the glosses rather than the images when they describe a pictorial history. For me, the pictorial evidence is always primary, because that is the information given by the manuscript's creator. Any added glosses must be considered a separate, although often valuable, text.

Most of the Mexican pictorials analyzed here are early colonial in date. The corpus of Mesoamerican pictorials includes only fifteen pre-Columbian examples that have survived over the centuries; only five of these are histories, all genealogical/historical screenfolds from the Mixteca.[13] Our principal evidence for the tradition of Mexican history painting thus comes in the form of more than 160 pictorial histories painted in the three generations after the conquest when the indigenous tradition of manuscript painting and pictorial documentation continued strong.

The strength of the manuscript painting tradition is notable, for it was the only major artistic form to survive any length of time after the importation of European images and techniques.[14] As discussed in Chapter 9, it survived because manuscripts of varying kinds continued to serve the documentary needs of the Mexicans, who continued to think and express themselves visually. The Spaniards, for their part, recognized the value of these painted documents and accepted them as valid records. Even during the conquest, Cortés relied on Aztec maps and painted reports. Early chroniclers lauded the care with which the painted records were executed. Charles V even ordered Spanish officials in 1530 to collect native tribute paintings so that they would know the amount of tribute he could expect, and we see Don Baltasar's history brought into an Inquisition case as a matter of course. The painted manuscripts continued to reflect the deep tradition of their pre-Columbian predecessors until eventually they were interpreted, assessed, and their stories reconfigured as European-style chronicles. Even some of the alphabetic texts, those in Spanish or Nahuatl that were close readings of painted documents, still preserve the pre-Columbian form.

History and Historians

Histories

Defining History

"History" is one of those common, comfortable words that pervades our thoughts, speech, and writing. We feel certain we understand its meaning and proper usage, and only if we are asked to define it might we hesitate; we would then be confronted with its fundamental ambiguity. One also reads it or says it in a specific context and is confident of its meaning, until the context expands or shifts even by a small degree; suddenly the history being read or said is something else entirely. History slides between a range of meanings, and it is this volatile quality, the ease with which it moves from one meaning to another, that confounds historiographical discussions.

History, in its broadest sense, means the past, that which has already happened. We say, "It is history," of something that occurred and is now behind us. History includes everything that happened, set against the field of everything that might have happened but did not. This seems obvious, but is it really so? Can we have a past, a history that is unstructured, unorganized, untouched by our cognition? Critics of history and narrative argue persuasively that we cannot. Their point is

that the past becomes history when it is organized. Just as all maps are selections and condensations of the features of an area (there are no maps that show everything at the original scale), there are no memories or recollections of the past that do not select and omit. It is impossible to speak of all of the past. Instead, when we think about the past, we organize and structure events to create threads of comprehension.

In examining the relationship between time and narrative, Paul Ricoeur (1984–1988, 1: 3, 52), has focused on "the temporal character of human existence." He argues that we make sense of the passage of time through narratives, that "time becomes human time to the extent that it is organized after the manner of a narrative." If we consider narrative here to mean a structure for understanding and speaking about the past, this is broadly true, for we cannot understand time without its passage, marked by the sequent occurrence of events.

Events, too, lack ontological meaning. They are defined by the structures in which they appear, by the organizational threads that tie them together. They come to us qualified according to these structures. As Hayden White (1981b: 251), summarizing Louis Mink's position, has said, "the transformation of events into stories endows them with cognitive meaning. In fact, as he [Mink] has argued, the very notion of event is so ambiguous that it makes no sense at all to speak of an *event per se* but only of *events under description.* In other words, the kind of descriptive protocol used to constitute event as facts of a particular sort determines the kind of fact they are considered to be. For Mink, narrativity is a mode of description which transforms events into historical facts by demonstrating their ability to function as elements of completed stories."[1] Although Mink and White are speaking of stories and narratives, their argument holds even if we speak only of mental structures that are created to link events.

Neurologists tell us that the brain's limbic system recollects the past by pulling memories from different parts of the brain and gathering them into a coherent whole (Conway 1996: esp. 76–82; Schacter 1996: 66–71). The individual memory parts are without meaning until they are assembled with others. This means that memory for humans is not something that is simply *there,* it is something that must be created, or structured, as a coherency each time, and because humans often vary the way they assemble the individual memory parts, humans can "remember" things differently than they actually happened. As Paul Connerton (1989: 27), speaking of memory, says, "literal recall is rare and unimportant, remembering being not a matter of reproduction but of construction; it is the construction of a 'schema,' a coding, which enables us to distinguish and, therefore, to recall."

It might be more accurate, therefore, to define history not as the past in all its fullness but as the selected and arranged past. Any time we think about the past, we necessarily choose to involve only a limited number of elements (events, locations, people, times, etc.) in the process. Their selection depends on the structure in which we will arrange them and ultimately on the construction of the past we seek. Since it is impossible for humans to consider everything at once, humans decide each time the subject they will consider.

History is not just the arranged past, however. By shifting our focus from the past itself to its structuring, we understand history to be a relation of the past. History in this sense is an account or a story. The story decides what parts of the past are chosen and how they are arranged. Generally histories are considered true accounts of the past. But historians more and more are paying attention to the narrative or literary aspects of

histories. As Hayden White (1985: 99) has argued, it behooves us not to ignore "the literary or fictive element in every historical account."[2] Histories not only select and structure the elements of the past, they interpret them, usually in the guise of explaining them, and they present a perspective on the past. Every history, like every story, combines facts, explanations, and a point of view. Historians are now more mindful of the points of view that so often drive the explanations.

Literary theorists are taking up some of these same concerns, seeking to understand the organization of narrative stories. Seymour Chatman (1978: 31), articulating a position shared by structuralist narrative theory, distinguishes between what he calls the story and the discourse. For him, "What is communicated is *story,* the formal content element of narrative [what Ricoeur would call the plot], and it is communicated by *discourse,* the formal expression element. The discourse is said to 'state' the story."[3] For Chatman, the story is the "what happened," and the discourse is the telling.

Chatman's two-level model of narrative is not without its critics—such as Barbara Herrnstein Smith (1981: 209–218), who argues that every telling of a story is a different version—but still his distinction can be useful. There are stories, or histories, that hold in their outlines but vary in their individual tellings. We call both the stories and the tellings histories. The Aztecs had a migration story (a migration history, if you will) that was recorded and spoken in various ways. The principal features of the story remained the same although the manuscript painters might paint it as a cartograph or annals; regardless, each document recorded the history of the Aztec migration and each was a migration history. Too, the Spanish version of Cortés' conquest of Mexico is a single story told slightly differently by Francisco López de Gómara and Bernal Díaz del Castillo in the sixteenth century, and told differently again by William Prescott in the nineteenth; thus there stands the history of the conquest, discoursed by the histories of López de Gómara, Díaz del Castillo, and Prescott, among others. Each writing has its own features and purposes, which do not conflict with the features and purposes of the conquest story.

Thus far we have reached three meanings of the word "history," each slightly more specific than the one before it and each closer to literature. The broadest history is the selected and arranged past; it is the thing presented by the story, what many people would call historical facts or real history: for example, the sequent acts related to the Aztecs' migrating. Then there is the story history, the structure and point of view that selects, arranges, and presents the past as a plot: for example, the history of the Aztec migration. Finally there is the discourse history, the individual document that records this story: the Mapa Sigüenza as a specific migration history.

There are other definitions of history, to be sure. History can be the past as an object of study, such as world history or Aztec history. In this case, it will comprise many histories or stories that together can reveal a distinct point of view or perspective, what White (1973) has called a metahistory. There is also the history tied to nature as in natural history. Other meanings of history narrow it, effectively restricting its usage and applicability from the Mexican pictorials.

There is the history that is true, which stands in contrast to myth, which is invented. This definition of history is one of the most common and has probably caused the most controversy in recent decades. It is fundamentally a western European construct, which presupposes that the facts of the past are knowable and can be recorded objectively. As Donald Brown (1988: 11) has explained it, "historians usually make their judgments in terms of the modern scientific standards of objectivity that date from the nineteenth century works of Leopold von Ranke," who was committed to writing about the past "as it actually happened." His point is that, although critics have pointed out that all accounts of the past are abstractions (even distortions) and all rest on subjective judgments about content and presentational manner, "real history" or "sound history" maximizes its objective content. If "historical materials produced by a given people are not based on the fundamental principles of modern historiography—do not conform, that is, to . . . the 'reality' rule— to that extent do those people lack a sense of history. An account of the past that is too remote from the historians' concept of history is then classed as legend, myth, folktale, or even as nonsense or deliberate falsehood" (Brown 1988: 11–12). Brown, like many other historians, distinguishes between history and myth (or legend) but acknowledges that the distinction is not a clear one; he sees history and myth as two poles of a continuum and acknowledges that actual accounts fall somewhere between the two.

If Brown's criteria for history are applied to the Aztecs, however, there would be no Mexican history until shortly before the conquest: all the migration histories from Aztlan and Chicomoztoc would fall away as being insufficiently factual. His definition of history is too narrow for our purposes here, and for most of the past outside of the European tradition. The Mexicans took pride in the veracity of their histories; they knew the migration story to be true even if it were not "factual" in Brown's terms. Paul Veyne's investigation of whether the Greeks believed in their myths helps us here. Veyne (1988: 22, 17) explains that the myths were "neither true nor fictitious because [they are] external to but nobler than the real world"; although myths might not record everyday reality, the "legendary worlds were accepted as true in the sense that they were not doubted." In the ancient Americas, we must include the fabulous and legendary in our understanding of history because the Mesoamericans saw no division between myth and history. Among Mesoamericanists, Dennis Tedlock (1985: 64) has solved the problem, and avoided unnecessary distinctions, by using the term "mythistory."

Another definition of history, widely shared among historians in the Western tradition, rests less on truth value than on presentational structure or the story value. This perspective sees the project of accounting for the past as having developed from a rudimentary form into a true history. In the Middle Ages there were the annals, whereby historians recorded events separately according to the years in which they happened. Then followed the chronicle where the events came in sequence without the need for an accompanying year-count. But true history came only with narrative history. Whereas annals and chronicles simply end, White, among others, argues that narrative history structures the past in a way that has a beginning and a story that "*concludes* with a moralizing ending." This view demands that a history be a narrative story about the past, a story that has closure. The "imperfect 'historicality'" of annals and chronicles, according to White, keeps them from attaining "full narrativity" and becoming "history proper."[4]

This definition of history, of course, cuts the Mexican annals and the Mixtec *res gestae* from the roster of histories. It is a view of history created specifically to address the concerns of historians of Europe about the development of historical reckoning in the Middle Ages and Renaissance. As Marilyn Waldman (1981: 240–242) points out, White has denied the presence of a story in the annals because he has not himself found one. She notes, coming from the perspective of an Islamic historian, that so many cultures have nonnarrative ways of recording history that "we must find a way to read [them] without reference to a relatively late Europocentric norm" (p. 242).

A final, restrictive definition attached to history is the sense, discussed in Chapter 1, that histories must be written alphabetically. This has given rise to the generally held notion that the human past has two stages, the first being ahistorical or prehistorical, and the second being historical, i.e., with alphabetically written histories.[5] I hope I have shown the error of this position, denying, as it does, history to a great many peoples of the world who had deep historical traditions.

In this volume I focus on the second and the third meanings of history: history as a story about the past and history as a specific document that carries that story. The first meaning of history—the selected and arranged past—is less a concern. This is not a book about Mexican history as such; this is not a book about the deeds and events in the Aztec and Mixtec past. Thus the truth value of episodes and stories is not a concern. It does not matter to me here whether the Aztecs really left Aztlan in the year 1 Flint (1168); it only matters here that their histories say they did. My purpose is to explain the stories painted about the past by the Mexican historians and to analyze the documents that record these stories. In Chatman's terms, I am looking at the stories and the discourses.

Support from the Past

It has been said that animals live in an eternal present, that they lack a historical consciousness and thus have no history. We humans, on the other hand, cannot escape our history. We see the present as having grown out of the past, and we see the future as yet a further growth once the present becomes the past. The past thus creates and defines the present and ultimately the future. We humans, therefore, feel that if we are to understand anything, outside the laws of nature, we must

principally understand and articulate the past. We do this by creating histories.

When in 1994 the lenses of the Hubble telescope were finally adjusted correctly, sights into deep space came to us for the first time. The astronomers who worked with this extraordinary piece of space-recording equipment were particularly excited about the possibility of discovering how the cosmos began. The popular press reported their belief that if we understood the origin of the cosmos and knew its subsequent history, we would understand its present organization and could tell its future.[6] In other words, they saw the history of the cosmos as the key to its future. If this is true for stars and matter, it is no less true for humans.

Human identity is inextricable from the human past. We are all those things that we have done and that have happened to us, and all those things we remember. As G. J. Whitrow (1961: 111), embracing Plotinus, has noted, "Memory has long been recognized as the concomitant of personal identity. . . . Memory is the means by which the record of our vanished past survives 'within' us, and this is the basis of our consciousness of self-identity." Personal pasts and memories form individual identities, but histories of groups create community identity. History, by tracing a shared past, brings people together and weaves solidarity. Families, ethnicities, and nations rely on their communal stories to affirm their identity.

Histories can both bolster and question the established power because they form the background for human claims. Speaking of the multiple histories, or images of the past, created by the different groups who populated Mexico, Enrique Florescano (1994: vii) explains: "They created those images to free themselves of the corrosive passage of time over human creation, to weave solidarity founded on common origins, to delimit the possession of a territory, to affirm identities rooted in remote traditions, to sanction established power, to back contemporary claims with the prestige of the past, to found on a shared past the aspiration of building a nation, or to give sustenance to plans laid toward the uncertainty of the future." By the slantings of many stories, humans affirm their existence and support their ambitions.

Multiple Histories

As Florescano notes, the images of the past created in Mexico were multiple. Histories are always being written and rewritten. Each is created by an author, at a particular time and place, and for a reason, and each is thereby governed by an underlying set of principles and assumptions. Each new recovery of the past carries its own point of view. These principles, assumptions, and points of view govern what features of the past are gathered and how they are arranged. They create hierarchies that characterize certain features as being central to the story while other elements are not, and they call forth structures to shape how the elements are presented. The recovery and recreation of the past has to be understood as an ongoing social process, one constantly in flux, and one that pulls new images into use as it discards others.[7]

A single event partakes in many histories. Depending on the story, the event may be the central feature or merely one of many secondary factors, it may come as the beginning or the climax, and it may be construed as a triumph or a defeat. The story in which an event occurs even determines what kind of event it is and what it is called. In the spring of 1994, the Smithsonian Institution's Air and Space Museum prepared to mark the fiftieth anniversary of an event they identified as the dropping of the atomic bomb on Hiroshima. The fuselage of the *Enola Gay,* the plane that carried the bomb, had been carefully and expensively restored over a several-year period in preparation for its display. Curators at the Air and Space Museum had planned an ambitious exhibition that would feature the *Enola Gay* and would carry messages about the destructive power of the atomic bomb, beginning with the devastation of Hiroshima and continuing with the military and social impact of the subsequent nuclear arms race. Almost immediately, great furor erupted from veterans groups and eventually Congress who wanted not a story of atomic destruction but a story of U.S. victory. The bombing of Hiroshima (followed soon by the bombing of Nagasaki) figured prominently in their stories of World War II as the event that ended the war; they characterized it as a justified and necessary strike against an aggressive enemy, an event that ultimately saved lives (mostly American but also Japanese).

But this was not the only alternative history in which the bombing figured. The Japanese saw the event in their own stories of the war as one of unfathomable devastation, when 80,000 civilians perished. Different parts of the Japanese population characterized the event in a variety of ways; representatives of Hiroshima called it "a nuclear attack" by the United States, and the mayor of Nagasaki compared the bombings to the Jewish Holocaust. In the United States, opponents of nuclear arms felt that the museum curators had not gone far enough in denouncing the nuclear arms race and the development of nuclear power; for them, the bombing was the beginning of a dangerous chapter in world armaments. In other histories, the bombing figures differently still. For the pilot of the *Enola Gay,* the bombing was a clean hit well delivered. In stories about the building of the first atomic weapons—when the great scientific minds gathered at Los Alamos in secret to develop the devices—the bombing itself comes as an epilogue to an extraordinary feat of science and engineering. For political historians, the event was the factor that gave the United States an edge in negotiations with the Soviet Union. In so many other stories, personal and communal, the event figures variously.[8]

As the drama was played out in newspapers and magazines, each side claimed its story as the one authentic version. Disagreements focused on the issue of authenticity, whether the Air and Space Museum was exercising historical standards and presenting the truth. Veterans groups and Congress charged the Air and Space Museum with historical revisionism because the museum had not planned to present the past as the veterans knew it. When the curators then tried to adjust the focus of the exhibition to address these concerns, other groups charged the curators with bowing to outside pressure and renouncing their objectivity. The arguments went back and forth. Everyone agreed on the importance of the event, but they could not agree on what kind of event it was. None of the sides openly acknowledged that this single event figured strongly in so many separate and conflicting histories, that it meant so many different things to different peoples, and that it was a fundamentally different event in each of their histories.

The uproar reminds us that all events take the meanings we give them. These meanings depend on how we structure the past into separate histories and on the place individual events then have in the armatures of these histories. The debate about the *Enola Gay* exhibition was so heated—such that the director of the museum eventually resigned—because the event was of such astonishing importance for so many people. It mattered deeply how the event figured in their histories and thus what kind of event it was.

Ancient Mexican Histories

Mexican Understanding of the Past: People in Time

There is nothing explicit in the ethnohistorical record to tell us how the Nahuas and Mixtecs understood the past. No chronicler addressed this issue or asked the question and recorded an answer. We therefore come to our understanding obliquely and piecemeal from hints in the existing documents.

It is clear that the ancient Mexicans shared the understanding that their present world was founded on the past. Aztec accounts of the five cosmic ages, or Five Suns, tell how the world was sequentially created and destroyed cataclysmically four times before it was created anew for the fifth time, which is their, and our, present. The great ages parallel each other in their characteristics: each created by the gods and running under the specific patronage of a divine being, each with its different humanity, and each destroyed by a natural phenomenon, namely, flood, hurricane, volcanic eruption, wind, with the fifth age to be brought down by earthquake. The previous four ages or Suns stood as imperfect experiments of existence that, by their precedence, made the fifth and present age merely the latest and most advanced one. As the Anales de Cuauhtitlan (León-Portilla 1992a: 5) tells us:

> It was recounted, it was said
> that already there had existed four [types of] lives,
> and that this one was the fifth age.

> As the old men knew,
> in the year 1-Rabbit
> the earth and sky were founded.
> And thus they knew,
> that when the earth and sky were founded,
> four kinds of men had already existed,
> four kinds of life.
> They likewise knew that each one of them
> had existed in one Sun [one age].

The present world of the Aztecs, then, was the latest segment in a historical sequence. The message these sequential ages conveyed to humankind was that the world had the characteristics it did because it was preceded by the four other ages. Its past, therefore, established its present.

The past not only established the features of the present, it was corporally carried into the present in the form of human beings. In each of the cosmic ages, the Aztecs understood that humankind was created anew and differently. Humans of the fifth age—being the Aztecs, their immediate cultural predecessors, and their contemporaries—were fashioned literally from the bones of the ancestors. The Leyenda de los Soles records how, after the gods had created the sky and earth, the divine culture-hero Quetzalcoatl went down into Mictlan, the underworld land of the dead, in search of the "precious bones" of the dead (León-Portilla 1963: 107–111). Quetzalcoatl underwent various trials (similar to those undergone by the Hero Twins in the Popol Vuh story) before he snatched up the piles of bones and raced out with them. Immediately he carried them to Tamoanchan, a place of origins, where the old goddess Cihuacoatl ground them into meal. Quetzalcoatl and other gods then bled themselves over the meal, their blood wetting and transforming it into the living dough that composes the common people (the *macehuales*).

This story of the creation of humankind is often used to explain the Aztec's debt to the gods for drawing their own blood to give humans life. But the story also shows that the Aztecs believed themselves to be formed out of the remains—the ancestral bones—of the past. Thus, the Aztecs did not simply hold the past within them as a factor of their consciousness, as we do; in addition to this, the Aztecs also understood their corporal selves literally to be composed of the past, brought to life by the blood of the gods.

On more specific and practical levels, too, the Mexicans understood that their present situations were established by the past. The Mexica, for example, held that their authority and might as an imperial power rested with the developmental events in their history. Their emergence from Chicomoztoc, their migration from Aztlan, and the hardships and various episodes during this long migration made the Mexica fit as a people to rule others (Boone 1991). It was the events in their past that endowed them with the authority they required. In southern Mexico, the Mixtecs also believed that authority devolved from the past, although for them it came largely through bloodlines rather than through sequent events of a migration. The status of the Mixtec ruling families rested on their genealogical histories, which began with divine ancestors who emerged from trees or openings in the earth. The Mixtec elite held office and power because of how they were descended and how their ancestors were descended (Spores 1967: 13–14). To them as to the Mexica, the past mattered greatly.

Time Travel. The past and future do not seem to have been permanently closed to the Mexicans. These temporal states were separated from the present, true, but their bounding walls were porous to the extent that the past could be visited if approached correctly, even if it could not be changed. The future could be known through prognostications and omens, and it could be seen in dreams and mirrors. The *tonalamatls,* or divinatory codices, revealed the supernatural forces that governed days and periods in the future; signs and portents signaled additional fates. Some humans could look into the future, such as when Moctezuma Xocoyotzin looked into a seeing instrument (like a mirror) that was miraculously located on a bird's head; he saw the image of Spaniards on horseback, well before their arrival.[9] I do not find any evidence, however, to suggest that humans actually entered the future.

They did go back to the past. The past, of course, was familiar because the recent past had been lived and the old past was kept alive in books, orations, and songs. There was never a difficulty with knowing about the past; the difficulty came with visiting it. Diego Durán (1994: 212–222) tells of the incident when Moctezuma Ilhuicamina sent emissaries back to Aztlan, their ancient homeland, in order to bring gifts and offerings to the god Huitzilopochtli's mother. As Durán records it, the Mexica ruler originally thought to send a contingent of warriors, but his counselor persuaded him that such a journey required not men of war but "wizards, sorcerers, and magicians, who with their enchantments and spells can discover that place" (p. 213). Moctezuma's royal historian explained how Aztlan was once a lush and fertile island in the middle of a lake, but that after the Mexica abandoned Aztlan, the place long ago became choked with thorns, brambles, and sharp stones, and it filled with vipers, poisonous creatures, and predatory animals, such that the Mexica would not be able to find it again. Moctezuma nevertheless selected sixty sorcerers—the wisest in the land—for the journey. The wizards went first to Coatepec, birthplace of Huitzilopochtli, where they conducted an elaborate ritual, invoked the supernatural forces, and were thereby transformed into their *nahuallis* (animal alteregos), taking the forms of birds and large carnivores. As beasts they miraculously and immediately reached Aztlan, where they reverted back to their human forms. They found Aztlan to be a fertile and verdant place, unchanged from its pre-migration days. There the wizards found that time had passed, but it had passed much slower than it had in Tenochtitlan. The people who had remained behind when the Mexica left centuries before were still there, although they were older, and they asked about those who had left as if they should still be alive. Huitzilopochtli's aged mother still waited for her son's return. The wizards eventually found their god's mother and conveyed to her their rich offerings. In return, she gave them maguey fiber clothing—gifts that reflected the Mexica's humble origins—for her son. Then the wizards took their leave: by repeating their earlier ritual, they transformed themselves into the same animals for their return to Coatepec. But at Coatepec, only forty of the sixty reappeared into the present; twenty had disappeared.

This episode tells us a number of things. It tells us that time travel was possible but not easy. Not everyone was able to visit the past; only the wisest priests, sorcerers, or day-keepers (calendrical diviners) could achieve it, and then only by performing the appropriate rituals and transforming themselves into their animal *nahuallis.* As animal spirits, but not as men, they might be able to pierce the walls of the past. The trip was so hazardous that not every wizard could expect to make it and return; fully a third of the wisest and most skillful men in Moctezuma's realm perished in the process. The journey back in time was also a journey from one place to another, for ancient Aztlan existed as a location inextricably tied to the period before the Mexica left it. One entered it and exited it through the portal of Coatepec, the place where Huitzilopochtli had been born. There in Aztlan time had still continued to run, but it proceeded at a much slower pace. The wizards reached Aztlan after the Mexica had already left but before it became uninhabitable with thorns, spikes, and ferocious beasts.

Books of the Past

The Mexica knew about ancient Aztlan because its features had been preserved in their historical codices. Although they also recounted long-gone peoples and events in oral stories, songs, and performances, the Mexica relied principally on the painted books to keep the past firm. A Nahuatl poem from the Romances de los Señores de la Nueva España collection (penned by the mestizo historian Juan Bautista Pomar) explains how the transience of life is preserved in the paintings (León-Portilla 1986: 68). Writing with flowers is a metaphor for poetry, just as the eagles and jaguars are metaphorically the warriors and/or nobles. Thus:

> With flowers you write,
> Oh Giver of Life!
> With songs you give color,
> with songs you shade
> those who must live on the earth.
>
> Later you will destroy
> eagles and tigers;
> we live only in your painting
> here, on earth.

This sense that the past endured through the medium of historical paintings is certainly not specific to the Mexicans; it may be a universal for those people who have a tradition of figural painting. On the other side of the Atlantic, the Italian humanist Leon Bautista Alberti expressed a similar sentiment when he declared, at the beginning of the second book of his 1435 compendium on painting, that "Painting possesses a truly divine power in that not only does it make the absent present . . . , but it also represents the dead to the living many centuries later" (Freedberg 1989: 44).

The Nahuas felt this deeply. The mestizo historian Fernando Alvarado Tezozomoc (1975: 4–5) opens his Crónica Mexicayotl with an invocation of the ancient history paintings.

> Thus they have come to tell it,
> thus they have come to record it in their narration,
> and for us they have painted it in their codices,

the ancient men, the ancient women.
They were our grandfathers, our grandmothers,
our great-grandfathers, our great-grandmothers,
our great-great-grandfathers, our ancestors.
Their account was repeated,
they left it to us;
they bequeathed it forever
to us who live now,
to us who come down from them.

> Never will it be lost, never will it be forgotten,
> that which they came to do,
> that which they came to record in their paintings:
> their renown, their history, their memory.
> Thus in the future
> never will it perish, never will it be forgotten,
> always we will treasure it,
> we, their children, their grandchildren,
> brothers, great-grandchildren,
> great-great-grandchildren, descendants,
> we who carry their blood and their color,
> we will tell it, we will pass it on
> to those who do not yet live, who are to be born,
> the children of the Mexicans, the children of the
> Tenochcans. . . . (León-Portilla 1986: 117)

A sufficient number of these painted histories survived the Spanish invasion to provide a treasured resource for the subsequent postconquest chroniclers. The mendicant fathers (e.g., Motolinía, Sahagún, Durán) as well as the Nahua and mestizo historians (e.g., Alvarado Tezozomoc, Alva Ixtlilxochitl, Chimalpahin) who investigated pre-Columbian history all speak of how crucial these paintings were to their own work, which could not have been written without them.

More than being an alternative medium (alternative to songs and poems) for preserving historical knowledge, paintings were the essential documentary evidence for history. As long as the paintings endured, knowledge of the past endured. The converse was equally true: when books were destroyed, knowledge of the past was lost. Sahagún's noble informants bring this point home to us. When recounting an episode in the distant Mexica past, they explained to Sahagún (1959–1982, bk. 10:191) that "No longer can it be remembered, no longer can it be investigated how long they [the Mexica] were left in Tamoanchan," because the ruler Itzcoatl later burned the history books and thereby destroyed memory of it.

Itzcoatl's (1427–1440) book-burning program did not totally erase the episode from Mexica history, however; enough of the story remained in the later history paintings for Sahagún's informants to recall it in the sixteenth century. The episode itself illustrates how the painted books—the histories, divinatory almanacs, and other genres—were understood to be models and guides for orderly and balanced living. The story goes that the Mexica, in the deep past, had followed their leaders to the "place named Tamoanchan, which is to say, 'We seek our home.' And there they tarried" (Sahagún 1959–1982, bk. 10:190). Shortly thereafter their wise men and priests left that place, carrying away their deity and all the books, leaving the people with nothing: "They carried the writings, the books, the paintings. They carried the knowledge; they carried all—the song books, the flutes." The four old, wise ones who remained behind with the people recognized that the sun would still rise and set, but they worried about humankind:

> "How will the common people live, how will they dwell? He is gone; they carried away the writings. And how will the common people dwell? How will the lands, the mountains be? How will all live? What will govern? What will rule? What will show the way? What will be the model, the standard? What will be the example? From what will the start be made? What will become the torch, the light?"
>
>   Then they devised the book of days, the book of years, the count of the years, the book of dreams. They arranged the reckoning just as it has been kept. (Sahagún 1959–1982, bk. 10:191)

Although the old ones in their lament noted that the god had gone, they focused their anxiety on the departure of the books. They were concerned with *what* would govern rather than *who* would govern, the implication being that the books themselves provided the model, the standard, the example. When they recreated the books, they metaphorically relit "the torch, the light," and started civilization, or culture, again.

The books were understood to be the foundation of knowledge. The metaphor for writings or books was *in tlilli, in tlapalli,* which translates literally as "the black [ink], the red [ink]" but is always used for its larger meaning. In the images of manuscript painters, preserved in existing codices, the scribes work with black and red ink.[10] Those who own and read books are con-

sidered to own and read "the black, the red." The black, the red, was also the metaphor for knowledge or wisdom. Where Sahagún talks about the books and knowledge (above), his Nahuatl text strings together the sequence of related words to build to the larger meaning: "they carried away the black, the red, the paper, the painting, they carried away the knowledge."[11] Those who were knowledgeable were possessors of books.

These several texts and episodes that help us understand the importance the Mexica ascribed to books also reminds us that song and poetry were similarly major media for retaining and conveying knowledge and were closely linked to the paintings. The metaphor for poetry, *in xochitl, in cuicatl,* literally translates as "the flower, the song." Thus, when the poem from the Romances de los Señores (excerpted above) speaks of the divine being who writes with flowers and gives color and shade with songs, it explains how past experiences and histories are orally preserved in songs and poems. As León-Portilla (1992a: 39–40) points out, the Nahuatl word for history, *ihtloca,* translates as "what is said about someone or something." Alonso de Molina translates "history of ancient times" as *yeuetlatolli* ("old, old speech" or, alternatively, "sayings of the elders"). For Molina, history is both *tlatollotl* ("speech or oral discourse") and *nemiliz amatl* ("life paper" or "life book"); a chronicle or a history is *nemiliz tlacuilolli, nemiliz tlatollotl* ("life painting, life saying"). In describing the concepts related to history and historians, Molina uses the words for painting (*tlacuilolli*) and speech or oral discourse (*tlatolli*) almost interchangeably.[12] It is clear that the spoken word is inextricable from and complementary to the painted document and that both together fill the category of knowledge that is history. The interpreters voiced the histories they interpreted from the documents.

Still, it remained for the documents to codify the knowledge and guarantee the authenticity of what was spoken. As the Franciscan friar Motolinía (1971: 5) remarked: "The memory of man is weak and sometimes forgetful, [and] the elders differ in recounting the things of the past, which require expounding to be understood, but of all the opinions and books that they have, as I have been able to ascertain and deduce, the history books are the most truthful" (author's translation). The Spaniards, although profoundly distrustful of most Aztec codices, especially admired these painted histories, which they considered less idolatrous than other genres. Motolinía (1971: 5) lists five kinds of books that the Aztecs had: the annals history, the book of days and ceremonies, the book of dreams and superstitions, the books of baptism and naming of infants, and the book of ceremonies and omens relating to marriage. All but the first are ceremonials and divinatory manuals of some kind and were clearly idolatrous to Motolinía's thinking. Of the historical annals, however, he says: "Only one of these books can be trusted, namely the first, which is of the years and times. . . . Thus they wrote and pictured the exploits and stories of war, and the succession of the principal lords, weather conditions and pestilences, and at what time and under which lord these things occurred. . . . All this they have written in symbols and figures. This book is called in the language of these Indians xiuhtonalamatl, which is to say the book of the count of the years" (p. 5, author's translation). *Xiuhtonalamatl* literally translates as "year-day-paper," meaning a book account of the years and days. Motolinía may well have meant to write *xiuhpohualamatl*, literally "year-count-book," which agrees better with his translation. Siméon (1981: 770) translates the related term *xiuhtlapoalamatl* as "papers, book of the count of the years, chronological history" and notes that the *xiuhtlacuilo* is "he who writes annals, [a] chronicler, [a] historian." For *xiuhtlacuilo,* Molina (1971: second pag. 159) gives simply "chronicler." Motolinía, like others of his mendicant colleagues (notably Molina, Olmos, Sahagún, and Durán), recognized in the history book, which for the Aztecs was largely the annals, a document that preserved the facts of the past. As Dana Leibsohn (1993: 183, 208, 245) has noted, the historical documents "imposed significant permanent outlines on contestable events" and functioned to guarantee that an oral narration was both authentic and comprehensive.

The Mexicans called up these painted histories to reveal their knowledge on a regular basis and whenever circumstances dictated, which may have been quite often. Deliberations over territory or sovereignty would necessitate a check of the pertinent manuscripts, as would any question about the past. According to Durán (1994: 213, 214), when the emperor Moctezuma Ilhuicamina had it in his head to send a contingent of men back to ancient Aztlan, he consulted "the royal historian, an aged man called Cuauhcoatl [Eagle Ser-

pent]." The emperor told the historian, "O ancient father, I desire to know the true story, the knowledge that is hidden in your books about the Seven Caves where our ancestors, our fathers and grandfathers, lived, and whence they came forth." Thereupon the historian told him about Aztlan before and after the migration, saying, "And this is the story told by our ancestors, it is what I have found [painted] in our ancient books." The history books stood ready to be interpreted and voiced when needed.

In the Mixteca, the genealogical histories of lineages were also consulted whenever members of the ruling class considered marriage. As Ronald Spores (1967: 13–14) and others have pointed out, lineage depth and the purity of the bloodline were of the utmost importance in determining rule of the Mixtec community kingdoms. "Only the offspring of the principal wife of a ruler who was herself of the ruling caste and necessarily descended in legitimate fashion from rulers could inherit title from either his or her father or mother. In the event of failure of a ruling line, it was often necessary to go back two or more generations to determine what particular living person stood in the closest degree of relationship to former rulers." For this understanding, the parties turned to the painted dynastic histories, where genealogies were carefully delineated. As Mary Elizabeth Smith (1973a: 32) notes, "We can be sure that no one goes to be married until his prospective mate is completely sure of where he 'comes from.'"

Throughout Mexico, the painted histories were prized by the nobles, the elite, and those in power, who wielded them effectively as social weapons. In the Mixteca, the friar Francisco de Burgoa reports that the painted histories were also hung on the walls of the nobles' palaces. In the valleys of Central Mexico, they were guarded in *amoxcalli* (book houses) or archives, many of which were attached to the houses of the rulers. The conqueror Bernal Díaz del Castillo remarked about the great house of books within Moctezuma Xocoyotzin's palace, and Fernando de Alva Ixtlilxochitl speaks of the extensive royal archive of Texcoco. Individual noble families and *capulli* heads also guarded their own collections of the books pertinent to them.[13]

The Physicality of the Painted Books

The books so carefully guarded were objects of paper, hide, or woven cloth that were painted on one or both sides and folded, rolled, or left flat. They could be protected with wooden end-pieces that, when folded back on the pages, made effective covers. Sometimes these wooden end-panels were also covered with decorative hide or a pattern of mosaics. An existing screenfold almanac in the Vatican Library (the Codex Vaticanus B) still retains its wooden cover and traces of turquoise decoration, and a screenfold history in the British Museum (the Codex Zouche-Nuttall) retains the imprint of feather and possibly turquoise decoration on its hide cover (Anders 1972: 29; Troike 1987: 39). We should keep in mind that some of these precious books must have been elaborately and expensively ornamented.

Of the eleven pre-Columbian manuscripts that have come down to us from central and southern Mexico, most are screenfolds of hide (Fig. 61). In creating them, the craftsmen took long strips of animal hide (which had already been stripped of hair and scraped smooth), glued them together to form a much longer strip, and folded this strip back on itself like an accordion or screen—thus its designation as a screenfold. The hide pieces, or skins (those that have been measured), tend to be 50–100 cm long,[14] and most people have assumed they are deer skin. Microscopic examination of the Codex Colombino hides (Fig. 63) suggests they are from the pronghorn deer (*Antiolocapra americana*) (Caso 1966: 101–102). Before being folded, the long strip was covered with a fine white gesso, which imparted a hard surface well suited for painting.[15] Not all the hide codices were folded screenfold-style. Some may have been folded horizontally and vertically, as a napkin, and others may have been rolled. For example, an extant ritual manuscript dating from before the conquest (Aubin Ms. no. 20) is composed of a single large panel of hide folded horizontally and vertically into quarters. Postconquest historical codices like the Codex Tulane and Selden Roll are rolls of hide (Figs. 75, 88).[16]

Although most of the pre-Columbian manuscripts that have survived are of hide, there is considerable evidence that the Mesoamericans thought of their books not as hide but as paper. The pictorials from the Valley of Mexico that are not of European paper are made of native paper, most of it from the inner bark of the fig tree. The Nahua word for book is *amoxtli*, which is derived from *amatl* (native paper) and *oxtli* (glue) and, taken literally, means "glued sheets of paper" (León-Portilla 1992b: 317). One read or voiced a book by reading or voicing the glued paper (the verb is *amoxitoa*), and owners of books were owners of this paper (*amoxoaque*; Sahagún 1959–1982, bk. 10:190). One might think that the confluence of "paper" with "book" or "codex" in Central Mexico reflected the fact that most extant native pictorials there *are* of paper. But the confluence is also found in the Mixteca, where the surviving preconquest pictorials are of hide. Like the Central Mexicans, the Mixtecs also used the same word, *tutu*, for "book" and "paper." When Father Burgoa recalled that the Mixtec elite hung books on the walls of their palaces, he was speaking of books made of paper. In both Nahua and Mixtec-speaking Mexico, books were paintings, and they were papers.[17]

To make paper screenfolds, craftsmen stripped the inner bark from one of several varieties of native fig trees.[18] They then soaked the bark, beat it thin, and pressed it into sheets, which, like the hides, were then glued together to create even longer strips. The strips could likewise be sized with a white gesso and were folded accordion-style.

Although most of the surviving paper books are of bark paper, a few are of maguey fiber paper; the Codex Huejotzingo, an economic document of c. 1531, uses both kinds. Maguey fiber books were a less common alternative to the *amatl* or bark fiber ones, for the papers are equally fine. The conqueror Bernal Díaz del Castillo (1956: 157) tells of how the Tlaxcalans had representations of their battles with the Mexica painted on "large henequen cloths." Motolinía (1971: 365) reports that much maguey paper was fabricated in Tlaxcala and transported throughout a large part of New Spain. Still today, maguey paper is fabricated and used in rituals in northern and western Mexico, and folkloric paintings on maguey paper remain a thriving craft industry.

Just as the hide books came in different formats, so apparently did the paper ones: as rolls and large sheets, the latter folded or not. Although preconquest paper screenfolds have survived only from the Maya region, abundant examples of paper books in Central Mexico have come down to us from the postconquest years. These take the form of screenfolds (C. Borbonicus,

Tonalamatl Aubin), single large sheets (Maguey Plan), rolls or strips (Tira de Tepechpan [Fig. 127], Anales de Tula), and sheets of various sizes that are now separate (C. Huejotzingo, C. Xolotl [Fig. 42]), which probably reflect the preconquest forms. Additionally, in the colonial period, the native paper sheets were sometimes bound together like European books (Matrícula de Tributos, C. Mexicanus [Fig. 34]).

The third medium for the historical documents was cotton cloth, in the form of great sheets, which could be folded, spread out on a floor, or easily hung on a wall (Fig. 44). They are usually referred to as *lienzos*, after the Spanish word for linen. The conquerors were the first to mention them in Central Mexico as the medium for maps. In the Mixteca, Father Burgoa recalls that the burial cave of the Mixtec rulers at Chalcatongo contained a number of "lienzos de pinturas" in addition to funerary bundles, altars, and cult figures.[19] Several dozen lienzos from the postconquest period, and one possibly from before the conquest, have survived to preserve the tradition.[20] These existing lienzos are sheets created by sewing together several strips of plain-weave cloth. The individual strips are roughly 35–55 cm. wide, a convenient size for a backstrap loom. Because of the flexible nature of the cloth, no sizing could be applied to smooth out the painting surface.

Careful examination of existing manuscripts and the few tests that have been conducted on the pigments allow us to understand something of how the painters worked. Speaking of the Codex Selden, Philip Dark and Joyce Plesters (1959: 536) explain that the artist first outlined his figures "in a thin solution of a red dyestuff, which is probably cochineal. The areas sketched out in pink were then colored. Finally, the figures and other objects were delineated with carbon black." In other manuscripts, the artists also pressed straight lines with a stylus to frame or guide their painting. When mistakes were corrected or changes made, the artist covered the figure with white paint or a second application of gesso and painted anew.

The colors were derived from minerals, animals, and plants. Carbon black gave a deep black; the crimson dye from the body of the cochineal insect provided that rich color; and minerals gave yellows, other reds, and some blues and greens. Vegetal dyes yielded other greens and blues. Some of these vegetal blues and greens are fugitive and fade over time to a dull tan,

which is why the quetzal feathers in the Mixtec codices are often this dull color. Although Father Sahagún devotes an entire chapter of his Book 11 to explaining how the many colors were made, we still know little about ancient Mexican pigments. Francisco Hernández reports that Mexican painters used a binder derived from the root of an orchid plant (*tzacutli*), but Dark and Plesters found that the specific painting medium for the Codex Selden was a protein similar to egg tempera.[21] Representations of painters that appear in the codices show them working with a brush and what looks like a reed pen.[22]

Scribes and Sages

These books circulated in a world of painters and scholars. The chroniclers tell us that the books were created by *tlacuiloque,* painters who drew and colored the books' images, and that the books were owned and interpreted by *tlamatinime*—scholars, wise men and women, or sages, literally "those who know something." Father Sahagún distinguishes between these two occupations, but the differences between them are far from clear. In ancient Mexico there were *tlacuiloque* who decorated walls, sculptures, and the like (sometimes with complex iconography), and there were those who worked as simple scribes under the direction of priests or governmental officials; such were probably the court reporters mentioned by Sahagún and Motolinía.[23] But there were also *tlacuiloque* who themselves authored the painted manuscripts; these painter/scribes had to have been sufficiently well versed in the esoteric content of the books to be counted among the *tlamatinime*. Neither the *tlacuiloque* nor the *tlamatinime* were necessarily members of the nobility, but some clearly were. The evidence for these roles bears reviewing, for they intersect in the person of the historian and author.

The *tlacuiloque* are presented in the ethnohistorical sources as artisans and craftspeople, the emphasis being on their physical skill and dexterity. When Sahagún (1959–1982, bk. 10: 24) describes the occupation of the *tlacuilo*, he focuses on its technical aspect: "The scribe: writings, ink [are] his special skills. [He is] a craftsman, an artist, a user of charcoal, a drawer with charcoal; a painter who dissolves colors, grinds pigments, uses colors." Sahagún clusters the *tlacuilo* with other artisans who create products valued especially by the elites. In Chapter 7 of his Book 10 on "the people," he describes the occupations of the craftsman, goldworker, copperworker, and lapidary; in Chapter 8 he explains "other ways of gaining a livelihood," covering the carpenter, stonecutter, mason, scribe, singer, wise man, and physician, respectively. If we consider this listing of occupations as a unit, we can notice how Sahagún has tied the scribe to a sequence of artisans; we notice also that Sahagún locates both the scribe and the singer between those crafts (carpenter, stonecutter, mason) that require more physical than mental skill and those occupations (wise man, physician) that require the opposite. In other sections of his *General History,* whenever the Franciscan father enumerates the artisans, he is sure to include painters among them (Sahagún 1959–1982, bk. 10:25–30, 73; bk. 6:224).

The pictorial evidence supports this assessment by placing the *tlacuiloque* with other crafts specialists. In the Codex Mendoza (70r), where the artist/author presents the trades taught by fathers to their sons, he pictures the carpenter, lapidary, painter, precious-metal worker, and featherworker. When the same manuscript (57r) explains how infants are presented with the insignia of their future trades, the implements depicted are those of the carpenter, featherworker, painter, metalworker, and warrior. In the Mapa Tlotzin, the painter is pictured as the first of seven craftsmen—followed by the pigment grinder, mosaic worker, metalworker, featherworker, lapidary, and fine carpenter—in a scene that shows the crafts being introduced into Texcoco during the rule of Nezahualcoyotl (Fig. 124). Here the painter is shown with twin bowls of red and black ink. In the Codex Mendoza, Mapa Tlotzin, and other representations of painters, the individual is always represented as a manuscript painter instead of a painter of murals or sculpture; usually he or she paints a rectangle decorated with the symbol for a day, which suggests that it is a day-count book or almanac that is being painted (Fig. 5). Manuscript painting was clearly embraced by the crafts. It was also tied to the performing arts, for children born on the day 1 Monkey were favored to be singers, dancers, or scribes or to produce some work of art (Sahagún 1959–1982, bk. 4:82).

Although the *tlacuiloque* described by Father Sahagún and represented in the Codex Mendoza and Mapa Tlotzin are treated more as commoners than as nobil-

ity, other manuscript painters were nobles or *pipiltin,* literally "children of someone [important]." In the Codex Telleriano-Remensis (30r), the wife of the Mexica ruler Huitzilihuitl is depicted as a painter, the only female scribe identified from ancient Mexico. In the Codex Xolotl (maps 4, 5), the leader of a group of people called the Tlailotlaque ("Those Who Came Back") is also identified as a manuscript painter, as is his third son. Fernando de Alva Ixtlilxochitl, who incorporated information from the Codex Xolotl into his alphabetic history, reported that the Tlailotlaque were of the lineage of the Toltecs who came from the Mixteca into the Valley of Mexico; he said they were craftsmen and were "consummate in the art of painting and making histories." Alva Ixtlilxochitl is also the one who says that "the greatest authors and historians . . . were [the deity] Quetzalcoatl, first, and, of the moderns, Nezahualcoyotl king of Texcoco and the two princes of Mexico, Itzcoatl and Xiuhcozcatzin, sons of the king Huitzilihuitl."[24]

These esteemed historians were *tlacuiloque,* to be sure, but they also were *tlamatinime,* learned persons. In Nahuatl-speaking Mexico, the *tlamatini* was a highly literate individual and a scholar, an embodiment of wisdom contained in the painted books; he or she was also a counselor and a teacher. Direct references to the *tlamatinime* are usually silent about whether they or someone else actually painted the books they had in their possession, but they are inseparable from the books and clearly controlled their content and production. The ethnohistorical sources consistently characterize the *tlamatini* as an owner of books. When Sahagún describes men's occupations, he says of the *tlamatini* (whom he calls "el sabio" in Spanish): "The wise man [is] exemplary. He possesses writings; he owns books. [He is] the tradition, the road; a leader of men, a rower, a companion, a bearer of responsibility, a guide." Elsewhere when Sahagún tells how the wise men left the Mexica at Tamoanchan and carried off the books, he identifies the sages as *amoxoaque,* which he translates as "men learned in the ancient paintings." After these learned men carried away the books, Sahagún reports that other wise men created them anew.[25]

When the Mexica lords defended their traditional

ways before the newly arrived Franciscans, they spoke movingly about the *tlamatinime:*

> There are those who guide us . . .
> The priests, those who make the offerings . . . ,
> The tlahtomatinimeh, sages of the word . . .
> who contemplate,
> follow the contents of the books,
> noisily turn the pages, who possess
> the red, the black inks,
> who keep with them the paintings. . . .
> They carry us, guide us,
> those who keep the order of the years
> and know how the day and destinies
> follow their own way. (León-Portilla 1992b: 317)

The *tlamatini,* owner of books and possessor of knowledge, was clearly a person to whom others turned for advice and guidance. They were counselors to the rulers; we remember that when Moctezuma Ilhuicamina thought to send messengers to ancient Aztlan, he summoned the royal historian for advice. Alva Ixtlilxochitl, in the prologue of his *Sumaria relación,* surveys the many subject specialties covered by these scholars and authors, who, he says, are "the most illustrious and knowledgeable people":

> They had writers for each genre: some who handled the Annals, putting in order the things that happened each year, by day, month, and hour. Others were in charge of genealogies and ancestors of the kings and persons of lineage. . . . Some of them took care of painting the limits, boundaries, and boundary lines of the cities, provinces, towns, and places, and of the lots and distribution of lands. . . . Others of the books of laws, rites, and ceremonies that they practiced as infidels; and the priests of the temple of their idolatry . . . and of the feasts of their false gods and calendars. And finally it was the responsibility of the philosophers and sages who were among them to paint all the sciences that they knew and attained and to teach from memory the songs that [preserved] their sciences and histories. (Alva Ixtlilxochitl 1985, 1:527, as translated in Florescano 1994: 35–36)

Alva Ixtlilxochitl's listing echoes Motolinía's (1951: 74–75; 1971: 5) enumeration of the different type of books the Mexica had: annals, almanacs and books of ceremonies, books of dreams and prognostications, books pertaining to baptism and the naming of infants, and books about the rites and omens relating to marriage. Although Motolinía emphasizes religious books, both he and Alva Ixtlilxochitl begin their surveys with the histories, which Motolinía admits are the only books that recount the truth.

History was taught, along with the other liberal arts and sciences, in the *calmecac,* the elite school where young men and women were trained for the priesthood. Sahagún reported that the *calmecac* accepted the children of "rulers, noblemen, and still others, well mothered, well sired, . . . and still others . . . who wished it." It was an institution into which the noble sons almost automatically went, as opposed to the *telpochcalli,* the young men's house that trained especially commoners in the arts of war. The *calmecac* was also open to the children of commoners "who wished it" and who had the aptitude for advanced learning. There in the *calmecac—*"a place of prudence, a place of wisdom, a place of making good, of making righteous"—the boys and girls were taught "the god's songs inscribed in books. And especially was there teaching of the count of days, the book of dreams, and the book of years." The children were taught all the *toltecayotl,* the arts said to have originated with the Toltecs.[26] In Aztec Mexico both commoners and nobles could learn to read and interpret the painted books. In the Mixteca also, according to Father Burgoa (1989: 210), both the children of nobles and those who studied to be priests were instructed in the painting of histories.

Most of the chroniclers, writing in Spanish, refer to the *tlacuiloque* and *tlamatinime* as males, and when they mention specific historians and painters, these individuals are all men. Sahagún treats the painter and sage among the men's occupations, as opposed to the women's professions of weaver, cook, and physician. Most of the pictorial representations of painters are males. Nahuatl, however, is a gender-neutral language, so *tlacuilo* and *tlamatini* mean painter and sage without specifying gender. Only when it is important to indicate that something pertains to women, rather than to men, is the affix *cihua* (woman) added, as in *cihuatlatoani* or "woman ruler."[27] Since Spanish requires a gender designation, the chroniclers automatically converted the neutral terms to masculine, and later scholars followed suit, so *tlamatini* has come simply to be "wise man." Given the preponderance of clearly male painters referred to in the ethnohistorical sources, I would venture that most of the painters and sages probably were males, but the female painter in the Codex Telleriano Remensis alerts us that women, too, were learned in this art. Both boys and girls were trained in the *calmecac* where such skills were taught.

Tlacuilo and *tlamatini,* whether male or female and of common or noble lineage, come together in the person of the manuscript painter. The key to understanding this intersection rests with the divine culture-hero Quetzalcoatl. Quetzalcoatl, according to the Nahuatl legends, was the ruler of the legendary Toltecs, a devout priest who brought the fine and applied arts, the crafts, and all knowledge to the Toltec people. The Toltecs themselves, according to the Mexica and other later peoples, were learned in crafts and exceptionally wise; they originated the year count, the day count, and the sciences. For the Mexica, Quetzalcoatl was patron of the artists and craftspeople—the workers in precious metal, the lapidaries, the featherworkers, the mosaic workers, the scribes. In the Mixteca, Quetzalcoatl was manifest as the culture-hero Lord 9 Wind, one of whose appearances was as a manuscript painter. In Central Mexico, Quetzalcoatl was patron of the *calmecac.* The two supreme Mexica priests, who presided over the *calmecac,* took "their manner of conduct from the life of Quetzalcoatl" and they took his name as their title; they were the Quetzalcoatl priests. They were also the *tlamatinime,* the sages who possessed and interpreted the painted books and guided the people.[28]

Painting/writing, including the painting of history, was a "Toltec" accomplishment in the sense that it was one of the *toltecayotl,* the arts of the Toltecs taught in the *calmecac.* So too was the reading, interpreting, and telling of history. A *tlacuilo* was a *toltecatl* or crafts specialist, and a *tlamatini* was equally a *toltecatl* in the office of priest and the possessor of knowledge. Neither a priest nor a scribe was required to be of noble birth, for as Sahagún's noble informants told him: "And though [the man] were poor, though he were in need, though his father, his mother were the poorest of the poor, if he well carried out the way of life, the precepts of the priests, this one was taken, this one was given the name of Quetzalcoatl. . . . Not lineage was considered, only a good life" (Sahagún 1959–1982, bk. 3:69; also bk. 10:166–169).

Both Diego Durán (1994: 503–505) and Fernando de Alva Ixtlilxochitl (1985, 1:286) mention that the professions of manuscript painter and historian were hereditary and that books passed from father to son. Several of the manuscript painters who came before the Inquisition in the years after the conquest were specifically identified in the court records as sons of important priests, who presumably dealt also with books (Procesos 1912: 115–119, 177–184); the implication was that these sons were destined to follow their fathers as priests and painters, and would have, had not the conquest intervened. After the conquest, a number of native historians mention ancient pictorial histories that were bequeathed to them by their ancestors. Scions of the old ruling families likewise took pride in having inherited their families' painted books (Alva Ixtlilxochitl 1985, 1:286; Schroeder 1991: 16–19).

Historians and rulers treasured the pictorial codices because the documents held explanatory keys to the Mexican social order. The books of hide, paper, and cloth told how the present and previous worlds were created and organized. Like community charters, they explained how the people came to occupy and control the lands they did and how their government was established. The books explained the relationships between peoples, their neighbors, and their enemies. These painted histories of the past held the evidence that supported the rights of the governing families to rule, and they kept true the stories of the heroic deeds of the ancestors.

Writing in Images

The Aztecs and Mixtecs never doubted that their books contained writing. Manuscript painting was simply their way of writing in books and on paper. It was the activity they knew as *tlacuilolli* in Nahuatl and *tacu* in Mixtec, the activity practiced by the scribe/painters, the historians, the day-keepers, and the sages.[1] It was the activity that fulfilled the written needs of the ancient Mexicans. It recorded the past, it preserved the prognosticatory guides that suggested the future, and it documented the many features of the present. The painted characters and figures that held memory and other forms of knowledge were relatively permanent (enduring long after the events they record and long after silence replaced spoken words), and they could be read and interpreted by readers other than their creators. These two features—permanency and readability—which are the features of any writing system, mean that the paintings functioned to establish ideas and to document facts. The painted images in the books gave accountability. As records, they were memory that could be inspected by others.

When Europeans first saw the painted books, they recognized them as such, as books that contained the indigenous Mexican version of writing. Cortés and his companions may have remarked that the books and writings were different from what they as Europeans were accustomed to, but they had no doubt of their function and efficacy. The manuscript painting tradition survived in postconquest Mexico for several generations precisely because it continued to function as the indigenous counterpart to European books written alphabetically and because some (although certainly not all) colonial authorities accepted this equivalency. Painted records were drafted for both native and Spanish-born leaders in the colonial period and were accepted as valid evidence in legal proceedings.

Along with this general acceptance of the painted records, however, came an ambivalence about the nature of the indigenous writing system. Motolinía recognized that the Aztecs had books, but he could not quite accord them writing, because to him, as to most of his contemporaries, writing was alphabetic script that recorded speech.

The Jesuit father José de Acosta, who would later, in his *Historia natural y moral de las Indias,* compare American, European, and Asian civilizations based on their writing systems, shared this uncertainty. We see this in his correspondence with Juan de Tovar in 1586–1587. Tovar had recently sent Acosta a copy of Tovar's chronicle of Mexican history, and Acosta wrote to thank him, saying that he had enjoyed seeing and studying the Mexican history and thought the people back in Europe would enjoy it also. "But," Acosta wrote also, "I wish you would satisfy certain doubts that have occurred to me. In the first place, what certainty or authority does this relation or history possess? In the second place, since the Indians did not have writing, how could they preserve such a quantity and variety of matters for so long a time?" Tovar replied by explaining, first, how his relation had been derived from the study of indigenous books interpreted by the indigenous historians. Then he said, "To the second question, how could the Indians retain so many things in their memory without writing, I repeat that they had figures and hieroglyphs with which they painted things in this way. Objects that could be represented directly were drawn in their own image. Whatever could not be represented directly was drawn with characters representing an image. In this way they drew what they wished. And as for their remembering the time in which each event took place, you have already read about the computation that these people used."[2] Tovar's answer must have persuaded, because Acosta ultimately included Aztec pictography (and Inka knot records) in his hierarchy of writings systems, although a few notches down on his scale. Acosta naturally gave first place to the alphabetic systems of western Europe; he gave second place to the ideograms of China; and in third place he put the pictograms of the Aztecs. His hierarchy served his purpose to distinguish those cultures that had alphabetic writing and history (and, therefore, civilization) from those cultures that did not, even though the latter were able to record the past (in painted books and khipus).

The ambivalence felt by Motolinía and Acosta, and shared by most of their contemporaries, has continued today among those who try to fit Aztec and Mixtec pictography with other writing systems throughout the world over time.[3] The scholars who have defined and categorized writing take a range of positions. Some, like John DeFrancis (1989), define writing strictly as visible speech or the record of spoken language. Others, like Geoffrey Sampson (1985) and Albertine Gaur (1992), expand the definition to include pictography and notational scripts. The majority opinion is represented by Ignace Gelb (1963: 12), who defines writing broadly as "a system of human intercommunication by means of conventional visible marks" but relegates pictography to the category "forerunners of writing."

Everyone who has studied the subject recognizes that language writing or phonetic writing is distinct from those systems that do not record language. When evolutionary models are proposed for the development of writing systems—charting its progress from ideograms, through logograms and syllograms, to the alphabet (e.g., Gelb 1963)—Mexican pictography is usually placed at an early, prewriting stage, or it is located as a dead end along a lateral branch. Never is it found to be "full" writing or "real" writing because it does not usually record words as human utterances in running speech. If one defines writing narrowly as spoken language that is referenced phonetically by visible marks, the Mexican system clearly does not fit.

Writing, Broadly Defined

As an Aztec specialist, I argue for a broader, more encompassing definition of writing, one that embraces nonverbal systems (Boone 1994b). Several of my colleagues, people whom I respect and whose opinions I trust, ask me why we need to do this, when such a broadening blurs the important distinction between phonetic writing and other forms. It is because the word "writing" is so loaded. Writing is not merely a type of notational system but an entire cultural category. It has been used to distinguish literate people from preliterates, people with history from those without, and even civilized people from barbarians or primitives. Writing, as a "cornerstone of the human heritage," to quote Schoville and Senner (in Senner 1989: vii), is seen as a basic element of civilized society. Gelb (1963: 12) represents this prevalent position when he states, "Writing exists only in a civilization and a civilization cannot exist without writing." Given these meanings, how can we deny that the Aztecs and Mixtecs had writing? They clearly had a notational system that allowed them to record the facts of the present and the past and to look toward the future. They were literate, historical, and civilized. Moreover, the broader definition of writing aligns with their own cultural category of writing. By recognizing their pictography as writing, we can begin to understand it more fully as a system with its own vocabulary and grammar, its own signifiers and structures.

The broad definition of writing embraces both verbal and nonverbal systems. It thus encompasses musical notation, choreographic notation, diagramming in chemistry and engineering, and such nonverbal scripts that record mathematical equations and the laws of physics. These notational systems all encode knowledge conventionally and permanently, and they are greatly superior to word writing for preserving certain kinds of information; the mathematical and scientific systems, in particular, are crucial to our understanding of the universe. Of the scholars who have put forward definitions of writing that encompass all these varied systems, Sampson (1985: 29–30) brings us closest, I think, to a good working definition.[4] Recognizing the limitations of seeing writing as "a phenomenon essentially parasitic on spoken language," Sampson wanted as broad a definition as possible but one that still distinguishes writing from art. Two of his definitions combined allow us to recognize writing as *the communication of relatively specific ideas in a conventional manner by means of permanent, visible marks.* This definition focuses on communication, on the use of conventions within an overall structure, and on a degree of permanency.

"All writing is information storage," as Gaur (1992: 14) has put it; "the information is stored mechanically, on an independent object, and can be retrieved and used at any time, in any place (in the case of moveable objects such as books, etc.), by all those who are able to consult and decode it." Permanency means that what is written at one time can be read days, years, or centuries later. Memory is a factor only in the sense that the reader must have learned and must remember the rules of a particular writing system to be able to retrieve the information it stores.

The visible marks, whether they be letters, hieroglyphs, or figural representations, operate and carry meaning according to their association with other marks within a structured system of relatedness. This structured system of relatedness is basically the grammar of the system; it tells us how to read a mark or an image—what meaning to give it—according to its association with other marks or images. As Sampson (1985: 12) argues, writing is like language in being able to communicate meaning by "*structures* of symbols defined by their interconnections." He continues, "What gives any particular element of a language its role in the language is not its superficial physical properties but,

rather, the relationships it enters into with the other elements of the language." Thus the meaning of a sound (in language) or a letter, mark, or image (in writing) is established by the system that relates all the sounds, letters, marks, or images together. Once a potential reader has mastered the grammar of the structure and has learned the vocabulary of letters, marks, or images that this grammar establishes, she or he should be able to read and interpret what is written.

Within this broad definition of writing systems, two basic kinds can be distinguished. One kind embraces what writing specialists have differentially called glottographic, phonographic, phonetic, and syllabic systems, which are systems that represent speech.[5] These are the notational systems that fill the narrow definition of writing. The other kind, which is of particular interest to us here, is what Gelb and Sampson after him call semasiographic systems, and what Hill calls discourse systems.[6] Semasiographic (based on the Greek word *semasia*, which means "meaning") refers to those systems that communicate information directly to the reader within the structure of their own system; these are systems of writing that do not detour through speech to be understood. They function independently of language, although they operate on the same logical level as spoken language and can parallel it. These are the systems that the broader definition of writing embraces.

Some discourse or semasiographic systems are composed of symbols or marks that are arbitrarily codified, where the marks have no intrinsic association to their meaning. Mathematical notation, for example, combines numerals, letters, and a variety of specialized signs that are conventionally understood to represent numbers, things, and actions. Marks having the configuration "$13 \times 4 = 52$" represent the action of multiplying an amount of thirteen unnamed things four times to reach fifty-two things; we know this because we have learned the conventional meaning of each numeral and its relative placement, the meaning of each sign, and how to relate them to each other. Few lay people, however, can read and interpret fully the formula in Figure 1, because we have forgotten or we never learned the complexities of the notational system in which it operates. The marks do not themselves look like what they mean, and their specific meaning also depends on their relative size and placement and on the overall spa-

$$\sigma_X^2 = \frac{1}{n}\left\{\sum_{i=1}^{n} X - n\overline{X}^2\right\}$$

Fig. 1. Formula for calculating the variance of a sample: symbol, size, and relative placement all contribute to the specific meaning.

tial arrangement of the component parts. Musical notation (Fig. 32) and some choreographic notations (such as Labanotation, Fig. 33) are other systems that rely on arbitrarily codified marks, which have no intrinsic association with their meaning outside of the grammar in which they operate (see Chapter 4). None of these systems can be penetrated even slightly unless one learns their specific conventions and grammar. Hill (1967: 94) has called these conventional systems.

Other semasiographic systems involve marks that bear some visual likeness to their meaning. Hill (1967: 94) has called these iconic systems to reflect the natural relationship between the mark and its referent. The mark is a stylized image of what it symbolizes. These systems are largely pictorial, and because they are pictorial, people who share the same visual culture find it easier to recognize and remember the meanings of the individual images than with conventional systems. Such pictorial writing systems are on the ascendancy at the opening of the millennium as Western culture becomes increasingly visual and increasingly multinational. Iconic writing systems are found in the growing body of pictographic signs for travelers in airports and other public places, in the corpus of international road signs, and even in the diminutive instructions for cleaning that appear on the labels of our garments. The icon-rich software systems developed for the Macintosh computer and then for IBM systems were championed as more user-friendly than the MS-DOS–based IBM systems precisely because they were more pictorial. All these pictographic systems instruct us and guide us without necessarily resorting to words.

Pictorial or iconic systems, like conventional ones, still must be learned, however. It is only that the visual resemblance between the marks and known objects make them easier to master for people who share the same visual culture. Context is also crucial to meaning.

The instruction panel for operating a hand dryer of the kind often found in public washrooms (Fig. 2), for example, successfully conveys information through the interplay of recognizable images, conventional abstractions, and the relative placement of these elements. Meanings are clarified by the context of the instructional panel. The two images of the hands would probably be recognized as hands by the intended audience in any context, but their activities might be unclear: the first could conceivably be read as signaling and the second as clapping, were it not for the circular disk, the three wavy lines (painted red in the original), and their placement on a forced-hot-air dryer. These additional visual elements and this context establish the actions as pressing a button and rubbing back and forth under hot air. We know to read the wavy lines as heat because we have learned to associate the color red with "hot," as opposed to blue, which is "cold" (when found as markers on plumbing), and we automatically know to read the panel from left to right because that is the way we have been trained to read most written texts. The instruction panel gives the potential user a quick, direct message about how the dryer works. Such pictorial instructions, short and to the point, are increasingly appearing as visual texts in public facilities and as labels on internationally traded merchandise. They work so well because they convey meaning regardless of the language one speaks, and they are quickly understood by those who share knowledge of this visual culture.

Mexican Pictography

Mixtec and Aztec writing is semasiographic in that it conveys meaning directly to the reader without usually having to form words. Largely pictorial, or iconic, it is composed predominantly of figural images that bear

Fig. 2. Instructions for operating a hot air dryer. Image courtesy of the World Dryer Corporation.

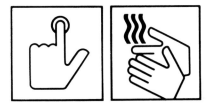

some likeness to, or visual association with, the ideas, things, or actions they represent. But like all pictorial systems, Aztec and Mixtec writing also contains abstractions and other marks that were arbitrarily assigned certain meanings, meanings unrelated to their likeness. In addition, Mexican pictography has a logographic or phonetic component used in appellatives, where some images intentionally represent voiced words or sounds. The pictorial writing of the Aztecs and Mixtecs is thus not purely one kind of writing or another. Instead, abstract conventions and phonetic referents join the fundamental pictography to form a composite system that could function across linguistic boundaries.

The whole point of this system is that it did not usually record speech and thus was not dependent on one language or another. I have been referring to it as the Aztec and Mixtec writing system, but it is also commonly considered to be the message-carrying aspect of the Mixteca-Puebla Horizon Style, a so-called "style" that spread over the central portion of Mexico in the Post-Classic period (A.D. 900–1520), carrying with it a distinctive graphic style, iconographic program, and pictographic writing system.[7] This horizon style was adopted by speakers of many different languages, including Nahuatl, Otomi, Totonac, Cuicatec, Chocho, Mixtec, Zapotec, and Tlapanec, to name just a range of linguistic groups whose painted documents share many features. Educated elites throughout Central Mexico understood and used the visual conventions of this style in their high-status ceramics, costume, mural painting, and manuscript painting. My sense is that a Mixtec-speaking painter/scribe who was well educated could read an Aztec history and understand the gist of the story, although he or she might not comprehend all the details. Likewise, a Tlapanec historian in distant Guerrero could paint a document (like the Codex Azoyu I or II [Fig. 133]) that was readily intelligible to his counterparts in Mexico-Tenochtitlan.

Although many of the pictorial elements comprising the vocabulary of the pictographic system have been deciphered, the grammar that drives it is not well understood. Few people have attempted to explain Aztec or Mixtec writing as a system of visual communication. A notable exception is Mary Elizabeth Smith (1973a: 20–35; 1983b: 238–245), who has given us a comprehensive overview and clear explanations of the pictorial

conventions used in the Mixtec genealogical histories. There is nothing comparably broad for the Aztec manuscripts. Aztec specialists have tended to acknowledge the pictorial character of the Aztec writing system but to concentrate on explaining the glyphic information, such as numbers, dates, and nominatives like place signs and name glyphs. As Maarten Jansen (1988a: 90–91) points out, scholars since the seventeenth century have focused on deciphering Aztec place signs, especially those in the Codex Mendoza.[8] Too, there has been a tendency to separate the Aztec material into two parts—the images (what Hanns Prem [1992: 54] and Prem and Berthold Riese [1983: 170] cogently call the narrative pictography) and the texts (the glyphic information)—and to see the glyphs either as the armature of the system (Berlo 1983: 9) or as captions to the images (Prem and Riese 1983: 170; Lounsbury 1989: 203; Marcus 1992: 29). This classificatory division between text and image helps us see the glyphs as wordlike texts, so scholars have most often concentrated on explaining their logographic or phonetic character; but this division often then makes it easy for us to ignore the fundamental meaning conveyed by the images. Mixtec manuscripts do not lend themselves to this kind of separation of glyphic and pictorial elements because the materials are too well integrated.

A student looking for overall explanations of Mexican pictography thus can turn to Smith's (1973a: 20–54; 1983b) analyses of the pictorial conventions in the Mixtec codices and to Maarten Jansen's (1988a) overview of the larger pictographic system. For brief and general coverage of the Aztec writing, beyond analyses of the place signs and appellatives, he or she can read two pioneering articles by Charles Dibble (1955, 1971) and, more recently, the good discussions by Miguel León-Portilla (1992a: 43–55), James Lockhart (1992: 326–330), and Hanns Prem (1992: 53–55). Joyce Marcus (1992) is perhaps alone in explaining many of the pictorial conventions for both Mixtec and Aztec materials, this in a broadly framed study that also includes Maya and Zapotec writing. Ultimately, of course, our understanding of the pictography rests with those who have studied and interpreted the messages of the pictorial manuscripts themselves.

Mexican pictography takes advantage of a range of pictorial strategies to hold meaning. These extend from figural representation, to abstraction and arbitrary conventions, to phonetic word writing. Although it can be useful to discuss these strategies individually—and I will do so—we should recognize that it is almost impossible on a practical level to separate one strategy from the other because their borders blend into each other. The situation is more like a sliding scale from figure painting, through conventionally understood images, to phonetic graphemes. The figural pictography may carry most of the story, as Prem and Riese (1983) have said, but this figural representation is itself shot through with ideographs of various kinds.

Pictorial Representation

Aztec and Mixtec writing is considered pictorial because much of the information is conveyed representationally. This presentational mode is what Prem and Riese call narrative pictography, what Lockhart calls depiction, what Jansen (1988a: 97) calls the iconic mode, and what León-Portilla calls pictographs. By any term, these are images of people, things, and events that have a recognizable visual resemblance to what they represent. Certainly the images are conventionalized and suppress any potentially confusing details, but we generally consider them to represent what they picture. The act of conquest, for example, is represented in both the Mixtec Codex Selden and the Aztec Codex Mendoza by a warrior grasping her or his foe by the hair (Fig. 3ab).[9] In the Codex Selden it is the ruler Lady 6 Monkey, who is identified by her day name, 6 Monkey, attached to her by a line. In the Codex Mendoza it is an unnamed warrior, whose identity is established by his short quilted cotton armor and his hairstyle of a warrior's topknot. In both cases the victor holds a shield and sword, and the vanquished demonstrates his powerlessness by his subservient body posture and limp arm gestures. These are straightforward depictions of conquest, although someone who has never previously looked at a Mexican pictorial history might have trouble reading the image. We also

---

Fig. 3. Pictorial representations and ideograms related to conquest and war: **a,** Lady 6 Monkey conquering Lord 6 Lizard; **b,** unnamed Mexica conquers unnamed foe; **c,** shield and spears as an ideogram for war; **d,** shield and club as an ideogram for war; **e,** burning of a temple as an ideogram for the conquest of a polity; **f,** Lord 13 Eagle standing on the chevron path (war path); **g,** chevron path signaling an enemy polity; **h,** *atl tlachinolli* (water/burned field), the Aztec metaphor for war. Drawings by John Montgomery. *Sources:* **a,** Selden 8a; **bce,** Mendoza 2r, 2v, 2v; **d,** Boturini 19; **f,** Bodley 28b; **g,** Selden Roll; **h,** Teocalli de la Guerra Sagrada.

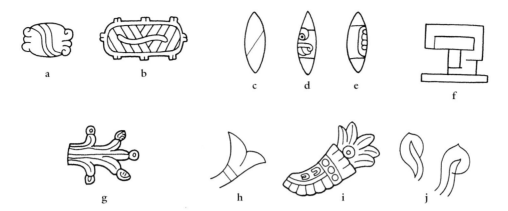

Fig. 4. Pictorial representations of material things: **a,** rock or stone in Aztec manuscripts; **b,** rock or stone in Mixtec manuscripts; **c,** flint knife; **d,** flint knife; **e,** flint knife; **f,** house; **g,** water; **h,** fire; **i,** fire; **j,** smoke. Drawings by John Montgomery. *Sources:* **acfghj,** Mendoza 18r, 3r, 10r, 32r, 3v, 3v; **bde,** Vienna 19b, 11a, 24b; **i,** Teocalli.

must know to read these images as the defeat of one polity by another rather than the victory of one warrior over the other.

The difficulty for the untrained reader is to understand the visual reference. Many, perhaps most, pictographs must be learned, although the resemblance between the image and its meaning usually becomes clear once it has been explained (Fig. 4). Depictions of rock or stone, for example, emphasize striations found in the geological matrix: as a cluster of S-curved lines in Aztec manuscripts and as crossed multicolored bands in Mixtec manuscripts; the series of curl-bump-curl motifs usually characterize images of stone and earth. When the painters represent a flint (knife), they draw a pointed lozenge and divide it diagonally into white and red sides or (in elaborate examples) enliven it with an anthropomorphizing fanged face; sometimes they instead add a row of teeth. The painters depict a house by drawing one half of the structure's facade, emphasizing one post and half the lintel over the entrance, and adding either a thatch or a concrete roof on top; Donald Robertson (1959: 19) has termed this a T-elevation. Water is identified by its internal striations and by its arms that end in shells or discs; it usually flows in the direction the arms reach. Fire appears often as a bifurcated tongue of red, although in elaborate examples it adopts the paneled body of the fire serpent. Smoke appears as curls or scrolls, often colored gray. All of these images are abstracted and conventionalized, but the general resemblance holds.

Ideograms

Another way of conveying meaning is through ideograms, where single images convey larger or unportrayable ideas, concepts, or things.[10] In Mexican manuscripts, there are two types, one representational and the other arbitrarily conventional.[11]

The first is the image that is related by natural association to its message, where the image may depict one element or a small part of the total message. For example, the picture of a round shield backed by either a cluster of darts or by an obsidian-edged sword is an ideogram for battle or war between one polity and another (Fig. 3cd). The image represents the weapons for war, which stand for the larger whole. The shield is typically round in Mexican manuscripts, and in Aztec ones it is usually decorated with evenly spaced balls or tufts of down. In some contexts, as in the Codex Mendoza, the ideogram also carries the meaning of victory, specifically the victory (military or not) of the Mexica over other *altepetl*.[12]

The image of a temple with its roof or superstructure askew, and often emitting red flames and gray curls of smoke, represents the defeat of a polity (Fig. 3e). The painters record this defeat by representing one of the most striking aspects of the event, that the victors often burned the temple of the loser and carried away its patron deity. This image is close to being an abbreviated figural representation, similar in kind to the example of a warrior capturing her or his enemy, but it is both more concise and more abstract as a visual statement. The difference between figural representation and ideogram is a small one, however, and indeed many images can be considered either.[13]

The second kind of ideogram, distinct from those that refer visually to what they symbolize, has no natural visual association with the meaning it conveys. The image is an arbitrary (as far as we know) referent to a thing, idea, or happening. In Mixtec codices and some Coixtlahuaca Valley pictorials, a path decorated by chevrons represents warfare when a warrior stands upon it brandishing weapons; without the warrior the path takes the general meaning of enemy (voiced as *yecu* in Mixtec), especially when associated with place signs (Smith 1973a: 33; Fig. 3fg). In Aztec manuscripts, the concept of a day can be represented in one of three ways (Fig. 5): by four plain disks clustered as a square, by a more complex disk characterized by a pinwheel of different colors and embellished with four small disks around the edge,[14] and by a rectangle decorated diagonally with two opposed scrolls (something similar to a percent sign), sometimes painted red. This latter image occurs as the object being painted by manuscript painters,[15] and it apparently represents not simply a day (as do the others) but a day accompanied by all the mantic associations that belong to it as part of the *tonalpohualli* (the sacred cycle of 260 days). When Aztec manuscript painters are shown painting, they are being shown painting a *tonalamatl* or sacred almanac of the days. Not one of these three ideograms bears any resemblance to the concept "day," although we know them to convey the meaning of day. The association of the images to their meaning is conventionally understood only because it has been culturally assigned; there is no visual similarity. Ideographs for movement and for gold belong to this category of arbitrarily assigned images, as do all the images that are day signs (discussed more fully below).

Metaphors also fall into this category of ideogram. They often appear as couplets and reflect metaphoric thinking that manifests itself both in spoken language and pictorial writing. The metaphor for war, for example, which is expressed in the Nahuatl language as

Fig. 5. Ideograms for "day" and a painter painting a *tonalamatl* ("day book") or divinatory almanac. Drawings by John Montgomery. *Sources:* Mendoza 7v, 19r, 70r.

in atl, in tlachinolli (the water, the burned field), is pictured in the codices and on Aztec relief sculpture as a band of water and a band of fire or burned field twisted together (Fig. 3h).[16] Another metaphor is expressed by the colors red and black; when they come together in pictorial codices (e.g., Mapa Tlotzin, Codex Vienna 48b, Codex Telleriano-Remensis 30r), they refer to manuscript painting, to the painted books, or to wisdom (or all these concepts); when the colors are voiced in Nahuatl as *in tlalli, in tlapilli* (the black, the red), they carry the same meaning. Visual metaphors are like arbitrarily assigned ideographs in that they bear no immediate resemblance to what they mean.

Phonetic Referents

At the other end of the representational scale from figural representation are those images or pictorial elements that function solely as phonetic referents. These almost always appear in place names either as a main sign or as an accessory element that qualifies the principal glyph. Phoneticism was relatively infrequent in pre-Columbian Mexican imagery but increased after the Spanish invasion when the Mexicans were faced with the task of representing Spanish names.

Before the conquest, most personal and place names were written pictographically or ideographically rather than phonetically. The glyphic image either represented or referred visually to the name and could be voiced in any language. For example, the Mexica emperor Ahuitzotl (Water Beast) is pictorially identified by a rodentlike beast with a characteristically long tail

Fig. 6. Name sign of Ahuitzotl (Water Beast). Drawing by John Montgomery. *Source:* Mendoza 13r.

that often has a water element attached (Fig. 6); the name glyph will yield the meaning Water Beast in all languages. Many place signs, too, can be voiced in both Nahuatl and Mixtec. An example is the Mixtec community kingdom known as Yucu Dzaa (Hill of the Bird) in Mixtec and as Tututepec (Bird Hill) in Nahuatl; it is pictorially named in both Aztec and Mixtec codices as a hill qualified by the image of a bird or bird's head (Fig. 7; Smith 1973a: 37, 246). As in most name signs, the visual elements are not functioning phonetically, although they do yield the words for the names.

Pure phoneticism occurs with names whose meaning might otherwise be ambiguous or with names that cannot easily be depicted pictorially. Phonetic qualifiers can be added to a name sign to ensure the proper reading. Thus, the place sign for Yucu Dzaa (Hill of the Bird) sometimes includes a human chin (*dzaa*) as a phonetic complement (Fig. 7b); this tells the reader to interpret the bird as *dzaa* rather than *yaha* or eagle (Smith 1973a: 67). Phoneticism plays a larger role in the place sign for the community kingdom of Teozacoalco, whose Mixtec name, Chiyo Ca'nu or Great Foundation, was not easily represented as a large platform. The painters of the Codex Bodley and the Mapa de Teozacoalco thus depicted the platform (*chiyo*) in the process of being bent or doubled by a person; this yielded the sound for doubled, *canu,* to reach Chiyo

Ca'nu (Fig. 8; Caso 1949: 153–155; Smith 1973a: 57–58).[17] Outside the realm of the place sign, Jansen (1988a: 98) has suggested that the image of a speech scroll with dots may represent ashes (*yaa*), which might be a phonetic complement in Mixtec for song (*yaa*). Byland and Pohl (1994: 111) mention that the image of a deer leg (*sii*) may represent "grandmother" (*sii*) in Mixtec when it appears with the priestess Lady 9 Grass, forming part of her title, Yan'si or Royal Grandmother.[18]

Aztec painters also relied occasionally on phonetic references to supplement pictorial representation in their place signs. The place sign of Culhuacan ("Place of the Culhua" or "Place of Those with Ancestors"), for example, has a phonetic main sign. Since it would be exceedingly difficult to picture the Culhua as distinctive people or to indicate the ancestors, the painters chose to represent the place as a hill sign (a conventionalized hill) that has a long curved top, not unlike a summer squash in shape (Fig. 9). The curved element yields the Nahuatl word *coltic* ("curved"), which effectively identifies the *cul* sound in Culhuacan.[19] In Central Mexican manuscripts, however, phonetic main signs are rare; instead phonetic indicators most often appear as accessory elements to represent qualities—such as "small," "near," or "on top of"—that defy representation. For example, the crouching lower half of a human figure yields the word *tzin* ("bottom or rump"), which also means "small." A set of two or three teeth gives *tlan* ("teeth"), which also means "near."[20] A banner yields *pan*, which is read as "on or over." Figure 10 identifies and illustrates some of the common phonetic qualifiers found in Aztec manuscripts.

This use of phoneticism by Mixtec and Aztec scribes before the Spanish invasion meant that the principle of phonetic transfer was known to them and was an acceptable if less common way of writing, even if it was not much used outside the genre of appellatives. Pho-

Fig. 7. Mixtec (**ab**) and Aztec (**c**) place signs of Yucu Dzaa or Tututepec (Hill of the Bird). Drawings by John Montgomery. *Sources:* **a,** Bodley 9c; **b,** Zouche-Nuttall 45d; **c,** Mendoza 13r.

a

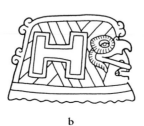

b

c

Fig. 8. Place sign of Chiyo Ca'nu (Great Foundation), renamed Teozacoalco in Nahuatl: the platform (*chiyo*) being bent or doubled (*canu*). Drawing by John Montgomery. *Source:* Bodley 15c.

neticism complemented pictorial and ideographic imaging.

After the conquest, the frequency of phoneticism increased even more when Aztec scribes found themselves needing to represent European names, which were strange and arbitrary sounding to them.[21] Occasionally the Aztecs renamed a person in Nahuatl or translated the name to Nahuatl and rendered it pictorially. This is the case with Cortés' captain, Pedro de Alvarado, whom the Aztecs called Tonatiuh, or Sun, because of his red-blond hair and fair skin; his name sign

Fig. 9. Place sign of Culhuacan. Drawing by John Montgomery. *Source:* Boturini 20.

became the image of the sun (Fig. 11a). The judge Alonso de Zorita was pictorially identified by the head of a quail, *zollin* in Nahuatl (Fig. 11b), which approximates "Zorita," considering that the Nahuas did not distinguish between the sounds *l* and *r*.

Most Europeans were not readily renamed, however, and their names were not easily pictured; so the native scribes turned to phonetic transfer to render their names as a cluster of pictographs. Thus Francisco was represented pictorially by a banner (*pan*), seashell (*cilin*), and pot (*com*) to yield *pan-ci-co,* a rough approximation of Francisco among those whose language did not recognize an *f* (Fig. 11c). The surname of the first viceroy, Antonio de Mendoza, was usually referenced by maguey leaves (*me*) and a gopher (*tozan*) to yield *me-toza,* although some scribes preferred to use a stone (*te*) and gopher (*tozan*) for *te-toza,* or they combined an eye (*ix*) with a bean (*e*) to render *ix-e* or "Virrey" (Fig. 11d–h; Boornazian 1996: 90–91). The pictographs for such Spanish names often vary considerably from manuscript to manuscript, for without a long tradition of writing these names pictorially, the scribes followed their own phonetic preferences. Then, as the Aztec scribes became accustomed to writing phonetically, they began in the late sixteenth century to represent their own names this way, too.[22]

Thus, phonetic referents join with ideograms and pictorial representation to give the Mexican manuscript painters a wide range of strategies for writing pictorially. Pictorial images, shaped by reduction and convention, are the foundation for the system, where, as Lockhart (1992: 328) has said, "fluidity [was] the keynote." The painter had many options, many choices to make in the way she or he described the past and the present. This means, also, that the same images could

Fig. 10. Phonetic indicators used in Aztec place signs: **a,** rump (*tzin*) for "small" in Tulanzingo (Little Place of Sedges); **b,** teeth (*tlan*) for "near" in Quauhtitlan (Near the Trees); **c,** speech (*nahua*) for "among" in Quauhnahuac (Among the Trees); **d,** banner (*pan*) for "on" in Tochpan (On the Rabbit). Drawings by John Montgomery. *Sources:* Mendoza 3v, 3v, 2v, 52r.

a   b   c   d

Fig. 11. Name signs for Spaniards: **a,** the sun (*tonatiuh*) for Alvarado, who was called Tonatiuh; **b,** the head of a quail (*zollin*) for Zorita; **c,** the combination of banner (*pan*), shells (*cilin*), and pot (*com*) for Francisco (*pan-ci-co*); **def,** maguey (*me*) and gopher (*tozan*) for Mendoza (*me-toza*); **g,** eye (*ix*) and bean (*e*) for Virrey; **h,** stone (*te*) and go-pher (*tozan*) for Mendoza. Drawings by John Montgomery. *Sources:* **a,** Telleriano-Remensis 46r; **b,** Osuna 16v; **c,** Galarza 1979: pl. 2.7; **d,** Aubin 48v; **e,** Telleriano-Remensis 46r; **f,** Tepechpan 17; **g,** Mexicanus 79; **h,** Cruz 3c.

be used and thus read in many different ways. In place names especially, as Prem (1992: 57–60) points out, many of the ideograms yield multiple readings. Thus, the place glyph of a hill with a bird can read generically as Tototepec or Yucu Dzaa (Bird Hill) or more spe-cifically as Yucu Yeza (Eagle Hill) or Hilotepec (Dove Hill).

Jansen (1988a: 97) gives the example of a banner to point out the different meanings a single image can hold. As a pictorial representation, a banner is simply that, a banner, perhaps one of a certain kind. On a more ideographic level, however, a banner may refer to the monthly feast of Panquetzaliztli, or a banner held by an individual can indicate that that person is des-tined to be sacrificed or already has been; the banner becomes an ideograph that refers to the monthly feast or to the sacrificial act. On a more abstractly ideo-graphic level, a banner can mean "20 things," because it is the usual symbol for 20 in Aztec manuscripts. As a phonetic referent, a banner (*pan*) can also mean "on,

above," as in the place name Tochpan or On the Rab-bit (Fig. 10d). In each case, the image of the banner is the same.

The difficulty with reading the Mexican manuscripts has always been, first, in understanding the pictorial abstractions and conventions and then, second, in knowing on what level to interpret them. It is a multi-valent writing system, for its elements carry meaning on many levels and can mean (or suggest) several things at one time. The conventions of pictorial representa-tion and the ideograms can be learned, but the mean-ing a particular image will have at any time depends ul-timately on its pictorial context. Context—an image's association with all the other images that come before, after, and around it (plus the function of the manu-script)—guides the reader to the meaning an image conveys. We thus cannot take an image or an element out of its context and understand all of its meanings.

Pictorial Conventions

Pictorial conventions are the basic elements of the Mexican writing system. Most are fairly well understood, thanks to the work of two centuries of codex scholars who have painstakingly compared and interpreted the imagery, although the meanings of some still elude us.

Many, perhaps most, conventions are shared among Aztec and Mixtec manuscripts. The conquest scenes of Figure 3ab, for example, are common to both, as are depictions of such things as houses, bodies of water, animals, and the like; manuscript painters from both cultures shared the same day signs and calendar. Some conventions, however, tend to be specific either to Mixtec manuscripts or to Aztec manuscripts and have come to be considered hallmarks of one tradition or the other. Often they relate to specific cultural metaphors (such as the combination of water and fire [*atl tlachinolli*] to mean war [Fig. 3h]) or to particular ways of doing things. Mixtec painters, for example, designate that a date is to be read as a year instead of a day by linking the date to what is now called an A-O year sign (discussed more fully below); Aztec painters designate a year by framing the date in a (usually rectangular) cartouche. A painter from the Valley of Mexico would not be likely to use the Mixtec convention, and vice versa, although I am sure they knew about them. When these characteristically Aztec or Mixtec conventions come together in the same manuscript, as many do in the pictorial histories from Puebla and northwestern Oaxaca, they signal the mixed cultural heritage of these codices.[23]

Because there are many more shared conventions than there are distinctive ones, I organize the pictorial conventions, below, not by culture but by subject matter. The pictorial contents of the codices are divided here into dates and time, persons, places, and various actions and events. These reflect the essential concerns of histories: to give the when, who, where, and what of a story. This review does not cover all of the conventions used in Mexican pictography but focuses on the information that appears in the pictorial histories.

Dates and Time

Mesoamericans from the Pre-Classic period through the Spanish invasion shared a single calendrical system. They conceptualized and recorded a cycle of fifty-two years, composed of a 260-day sacred calendar that interfaced with a 365-day "solar" year. Different Mesoamerican peoples represented and named the signs for the days, "months," and years differently, but they all used the same system.[24]

The 365-day vague year is the least important ideologically and historiographically. It approximates the solar year and functioned primarily to time agricultural events and organize the solar year into a series of festivals. It was composed of eighteen "months" of twenty days each, with five useless and generally unlucky days left over at the end. The Aztecs represented the months in three ways: by depicting the activities of the feasts that dominated these twenty-day periods, by portraying the patron deities of these feasts, or by painting ideograms that referred either to the feast or the patron. Representations of the festival activities and depictions of their patron deities appear only in early colonial manuscripts that were created to document the Aztec calendar; they do not figure in the historical manuscripts. Glyphs that refer to the months appear in tribute rolls to indicate the frequency that tribute was expected, but they do not have an active role in the pictorial histories. Aztec scribes did not use the month glyphs to date events in their painted histories.[25] Mixtec painters, to my knowledge, did not represent these months at all.[26]

The calendar that *was* used for dating was the 260-day ritual cycle, composed of a count of twenty days that repeated thirteen times. The Aztecs called it the *tonalpohualli*, which means simply the "day count"; we do not know the corresponding Mixtec term. It was the only count that truly mattered to the Aztecs and their neighbors because the days carried augural meaning that governed all natural and cultural happenings. Each of the twenty days had its symbol and corresponding name, and each followed in an established sequence from Crocodile through Flower (Fig. 12), which repeated in perpetuity. Each day also had a number, from 1 through 13, which also repeated. In this way, the day 1 Crocodile was followed by 2 Wind, 3 House, 4 Lizard, and so forth until the numbers arrive at 13

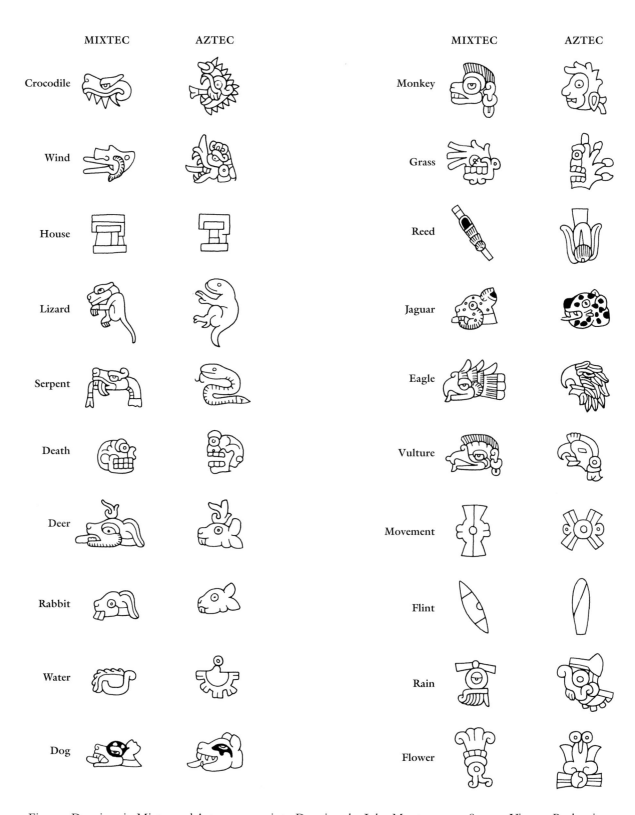

Fig. 12. Day signs in Mixtec and Aztec manuscripts. Drawings by John Montgomery. *Sources:* Vienna, Borbonicus.

with 13 Reed, after which day number 1 occurred again, to give 1 Jaguar, 2 Eagle, and so forth. We should keep in mind that these numbers were never considered to be amounts—5 Flower did not mean five flowers, although sometimes the day names were mistakenly translated into Spanish as such—rather they were numbers attached to sequent days.

Painters throughout Post-Classic Central Mexico recognized the same day names and signs, although they voiced them in their own language and they drew some of them a little differently. The day signs Wind, Water, Grass, and Reed occasion the greatest variation, even within the same manuscript. The painters represented the numbers as a string of disks, often grouping the disks five at a time, if there were many. Mixtec painters sometimes grouped them in smaller strings and often colored them in different hues, even within the same string. The Mixtecs also had a special verbal vocabulary for the day signs and numbers, a vocabulary that is thought to be an archaic form of Mixtec.[27] This suggests that the numbers of the days belong to a different conceptual category than numbers for amounts (discussed below).

Days and Years. Throughout Mexico four of the day signs were also year signs, for the 365-day year took its identity either from the day that began it or the day that ended its last month. Many have argued that the year was named for its first day—a year beginning on the day 1 Rabbit would be named 1 Rabbit, for example—although Caso (1971: 346–347) has suggested instead that the year was named for the last day of the last "month," before the five useless days. Among the Aztecs and Mixtecs, these year bearer signs were Rabbit, Reed, Flint, and House (Fig. 13). Among the Tlapanec and Cuicatec, the year signs were Deer, Grass, Movement, and Wind.[28] The year signs, like the day signs, repeated serially, as did the numbers 1 through 13 that accompanied them, so that the year 1 Rabbit was followed by 2 Reed, 3 Flint, 4 House, 5 Rabbit, 6 Reed, and so forth.[29] This great cycle, created by the correspondence of the 260 days of the sacred count and the 365 days of the vague year, contained fifty-two years (or four year signs × 13 numbers), after which 1 Rabbit would come around again, and the year count would then continue again with 2 Reed. The Aztecs called the years *xihuitl,* which means both year and turquoise, and when they represented an unnamed year,

they painted it as a disk of turquoise, often a disk of turquoise mosaic.[30]

People in the central valleys of Mexico began their fifty-two-year cycle on the year 2 Reed. When one cycle ended, they extinguished all fires throughout the land, and then drilled a new fire to bring in the new cycle. Aztec painters, much more so than their Mixtec counterparts, record these cyclical New Fire ceremonies in their histories (discussed below under Events and Action).

Some day names—for example, 5 Flower—could only be days; but others—such as 1 Rabbit—could be either days or years. The history painters solved the problem of identifying a date as a day or a year by marking it as a year when appropriate. The Mixtec painters used what has been called an A-O sign, a symbol that interlocks a pointed ray and a flattened circle

Fig. 13. Year signs in Mixtec (**a**) and Aztec (**b**) manuscripts. Drawings by John Montgomery. *Sources:* Vienna, Mendoza.

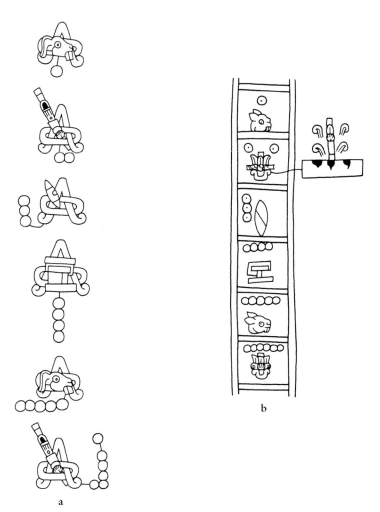

a

b

(Fig. 13a); they either attached the year name to it or embraced the year sign in the arms of the A-O (Smith 1973a: 22). The Aztecs enclosed the year name in a rectangular cartouche, one that was almost always painted blue or turquoise (Fig. 13b). Some variation to this rectangular cartouche was allowed, however, for the painter of the Tira de Tepechpan (Fig. 127) enclosed the year names in circular cartouches of different colors.[31] Similarly, the painter who designed the cosmogram on page 1 of the Codex Fejérváry-Mayer painted circular cartouches with yellow frames around the four year bearers.

The vast majority of dates appear in the pictorial histories in order to place an event firmly in time. They signal to the reader when an action or activity occurred. But both Aztec and Mixtec histories also contain dates that are so wrapped in strong associative meaning that these metaphorical signals dominate the temporal ones. The Aztecs, probably the commoners as well as the intellectuals, associated the year 1 Flint with great beginnings. This year, 1 Flint, was the year the Mexica left Aztlan to begin their long and arduous migration; this 1 Flint year initiates the year count, so that in the Codex Mexicanus (Fig. 142) the Mexica are depicted actually stepping up on the ribbon of time, which begins when they leave Aztlan. On 1 Flint years the Mexica also seated their first monarch, Acamapichtli, and their third monarch, Itzcoatl, who established the empire (Boone 1992: 152–153). The year 1 Flint is the date used in the Codex Xolotl to mark the founding of polities, where it functions less as an actual year than as a signal that the polity is being founded (Figs. 42, 120). The year 1 Rabbit carried strong, but dire, associations. It was the year of the great famine of 1454, when droughts and pests had destroyed the crops and many of the people in Central Mexico perished or sold themselves into slavery in order to survive. The year name 1 Rabbit came thus to carry this meaning, and one finds that 1 Rabbit years are often associated with droughts or famine in the histories. The years absorbed meaning from the outstanding events or individuals linked to them.

This is even more true in the Mixteca, where certain day and year combinations carry metaphoric meaning that outweighed any chronological import. Two dates in particular appear frequently in the Codex Vienna Obverse, where the painter describes how the Mixteca was created and geographically arranged. The year 1 Reed, day 1 Crocodile (combining the first number, the first year sign, and the first day sign), appears twenty times in the Vienna Obverse and is frequent in other manuscripts; it has been identified as a metaphor for beginnings, especially the beginning of royal dynasties. The year 13 Rabbit, day 2 Deer, appears eight times in the Vienna Obverse; it, too, is associated with beginnings, as well as with actions, place signs, and attendants of the archetypal priest Lord 2 Dog. Other metaphorical dates are 5 Flint, 5 Flint; 7 Flint, 7 Flint; 1 Rabbit, 1 Rabbit; 9 Rabbit, 5 Wind; etc. Most, if not all, of the year and day date combinations in the Vienna Obverse are metaphorical rather than chronological. Many are associated with particular place signs, either being the date of their founding or combining the day names of their founding couples (or both at the same time). When these nonchronological dates appear in the historical manuscripts, they are functioning not as factually secure temporal markers but as signals of larger metaphorical messages.[32]

Calendrical Correlation. Although scholars are still debating which is the first "month" of the Aztec year and when this year began, there is agreement about the general correlation of the Mexica and Spanish calendars. Tenochtitlan fell on August 13, 1521, in the Julian calendar; this was the day 1 Serpent in the year 3 House (Caso 1971: 346–347). That year in the Mixteca was 2 House (Smith 1973a: 22), however, for there is a 40-day difference between the year bearers of the two counts (the Mixtec 2 House is 40 days before the Mexica 3 House). The Aztec year 2 Reed (the time of the New Fire ceremony and the beginning of the Aztec cycle) was the Mixtec year 1 Reed (the beginning of their cycle). Several scholars have proposed even more variation in the year counts employed throughout Central Mexico in the fifteenth and sixteenth centuries, saying that as many as thirteen different year counts were simultaneously in operation, including separate ones in the neighboring cities of Mexico-Tenochtitlan, Texcoco, Cuitlahuac, and Culhuacan (which allegedly had two different ones). I am not convinced by these proposals, however, and elsewhere have argued against them; certainly, one does not see such variation in the pictorial codices.[33]

Amounts. For amounts of things—but not for date numbers—the Post-Classic Mexican painters drew upon a slightly larger repertoire of signs. In the Codex

Selden (3a), the painter took advantage of a symbol characteristically used among the Maya and Zapotec (among other peoples): a bar to represent 5. He explained the preparation of twenty sacred bundles by painting four bars to indicate the amount of 20 (Caso 1964a: 29, 76; Pohl 1994b: 28). This use of the Maya and Zapotec bar is relatively rare in the Mexican pictorials, however.[34] I do not know of an instance where an Aztec painter used it. Instead the painters of the central valleys usually linked five disks together with an underline, or occasionally they would link five strokes with a bridge (this especially in cadastral registers, where it may represent a postconquest variation on the linked disks [Fig. 14ab]).

For quantities of 20, Mexican painters usually used banners, stringing the banners together to reach higher numbers. For example, in explaining how the Mexica ruler Cuitlahuac died after eighty days in office, the painter of the Codex Aubin attached banners to four blue disks symbolizing 20 × 4 days (Fig. 14c). In what seems to be a regional variation of this, the painters of such Texcocan manuscripts as the Codex Xolotl and Mapa Quinatzin replaced the banner with something

very much like a corn cob to represent 20 (Fig. 14d). Aztec painters indicated amounts of 400 with a stylized feather and 8,000 with a bag of incense (Fig. 14ef).[35] All these numerical symbols only appear occasionally in the historical codices when the painters must indicate great quantities of a thing, as, for example, in the Codex Telleriano-Remensis (39r), where the painter records that 20,000 victims were sacrificed at the dedication to the Templo Mayor. Most of the time there was no need in the painted histories to record large quantities of people or objects. One finds these symbols much more frequently in economic and cadastral documents.

The scribes never used bars, flags, feathers, or incense pouches with dates or day names, which belonged to a different conceptual category, at least among the Mixtecs. The painter of the Codex Selden, for example, may have used four bars to indicate an amount of twenty bundles, but when he identified the Tilantongo heir, Lord 2 Rain, with his personal name of 20 Jaguar, the painter drew twenty separate black disks (Selden 6b). Apparently Aztec and Mixtec manu-

Fig. 14. Signs for quantities: **ab,** 5; **c,** 4 × 20 days; **d,** 5 × 20 days; **e,** 400; **f,** 8,000. Drawings by John Montgomery. *Sources:* **a,** Osuna 16v; **b,** Kingsborough 207r; **c,** Aubin 75r; **d,** Quinatzin 1; **ef,** Mendoza.

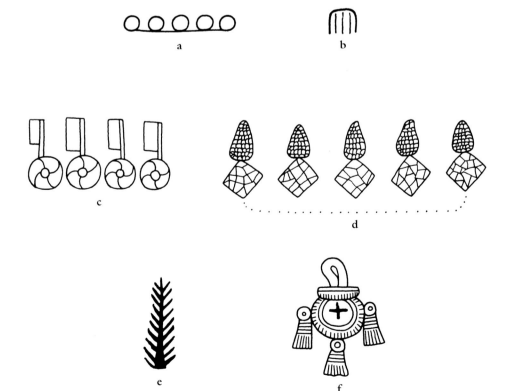

Fig. 15. Males in the Mixtec (**ab**) and Aztec (**cd**) codices. Drawings by John Montgomery. *Sources:* **ab,** Zouche-Nuttall 63a, 74d; **c,** Boturini 1; **d,** Mendoza 61r.

script painters used only disks when they indicated numbers in names and dates.[36]

Duration. Occasionally in the historical codices, the painters wanted to indicate the passage of a quantifiable amount of time, although they did not necessarily want to give beginning and ending dates. In these instances they used the symbols for "day" and "year," repeating them, employing the conventions for amounts, or some combination of the two to yield amounts. The Mapa Sigüenza painter recorded the number of years the Mexica lingered in different locations during their migration by painting the appropriate number of blue disks near the place signs. The painter of the Codex Aubin (72v) indicated that Moctezuma Ilhuicamina ruled for twenty-nine years by depicting nine mosaic disks of turquoise and a tenth disk with a banner attached.

Persons

Persons, whether human or supernatural, were identified in the codices according to different levels of specificity. Their character or nature was usually indicated through their physical features, costume, or pose. The manuscript painters always identified individuals as being male or female, and they additionally could charac-terize them as having a particular rank, status, or occupation (elder, ruler, warrior, priest, etc.) or a particular ethnicity. Moreover, most of the individuals appearing in the historical codices were named—with personal names or calendrical names or sometimes both.

Gender. Males and females are distinguished by their hair and costume (Figs. 15, 16). Males usually wear their hair shoulder-length or shorter, usually with bangs. Both males and females can wear earrings, necklaces, and nose ornaments, but only men wear lip plugs. Men always wear loincloths, usually white, that are tied in the front and have panels hanging down (Fig. 15). Although these loincloths are not always visible, usually one sees the panels hanging beneath other garments (such as the hip cloth or tunic) or jutting out between the knees in seated figures, or one sees the loincloth band around the waist. Aztec, but not Mixtec, men usually wear a distinctive cotton cloak that was knotted over one shoulder (the *tilmatl;* Fig. 15cd); it and the loincloth were the fundamental garments of the Aztec man. Both Aztec and Mixtec men often have decorative bands around their calf muscles but are otherwise bare-legged.

Women wear their hair longer: down to the middle of the back when it hangs loose. Usually, however, women's hair either is gathered in a low bun at the nape

Fig. 16. Females in the Mixtec (**ab**) and Aztec (**cd**) codices. Drawings by John Montgomery. *Sources:* **a,** Bodley 3b; **b,** Zouche-Nuttall 9a; **c,** Boturini 1; **d,** Mendoza 61r.

of the neck or is twisted or braided into two separate cords that are pulled from the nape of the neck around the sides of the head to the forehead where they are intertwined (Fig. 16acd). The result is that women often look like they have two horns of hair emerging from near their temples. In some Mixtec depictions, these cords of hair are laced with brightly colored ribbons (Fig. 16a). Women always wear a long, ankle-length skirt, their bodices covered by a *huipil* (like a tunic, with closed sides under the arm; Fig. 16cd) or a *quechquemitl* (like a poncho, open under the arms, sometimes with the points in the front and back; Fig. 16b).[37] These same clothes and hairstyle continue to be worn in traditional communities today. Both males and females can be shorn or barefoot, and both wear a vast array of headdresses.

Men sit on the ground or a raised surface with their legs bent at the knees in front of them (Fig. 15). In Mixtec manuscripts women usually sit this way, too. Very occasionally Mixtec women sit with their legs bent beneath them, in a manner that has been called the "Aztec women's pose." Since Aztec women uniformly sit this way in the codices, this pose is considered a marker for Valley of Mexico influence on a codex (Fig. 16c).[38]

Age. The individuals are almost always represented as adults, neither particularly young or old. Infants and children only figure in the histories if they are actively pictured being born or are being held by their mothers as part of the presentation of a dynastic founding; and in these relatively rare cases they appear as small, unclothed adults.[39] Occasionally the history calls for a woman to be marked as being mature and nominally of

Fig. 17. Aged persons in the Mixtec (**a**) and Aztec (**b**) codices. Drawings by John Montgomery. *Sources:* **a,** Vienna 49a; **b,** Mendoza 61r.

child-bearing experience; then she is shown without her clothes (but with jewelry and headdress), with pendent breasts and folds of skin over her abdomen, the result of her prior pregnancies. This marking may be more related to the events being described than to her actual condition, however.[40]

Old age carries its own marking and its own meaning (Fig. 17). Aged individuals are shown toothless or with one snaggly tooth, their lower lips sagging. They might also have scraggly hair and, in Aztec manuscripts, wrinkles on their face. Age marking can indeed refer to old age, but more often it carries the respectful meaning of an elder or an esteemed one. In Mixtec manuscripts, as Smith (1973a: 32) points out, only priests, special advisors, and mythological persons are marked as aged. The primordial couples in Aztec and Mixtec manuscripts are always aged. Death is signaled by an individual having closed eyes or being wrapped as a funerary bundle (Fig. 18).

Fig. 18. Dead persons in the Mixtec (**ab**) and Aztec (**cde**) codices. Drawings by John Montgomery. *Sources:* **ab,** Bodley 3c, 4c; **c,** Tepechpan 12; **de,** Mendoza 2v, 4v.

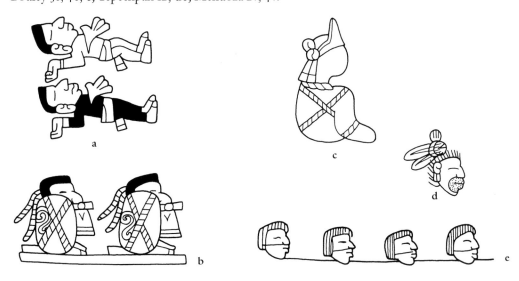

Rank, Occupation, and Temporary Status. Certain ranks, occupations, and temporary states of being were pictorially identified in the codices. Generally rulers, priests, and sacrificial victims are so designated, and occasionally warriors are.

Aztec rulers usually wear a pointed turquoise diadem (the *xihuitzolli*), sit on a woven mat or throne, and have a speech scroll issuing from the mouth to signal they are a "speaker" or *tlatoani* (Fig. 19a). Mixtec rulers are not usually distinguished from other lords, except that two Mixtec rulers, Lords 8 Deer and 4 Wind, went to great efforts to gain a Mexican symbol of office, the turquoise nose ornament that identified a lineage head, which they subsequently wore as a symbol of this rank (Fig. 19c).[41]

Priests are identified in both Aztec and Mixtec codices by their costuming, accoutering, and body coloration. Specifically, priests wear a short fringed tunic, carry on their backs a distinctive gourd for holding tobacco, and usually have black skin (from applications of ashes); often they are marked as aged (Fig. 19de).[42]

A special type of priest, the sacrificer or *yahui*, appears in Mixtec codices configured as a fire serpent and turtle combination (Fig. 19f).

Sacrificial victims are characterized by the white banners they carry, the distinctive white headband they wear, and a black line painted horizontally across their eyes (Fig. 19h). In Aztec manuscripts the headband is embellished with balls of eagle down and the body is covered with white chalk.[43]

Warriors, when they are distinguished, carry weapons, wear short tunics that represent their quilted cotton armor, and have their hair cut and bound up in the warrior's topknot (Figs. 3b, 19g).[44] High-status warriors are further identified by their elaborate costumes: full body suits of brightly colored feathers, great headdresses or zoomorphic helmets, and intricate standards attached to the back, which together signal rank. These military distinctions appear especially in manuscripts of the Aztec realm, where the warrior's occupation was an established career. They tend to be absent in the Mixtec histories, which show rulers conventionally go-

---

Fig. 19. Indications of rank, occupation, and status: **a,** Aztec ruler; **b,** Aztec ruler identified as the *cihuacoatl;* **c,** Mixtec lord wearing the turquoise nose ornament; **d,** Aztec priest wearing a *xicolli* with a tobacco gourd on his back and carrying a long-handled incense burner and incense pouch; **e,** Mixtec priest wearing a *xicolli;* **f,** Mixtec *yahui* priest sacrificer; **g,** Aztec warriors; **h,** Mixtec sacrificial victim. Drawings by John Montgomery. *Sources:* **abdg,** Mendoza 3v, 2v, 63r, 64r; **c,** Zouche-Nuttall 75; **e,** Bodley 7c; **f,** Vienna 8c; **h,** Selden 5d.

ing to war or doing battle without changing their regular costume.

Although most occupations are not separately specified in the pictorial histories, the titles of a few important offices are occasionally noted in Aztec manuscripts by the use of glyphs. For example, the title of the *cihuacoatl* (woman serpent), who was the empire's second administrator (after the emperor), was rendered as a glyph of a serpent with a female head (Fig. 19b).[45]

Ethnicity. Ethnicities, too, could be distinguished by physical features and costuming. One of the most dramatic markings identifies the so-called "Stone Men," who apparently were earlier (Classic period) inhabitants of the Mixteca and whose defeat led to the rise of the dynasties recorded in the Codices Bodley and Zouche-Nuttall; the Stone Men are characterized by the colored crossed bands and bumps typical of stone (Fig. 20ab). Other ethnic identifiers are more subtle. For example, Zapotecs in the Mixtec codices are identified by their distinctive face paint and headdress that are usually associated with the deity Xipe Totec; Chochos in the Codex Zouche-Nuttall (14) are identified by their headdress; Tlaxcalans in the Mixtec and Aztec codices have what Nicholson has called "the royal headband of the Tlaxcalteca," a twisted cord of red and white; and Lord 4 Jaguar and his colleagues are identified as "Mexicans" associated with the cult of Mixcoatl by their headdress, leg bands, and black eye paint (discussed in Chapter 5).[46]

In Aztec documents, the principal distinction was between Chichimecs and those people of Toltec ancestry who were civilized. This distinction is not so much between ethnicities but between ways of life, the Chichimecs being barbarian hunters and gatherers who had not yet mastered cultivation and had not yet adopted the social ways of the settled peoples. In the Aztec migration histories (see esp. Chapter 6), the people (Mexica and Acolhua alike) tend to begin as Chichimecs and end as cultured, civilized people, a transformation signaled by a change in costume and appearance. Chichimecs are characterized by the bow and arrows they carry, their clothes of animal hide, and their unkempt hair (Fig. 20c); "Toltecs" or civilized people wear cotton clothing (the men wear the *tilmatl*), are neatly coiffed, and use swords or spearthrowers for weapons (Fig. 20d). This same kind of cultural distinc-

Fig. 20. Indications of ethnicity: **ab,** Mixtec stone men; **cd,** Chichimec conversing with Toltec; **e,** Spanish official; **f,** indigenous ruler of Tepechpan who has assumed Spanish ways. Drawings by John Montgomery. *Sources:* **a,** Zouche-Nuttall 3b; **b,** Vienna 37a; **cd,** Quinatzin 1; **e,** Telleriano-Remensis 46v; **f,** Tepechpan 17.

tion is made between Aztecs (or Mixtecs) and Spaniards in colonial manuscripts. The native rulers dress in traditional costume and sit on woven mat seats (Fig. 19a), while the Spaniards appear in their own traditional garb and sit on wooden chairs of authority (Fig. 20e); as the native rulers became more Hispanized, they, too, took up European costume and ways (Fig. 20f).[47]

No pictorial distinction is made between the ultimate ethnicities: humans and supernaturals. In the

Mixtec codices, where supernaturals often figure in the stories, the gods are not visually differentiated from the humans. We know they are supernaturals only because they live longer than a human lifespan and are often consulted by the rulers of several polities or because they appear with other supernaturals in the early part of the cosmogony in the Codex Vienna Obverse. The supernaturals who figure largest in the existing Mixtec pictorials are Lady 9 Grass of the Skull Place (Chalcatongo) and Lord 1 Death (the sun deity) of the Temple of Gold and Jade at Sun Place. Aztec supernaturals are usually absent from the histories, with the exception of the Mexica tribal patron Huitzilopochtli, who is identified by his hummingbird costume.

The Mexican painters thus were able to say much about the nature of individuals according to how they were rendered physically and how they were dressed. Costume and physical attributes told of gender, rank and occupation, and ethnicity. When the individuals needed to be identified precisely, they were named.

Names: Calendrical and Personal. All civilized Mexicans in the Post-Classic period were named according to the day on which they were born. They took their birthday as their calendrical name unless their birthday augury was so poor that the day-keepers delayed their naming ceremony for a more auspicious day. Lady

6 Monkey, for example, was born on the day 6 Monkey (Fig. 21a). Individuals in the Mixtec codices are always identified by their calendrical names, which appear as a date either attached to the individual by a line or unattached nearby. The Aztecs had day names, too, but these calendrical names almost never figure in the pictorial histories.[48]

Instead the Aztecs identified people only by their personal names (Fig. 22). The Mixtecs used personal names, too, in conjunction with calendrical names. Personal names may take the form of objects, plants, animals, or qualities. Aztec names always appear as a glyph attached to or near an individual. For example, Moctezuma Ilhuicamina's personal name, Archer of the Sky, is represented by a sky band pierced by an arrow (Fig. 22). Mixtec personal names may be attached or floating nearby, too, but they can also be incorporated into the individual's costume or be held in the hand (Smith 1973a: 27). For example, Lord 8 Deer's personal name, Jaguar Claw or simply Jaguar, appears as his helmet, his body suit, a glyphic jaguar's paw, or simply a curved claw (Fig. 21cde). A priest, Lord 10 Flint, who figures in the early history of Jaltepec, is disfigured by his personal name, which is Earth Monster (or some variant); the conventional but grotesque open mouth of the Earth Lord replaces his own facial features (Fig. 21b).

Personal names may not have been as important for the Mixtecs as they were for the Aztecs. The Aztecs always used them, but in colonial Mixtec codices, the personal names have tended to fall away, leaving only the calendrical names.[49] In manuscripts that share cultural traditions, some individuals are identified only by their calendrical names (and are assumed to be Mixtec) while others are identified only by their personal names (and are assumed to be Aztec or another ethnicity).

Most of the people in the Mexican pictorial histories are named in one way or another. In the Mixtec histories, as Smith (1973a: 3, 21) has pointed out, virtually everyone is named, being either a noble or a priest; there are no crowds of people, no attendants, no workers. The Aztec histories are populated with an equally narrow range of people, although the Aztec painters would occasionally use unnamed humans to represent an event or an action (conquest, for example, as in Figure 3b).

Fig. 21.   Mixtec name signs: **a,** Lady 6 Monkey, Serpent Quechquemitl; **b,** Lord 10 Flint, Earth Monster; **cde,** Lord 8 Deer, Jaguar Claw. Drawings by John Montgomery. *Sources:* **ab,** Selden 6c, 1c; **ce,** Bodley 10d, 29d; **d,** Zouche-Nuttall 26b.

a   b

c   d   e

Places

In the same way that persons were almost always identified by their name signs and sometimes were distinguished from one another by their physical characteristics and costumes, locations, too, were almost always identified by place signs and were sometimes depicted via a pictorial description. Both methods employed conventional imagery, but in the place signs the imagery is more linguistic than representational. By this I mean that the image of a serpent in a place sign refers to the name of the place, whereas a serpent in a pictorial description is likely to indicate the actual presence of serpents.

Place Signs. Place signs are usually composed of a topographical element (what Smith has called a "geographical substantive") that serves as the foundation for one or more qualifiers (Fig. 23). The most frequent foundation elements in both Mixtec and Aztec codices are hills, platforms, fields or plains, and bodies of water (Smith 1973a: 38–41). The hill element is by far the most common. It can actually refer to a hill, but it often simply serves as the foundation on which identifying elements are put (Fig. 23a). The basic form is drawn as a rounded green triangle punctuated with what I call "earth bumps" (symbolizing its stony nature), on top of a distinctive base that has a red band over a yellow band, the yellow occasionally scalloped.[50] Variations

Fig. 22. Aztec name signs of the Mexica rulers. Drawings by John Montgomery. *Sources:* Mendoza 2v, 3v, 4v, 5v, 7v, 10r, 12r, 13r, 15v, Tepechpan 15.

Acamapichtli
Handful of Reeds

Huitzilihuitl
Hummingbird Feather

Chimalpopoca
Smoking Shield

Itzcoatl
Obsidian Serpent

Moctezuma Ilhuicamina
Angry Lord, Archer of the Sky

Axayacatl
Water Face

Tizoc
Blood Letter

Ahuitzotl
Water Beast

Moctezuma Xocoyotizn
Angry Lord the Younger

Cuitlahuac
Dung

Cuauhtemoc
Descending Eagle

occur. In the Codex Xolotl (Fig. 25i) the "earth bumps" are missing, but the hill is patterned as a wavy net-and-dot design that recalls the scales of the earth crocodile or *cipactli;* in the Codex Bodley (Fig. 24g) the base is elaborated with other patterns.

Platforms, which are especially common in Mixtec codices, are low rectangular friezes decorated with geometric patterns usually in a stepped design (Fig. 23b).

This element refers not simply to a platform but to a city, town, or settled place. Fields and plains are long rectangular strips decorated either with feathers (a phonetic reference to the Mixtec word for a plain) or (in Aztec manuscripts) with a distinctive motif of dashes and U-shaped elements (Fig. 23cd); both tend to refer to agriculturally rich areas. Flowing bodies of water, whether they be rivers or lakes, appear as the profile of

Fig. 23. Foundation elements for Mixtec and Aztec place signs: **a,** hill; **b,** platform; **c,** plain; **d,** plowed field; **e,** bodies of water; **f,** current of water; **g,** spring or small lake; **h,** marketplace; **i,** ball court; **j,** stone; **k,** sky band. Drawings by John Montgomery. *Sources:* **a,** Mendoza 7v, Vienna 40a; **b,** Vienna 52a; **c,** Vienna 52a; **d,** Mendoza 7v; **e,** Mendoza 18r, Vienna 47b; **f,** Mendoza 24v; **g,** Mendoza 49r; **h,** Vienna 7c; **i,** Mendoza 36r, Vienna 19b; **j,** Mendoza 18r, Vienna 49c; **k,** Vienna 52b, 48c.

a canal or river, the water being enclosed on three sides by bands of varying degrees of elaboration (Fig. 23e). Currents in the water manifest themselves as straight or wavy lines (usually in combination) and as fingers that reach outward or upward, ending in shells or disks (Fig. 23f).[51]

Other topographic elements are circles of swirling water (probably small lakes or springs), markets (circles of footprints, usually divided in quarters), and ball courts (wide H-shaped structures; Fig. 23ghi). Stones or rocks usually take the shape of fat ovals with elaborate "earth bumps" on the ends (Fig. 23j). In Aztec manuscripts they are decorated with curved stripes colored in tan and brown; in Mixtec manuscripts they are decorated with brightly colored diagonal bands.

The sky appears more often in pictorial descriptions of location than it does in place signs. It is represented as a wide band that has "star" symbols hanging down from the top (Fig. 23k). The simplest stars are white circles painted red on the upper half or third and with a small half-circle just below the red. As "night eyes," stars are visually the same as the lidless eyes that characterize skulls and certain supernaturals. The more elaborate stars are embellished with a U-shaped scroll that emits two or three pointed rays.

The qualifiers that accompany these topographical elements and carry much of the identity of the place sign cover a wide range of objects, conceptions, and qualities (Figs. 24, 25). They include animate and inanimate objects like plants (trees, grasses, reeds, and the like), animals (birds, serpents, monkeys, jaguars, etc.), and utensils (weapons, digging sticks, flint [knives]). Coatepec (Serpent Hill), for example, appears as a hill qualified by a serpent (Fig. 25c). The place sign of Coixtlahuaca (Plain of the Serpent) is a field or plain on which a serpent is stretched (Fig. 25d). Tenochtitlan (Nopal Cactus on Stone) is represented by a nopal cactus growing from a rock (Fig. 25g). Humans figure as qualifiers by representing ethnicities or by virtue of being engaged in activities (such as dancing, swimming, crying, pushing). The place sign of Zahuatlán, or Yucu Nicata (Hill That Danced) in Mixtec, is represented by a dancing human in or on top of a hill sign (Fig. 24b). Supernaturals occasionally appear as qualifiers, a noted example being the rain deity whose head dominates the hill element and refers to Yucuñudahui (Hill of Rain or Hill of the Rain Deity) (Fig. 24c). Sometimes place

signs lack the topographic foundation and are composed only of the qualifier, such as Azcapotzalco (On the Ant Heap) in the Valley of Mexico, which appears as an ant surrounded by sand and pebbles (Fig. 25a).[52]

Most place signs can operate across language boundaries because they convey meaning directly through the pictorial elements. A hill with a bird on it is Tututepec (Bird Hill) in Nahuatl and Yucu Dzaa (Bird Hill) in Mixtec, which are names for the same location (Smith 1963: 277–279; 1973a: 37, 67–68; Fig. 24a). Other place signs, however, are tied to language because they involve homonyms to convey meanings that cannot easily be represented pictorially. I have already mentioned the situation with Culhuacan, where the curve (*coltic*) signals the sound *cul* for the Place of the Culhua, as well as Teozacoalco (Chiyo Ca'nu or Great Foundation), where a man bending a platform yields the pun for "great" (Figs. 25e, 24k). Apoala, one of the Mixtec places of origin, combines a river (*yuta*) with a hand holding feathers (*tnoho*) to yield Yuta Tnoho or River of Lineages (Fig. 24d).

Phoneticism occurs especially in locatives and diminutives, where the meanings of "near," "on," "place where there is an abundance of," "little," and the like, are not so easily pictured (Fig. 10). These locatives and diminutives belong to the Aztec realm. The Mixtecs rarely used them (Smith 1973a: 41–43). An exception is the locative *a* (place where something exists), which, in the region of the Nochixtlan Valley, was represented by a human jaw with an open mouth. The element figures prominently in the place sign of Magdalena Jaltepec, whose Mixtec name was Añute (Place of Sand), where the open mouth spews forth sand (Fig. 24j); because of this spewing feature, generations of scholars called the place Belching Mountain until Smith (1983a: 252–253) determined its correct meaning.

We know the names and identities of the most prominent Aztec place signs, thanks to two centuries of scholarly research on the subject and to such manuscripts as the Codex Mendoza, which contains identifying glosses for its 612 place signs (Berdan 1992a: 163). The Mixtec place signs have been much harder to identify for several reasons. The Mixteca was not so intensively documented in the colonial period, so comparative alphabetic material is scarcer than in the Valley of Mexico. Too, many Mixtec towns were renamed in pre- and post-conquest times with Nahuatl names that

Fig. 24. Mixtec place signs, including those that figure prominently in the histories: **a,** Tututepec or Yucu Dzaa (Hill of the Bird); **b,** Zahuatlán or Yucu Nicata (Hill That Danced); **c,** Yucuñudahui (Hill of Rain or the Rain Deity); **d,** Apoala or Yuta Tnoho (River of Lineages); **e,** Cerro Sazmín, Suchixtlan (Hill of the Monkey, Place of Flowers); **f,** Red and White Bundle; **g,** Hill That Opens/Insect; **h,** Tilantongo or Ñuu Tnoo Huahi Andehui (Black Town, House of Sky); **i,** Place of Flints; **j,** Magdalena Jaltepec or Añute (Place of Sand); **k,** Teozacoalco or Chiyo Ca'nu (Great Foundation); **l,** Place of Cattail Reeds; **m,** Skull (home of Lady 9 Grass); **n,** Santa María Tataltepec or Yucu Quesi (Flame Frieze); **o,** Tlaxiaco or Ndisi Nuu (Visible Eye). Drawings by John Montgomery. *Sources:* **a,** Zouche-Nuttall 45d; **b,** Selden 11b; **c,** Zouche-Nuttall 3a; **d,** Zouche-Nuttall 1, Bodley 13d; **e,** Zouche-Nuttall 5b; **f,** Bodley 11a; **g,** Bodley 4b; **h,** Zouche-Nuttall 68b; **i,** Bodley 11c; **j,** Selden 6b; **k,** Bodley 15c; **l,** Colombino 13; **m,** Zouche-Nuttall 55d; **n,** Bodley 23c; **o,** Selden 14a.

do not correspond to the Mixtec originals, so it has been harder to correlate a name with a site (Smith 1973a: 61). Additionally, place-sign research is younger in Mixtec studies. Caso's 1949 article on the Mapa de Teozacoalco may have pioneered the investigation of place signs, but Smith's 1973 book was the first to treat Mixtec place signs in any depth. With her work (1973a, 1973b, 1983a, 1983b, 1983c, 1988, 1994; Smith and Parmenter 1991) and studies by others (e.g., Jansen 1982, Furst 1986, Parmenter 1982, Byland and Pohl 1994), we now can identify with some certainty perhaps fifty of the several hundred Mixtec place signs. The place signs that figure most prominently in the Mexican pictorial histories are illustrated in Figure 24, for the Mixtec codices, and Figure 25, for the Aztec manuscripts.

All of these place signs name community kingdoms or *altepetl* (to use the Nahuatl term). They refer to specific locations, in the sense that a city or town is located somewhere, but they convey the larger meaning of a polity and its people. Lockhart (1992: 14, 577 n. 6) has even argued that the names of *altepetl* should not be called toponyms, as they so often are, because they do not actually name geographic features. Place signs may refer, not just to *altepetl,* but to subject towns and to ceremonial centers, such as Skull Place (probably Chalcatongo [Jansen 1982, 1:252–254]), the home of the supernatural Lady 9 Grass (Fig. 24m), and Sun Place, the home of the sun deity Lord 1 Death. They can also be true toponyms, in that they identify uninhabited but named locations, such as springs, rock outcroppings, cultivated fields, and the like. These signs occur especially in maps and lienzos, where they are often

Fig. 25. Aztec place signs that figure prominently in the histories: **a,** Azcapotzalco (Ant Heap); **b,** Chapultepec (Grasshopper Hill); **c,** Coatepec (Serpent Hill); **d,** Coixtlahuaca (Plain of the Serpent); **e,** Culhuacan (Place of Those with Ancestors); **f,** Cuauhtinchan (Place of the Eagle); **g,** Tenochtitlan (Nopal Cactus on Stone); **h,** Tepechpan (On the Large Stone); **i,** Texcoco (Place of Pot/Alabaster Stone?); **j,** Tlatelolco (Earth Mound); **k,** Tollan (Place of Reeds). Drawings by John Montgomery. *Sources:* **abce,** Boturini 11, 18, 5, 20; **dgjk,** Mendoza 43r, 19r, 6r, 8r; **f,** Mapa Pintado; **h,** Tepechpan 3; **i,** Xolotl 3.

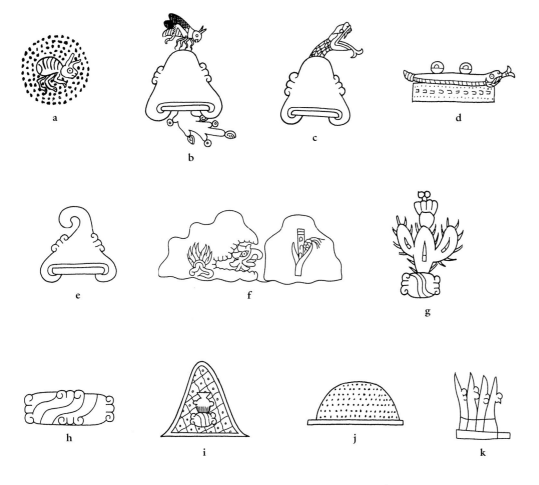

strung together to form boundary lines (Fig. 44; Smith 1973a: 43–44).

One cannot tell by looking at a place sign what kind of place it names or its size. Nor do the codices indicate the distance that obtains between locations. Tenochtitlan was an immensely larger city than the minor town of Tepechpan, for example, but their place signs do not tell us this. In the Codex Nuttall, Lord 8 Deer conquers a series of places, but we do not yet know whether these were inhabited or how close they were to each other; was this a grand expansionist program, or was 8 Deer merely laying claim to named locations within a limited region? Recent research, especially by Pohl and Byland (1994), suggests that these conquests were more local than previously thought.

Pictorial Representation. Pictorial representation or pictorial description was an alternative mode for indicating location. The Mexican painters always relied on the place sign when they wanted to name a place, but they turned to pictorial description when they wanted to convey its character. When they needed to tell what kind of a place it was, they painted its physical and ecological features. These paintings of places are not naturalistic landscapes in any European sense, for they make use of the standard pictorial conventions, but they differ from place signs because they represent real or imagined space. The painters used pictorial description in three ways: as an alternative to the place sign, as a complement to the place sign, and as a structure in which a number of place signs are brought into a spatial arrangement.

In the first mode, no place sign names the location. Instead, description replaces appellation, and the place is identified only by its physical features. These described places can be specific or vague. For example, the origin point for many of the people in the central valleys, Chicomoztoc (Seven Caves), is rarely named glyphically in the pictorial histories.[53] Instead it almost always appears as a (usually elaborate) rendering of a hill or mountain with a seven-lobed cave from which people emerge (Figs. 95, 97, 114, 143, 144); we know it to be Chicomoztoc because of these physical properties. Celestial origin points, such as one finds in the Codices Vienna and Zouche-Nuttall and the Selden Roll, also tend to be pictorially described rather than named (Figs. 49, 53, 95).

Pictorial description also works well when the painter wants to give a general ecological impression of an area. In several early colonial codices from the Valley of Mexico, the painters show migrating Chichimecs moving through a dry and rough environment, one dotted with different kinds of desert flora and fauna (Figs. 122, 125). These scenes represent no place in particular; instead they characterize the unnamed terrain through which the Chichimecs moved. Impressionistic landscapes like these may well be a colonial adaptation of European ways of painting; if so, the manuscript painters clearly found them a useful alternative to the place sign.

The second mode employs both a place sign and a painted description. In these instances the painters clearly wanted to name the place but also to indicate what kind of a place it was. The representation of the Aztec capital of Tenochtitlan at the time of its founding, for example, is both named and described pictorially in the Codex Mendoza (Fig. 134). The painter presents it as a swampy area, bounded on four sides by water and cut diagonally into four quarters by canals; reeds and rushes abound. Aztlan, the Aztecs' ancestral homeland and the starting point for their migration, is also both named and pictured in the migration histories. In the Mixtec codices, certain places that figure especially in Lord 8 Deer's life are named and pictured. Such is the Place of the Loincloth (Codex Zouche-Nuttall 75), where Lord 8 Deer and his companions boat across the body of water (inhabited by shells, fish [?], crocodiles, and serpents) that surrounds the island city; below the sky band, the island itself is pictured as having five caves (Fig. 66). As a tentative hypothesis, I would suggest that these places are rendered as scenes because they figure so large in the historical narratives. The scene allows the reader to understand the character of the place and invites him or her to linger over the telling.

The third way that Mexican painters employed pictorial description was by creating a matrix that locates a group of place signs in space and relates them to topographical features. One sees this especially in the "mapas," lienzos, and other cartographic histories where the painters produce what is essentially a map of an area, usually an area of some size. The painter arranges the place signs spatially and pictures such natural features as mountains and rivers. Such is the Lienzo of Zacatepec, where the boundary of the community kingdom is drawn as a cartographic rectangle studded by place signs (Fig. 44). Rivers and canals run through at specific points. Actual geographic space is ambiguous because it is unclear how far apart the actual places are or how their location on the ground might deviate from the structured presentation. But there is no doubt that a geographic area is being represented, for the topographic features anchor the territory to the earth. The relative placement of the place signs and geographic features means that all the empty space between the signs and features should be read as "distance" or geography. This is a very different presentation than is achieved in the screenfold manuscripts when the painters list a series of individual place signs; there the empty space between the place signs is as likely to indicate the passage of time.

Events and Action

Events and action may have posed the greatest challenge to the manuscript painters who were recording the past. The painters could set dates and identify people and places with relative ease simply by using glyphs—calendrical signs and numbers, name glyphs, and place signs—but events were not so easily represented glyphically. Instead, most events called for a pictorial presentation or visual description of the happening. This description could be elaborate, as in some marriage/foundation scenes in the Mixtec codices (i.e., Zouche-Nuttall 18b [Fig. 54]), or it could be condensed to its barest convention, as in other Mixtec marriage statements, but it tended always to be more pictorial than glyphic. Events are the most pictorial in the cartographic histories and Mixtec screenfolds, and they are the most glyphic in the Aztec annals.

The problem for the history painters was how to render the painted events as concisely as possible. They often did this by condensing the event to one or two telling referents and using those referents to stand for the whole. For example, in the years 2 Reed, the Aztecs marked the end of one fifty-two-year cycle and the beginning of another by binding their years (actually tying fifty-two reeds together) and then drilling a new fire. The painter of the Codex Mendoza (as did many of the Aztec history painters) always signaled the binding of the years by adding a knotted cord to the Reed sign for the years 2 Reed (Fig. 13b). He represented the

New Fire ceremony by painting a drilling board and drill with smoke curling forth. These two referents, or just one singly, called forth the larger meaning of the cyclical change and the events that embraced it. In this same way, a white banner held in the hand represented the sacrifice of the person who held it (Fig. 19h).

Events, more so than the other classes of elements, almost never exist independently. They involve people or supernaturals who do the deeds, and they almost always involve places where the events happen. Understanding this dependence, the painters usually used people and places to represent the events associated with them. In this way the painters recorded the conquest of an enemy polity by showing the destruction of that polity's temple (Fig. 3e) or by painting an arrow piercing the polity's place sign. They signaled the accession of a ruler by showing him seated, appropriately costumed and accoutered, at his polity (Fig. 19a). With the exception of natural phenomena (such as eclipses and the like, which are represented glyphically), events are revealed by descriptive pictures of people and places that are doing things or having things done to them.

Life Events. Only a few life events were sufficiently important to be mentioned in the painted histories; these are birth, marriage, the associated aspect of parentage and lineage, and death. The Aztec and Mixtec painters favored slightly different conventions for representing them, with some overlap. Mixtec painters signaled the birth of an individual by painting that person immediately following the marriage presentation of the person's parents. Thus the marriage of Lord 8 Deer and Lady 13 Serpent is followed by the appearance of their two sons Lord 4 Dog and Lord 4 Crocodile (Fig. 26a). This was the basic way of indicating birth. The painters could embellish it by adding the year date or by attaching a wavy yellow umbilical cord and red placenta to the bottom of the figure (Fig. 26b); sometimes the placenta is dropped when the umbilical cord links the child to its parent or to the year sign (Fig. 26c). Birth was a major event in the Mixtec screenfolds, but not so in the Aztec codices, where it appears infrequently and unconnected to an individual's parents. When Aztec painters did record births, they pictured a cradle board with the individual's personal name sign attached (Fig. 26d; Codex en Cruz, Codex Azcatitlan).

Marriage is naturally one of the principal events in

the Mixtec screenfolds, which, after all, are dynastic histories. Two marriages—between Lady 3 Flint and Lord 12 Wind of Hill of the Wasp (Nuttall 19ab) and between Lady 6 Monkey of Jaltepec and Lord 11 Wind of Xipe Bundle (Selden 6–7 [Figs. 37, 38], Bodley 36bc)—were so important that the painters elaborated the ceremony itself. But the painters reduced all the other marriages to the conventional presentation of a man and woman seated and facing each other on a shared platform; sometimes the partners have between them a frothy jar of pulque or chocolate, reflecting the Mixtec idiom for royal marriage, which is "a royal vessel was placed before the nobleman" (Fig. 26a); some-times they sit on a woven mat, reflecting another marriage idiom: "there is a royal celebration of the petate [woven straw mat]" (Fig. 26e; Smith 1973a: 30–31, 34–35). Sometimes, too, the couple is seated within or in front of their palace (Fig. 26a). The Aztec recording of marriage is similar but more fluid: the man and woman are seated facing each other, sometimes joined together by a line (Fig. 26f).

Marriage presentations easily flow into presentations of lineage or descent. In the Mixtec screenfolds, the appearance of a marriage presentation alerts the reader that the offspring will follow. Then when these offspring marry, the painters often added a separate

Fig. 26. Expressions of birth, marriage, and parentage: **a,** the marriage statement of Lord 8 Deer and Lady 13 Serpent (year 13 Flint day 12 Serpent), followed immediately by the birth statements of their first two sons (in years 7 Rabbit and 9 Flint); **b,** birth of Lady 6 Monkey; **c,** birth of Lord 4 Wind; **d,** birth of Texcoco's Nezahualcoyotl (Fasting Coyote) in year 1 Rabbit day 1 Deer; **e,** marriage statement of Lord 4 Wind and Lady 10 Flower (year 8 Flint day 7 Eagle) with Lady 10 Flower's parentage statement, on the right, showing her to be the daughter of Lord 8 Deer and Lady 13 Serpent of Tilantongo (Black Town); **f,** marriage statement of Lord Nopaltzin (Precious Nopal) and Lady Azcaxochitl (Ant Flower) with their three offspring Tlotzin (Falcon), Rabbit Digging-Stick, and Leather-Knot Water-Jar. Drawings by John Montgomery. *Sources:* **a,** Zouche-Nuttall 26; **b,** Selden 6a; **c,** Selden 8d; **d,** Cruz 1a; **e,** Bodley 29d; **f,** Xolotl 2.

parentage statement for the spouse; they did this by picturing or simply naming these spousal parents as facing in the same direction over the place sign of their polity (Fig. 26e). In Aztec pictorials, the offspring are pictured and named below their parents, with descent lines assuring the reader of the relationship (Fig. 26f). In both Aztec and Mixtec histories, descent can be indicated by footprints that run from the parent to the child.

Death is not a common event in the Mixtec codices. The persons whose births and marriages are so carefully recorded are not recalled when they died of natural causes; instead, they simply drop from the story, which continues with the deeds of their offspring. When people were killed, however, and especially if their deaths led to other upheavals in the dynastic reckoning, their deaths are recorded.[54] The deceased is pictured with closed eyes (Fig. 27a); the body can be wrapped as a funerary bundle (Figs. 18b, 27c); or the body can descend head first into the earth. In most cases, the individual is actually sacrificed, usually by having his or her chest cut open and the heart removed

(Figs. 18a, 27b). Death in the Aztec histories is more common. The annals almost always picture the wrapped funerary bundle of the deceased ruler prior to the accession image of his successor (Figs. 18c, 27d). When a ruler is killed in a spectacular manner, the details are elaborated; Cuauhtemoc, for example, is pictured being hung upside down from a tree in the Tira de Tepechpan (Fig. 27e). Of the life events, the Mixtec genealogical histories focus on birth, marriage, and lineage, whereas the Aztec annals focus on the rulers' accession and death.

Accession and Foundings. The painters represented a ruler's accession by picturing the ruler seated. In the Mixtec histories, he is seated on his place sign, with or without his spouse (when the spouse is present the scene doubles as a marriage statement; Fig. 28a). In the Aztec histories the ruler is usually seated on a woven straw throne (often with a high back); he wears a cloak over his torso and legs and a pointed turquoise diadem (the *xihuitzolli*), and he often has a speech scroll emitting from his lips to signal the rank and responsibility of *tlatoani* or "speaker" (Figs. 27d, 28b). These are the

Fig. 27. Expressions of death: **a,** death of the Mixtec Lord 8 Deer (year 12 Reed day 1 Grass); **b,** death by heart sacrifice of Lord 8 Deer at the hands of 9 Wind; **c,** Lord 8 Deer's funerary bundle; **d,** death of the Aztec ruler Moctezuma Ilhuicamina (Angry Lord) just prior to the accession of his successor Axayacatl (Water Face); **e,** death by hanging of the Aztec ruler Cuauhtemoc (Descending Eagle). Drawings by John Montgomery. *Sources:* **a,** Vienna Reverse 9b; **bc,** Bodley 14e, 14d; **de,** Tepechpan 12, 15.

Fig. 28. Accession of rulers: **a,** the Mixtec Lord 4 Wind at Place of Flints; **b,** the Aztec ruler Acamapichtli (Handful of Reeds); **c,** Lord 8 Deer at Tilantongo (Black Town). Drawings by John Montgomery. *Sources:* **a,** Bodley 31c; **b,** Mendoza 2v; **c,** Zouche-Nuttall 53d.

basic conventions of accession to rule, for which there are elaborations.

The founding of a new polity or the establishment of a new rule is often marked by the more complex presentation of ceremonies. For important foundings, the Aztecs present a gathering of clan leaders (with one identified as the *tlatoani*) around the place sign of the polity, as in the Codex Mendoza presentation of the founding of Tenochtitlan (Fig. 134). The Mixtecs focus instead on the placement of staffs of office (Fig. 28c), the drilling of new fire, and the offering of quail, incense, and the like, as on Codex Nuttall 18b (Fig. 54), where Lord 12 Wind and his companions carry the distinctive staff of rule, other staffs, a temple, a cult bundle, a fire drill and board, and offerings to a place and there establish a polity. Foundation rituals are discussed more thoroughly in Chapters 5, 6, and 7.

Speech and Interpersonal Communication. Painters throughout Post-Classic Mexico noted speech by drawing a scroll coming out of the mouth of the speaker. These speech scrolls can be qualified, where desired, by adding such elements as a flint knife to signal cutting speech or a mortal threat (Fig. 29a; Jansen and Pérez Jiménez 1986: 188) or a flower to indicate poetry or song (Borbonicus 4). In the Codex Zouche-Nuttall (Fig. 29b), a speech scroll modified by the day sign 7 Flower may identify the subject of the speech as the Lord 7 Flower who was sacrificed earlier in the War of Heaven.[55] Modified speech scrolls are rare in the existing pictorial histories, however.

Conferences are similar to marriages in that they involve two persons who face each other. But conference participants may be of the same sex, they can be seated or standing, and they usually do not sit together on the same place sign (Fig. 29c). In the Mixtec codices, if one person sits on a place sign and the others do not, the former is being visited by the latter (Smith 1973a: 30). Gestures can point to the nature of the meeting.

Fig. 29. Speech and meetings: **a,** threatening speech; **b,** Lord 10 Rain's speech scroll ends in the day (name?) 7 Flower; **c,** Lady 6 Monkey meeting with the priest Lord 6 Vulture; **d,** Lord 8 Deer (*left*) accepting the request made by the sun deity 1 Death (*right*). Drawings by John Montgomery. *Sources:* **a,** Selden 7c; **b,** Zouche-Nuttall 20b; **c,** Selden 6c; **d,** Becker I 3c.

Although most gestures have not been interpreted, Nancy Troike has pointed out that in the Colombino-Becker a meeting where one person holds his hand horizontally or downward while the other raises his hand to point upward means that the former has made a request of the latter, who has accepted it (Fig. 29d).[56]

Travel, War, and Conquest. The painters indicated travel by painting a figure walking, usually on a road and often with footprints before and after. A succession of place signs tells the reader where the person went. By themselves, footprints and the road can signal movement literally and figuratively: a line of footprints carries Lady 6 Monkey into battle (Fig. 3a), whereas another group of footprints tells the reader Lady 10 Flower came from Tilantongo, the daughter of Lord 8 Deer and Lady 13 Serpent (Fig. 26e). In this latter case, the footprints signal both descent from her parents and travel from her town of origin to her husband's home.

War and aggression are easy to identify in the histories, for the participants are usually pictured as brandishing weapons or actually fighting (Fig. 3ab). Aggressors in the Mixtec codices usually stand on chevron bands, which have thus been called warpaths, that carry them into battle (Fig. 3f).[57] Conquest can be signaled in several ways: a victor holds his defeated foe by the hair, the defeated foe is sacrificed, the conquered place sign is shot with an arrow,[58] or the conquered place has its temple in flames with the roof unseated (Fig. 3abe). Glyphic references to warfare are frequent in the Aztec annals, where the convention for war is a round shield backed by spears or an obsidian bladed club (Fig. 3cd).

Other Human Activities. Other actions performed by humans are usually indicated pictorially. Humans are shown hunting, quarrying stone, laying out land, and building new towns. When it is important to the story that a specific individual does these deeds, he or she is clearly named. When the history only records the activity, unnamed humans perform the jobs.

Natural Phenomena. Natural and climactic phenomena, such as earthquakes, eclipses, comets, hailstorms, and droughts, appear in the Aztec annals but not in the Mixtec genealogical histories or in the Aztec cartographic histories (Fig. 30). The Aztec painters pictured them conventionally, indicating an earthquake by the symbol for movement over or within a rectangle of earth, or an eclipse by a partially blackened sun disk (sometimes with the appearance of stars in the darkened sky). Comets were visualized as colorful worms, hailstorms or snowstorms as clusters of dots; floods and droughts were respectively recalled by strips of water and sun disks. When rodents or grasshoppers appear in the annals, the painters are recording their devastating attacks on the crops. In the postconquest

sections of the Aztec annals, the painters recorded epidemics in similarly shorthand fashion. They represented the devastating epidemic of smallpox in 1520 by painting a human or human head dotted with spots. They told of the great deaths later in the century simply by painting skulls next to the year signs.

It is clear in reviewing the presentation of events in the Mexican histories that some pictorial representations have clear linguistic parallels. As Smith (1973a: 30–35; 1983b: 241, 244–245) has pointed out, idioms in the Mixtec language are reflected in some of the pictorial representations of marriage, of warfare, and of conquest; there are surely others, too. Research on the Aztec codices has not focused on this aspect as much, but we have the ready example of the ruler with a speech scroll before his mouth, which recalls the Nahuatl word for ruler, *tlatoani* or "speaker." This corre-

---

Fig. 30. Natural and climatic phenomena: **a,** earthquake; **b,** solar eclipse; **c,** comet; **d,** snowstorm; **e,** flood; **f,** drought; **g,** rodents ruining crops; **h,** grasshoppers descend to devour corn; **i,** smallpox epidemic; **j,** epidemics of 1576 and 1577. Drawings by John Montgomery. *Sources:* **abcdg,** Telleriano-Remensis 38r, 42r, 39v, 32r, 41v; **efh,** Mexicanus 73, 72, 72; **ij,** Tepechpan 15, 19.

spondence between the visual and verbal modes of communication points up the importance of understanding the language spoken by the manuscript painters and readers, but it does not mean that the imagery in the pictorial histories is replicating speech. Rather it tell us that the ancient Mexicans thought idiomatically and that they expressed these idioms both verbally and pictorially.

Reading Orders

Although precise reading orders vary from manuscript to manuscript, there are two basic kinds. One is unidirectional, where the story follows a single line, although this line might start and stop or, very occasionally, be paralleled by another line. The other is open, as in a cartographic history, where the reading order or story line is left to the discretion of the reader, who chooses which part to read first. A few general rules guide the reader through the narrative.

Unidirectional manuscripts are the Aztec annals and the Mixtec genealogical/historical screenfolds. The annals feature a continuous count of the years, presented as a ribbon of time, that controls the reading order. Usually this ribbon begins at the left and runs to the right, with all the year signs facing in the direction of the count (Figs. 34, 127). Some other annals, like the Codex Saville (Fig. 128), run from bottom to top. The years of the imperial history in the early colonial Codex Aubin (Fig. 129), painted on European paper, are organized as strips that run from top to bottom on each page. Except in those annals that are so governed by the format of a page of European paper, an annals story flows evenly across the long strip or tira irrespective of any page folds; there is usually no sense of the page as a unit.[59] Time marches regularly forward, the year count broken only to allow the painter space to elaborate a major event; when this happens, the universal time of the year count gives way to the experiential time of the event, as is discussed more fully in Chapter 8.

King lists or lists of successive ruling couples are like annals in that they have an unwavering reading order. They usually run from bottom to top, as in the Mapa de Teozacoalco from the Mixteca, the Codex Tulane and Coixtlahuaca manuscripts from Puebla and Oaxaca (Smith 1973a: 10; Smith and Parmenter 1991: 18–

19), and the Maguey Plan from the Valley of Mexico (see Figs. 76, 75, 80, 86, 87). A few, however, read left to right (e.g., Codex Baranda [Fig. 74]) or top to bottom (e.g., Mapa Tlotzin [Fig. 122]).

The Mixtec genealogical histories conceived in screenfold format follow a boustrophedon pattern. The stories flow back and forth, the way an ox plow would work a field, across one or two pages. The painters used red lines to divide the pages into registers, leaving the lines open on those ends where the story flows onto the next register. Mary Elizabeth Smith's classic diagram of the reading order of the Mixtec screenfolds presents this clearly (Fig. 31).[60] As her diagram also shows, there is considerable variation in the actual reading order between manuscripts and even within the same manuscript. The Codex Selden reads bottom to top (Figs. 37, 38, 39), whereas most of the others read horizontally either from the right or from the left.

It is not always easy to understand the reading order when one opens a Mixtec screenfold in the middle. The usual rule is that the figures face in the direction the story moves, but manuscripts like the Codex Zouche-Nuttall are flexible in this regard; and in other manuscripts, conferences and confrontations between people cause many individuals to face against the flow. Also, individuals in parentage statements always face the offspring.[61] One might think that the day signs would face in the direction of the flow, as they do in the divinatory codices, but this is not the case. The day signs usually face to the left, although they occasionally face up, down, or to the right. In codices like the Colombino and Bodley that read across two pages, the reader may have to interpret a section of the story before recognizing the reading order. Three of the Mixtec codices have dual registration: the main story line is paralleled by a concurrently running story that offers supporting or background material.[62] These supplementary registers are almost like footnotes to the principal narrative.

Donald Robertson (1983: 214) felt that the boustrophedon manner of Mixtec screenfolds was probably a condensation of an older, single-file form effected to save space, and he presented for discussion the idea that the Aztec annals preserve this older form, as one might expect to find in a regional or provincial survival. Robertson's argument was based on his opinion

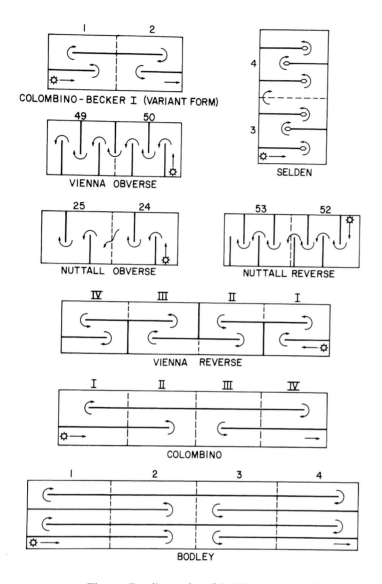

Fig. 31. Reading order of six Mixtec screenfolds. An asterisk marks the beginning of the sequence in each example, and the numbers identify the pages from which the examples were taken (from Smith 1973a: fig. 1). Reproduced courtesy of the University of Oklahoma Press.

that the Mixtecs brought the art of manuscript painting to the Valley of Mexico, where the early form was retained; then the painter's art continued to evolve in the Mixteca, resulting in the boustrophedon screenfold. My own opinion is that we have insufficient evidence to know the origin and history of these formats. Certainly, I do not feel the boustrophedon format developed from the straight line of the annals: the genres

are simply too different. Arguing on the other side of the matter, Smith (Smith and Parmenter 1991: 1) has suggested that the extant tiras and rolls, with their straight narrative line, may themselves be later versions of preconquest screenfolds. Smith may be correct, but again, as she notes, we lack clear evidence.

Annals, ruler lists, and event-oriented screenfolds all are unidirectional, as are tiras, where the story runs from one end of the long strip to the other. The narrative is clearly linear. I stress this because scholars have had a tendency to conceptualize Mesoamerican patterns of thought as nonlinear and to contrast the pictorial histories with the linear narratives of alphabetic chronicles.[63] One hears much about the Mesoamerican cycles of time—what we have come to call the Calendar Round—but it is often forgotten that the year count runs as a single ribbon in the annals, that the stories in the Mixtec screenfolds run as a linear narrative, and that the Maya long count is a straight reckoning of an ongoing flow of days. The pictorial histories are indeed different from alphabetic histories, but the stories in many of the pictorials flow in a similar way.

Other pictorial histories, those that I call cartographic, have no predetermined reading order. These histories conceptualize the story within a spatially presented territory, and they can be read in a number of ways. As explained in Chapter 4, the reader of map 1 of the Codex Xolotl (Fig. 42), for example, can begin the reading in the lower left corner, where Xolotl and his followers enter the valley, or on the right side of the map where the painter describes the people who are already settled in the valley. Footprints and the direction in which the figures face may guide the reader from point to point in the presentation, but he or she must choose which of several competing lines to follow, and which part of the story to voice next. The cartographic history excels at presenting simultaneous occurrences and leaves the exact narrative line up to the interpreter.

Space takes on different meanings in the unidirectional and open formats. In an annals or an event-oriented history, the empty space between events is often a reflection of time. An event occurs, and sometime later (a year later in the annals) another event occurs; the space between the individual presentations or scenes functions to separate these occurrences temporally. If any location is changed, that change is signaled by a change of place signs. In the cartographically structured histories, however, the space between events may well reflect the physical distance between locations. Empty space is more ambiguous in these histories. The appearance of a single individual at two places on the map certainly means that the two appearances are separated by time, since an individual cannot be at two places at once, but these two appearances are often also at different locations. The space between the two places therefore stands for all the land in between where the individual did not appear, and where nothing happened. As Dana Leibsohn (1994: 173–175) has pointed out, the empty spaces in cartographic histories are the empty moments and empty places in a story, times and places that do not figure in the history.

4

Structures of History

Thus the Mexican painters had devised the pictorial conventions and visual elements that would allow them to tell about the past. Persons and places could be named glyphically or described through visual characterization. Time could be controlled by day dates and year dates and by symbols of duration. And events, those elements that are the core of any history, either could be signaled by brief pictorial convention or could be represented by a more detailed painting. The painters had the easy means to control the four essential elements of a history: the participants, locations, time, and events—the who, where, when, and what. The why—the causal factors that drive events—would be revealed through the unfolding of the story. The painters had only then to decide how to transform these isolated elements into a story: how to arrange and structure the pictorial conventions and visual elements into a viable account of the past.

In this the Mexican history painters were no different from their historical and literary counterparts writing alphabetically or logographically on the other sides of the Atlantic and Pacific Oceans. Although the Mexicans wrote with images, they shared the same need to structure the elements that make up a story, whether that story was a history or a fictional tale, and they shared some of the same options for structuring it.

Historiographers and literary theorists have pointed out that alphabetic writers in medieval Europe structured the past in three different ways: as an annals account, a chronicle, or a narrative. The annals account lists sequent years and includes next to the years any significant events that then occurred; the chronicle is a sequence of described events; and the narrative is a motivated sequence of related events, generally considered to culminate in a conclusion that imposes meaning on those events.[1] As Hayden White (1981a: 5) explains, it has been traditional for historiographers of western Europe to view the annals and the chronicle as earlier, imperfect historical forms that developed into the narrative, which is usually equated with history proper. The relative historicity of these three forms, which has been under debate, is largely irrelevant for us who are interested in the Mexican pictorial histories, for the issues we confront are not so circumscribed that we can define "narrative" so narrowly. I would consider all these forms as histories of one kind or another, and I consider a narrative to be the structured presentation either of the past or of a story, whether or not that story has a conclusion.[2] What is relevant for us is that medieval European historians could choose between ordering the past according to time (as in annals) or event (as in a chronicle).

Alphabetic writers are not alone in their concern with structuring events over time. Events that are not easily recorded alphabetically, such as musical sounds and human movement, also call forth efforts to document their passage, which have led to the creation of various notational forms to record music, dance, and human geography. All the people who develop and use these notational systems (or semasiographic writing systems) are faced with the fundamental question of how to record events over time. Events and three-dimensional objects can be represented easily enough on a writing/painting surface, for we have learned to read the two-dimensional graphic image as the three-dimensional whole, but the fourth dimension of time makes the situation that much more complex and problematic. Semasiographic writing systems must then achieve a four-dimensional narration of space-time on a flat surface.

Recorders of music, dance, and human geography—and graphic designers, of course—have solved this problem variously, taking one of three approaches. They configure the narrative as a time line (like the medieval annals), as a string of events (like the medieval chronicle), or as a map. The Mexican history painters did likewise, structuring their histories in the same general ways. We can think of these three ways of presenting actions in space over time as being annals, *res gestae* (or event-oriented) histories, and cartographic histories. It can help us understand the Aztec solutions if we also consider the parallel solutions reached by other ancient and modern thinkers.

Time-Line Presentations

Time-line or time series presentations link events to a constant and ongoing measure of time. This measure, like a ribbon of time, is the armature to which the events are attached. Time proceeds usually at an unchanging pace, neither slowing down nor speeding up, regardless of the events associated with it. It goes forward whether or not there are any events, ceasing only when a foregone ending is reached. We are all familiar with "time lines," those historiographic charts that order events, usually by year, from some beginning to some end.

Musical notation, at least the form almost universally used today, is a time-line presentation (Fig. 32). A horizontal ribbon of parallel lines, called a staff, reads left to right, divided vertically by bar lines into equal and repeating units of time. Numbers (e.g., 4/4, 3/4, 2/4) signal the pace of these units of time at the beginning (on the left) and whenever their pace should change. Thus, time is marked. The events that occur therein are the notes that dot the staff. Their formal configuration, color, and placement tell the reader what kind of notes (what kind of events) they are. The shape of the notes (whether they have stems, beams, and other accompanying marks) and their color (black or white) identify them as being short or long events, and lines (beams and slurs) that join them tell us that the events themselves are joined. Their placement high or low on the scale sets their pitch and thereby identifies them as higher or lower events; the specific value of the scale (its own placement within the full range of pitch) is signaled at the beginning by the conventional motifs of clefs. When units of time are incompletely filled with notes, or events (where there are rests), other conventional marks identify this absence. Thus the musician, who knows the individual elements that compose the score and understands the structure that gives it shape, can follow the recorded concerto.[3]

One of the major notational systems for recording choreography—Labanotation—is also a time series system (Fig. 33). Developed by Rudolf Laban in the 1920s (Hutchinson 1966: 3), it focuses on time and duration of movement, and it draws its general structure from musical notation, from which it is derived. Time, in Labanotation, proceeds from bottom to top along a set of three parallel vertical lines (the staff), which are segmented by horizontal lines into regular and repeating rectangular units. In this, it is structured like a musical score turned on its end. With the central vertical line representing the center of the human body, the spaces between and outside the parallel lines identify which fields of the body are active (e.g., left and right support, leg, torso, arm, head). Actions themselves are indicated by the appearance in these spaces of different geometric forms, differently shaded and marked. The shape of these symbols indicates the direction of the action, the shading indicates which level (high, middle, low), and the length of the symbol indicates duration. Describing movement, these geometric codes are the events of the choreography, which are pinned to the human body that exists through time. As time proceeds regularly, Labanotation tell us what parts of the body are engaged in what movements (Hutchinson 1966: esp. 11–20; Laban 1974; Guest 1984: 60, 81–88).[4]

Like musical notation, Labanotation is unconcerned with documenting actions over space. It does not record where the movements of the body carry the dancer across the floor. Instead, it assumes that the movements (events), properly read and executed, will themselves direct the dancer to the correct floor location. Labanotation takes the human body, the dancer, as its referent; the notational system presents actions from the body's point of view, moving through time but not necessarily through space. The place that this action occurs is always directly below the body.

Because Labanotation records the movements of individual dancers (or uniform groups), the score for one dancer is silent about all the others potentially on the floor at the same time and moving differently. These other dancers have their own choreographic scores. Musical notation shares with Labanotation this singular point of view, for it, too, views events (notes) from the point of view of the individual musician. It requires that each part of a musical group (from duet to symphony) have its own score. If we are to see musical notation and Labanotation as histories, we recognize that the assumed subject or protagonist of these histories is the individual dancer or musician.

The Aztec annals, as time-line presentations, share many of these features with musical notation and Labanotation. The annals ignore space to concentrate on the presentation of events over time. The protagonist, usually unspecified, is understood to be the polity whose annals it is, such that every action in an annals account is an event that pertains to the originating *altepetl*, just as every note in a musical score pertains to the musician (and instrument) for whom the score was written.

In Aztec annals, the history painters create a ribbon of time by drawing all the year signs one after another, usually joined side by side along the axis of a long strip of paper (*tira*). The paper can be rolled or folded

Fig. 32. Musical notation: beginning of stanza 2, Dumbarton Oaks Concerto, by Igor Stravinski, 1938. Photograph courtesy of Dumbarton Oaks.

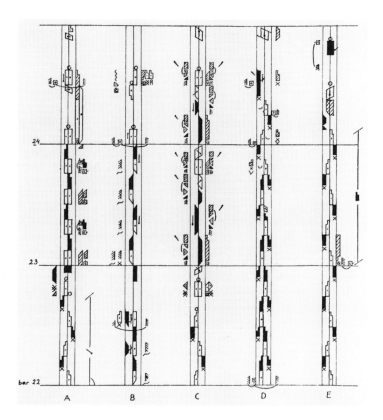

Fig. 33. Labanotation: excerpt of "Gentleman in Black" from the ballet *The Green Table*, by Kurt Jooss; notated by Ann Hutchinson, 1939 (from Guest 1984: fig. 12.10). Reproduced courtesy of Ann Hutchinson Guest, Director, Language of Dance Centre, London.

accordion-style as a screenfold, but the time line is usually continuous.[5] Time, measured by its divisions into years, runs along the length of the strip either left to right or bottom to top in the same way as do the scores of musical notation and Labanotation. Since the historian has little room to elaborate on events (even great ones) or to delve into detail, he or she records the happenings by brief, conventionalized images, conceptually equivalent to musical notes and the geometric shapes of Labanotation.

The Codex Mexicanus illustrates the features of the typical Aztec annals well (Fig. 34). Time proceeds left to right, six years to a page, from 4 Reed to 9 Flint on one page and then from 10 House to 2 Rabbit on the next. Above the year 4 Reed, a funerary bundle (only partially visible on the far left) signals the death of the ruler Axayacatl, who had been in office up to that time. Within the same year, the painter records the accession of his successor Tizoc, pictured in the conventional manner of a ruler on this woven straw throne and spe-

cifically identified by the name sign attached to his head. The elements that compose his name sign—a striped leg, ball of copal, and bound sticks—are all related to sacrifice and yield the name Tizoc, roughly translated as "Bloodletter" (Berdan 1992a: 235). That same year, the scribe records a renovation of the Templo Mayor. The next year, 5 Flint, was characterized by a quantity of 160 (8 × 20) unidentified things, perhaps defeated warriors related to the events of the year 6 House. In 6 House the Mexica were defeated by the Matlatzinca: a warrior identified by the name sign for Matlatzinco (a hunting net [*matlatl*] combined with a lower body [*tzin*]) has captured and defeated an unnamed and presumably Mexica foe; conventionally the Mexica's eyes are closed in death while the victorious Matlatzinca grasps him by the hair.

The historian notes that Tizoc died in the next year, 7 Rabbit, where the ruler's funerary bundle and name sign identify the event. Succession passed immediately to Ahuitzotl, who is pictured conventionally on the

Fig. 34. Annals history from 4 Reed (1483) to 2 Rabbit (1494), Codex Mexicanus 71–72. Photographs courtesy of

throne and is identified by his name sign, a water beast (combining the elements of a rodent and water). The next year, in 8 Reed, the historian recorded the dedication of the newly renovated Templo Mayor.

Moving to the next page, the annalist uses a combination of conventions and pictorial representations to record a series of natural disasters. In 10 House, the convention for "movement" surrounded by angular shapes and rubble indicates that an earthquake rocked the land. Then in 11 Rabbit the painter describes a devastating hailstorm that was so severe that the fish in the lake died: we see the heavy clouds, the fierce rain and large hailstones, and the fish floating belly up. Disaster struck again in 12 Reed, where a descending footprint, a grasshopper, and a maize plant together describe how a plague of grasshoppers swarmed down to devour the crops. Finally, in 13 Flint, the image of the sun (drawn in a European manner, it is true) signals a drought that parched the land.[6]

In these annals, history is structured around time, the events arranged as pictures and conventions around the year count, and often directly linked to specific years by a line. The events are clearly presented, but the par-

ticipants in the story—those who do the deeds or who are affected by the events—are not highlighted. Rulers and other important persons will be pictured and named, to be sure, but ordinary humans are absent unless they have been placed there to symbolize the actions they perform, such as the Matlatzinca and Mexica warriors. To discover the subject or protagonist of the history, we must look for the entity that is involved in all these events. That entity is not an individual person or a family but the community as a corporate body. Just as Labanotation records the movements of the different parts of a human body over time, the Aztec annals record the varied events that affect the community, the *altepetl,* over time. *Altepetl,* the Nahuatl word for community kingdom or city-state, translates into Spanish as *pueblo,* and like *pueblo,* it carries the meaning of a place (a town or city and its surrounding lands) and a people.

The place where all this action occurs is not usually specified because the events are assumed to take place in the *altepetl* whose history it is. The exceptions are events that involve other *altepetl* or other places, and in those cases, the other polities are named. Conquests,

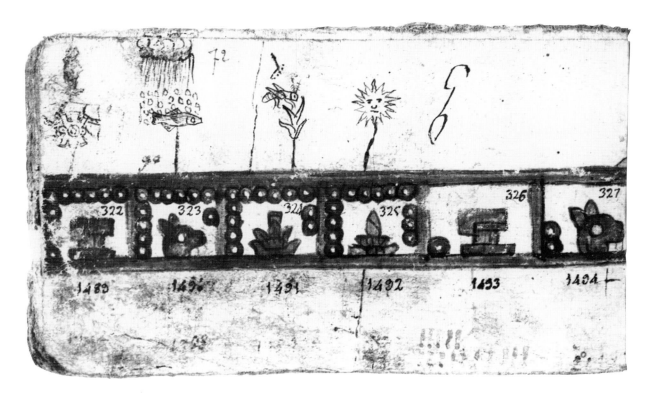

the Bibliothèque Nationale de France, Paris.

for example, where Aztec armies were victorious over near or distant peoples, are always accompanied by the conquered place signs, because the identity of the conquered polity is a fundamental part of the event.

These features of the Aztec annals might seem to form a unique genre for writing history pictographically, one that is particular to the Mexica and their contemporaries. This is not the case, however. Other historians in other times and places have solved the problem of painting a history in a similar way. A comparison with other painted annals forms can help to put the Aztec features in sharper perspective.

The same structural features we noted in the Aztec annals characterize the painted history of the College of William and Mary, which was crafted on the occasion of the college's 300th anniversary and printed on tee shirts (Fig. 35). The alumni office billed it as the William and Mary "Time Tee." The story of the college begins in the lower left, then runs to the right, up and to the left, and so on in a boustrophedon pattern that carries the story to its grand finish at the top. Although all the years are not individually named, they

are marked according to forty-year intervals, so that each loop of the time line equals eighty years.

The anonymous college historian represents the founding of the college as the momentous event it was, an event from which the entire history stems. He or she depicted it larger than the other events and dated it precisely to 1693. The royal charter that established the college is represented by the picture of the two British monarchs, William and Mary, sitting on their thrones. The abbreviations "QM" and "KW" are their name tags (equivalent to name glyphs), which identify them conventionally as Queen Mary and King William in case there would be any confusion. Soon thereafter, the painter notes that the first building was constructed in 1695–1697.

As in the Aztec annals, significant events in the college's history are recorded by conventionalized depictions of persons or by iconic images. Important early events include Benjamin Franklin's honorary degree, George Washington's chancellorship, and the first law degree. Crossed rifles (equivalent to the Aztec convention for war) signal that the college was occupied by Federal troops during the Civil War, when Union sol-

Fig. 35. "Time Tee," an annals history of the College of William and Mary printed on tee shirts for its 300th birthday celebration in 1993. Reproduced courtesy of the Society of the Alumnae, College of William and Mary.

diers burned the Wren Building. The subject of this history is understood to be the College of William and Mary, and the location of all the action is understood to be the campus in Williamsburg, Virginia. The one exception is the 300th anniversary celebration. The historian signals in alphabetic script that it took place not on campus but at nearby Busch Gardens. Like the Aztec annalist, the college historian is careful to indicate the change in location.

This William and Mary annals history is close conceptually and structurally to the Aztec annals, where the subject is the corporate body and where a ribbon of time is the armature on which events are attached. Time moves forward at a constant rate, and events are signaled pictorially or by conventional images whenever they occurred. In such annals, there may be long periods when nothing noteworthy happened, and there may be times that are crowded with action.

Event Series or *Res gestae* Presentations

In this second category of historical presentation, the events themselves pull the story along. This category covers those histories structured as a linked series of events that are related to each other by virtue of pertaining to the same subject. We can call them event-oriented histories. The Romans called them *res gestae*, literally "deeds done," where the story proceeds from event to event, irrespective of time or place. Such are the medieval chronicles. *Res gestae* histories can sometimes look like time-line histories, but without the tight control of an inflexible time count. Like annals, they excel in presenting sequence, but unlike annals they emphasize the sequence of events rather than the passage of time. Thus, they leave no gaps between the recorded events. *Res gestae* histories consider time and location only secondarily, for time and location are not themselves incorporated into the structure of the presentation. Instead, specific dates and place names are added to the events when needed.

Most of the alphabetically written histories with which we are familiar have a *res gestae* structure, as do most novels and short stories. Writers of history and fiction have found that their stories are best told by moving from event to event. With the added features of a beginning, development, and conclusion, these event series presentations are what we come to think of as histories.

Pictorial *res gestae* stories are all around us also. The set of graphic instructions for operating a hot-air hand dryer, illustrated in Chapter 3 (Fig. 2), serves as a simple example, if we approach the images as a description of the past actions (a history) rather than a prescription for future actions (instructions). Two panels, each one depicting an event, are presented side by side. Our cultural training, however, tells us to read them left to right. Interpreting the pictorial and iconic images, we then read that an unnamed individual pushed the button and then rubbed his or her hands under the hot air. We do not know how much time elapsed between the first and the second events, because that time interval is not sufficiently important to have been specified. The location of these events is specified only indirectly by virtue of the button, which represents the actual button on the machine below the panel.

Because the panel appears on a dryer in a washroom, we recognize the message not as a story of something that happened in the past but as an instruction for our actions in the future: we ourselves then become figuratively the unnamed protagonist. If the panel were in an entirely different context, however, and were elaborated with other elements, we might well read the sequence as a brief history.

Comic strips and children's picture books, such as the Good Dog Carl series by Alexandra Day, are also event-oriented presentations. Like the dryer instructions, they structure events as a series of separate scenes, but they are more complex both in their imagery and in their stories. Bill Watterson, author of the Calvin and Hobbes comic strip, has organized a simple story in three distinct scenes, separated from each other by a vertical line (Fig. 36). Each scene has its own internal

space in which the figures do things and speak to each other, their words recounted alphabetically in "balloons." These actions are the individual events of the story. The first and last scenes also have multiple events presented sequentially within them. The boy Calvin, as he grabs the letter from the mailbox in the first scene, tells the tiger Hobbes that he got the letter he wrote himself; then Hobbes asks what he wrote. Watterson has placed Calvin's speech above Hobbes's because he knew the reader would read the top speech first. Then in the final panel, where Calvin's speech also precedes Hobbes's, Watterson has put Calvin's on the left.

The persons are not named, except alphabetically in the title of the comic strip and in Calvin's speech in the second scene. Instead they are pictorially described. Hobbes, who has two personas, appears here as the living tiger who plays with Calvin rather than as the stuffed animal toy that Calvin's parents see. Thus, the visual attributes of the tiger signal his status, in the same way that the *yahui* priest costume worn occasionally by Lord 8 Deer in the Mixtec screenfold histories signals that hero's intermittent role as a *yahui* priest. Location in the comic strip is also referenced in a way that is similar to the representation of locations in the Mexican codices: locations are either precisely identified, left ambiguous, or characterized pictorially according to what kind of places they are. The action in the first scene takes place around Calvin's mailbox, which is unambiguously represented, like a Mixtec or Aztec place sign. Watterson did not specify the location of the second scene because it is immaterial, but for the third scene he added a tree trunk to indicate that Calvin and

Fig. 36. Calvin and Hobbes comic strip, by Bill Watterson, an example of a *res gestae* history. CALVIN AND HOBBES © 1995 Watterson. Reprinted with permission of UNIVERSAL PRESS SYNDICATE. All rights reserved.

Hobbes have moved away from the mailbox and are crossing what we then assume is a yard, garden, or woods. The place is not specified; instead, it is characterized visually in the same way that desert areas in Aztec migration histories might be pictorially described. Time is not treated at all except as sequence and except for the sense that one scene follows the other without much delay. Precise time is not an issue for this story.

In the Codex Selden, the Mixtec historian is telling a very different and much more complex story, but he tells it in roughly the same manner as a series of events (Figs. 37, 38, 39). The codex recounts the dynastic history of the ruling family of Magdalena Jaltepec, known as Añute in pre-Columbian times, a Mixtec town in southern Mexico on the edge of the Aztec empire. By reading a section of it, the three pages covering the life of Lady 6 Monkey, we can see clearly how the Mixtec event-oriented histories present the past as a sequence of events. The codex reads from bottom to top, back and forth in a boustrophedon pattern, with red guidelines to separate the registers and establish the stream of events. There are no vertical lines to separate the individual scenes, which often flow into adjacent ones, and some scenes continue upward from one register to the next.

Lady 6 Monkey's life begins at the bottom right of page 6 (Fig. 37), with the conventional image of her birth, seated with a red umbilical cord attached to her rump from a yellow placenta. Her calendar name, 6 Monkey, floats above her, while her personal name, Serpent Quechquemitl, covers her chest and shoulders. Her birth is one event, but she also faces and is therefore in conference with an old man, a priest (by his costume) who has the calendrical name 10 Lizard and the personal name of Jeweled Axe.[7] The time that has elapsed between 6 Monkey's birth and this conference is not specified. In the second register (register b), the action shifts to 6 Monkey's father, 10 Eagle, who is actively engaged in defending Jaltepec from the attack of Lord 3 Lizard, whose invasion is indicated by the footprints on the road under him. Both 10 Eagle and 3 Lizard carry the shields and obsidian clubs of war, but 10 Eagle has 3 Lizard by the hair and has clearly defeated him. Jaltepec, or Añute (Place of Sand), is identified by pictorial elements in the place sign (the scroll of sand and the mouth element that carries the phonetic reading of "a"), and it is visually described as

a place ringed by clouds (Smith 1983a: 252–255). The date attached to Jaltepec's place sign tells us that 10 Eagle's victory occurred on the day 4 Wind in the year 4 House. Immediately thereafter the story shifts to a new scene in a new place: Lord 2 Rain, 20 Jaguar, appears at a cave containing sacred objects. From other sources, we can surmise that he was responsible for this attack on Añute, although the Selden historian does not tell us this directly. In any case, Lord 2 Rain does not again figure in the story told in the Selden.

The narrative then returns to 6 Monkey, the daughter. Accompanied by the old priest 10 Lizard (6c), 6 Monkey meets with the wizard or sorcerer named 6 Vulture, who advises her to go into hiding, his words rolling from his mouth in speech scrolls. Lady 6 Monkey follows his advice and pictorially dives into the earth, which is identified by the square of wavy diamonds and circles that reflect the scales of the earth crocodile. Footprints direct her into the earth and back out. These three events—the consultation, her hiding, and her emergence—flow into each other to span the entirety of register c.

The uppermost register (d) of page 6 pictures her and Lord 11 Wind in a conference with the supernatural Lady 9 Grass, who resides at Skull Place (Chalcatongo). Speech scrolls from the mouth of 9 Grass unite 6 Monkey and 11 Wind as betrothed. The date of this conference and engagement appears on the register below, attached by a line to Skull Place; the day is 6 Lizard in the year 5 Reed. The offerings the couple have brought to 9 Grass follow on the top register and onto the first register of page 7 (Fig. 38). Then, on the day 10 Wind in the year 10 Reed, seven individuals—including the engaged couple, 9 Grass, and perhaps the priest 10 Lizard—dance around a man playing a slit gong drum. What follows next is the actual marriage of 11 Wind and 6 Monkey, who are shown bathing together (a convention for marriage) in the year 12 House, the day 7 Flower (7a). Gifts—likely the male and female costumes of rule—follow in register b. The individual scenes of betrothal, dancing, and marital bathing might seem part of the same marriage ceremony, except that the dates tell us that these separate events took place over a seven-year period.

The narrative shifts again in register b to a scene at Añute where the old priest 10 Lizard holds gold and jade before Lords 2 Flower and 3 Crocodile and

Fig. 37. Codex Selden 6, a Mixtec *res gestae* history recording the life of Lady 6 Monkey. The page traces her story from her birth to her betrothal to Lord 11 Wind:

a Birth of Lady 6 Monkey; she confers with 10 Lizard.

b (y4 House d4 Wind) 6 Monkey's father 10 Eagle defends Añute; 2 Rain visits cave shrine.

c 10 Lizard and 6 Monkey confer with 6 Vulture, who advises her to go into hiding; she does so and then emerges later.

d (y5 Reed d6 Lizard) 6 Monkey and Lord 11 Wind are betrothed by Lady 9 Grass at Skull Place (Chalcatongo); offerings follow.

The Bodleian Library, Oxford, MS. Arch. Selden. A.2.

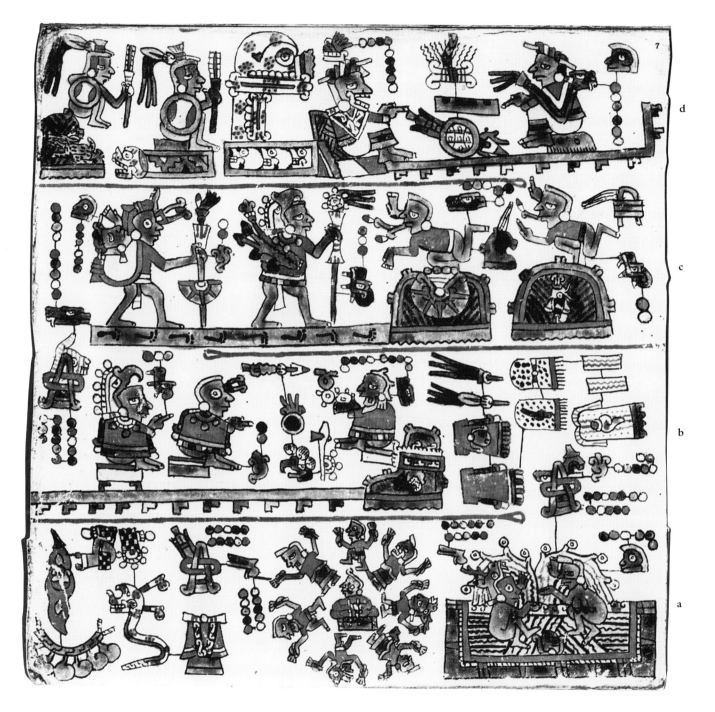

Fig. 38. Codex Selden 7, tracing Lady 6 Monkey's story from her betrothal and marriage to Lord 11 Wind to the time she prepares for war against enemy polities (after Caso 1964a):

a More offerings; (y10 Reed d10 Wind) dance; wedding of 6 Monkey and 11 Wind (y12 House d7 Flower).

b Costumes of rulership; advisor 10 Lizard instructs two ambassadors (2 Flower and 3 Crocodile) to go forward.

c (y13 Rabbit d9 Lizard) Ambassadors carry name

(or person) of 6 Monkey and her insignia to towns of Hill of the Moon and Hill of Bee, where rulers (6 Lizard and 2 Crocodile) threaten them.

d 6 Monkey speaks of war with 9 Grass at Skull.

The Bodleian Library, Oxford, MS. Arch. Selden. A.2. Facsimile reproduction courtesy of Sociedad Mexicana de Antropología, Mexico City.

thereby sends them as ambassadors on a journey. In the next register (7c), 2 Flower carries the head and calendar name of 6 Monkey in a pouch on his back, while 3 Crocodile carries instruments of rulership; either they are actually bringing 6 Monkey with them, or they are carrying her good name and office. The journey, marked by footprints, leads to the Hill of the Moon and the Hill of Bee, where the rulers of these polities either insult 6 Monkey's ambassadors or threaten her (Jansen and Pérez Jiménez 1986: 188). Poised aggressively on their place signs, the rulers 6 Lizard and 2 Crocodile speak sharply to the visitors, their harsh or threatening message indicated by the red and white flint knives on the ends of their speech scrolls.

Provoked by this, 6 Monkey seeks 9 Grass's advice in register d, where the two women face each other with implements of war between them. Behind 9 Grass, warriors from Skull Place and Place of Deer gather. In register a of page 8 (Fig. 39), Lady 6 Monkey attacks and defeats the offending rulers in a battle or series of battles that lasted two days, from 3 Grass to 4 Reed in the year 13 Rabbit. Lord 2 Crocodile is taken to Añute where he has his heart cut out. Then the ambassadors (again carrying 6 Monkey and her emblems of rule) march the second ruler to Red and White Bundle (home of 6 Monkey's husband 11 Wind) where that ruler is also sacrificed. Lady 6 Monkey's victory ceremony follows on register c, where her ambassador 2 Flower holds aloft her emblems of rule, while 6 Monkey bows. In honor of her victory, she has received a new name, Warband Quechquemitl, which she wears; her old name still appears behind her, however.

These trials and victories thus recounted, the historian is at liberty to bring Lady 6 Monkey's story to a close and to proceed with the story of her offspring. He does this by picturing the marriage statement of Lady 6 Monkey and Lord 11 Wind in register c, which shows them ruling at Red and White Bundle. Since the appearance of this marriage statement requires that any offspring follow, we immediately see the birth of the couple's two sons, Lord 4 Wind and Lord 1 Crocodile, both births dated. Thus 6 Monkey drops from the story, which continues with her offspring.

This *res gestae* form, like the Calvin and Hobbes cartoon, concentrates on presenting the participants and events of the story. The people are all identified—in this case they are both named and pictorially character-

ized—and the principal actors appear again and again. The events are clearly presented, and if we do not yet understand the full meaning of each event, it is because we have not yet mastered the pictorial conventions and the larger context of the story. Whereas the individual events are framed and thus separated by vertical lines in the cartoon, in the Selden their separation is less immediately obvious. Distinct events are unconnected to each other, they do not share a platform or foundation, and often the figures in each face in opposite directions; they can also be separated by year dates and a change in location. Events in the Calvin and Hobbes cartoon and in the Codex Selden can also blur into each other in order to share an actor or a place that the painter does not want to have to repeat.

Ambiguity comes with the elements of time and space. Time is not the universal time of an annals account, where it proceeds at an established pace according to quantitatively equivalent units (e.g., years). Instead time is built up of units that are qualitatively equivalent, these units being the events that drive the story.[8] Time proceeds according to these happenings and not according to the calendar, so the events themselves determine how fast time passes rather than the converse. This means that time can leap quickly from one distant event to another, from 6 Monkey's birth to her conference with the priest 10 Lizard, for example. Or it can slow to allow the elaboration of a series of events that occur in a short span, such as 6 Monkey's attack on Hill of the Moon and Hill of Bee and the subsequent defeat and sacrifice of their rulers. There are occasions, too, in *res gestae* where time is immaterial, such as the year of 6 Monkey's birth, which the Selden painter never indicates.

Place can be equally ambiguous. Place signs seat the action of some events, while the absence of place signs allows other events to float. The Selden painter does not indicate, for example, where the dance preceding 6 Monkey's marriage was held, or where 6 Monkey received her new name (Warband Quechquemitl) after her victories; apparently these places were not important.

Mixtec historians almost always used this event series form, and Aztec historians often preferred it too when they recorded the distant past or told of the long migration into the Valley of Mexico. This allowed the historians both to skip by the many uneventful years

Fig. 39. Codex Selden 8, tracing Lady 6 Monkey's story from her defeat of enemy rulers through the birth of her children:

a 6 Monkey captures the two enemy lords (y13 Rabbit d3 Grass and 4 Reed), sacrifices one (2 Crocodile) at Añute.

b Ambassadors carry 6 Monkey and insignia to Red and White Bundle, where other enemy lord (6 Lizard) is sacrificed.

c 6 Monkey receives new name; (y13 Rabbit

d6 Eagle) 6 Monkey and 11 Wind in marriage statement.

d Birth of first son 4 Wind (y2 Flint); birth of second son 1 Crocodile (y5 Flint); Lord 4 Wind (first son) seated at Flints marries Lady 10 Flower.

The Bodleian Library, Oxford, MS. Arch. Selden. A.2.

and also to elaborate the treatment of the major episodes. In the case of migration stories organized according to events, the events are the stopovers at different locations, whose circuit effectively defines the migration route. Thus, the painters presented the Aztec migration as a series of places passed through, and where things happened, although the painters did not arrange these places geographically: the places appear as a sequence. Many migration stories were structured this way as a series of events, up to the point that the migrating people approach or reach their intended territory. Then the painted stories often shifted structure. They shifted from an event-oriented history to a cartographic one. The events still occur, it is just that the historians painted them as occurring in real space.

In explaining the structure of the Cuauhtinchan maps, Dana Leibsohn (1994: 166) has noted Michel de Certeau's (1984: 115–130) distinction between a tour and a tableau. Speaking of stories told spatially, de Certeau sees the tour as a route where space is revealed by movement, whereas he describes a tableau as a presentation of stable geographic territory independent of any action in it. A migration ordered as a series of places visited is a tour, while an ordering of events over a map, as in a cartographic history, is a tableau.

Cartographic Presentations

Cartographic histories are map based. They present events as occurrences that happened in real space, and they relate these events to each other spatially. Time is usually shallow in these cartographic presentations because they make it impossible for the painter to represent a great many events happening over time in the same place; such a situation calls for an annals treatment or a *res gestae*. But in those situations where the spatial relationship between events is of primary importance, the map-based structure is ideal. In this genre, therefore, the story being told is usually the movement of people or things across real space.

In the modern world, cartographic presentations have been used by choreographers and dance teachers to record and teach dance movement; they have been used by the military to plan and record battles; they have also been used by human geographers to plot the normal movement of individuals. The Mexican histori-

ans used them to tell how people came and established themselves in a particular territory.

The Feuillet system of dance notation was the most prominent of the systems developed in the late seventeenth century when accomplished dancing was a highly valued social grace (Guest 1984: 62–64). The system shows not so much the movements and attitudes of the dancer over time, as does Labanotation, but the dancer's movements over space. The action proceeds along a circuit from one point to another on the real space of the dance floor; the space is condensed, and the actions are conventionally presented as marks along the line of travel. In Figure 40, which records the movements of a couple dancing "The Pastorall," the couple begins side by side in the bottom center; they proceed forward, sideways, around, and back again along separate but symmetrical courses until they come to rest again side by side at the bottom. A continuous line tracks the body's movement; a dotted

Fig. 40. The Feuillet system of dance notation, recording the early eighteenth-century dance "The Pastorall" (from Guest 1984: fig. 10.1). Courtesy of Ann Hutchinson Guest, Director, Language of Dance Centre, London.

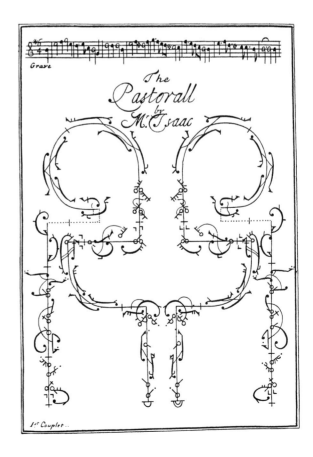

line shows where the dance recorder had to shift the actual line to an empty area in order to avoid crossing and obscuring the earlier movement. On each side of the tracking line, the intricate footwork of this dance is recorded by small circles (which indicate the origin of each step) and lines stemming from them (which indicate the direction and duration of the step), while short branching lines signal the step embellishments. As here, many of these dances concentrated on the foot and leg movements, knowing that a fine carriage and graceful arm movements would automatically accompany them (Guest 1984: 62–67).

The system itself shows the length of each movement but not the temporal duration of these movements. Time in general, however, is indicated by the short lines running perpendicular to the track, which correspond to the bars in the musical score at the top of the sheet (Guest 1984: 58). Although the recorder could not easily build precise time into the spatial system he used, he was able to key cartographic progress to a separate time-line system. He told the reader what kind of events happened or should happen where, and he indicated roughly when.

Such cartographic, or floor plan, systems of recording dance are more limited in the information they can carry than systems like Labanotation that concentrate on the work of the body's musculature. Floor plans excel in tracing footsteps and leg movements, but they can easily be overburdened if much other information is added. They also fail in their ability to note different events that occur in the same place. Yet floor plans give an immediate message and have a clarity that makes them easy to understand, which is why they often accompany and complement other forms of dance notation (Guest 1984: 55).

This clarity and immediacy characterize the classic graphic drawn by the French engineer Charles Minard in 1860 to illustrate the tragic fate of Napoleon's armies in the Russian campaign of 1812–1813 (Fig. 41). Edward Tufte (1983: 40) has described the chart as perhaps "the best statistical graphic ever drawn," one that exemplifies the power of a spatially presented story. Geographically, the chart covers the region from the Polish-Russian border, which is located on the far left, to Moscow, on the far right. The thick, lightly hatched band shows the route of Napoleon's march to Moscow as well as the strength of the French army, first as it invaded Russia with some 422,000 men (on the left) and then as it diminished along the approach to Moscow. The width of the band indicates the size of the army at each place on the map. Auxiliary numbers printed perpendicular to the band specify the size more exactly at various places, but these numbers fail to convey the immensity of the loss.

Fig. 41. Chart of the route of Napoleon's army to and from Moscow during the 1812–1813 Russian campaign, by Charles Minard, 1860 (from Tufte 1983: 41). Reproduced courtesy of Graphics Press, Cheshire, Conn.

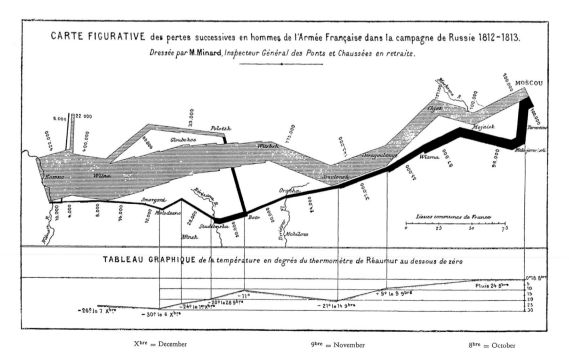

Reaching Moscow in September of 1812, with only 100,000 men, Napoleon found the city sacked and deserted. The smaller black band then shows both his route home and the decreasing size of his army as it struggled home during the bitterly cold winter. This black band is linked to a temperature scale and written dates, both presented at the bottom of the chart, that show clearly how drops in the temperature killed many of the men.[9] The crossing of the Berezina River, when the temperature dropped to 20 degrees below zero, was disastrous; 32,000 men were lost. Only 10,000 of the original 422,000 soldiers made it back to Poland after that devastating winter. Also shown on the left side are the movements of auxiliary troops, first as they tried to protect the advancing army and then as they, too, retreated.

This cartographic history effectively combines space, time, event, and subject to recount the route and ruin of Napoleon's army during that 1812–1813 campaign. The events are the deaths of his men. Because the geography of the story is fixed, time has to be flexible; when it matters, Minard added exact dates.

The same principles operating in the diagrams of the Pastorall dance and of Napoleon's losses during the Russian campaign also govern the cartographic histories painted by the Aztecs. An example is map 1 of the Codex Xolotl, which tells how the Chichimecs, under their leader Xolotl, moved into the Valley of Mexico and settled at Tenayuca (Fig. 42).[10] The map replicates the geography of the Valley of Mexico, with east at the top. There the undulating band of brown hills locates the volcanic mountain range on the valley's eastern edge, with the prominent peak of Popocatepetl at the far southern (right) end; above that range is Puebla to the east. Just below the center of the map, blue waters describe the curving form of the valley lake system: the "loop" of Lake Xaltocan on the left (identified also by Xaltocan's place sign, a spider), then the length of Lake Texcoco, which joins the cuplike shape of the combined lakes Chalco and Xochimilco on the far right. Other hills and bodies of water are represented pictorially, and definite places are precisely identified by the place signs: the curved hill of Culhuacan on the far right, the grasshopper hill of Chapultepec in the lower right corner, the deer's leg that identifies Cholula at the top on the other (Puebla) side of the volcanic range, and so on. Framing the map is a ring of place signs

(many unfortunately lost because of wear) that sets the effective boundaries of the territory. By this combination of described and named places, the artist has spatially set out the area and features of the valley and its environs.

Then the artist added the preexisting cultural component by picturing, describing, and naming the peoples who were already settled at different polities. At Cholula and at five other sites along the right side of the map, male and female couples sit together, the woman holding an infant in a scene that is a conventional representation of the founding of a polity. The adults are identified by name signs; they wear the white cotton clothing that identifies them as civilized and generally "Toltec" people; and the males also usually have a glyph that specifies they are of Toltec ancestry. The glyph combines a bunch of rushes (*tulles*) with a human mouth and chin (*ten* or mouth) to yield *tolte[ca]* (Dibble 1980, 1:18). The scenes are thus conventional representations of the founding of these polities, and the date 1 Flint that accompanies them is a metaphoric reference to these foundings. In this manner, the painter presents the natural and cultural features of the Valley of Mexico and part of Puebla.

Into this world, the historian pictures the Chichimecs entering. They arrive in the lower left corner, where a series of footprints trace their journey upward past a series of five locations to a hill sign where the ruler Xolotl stands wearing the animal skins and carrying the bow and arrow that are the Chichimec hallmark. His name sign is the head of the beast called Xolotl, and that same name is attached also to the hill sign (Xoloque). Below the hill, the date 5 Flint indicates the year Xolotl and his people arrived. Speech scrolls coming from Xolotl's mouth indicate that he is conversing with his son Nopaltzin (named by a nopal cactus), who is seated opposite him and who returns the speech with comments of his own. Three stylized eyes that rise vertically from Xolotl's mouth signal that the father and son are speaking about looking; specifically they are deciding how to reconnoiter the valley. The pair then adjourn; footprints tell us that they travel eastward, up the left side of the map past a series of five other place signs. Another scene of conversation between father and son in the upper left indicates that they are conferring again about the exploratory mission.

At this point, according to the seventeenth-century

historian Fernando de Alva Ixtlilxochitl (1985, 1:294), who based part of his own history of Texcoco on this codex, the father and son separated. Footprints carry Nopaltzin in a meandering path to the right, traveling southward into the valley between the mountains and the lake. In the center of the right side of the map, Nopaltzin stops his rambling southward journey at a hill sign identified by a jar (Alva Ixtlilxochitl says he climbed the high hill), where the painter pictures him bending over and looking (note the stylized eyes) over the southern lake area. From there, footprints carry Nopaltzin in a straight line to the left (northward), past the site of Teotihuacan (identified by the twin pyramids and cave), and then down again to where he and Xolotl began their travels. Meanwhile, while Nopaltzin was traveling, another set of footprints signals that Xolotl continued up the left side of the map (eastward) to visit a ruined Toltec site and then himself returned to where he began at Xoloque.[11]

Footprints then carry both the father and son to

Fig. 42. Codex Xolotl map 1, which traces Xolotl's entrance into the Valley of Mexico (*lower left*), his and Nopaltzin's reconnaissance of the area, and finally his settlement at Tenayuca (*lower center*). Photograph courtesy of the Bibliothèque Nationale de France, Paris.

Tenayuca, the large place sign below (west of) Lake Texcoco, where Xolotl sits surrounded by his son, wife, and six vassals in a scene that signals he has taken possession of the valley and established his polity there. Since taking possession of this land has also involved walking its boundaries literally or figuratively, another series of footprints carries the ruler from Tenayuca down to the bottom of the map and then to the right in a counterclockwise circuit from place sign to place sign that frames the map. We see the traces of this circuit especially well on the upper part of the map where the edge is less worn. The story effectively told on this map is of the Chichimec arrival, exploration, and settlement under the ruler Xolotl.

Such a map-based history is an ideal form for representing migrations, where the principal story is the movement of people across the land, for the cartographic form excels at showing actions taking place in different locations. History flows much like it does in an event-oriented story, in that the narrative moves from event to event, except that in a cartography the events are tied to real space, and the story moves from place to place. Geography is the all-governing factor, for all the events have to be adjusted to fit visually in the space left available by the features of the map. Some events are indicated conventionally—such as the footprints that mark travel or the combination of footprints and a conventionalized eye to indicate reconnoitering—whereas other events appear as discrete scenes.

When the historian relies on scenes to portray events, he or she is forced to abandon the spatial field of the map and to substitute another spatial projection entirely. This is because each scene automatically has its own internal space: the space that the human figures or other forms themselves occupy, together with the space that exists between these forms. We can think of this internal space of the scenes as experiential space, which necessarily is at a different scale than the universal space of the map. Thus the scene of Xolotl surrounded by his vassals at Tenayuca occupies a relatively large part of the map because it is a complex scene with many actors. Although in universal terms the event took place in one spot, it has come to occupy space on the map that would otherwise be devoted to the geography of the land west of Lake Texcoco. In this case, as with any scene, the historian chose to sacrifice geographic space for experiential space.

In such cartographic histories, time is the most ambiguous element. It is present in the sequences of the actions, especially in cases where the sequence is clear, as when footprints carry the story from one place and event to another. It can also be established more precisely by the addition of dates or duration markers to various events, but this is done sparingly in the Aztec histories. Usually the historian chose this format because space was more important for the story than time. Too, the cartographic form excels in its ability to show contemporaneous events. The Codex Xolotl painter can explain how Xolotl traveled east to visit an old Toltec ruin while Nopaltzin was rambling south to explore the valley and still inform the reader about the already settled people then living in the region. In contrast, it is virtually impossible in a cartographic history to portray or even signal a series of events that occurred over time in the same place. Unless the story moves from place to place, time is shallow. Maps, in and of themselves, present all their data at once, so any temporal dimension in a cartographic history is always at war with the governing spatial dimensions.

This difficulty of representing the passage of time over geographic space has been a particular challenge to human geographers who study the human use of space and wish to develop theories of human time allocation as well. The Swedish geographer Torsten Hägerstrand approached this challenge by developing a time-geographic model of human paths in time-space. His approach views each individual's activities as forming a life path that can be plotted both spatially and temporally.

The model for tracking this path is founded on a two-dimensional map, to which Hägerstrand has added the dimension of time as a vertical element (Fig. 43).[12] An individual's daily activities, from home, to office, to shops, and back to home can thus be plotted, not just in space but also in time. As Alfred Gell cogently explains, this model has allowed Hägerstrand and his colleagues to show "the population as a network of individual 'paths' in time and space. Paths are always inclined upwards relative to the place, to reflect the fact that movement in space is time-consuming. Vertical lines indicate stationary objects or temporarily stationary people or things. Spatial relationships are projected on the horizontal plane, temporal relationships, interactions, etc., on the vertical plane. Using this kind of cartographic convention, it is possible to indicate social occasions involving the interaction between many individual paths as 'bundles', and spatial locations such as houses, schools or factories, as 'stations' between which paths move and crisscross one another" (Gell 1992: 193). The model works well in revealing spatial and temporal relationships. Its drawback, for us who are concerned with representing time and space

Fig. 43. Time-geographic model tracing the activities of a Swedish family over a single day. From *Times, Spaces, and Places* by Don Parkes and Nigel Thrift, fig. 6.6. Copyright John Wiley & Sons Limited. Reproduced with permission.

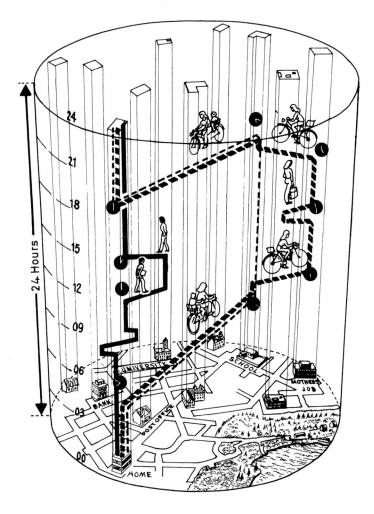

Father:	0900	leaves home	Mother:	0750	leaves home
	0930	bank		0820	drops off child at schoo
	1000	post office		0830	work
	1015	home		1100	shopping
	1210	lunch at university		1130	returns from shops
	1300	home		1700	leaves work
				1720	picks up child
				1800	home

	Child:	0820	school
		1720	leaves school
		1800	home

on a hide or paper surface, is that it is essentially a three-dimensional model that must be rendered on paper in two dimensions. Thus the map comes to be represented as a flat surface having depth but no significant height, and its perceived depth depends on our ability to read diagonals as receding into space according to the principles of linear perspective. This innovative attempt to weld time and space points up the profound difficulty of doing so with paint on paper.

Blended Structures

Many Mexican pictorial histories are more a blend of structures than they are classic examples of one type or another. Annals sometimes assume some of the characteristics of event-oriented histories, when the painters cluster and interrupt the sequent years in order to represent the events in more detail. Cartographic presentations can also merge with event-oriented histories, especially when they describe the events leading to and accomplishing the foundation of a polity.

Res gestae and Cartographs

Most of the lienzos painted by Aztec and Mixtec painters combine a *res gestae* format with a cartographic one, which allows the painter to achieve the important blend of event and place. The Lienzo of Zacatepec (Fig. 44), for example, overlays a *res gestae* history on top of a map of Zacatepec's territory. The string of events thus brings a temporal dimension to this mixedform history.

The map in the lienzo delineates the lands of Zacatepec as a large rectangle, a convention that Mary Elizabeth Smith (1973a: 92) has called a "cartographic rectangle," which is framed by the place signs of Zacatepec's boundaries, their bases oriented inward.[13] The painter oriented east roughly at the top and placed Zacatepec's place sign, prominently sized, in the upper center. Rivers and canals locate important natural features of the terrain. Outside the rectangle, the painter rendered the place signs of Zacatepec's neighbors, usually oriented with their bases outward toward the edge of the lienzo. Within the rectangle are other place signs, some of which are cartographic and others of which are not. Of these interior place signs, the cartographic ones

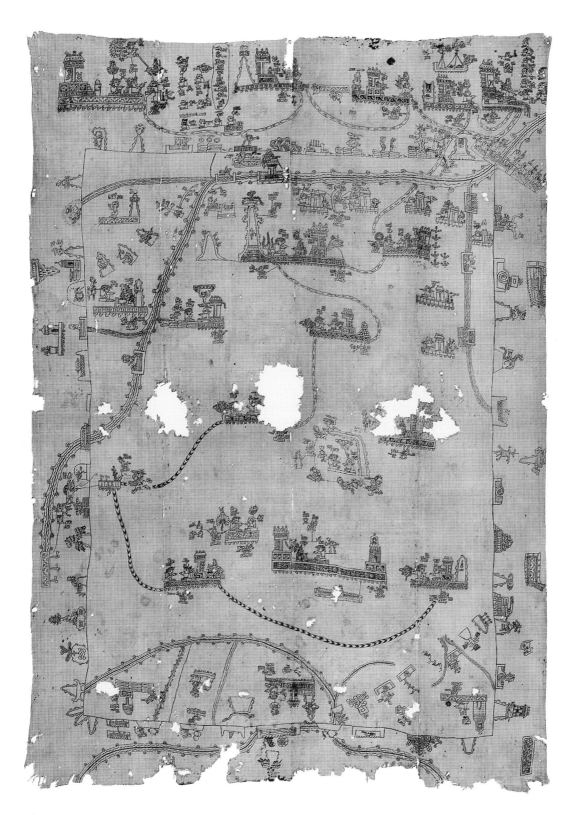

Fig. 44. Lienzo of Zacatepec I, a blend of *res gestae* and cartographic presentations that records the founding and consolidation of Zacatepec. CNCA.-INAH.-MEX; reproduced with permission of the Instituto Nacional de Antropología e Historia.

(those that are part of the map) are either of subject communities (where a single ruler sits on the place sign) or of unoccupied places (where no humans are pictured). These cartographic elements—the boundaries, internal place signs, and aquatic features—reflect, roughly, the geography of Zacatepec and establish it cartographically.

To this basic map the painter also added noncartographic place signs (on which ruling couples sit) that represent Zacatepec's neighboring polities. Although these towns lie geographically outside Zacatepec's boundaries and although some of the place signs appear again outside the rectangle, the painter located them inside the rectangle. The painter did so because these place signs, accompanied by their ruling couples, are less places than events: they signal either the founding of these neighboring polities or their *a priori* existence and rulers, and thus are part of the history unfolding within the rectangle.

The historical narrative itself begins in the upper left corner of the lienzo, outside Zacatepec's territory. There in an elaborate scene the dynastic founder of Zacatepec, Lord 11 Jaguar, receives the accouterments of rule from the great Mixtec lord 4 Wind, ruler of Place of Flints. A ribbon of footprints then carries the founder from left to right across the top of the lienzo as he journeys to a series of four places, places that Jansen (1982, 1:253–254) suggests are in the Mixteca Alta en route from Place of Flints to Zacatepec near the coast. At each site 11 Jaguar makes offerings and performs rites. On the far right, another elaborate ceremony confirms his rule. Then 11 Jaguar enters the land that will be Zacatepec, footprints carrying him inside the cartographic rectangle to a place named Siete Ocotes (Seven Pines) where he appears in a marriage and rulership scene with his wife. The narrative then leaves 11 Jaguar and continues with his son, 8 Crocodile, who is painted ruling Zacatepec with his wife; both sit together on the large place sign of Zacatepec in the upper center of the lienzo. Later the narrative follows 11 Jaguar's grandson, 3 Reed, in his efforts to conquer and consolidate Zacatepec's territory.

Smith (1973a: 92) points out that some of these places in the *res gestae* history are not in their correct geographic location and thus do not function cartographically. The painter located Siete Ocotes, for example, in the upper right corner of the rectangle, when its correct geographic location is on the other side of the river in the upper left, where two pine trees mark its spot (Smith 1973a: 115). I suggest the painter put Siete Ocotes in the upper right because he or she needed to locate the marriage and rulership scene of Lord 11 Jaguar within the sequence of events that led from his entrance into Zacatepec's territory to the founding of Zacatepec itself. The implication is that Siete Ocotes' place in the sequence was more important than its place on the map.

In the case of another town, Putla, however, the painter could approximate its correct location more closely. Putla (a platform with three metal axes) is cartographically placed outside Zacatepec's boundaries along the lower left side of the lienzo. When 11 Jaguar's grandson, 3 Reed, conquers it, however, the painter drew it just inside the rectangle near its repeated, cartographic location (Smith 1973a: 97–98). Unfortunately, the other three place signs in the narrative have not yet been surely identified with known locations, so we cannot now say whether they, like Zacatepec and Putla, were placed on the map roughly in accordance with their geographic location.

The narrative of Zacatepec's founding thus begins as a *res gestae* and maintains that structure throughout. After the protagonist enters Zacatepec, however, cartographic forces begin to pull some events closer to their geographic location. These events then have a partially geographic relationship to each other and are no longer merely part of an autonomous sequence; they must now contend with the cartography of a single place. The painter has effectively blended the *res gestae* and cartographic structures.

Other lienzos and *mapas* utilize both structures without blending them as thoroughly. As explained in Chapters 6 and 7, the Selden Roll, Mapa Sigüenza, and Cuauhtinchan Map 2 begin with an event-oriented narrative that proceeds along a sinuous circuit in undefined space (Figs. 88, 105, 111, 112). Once the narrative arrives in the valley or territory where the polity will be founded, the structure shifts to a map, and the subsequent events are portrayed as taking place in spatial relation to the cartographic features that define the territory. The Mapa Sigüenza (Fig. 105), for example, traces the Mexica migration from Aztlan as a road of footprints that winds around the right half of the *mapa*; the action moves from place sign to place sign, but the place signs are not cartographically arranged. Then when the Mexica are finally portrayed as arriving in Chapultepec, on the left side of the *mapa,* the painter arranges the pertinent place signs cartographically and then pictures the actions as occurring in these places. As explained in Chapter 6, many lienzos—such as those of Tequixtepec, Tlapiltepec, Ihuitlan—and the Map of Teozacoalco juxtapose event-oriented histories with maps without blending the two.

Clustered and Interrupted Annals

Aztec painters, impatient with the rigidity and inefficiency of the annals structure, adjusted this form as well. They brought it closer in line with a *res gestae* narrative by clustering some of the years in blocks and opening up space between these year blocks for the pictorial representation (Fig. 45). All the years are still present visually, but they rob less space. The Codex Boturini and the first parts of the Codex Aubin, Codex Azcatitlan, Aubin-Goupil 40, and Aubin-Goupil 85 are all clustered annals (discussed in Chapter 8; see Figs. 137, 138, 139). It should be pointed out that these clus-

tered annals are all migration histories. The second parts of the Codex Aubin and Aubin-Goupil 40, which are imperial histories, revert to the standard annals structure (Figs. 129, 149).

The migration story, as it is recorded in the pictorials, documents the Aztecs' move from place to place, most of the action being either the act of moving or the act of residing. The manuscript painters chose to cluster the many years of residence, which allowed them more space to present the relevant events (Fig. 45). In the Azcatitlan (Fig. 139), the years accompany the continuing *res gestae* narrative as a secondary element; in the Boturini, Aubin, and Aubin-Goupil documents (Figs. 45, 137, 138), the year blocks alternate with the representations of the events.

Structural Selection

Each of the principal narrative structures—the time line, the event series, and the cartograph—emphasizes some elements of a story at the expense of others. All narratives, as Seymour Chatman (1978: 30) has pointed

Fig. 45. Codex Boturini 13, a blend of annals and *res gestae* structures that records the Aztec migration. The page shows the Aztecs arriving in Coatitlan for a protracted stay that begins in the year 1 Flint. CNCA.-INAH.-MEX; reproduced with permission of the Instituto Nacional de Antropología e Historia.

out, have both determinacies and indeterminacies that occur because of the media in which they are presented. As examples, Chatman mentions that the cinema easily and regularly presents a character's physical demeanor and costume without usually presenting the contents of that person's mind, which must then be inferred from speech or action. Conversely, verbal narrative can easily ignore such visual attributes but would find it difficult not to describe a person's thoughts. What one medium features, other media restrict.

The time-line or annals form emphasizes the regular passage of time and is unmatched in its ability to place events firmly within time and relate them temporally to each other. The annals form, however, is ill suited to conveying spatial relationships or to presenting many contemporaneous events, and its strict time line means the painter must forgo representing the details of individual action.

In contrast, the *res gestae* or event series structure focuses on the events themselves and creates a history that is a string of related events. The emphasis is on the relationship between sequent events, which can themselves be rendered in some detail as scenes of varying degrees of complexity. Although the events can each be precisely dated by the addition of dates, when they appear without such dates they often float somewhat in time. The exact dating of events in the Mixtec screenfolds, for example, has been a concern of scholars ever since Alfonso Caso proposed a tentative scheme, precisely because the *res gestae* stories do not make the exact chronology clear. When John Pohl put forward a revised chronology, building on the work of Emily Rabin and others, he used an annals format to present it (Pohl 1994b: 131–136; Byland and Pohl 1994: 233–264). Duration and continuity, too, are difficult to express in *res gestae* histories.

Cartographic histories also deemphasize time, but they focus less on the pure sequence of events than on their spatial relationships. Cartographic histories are like *res gestae* histories that are embedded in a geographic template. Scenes can be used to picture events, but these scenes must be sufficiently abbreviated to fit into space left between the geographic features. Map-based histories can also easily present contemporaneous events occurring at different locations, which the other structures cannot.

The relative merits and liabilities of these structures shaped the kinds of stories they told. Mixtec historians consistently relied on the *res gestae* structure to record the dynastic histories of their ruling families. Aztec painters looked to the annals form to document their imperial history, from the founding of Tenochtitlan through the Spanish invasion and beyond. Painters in both spheres turned to cartographic histories and to mixed *res gestae* and cartographs to tell about the founding of territories. The Mexican painters also merged the different structures when they found it necessary to achieve a better presentational balance.

5

Mixtec Genealogical Histories

The Mixtec pictorial histories, and especially the *res gestae* screenfolds, document the histories of the Mixtec royal families, explaining how they came to rule their respective polities and how this rule was passed down through subsequent generations. The documents are more family histories than they are community histories. By far the greatest proportion of the information in the codices is genealogical in that it tracks the lines of biological descent of the rulers from the distant past (often beginning with a supernatural ancestor) to the "present" (roughly contemporaneous with the painting of the manuscript) or to some intermediate point. These genealogies, in turn, flow out of and are interposed with historical episodes that explain the sources and trace the threads of the families' power, whether this power derives from divine origins or from the military and diplomatic activities of individual rulers. Combining such genealogical and historical material, the pictorials explain long-standing interrelationships between the Mixtec royal families.

They do so usually from a local point of view. As Smith (1973a: 82) has pointed out, "The story told in any one historical manuscript undoubtedly expressed the regional viewpoint of the town or towns whose rulers commissioned the painting of the manuscript." The manuscripts usually focus on their own dynasty's past, omitting material that may be part of a larger and widely known story but extraneous to that dynasty's interests.[1] For example, the Codex Colombino, which was owned by the ruling family of Tututepec in the Mixteca Costa until 1717, tells a coastal version of Lord 8 Deer's biography (Smith 1966: 171; 1973a: 82). The Codex Selden, to the contrary, mentions 8 Deer only as a parent of one of the wives of a Jaltepec ruler (Smith 1983c: 260–261).

The first events in the Mixtec histories that can be placed in real time date to about A.D. 950, when the old Classic political structure ruptured and made way for the new Post-Classic dynasties and community kingdoms. The last events in the codices occurred in the middle of the sixteenth century, a generation or more after the Spanish invasion.[2] Four of the extant screenfolds (the Codices Bodley, Colombino-Becker, Zouche-Nuttall, and Vienna) predate the conquest, but the Codex Selden was painted about 1556 (Caso 1964a: 61), although in a preconquest style. Additionally a number of screenfolds, tiras, lienzos, and *mapas* from the sixteenth century retain much of the pre-Columbian tradition while incorporating European pictorial elements or information.

The particular nature of these pictorial histories reflects the social and political structure and the sources of political power in the Mixteca. The region was politically organized into autonomous community kingdoms, equivalent to the Nahuatl *altepetl* but generally smaller in scale (such that a community could be traversed in a day) and clustered more closely together (Spores 1967: 101, 184; 1974: 302; Pohl and Byland 1990: 123; Byland and Pohl 1994: 36). Each was under the domination of a hereditary ruler, who traced his descent from the polity's ancient founders, who themselves were indigenous to the area, having emerged from the earth or from a tree or having received the right to rule from supernaturals. Rulership was locally based, and the rulers, although they were not themselves divine, shared with deities the titles *iya* (lord) and *iyadzehe* (lady).[3]

The kings and queens were not simply nobles but were specifically the sons and daughters of kings and queens, for rulership passed directly from parent to offspring. Although the preferred pattern was from father to first son, the vagaries of birth and death meant that another son or daughter often inherited and that occasionally the inheritance passed to a more distant relative who was the nearest direct descendant. When daughters acquired polities, they brought these polities with them to a marriage. Multiple kingdoms controlled by a ruling couple might then pass together to the principal heir, be separated among the offspring, or revert back to the originating families, depending on the situation. The rules of direct inheritance made it essential that the royal families keep careful genealogical records, for one's eligibility to assume rule was based directly on one's genealogical position (Spores 1967: 13–14, 67; 1974: 298, 302–303).

Rulers of these community kingdoms dealt with each other as equals and often as kinsmen, linked by many generations of intermarriage. Still disputes arose, sometimes erupting into military aggression and conquest. Following such a conquest, however, the new arrangement was often consolidated by a marriage between the respective royal families. As Ronald Spores (1974: 298) has noted, "Marital alliance was a customary and persistent form of political integration."[4] The interrelations of the ruling families, moreover, were mediated by supernaturals, whose representatives Pohl identifies as oracular priests, individuals positioned outside the ruling families but to whom the rulers turned for support and counsel. The principal super-

naturals appearing in the codices were Lady 9 Grass of Skull Place (identified as Chalcatongo, where the ancestors of Tilantongo were buried) and Lord 1 Death of Sun Place (perhaps Achiutla), as well as Lord 13 Flower of Mitla.[5]

The community kingdoms that figure most prominently in the existing Mixtec codices are today the small towns of Tilantongo, Teozacoalco, Jaltepec, and Tlaxiaco. The Dominican father Burgoa noted that the Tilantongo dynasty was the most prestigious of all, which is surely why Tilantongo lords and ladies intermarried with so many other families and thus why the Tilantongo line is mentioned in all of the surviving Mixtec screenfolds (Spores 1967: 184; Smith 1973a: 57; Byland and Pohl 1994: 126). Teozacoalco came to control Tilantongo through interdynastic marriage (Smith 1973a: 10), and Jaltepec was alternately a principal ally or opponent in political affairs. Tlaxiaco, along with Yanhuitlan, Coixtlahuaca, and Tututepec, was one of the four largest communities at the time of the conquest (Spores 1967: 101). Other communities, such as those whose place signs are noted in Chapter 3 (Fig. 24), also appear frequently.

Scholars generally refer to the eight Mixtec screenfolds, but this number can contract or expand depending on how one views the manuscripts. Two of them, the Colombino and Becker I, have been shown to be parts of the same original (Seler 1902–1923, 1: 155–156; Caso 1966; Troike 1974: 48–106). Three others, the Vienna, Bodley, and Zouche-Nuttall, have an obverse side that differs in content from the reverse side; the obverse and reverse of the Vienna and Zouche-Nuttall are painted by different artists and are sufficiently different that they can almost be considered separate documents. The principal screenfolds and their contents are as follows:

VIENNA (Vindobonensis): 52 leaves (c. 22 cm × 26 cm), with different stories by different artists on the two sides (Caso 1950; Furst 1978a; Jansen 1982; Anders, Jansen, and Pérez Jiménez 1992a).

   OBVERSE (Figs. 46–52): cosmogony of the Mixteca; reads right to left from p. 52 to p. 1.

   REVERSE: the genealogy of Tilantongo from its founding to the fourteenth century; reads right to left from p. 1 to p. 13.

BODLEY: 23 leaves (c. 26 cm × 29 cm), with different genealogical histories on the two sides (Caso 1960b; Smith 1998: 185–188).

OBVERSE (Figs. 55, 59, 61, 73): dynastic history of Tilantongo with the biography of 8 Deer embraced, ending with the Tilantongo rulers at the time of the Spanish invasion; reads generally left to right in a horizontal boustrophedon from p. 1 to p. 20.

REVERSE: dynastic history of Tilantongo and Flints, focusing especially on the life and paternal ancestors of 4 Wind; includes dynastic histories of Achiutla and Tlaxiaco and ends with Tlaxiaco rulers of the fifteenth century; reads generally right to left in a horizontal boustrophedon from p. 40 to p. 21.

ZOUCHE-NUTTALL (Nuttall): 47 leaves (19 cm × 25.5 cm), contains different stories by different artists on the two sides (Nuttall 1902, 1975; Troike 1987; Anders, Jansen, and Pérez Jiménez 1992b).

OBVERSE (Figs. 53, 54, 58): dynastic histories of Tilantongo, Teozacoalco, and probably Zaachila; reads right to left in a vertical boustrophedon from p. 1 to p. 41.

REVERSE (Figs. 62, 64–68, 70–71): partial biography of 8 Deer from his father's marriage to the death of his genealogical rivals Lords 10 Dog and 6 House; reads right to left in a vertical boustrophedon from p. 42 to p. 84.

COLOMBINO-BECKER I (Figs. 63, 69): fragmentary manuscript now composed of 24 Colombino leaves and 16 Becker I leaves (19 cm × 26 cm), painted on one side with partial biographies of 8 Deer and 4 Wind from the coastal (Tututepec) point of view (Caso 1966; 1996; Smith 1963; 1966; Troike 1974).

SELDEN (Figs. 37–39, 56, 57): 20 leaves (27.5 cm × 27.5 cm), painted on one side with the dynastic history of Jaltepec from the founding to rulers in 1556; reads bottom to top from p. 1 to p. 20 (Caso 1964a; Smith 1994).

BECKER II (Fig. 60): 4 leaves (26.5 cm × 28.5 cm), to which the Hamburg fragment (one and one-half leaves) was attached at the front, painted on one side with the genealogy of a town in the Mixteca Baja (probably Santos Reyes Yucuna), beginning

with its founding (Nowotny 1964, 1975; Smith 1979; Jansen 1994: 193–214).

EGERTON (or Sánchez Solís): 16 leaves (21.5 cm × 27.7 cm), painted on both sides with the genealogy of an unknown place beginning with its founding; reads left to right from p. 2 to p. 17 (obverse) and p. 19 to p. 31 (reverse) (Burland 1965; König 1979; Jansen 1994: 143–191).

MURO: 11 leaves (14.5 cm × 19 cm), painted on one side with the genealogy of Adeques, a town to the south of San Pedro Cántaros (Ñunaha) in the Mixteca Alta; reads right to left from p. 1 to p. 11 (Smith 1973b, n.d.a, n.d.b; Jansen 1994: 47–77; Hermann Lejarazu 1997, 1998).

These codices and the other screenfolds and tiras, as a corpus, cover a broad range of history: they record the creation of the Mixteca, the origins of the ancestors, the founding of the community kingdoms, the diplomatic and military exploits of key rulers (such as Lady 6 Monkey, Lord 8 Deer, and Lord 4 Wind), and the genealogies that carry the dynasties forward. Although it is important to consider each document in its own terms as a particular creation, it can help us understand the nature of Mixtec history if we consider the pictorials thematically.

Origins

Cosmogony of the Codex Vienna

Were it not for the Codex Vienna, our understanding of Mixtec cosmogony would be much poorer than it is. The obverse side of the Vienna is a Mixtec Genesis: it summarizes the formation of the Mixteca, from the first stirrings out of a presumed void to the establishment of the political landscape. The Vienna Obverse explains how ritual acts generated a sequence of progenitors, who in turn begot or caused to appear deities and other supernaturals, natural features, and aspects of the human condition; it also documents the birth of the Mixtec polities, describes the beginnings of important ceremonies, and shows how supernaturals organized the Mixteca territorially.

Because the Vienna Obverse does not feature the activities and genealogies of the rulers, it has often been treated separately in Mixtec studies, considered to be ritual rather than historical. But as Furst (1978a) and Jansen (1982) have made clear, the Vienna Obverse is figuratively the springboard for the political and dynastic histories that follow. Individuals who are born or who first appear in the Vienna Obverse later function in the genealogical histories as gods, divine patrons, or sacred cult bundles. The Vienna Obverse is indeed a historical manuscript; it is just that the history it records is the creation of the Mixteca's supernatural, natural, and cultural features.

Like several of the other screenfolds, the Vienna Obverse reads right to left in a vertical boustrophedon pattern. Unfortunately its pages were later numbered left to right, so that one now reads the manuscript beginning with page 52 and continuing to page 1. Its narrative is structured as a series of creation or "beginning" episodes, which start out being conceptually abstract or ceremonial and then become more concrete and geographical as the manuscript progresses. For the purposes of discussion, the episodes can be clustered into three sections: the first takes place in the celestial realm (52–49), the second is dominated by the earthly actions of the supernatural culture hero 9 Wind and then by the prototypical priest-shaman 2 Dog (49–23), and the third explains how the gods organized the Mixteca world politically and territorially (22–1).[6]

Celestial Beginnings. The Vienna Obverse opens not with deities, humans, or physical features but with relative intangibles: song (or prayer) and offering (Fig. 46). In the bottom right corner of page 52, two unnamed human figures represent these actions, followed by four other pairs of black figures who symbolize other fundamental concepts: the 20 nights and days on which the calendar is founded, the coming and going of the

Fig. 46. Codex Vienna Obverse 52, the first page of the creation story. After song and offering (*lower right*), there follow night and day, other concepts in pairs, and the structures and places where songs and offerings occur. Photograph courtesy of the Österreichische Nationalbibliothek, Vienna.

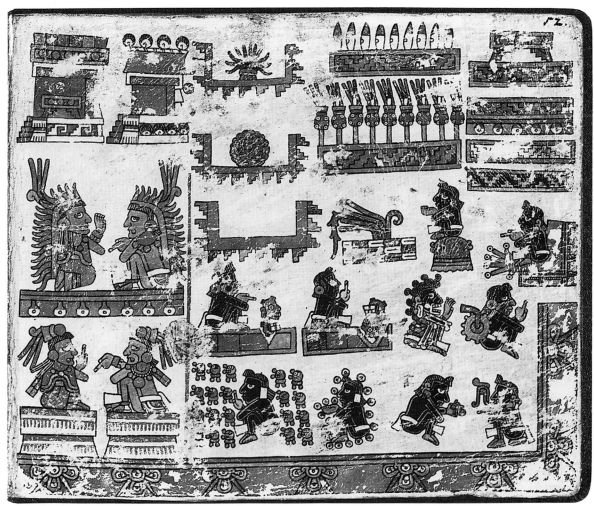

ñuhu (earth spirits), death and priests, and water and hill (the metaphor for community kingdom). Thus, before anything else, before the gods or even the days, the Mixtec cosmos opened with the principal elements of ritual: song/prayer and offering. There follows a series of enclosures, platforms, and temples (places where songs and offerings might occur). A great sky band framing the bottom and right sides of the page figuratively locates all these elements, and probably those that follow, in the heavens.[7]

Next, the primordial couple, Lord 1 Deer and Lady 1 Deer, make their first appearance, preceded by two unnamed pairs of ancients who may well represent their titles (Fig. 47). The couple make offerings of copal incense and powdered tobacco (51a bottom), which generate a series of 52 physical and cultural features, represented by pairs of named and unnamed figures (51–50). Jansen (1982, 1:89, 136–138) sees these figures and features as supernaturals and qualities of the earth. Included are varying kinds of serpents, stone men (two

---

Fig. 47. Codex Vienna Obverse 52b–51a. The primordial couple Lord 1 Deer and Lady 1 Deer, preceded perhaps by their titles, make offerings to create pairs of physical and cultural features. Drawing by John Montgomery.

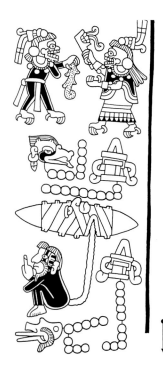

Fig. 48. Codex Vienna Obverse 49d. After a skeletal pair make offerings, Lord 9 Wind is born from a great flint knife. Drawing by John Montgomery.

---

representing the smoke and movement of volcanic eruption [50a]), tree men, warriors, and two black painted priests holding incense bags (who figure several times later in the story). A jeweled A-O year sign and the number 1 (symbolizing the first year), followed by the ritual date year 5 Flint day 5 Flint, signal a beginning. Then some of the figures gather to make offerings to a tree growing from a plain of smoking copal balls (50d); this tree will also figure later as the source from which many Mixtec lords were born (i.e., Vienna 37–35). Year 5 Flint day 5 Flint is the first full date in the manuscript, and it, like almost all the dates in the Vienna, should be read metaphorically rather than literally (Furst 1977: 208–210; 1978a: 315; 1978c). Other dates that mark episodes of beginning are the year 1 Reed day 1 Crocodile and year 13 Rabbit day 2 Deer.

The year 1 Reed day 1 Crocodile on the bottom of page 49a introduces another ancient pair (Lady 4 Dog and Lord 8 Crocodile), whose offerings generate a series of variously described stones.[8] When a skeletal couple makes another offering (49d), the final stone (shaped as an animated knife) gives birth to the Mixtec culture hero Lord 9 Wind, the Mixtec equivalent of the Aztec Quetzalcoatl-Ehecatl (Fig. 48). The birth of 9

Wind brings to a close this first section, which starts the creation in motion by bringing into being the essential intellectual and cultural concepts that sustain Mixtec life (the practice of making offerings, twenty days and nights, community, supernaturals), as well as creating the fundamental elements of vegetation and the as yet undefined earth. I suggest that all these cultural and natural features are not simply born as progeny of the two primordial couples but are realized as the result of the offerings the first couples make.

The Works of Lord 9 Wind. Lord 9 Wind's birth from the great stone knife (Fig. 48) opens the account of his successful efforts to bring the Mixteca and its ceremo-nial life fully into being; this second section, of nearly a dozen episodes, spans pages 49 through 23. His birth is immediately followed by sixteen figures, who represent either his titles or the qualities he possesses (Fig. 49): one can almost hear the litany of these phrases, which might have been something like "he of white cotton, he of jade, he of gold, Lord 9 Wind, his twin, the sacrificer, he who makes offerings, the twisted one (shaman?), the hunter, the warrior, the man of stone, the jaguar singer, he who has poetry/prayer/song in his heart, the painter/writer, he who has the earth spirit in his heart, he who has the 'Xipe' bundle in his heart."[9]

Thus titled, 9 Wind next appears on a platform in

Fig. 49. Codex Vienna Obverse 48. Following a listing of 9 Wind's qualities, presented as couplets, 9 Wind descends from the heavens carrying with him the accouterments of rule. Photograph courtesy of the Österreichische Nationalbibliothek, Vienna.

the sky (48c), seated between two ancient males who confer on him the costume and attributes that will be important to him thereafter (Fig. 49). Wearing this costume, he descends from the sky via a white rope that is adorned with the down balls that signal sacrifice. He is dressed equivalent to the Aztec Quetzalcoatl-Ehecatl, he carries the "quincunx" staff of rule, and he is accompanied by his eagle and *yahui* manifestations, who carry temples on their back. Thereby, Lord 9 Wind descends from the sky bringing with him the accouterments of rule necessary to found polities (Jansen 1982, 1:89–90, 146–180; Furst 1990: 129–130). On the next page (47a), he is greeted by the primordial couple Lady

4 Dog and Lord 8 Crocodile and their three offspring (seen earlier). After conferring with an ancient pair (first seen on 52), 9 Wind is then shown supporting the sky and water on his shoulders (47b top).[10]

Lord 9 Wind's sky/water-bearing scene initiates an extraordinary series of over 200 place signs, many accompanied by day and year dates, that fills pages 47c through 38b (Fig. 50). These are places 9 Wind brought into being or allowed to come into being by his actions, and the dates that accompany them are considered to be the metaphoric dates of their founding.[11] Polities mentioned in the other Mixtec histories are found in this list, as are some that may lie well outside the Mix-

Fig. 50. Codex Vienna Obverse 42bcd. Places brought into being by 9 Wind, accompanied by the dates associated with their creation. Photograph courtesy of the Österreichische Nationalbibliothek, Vienna.

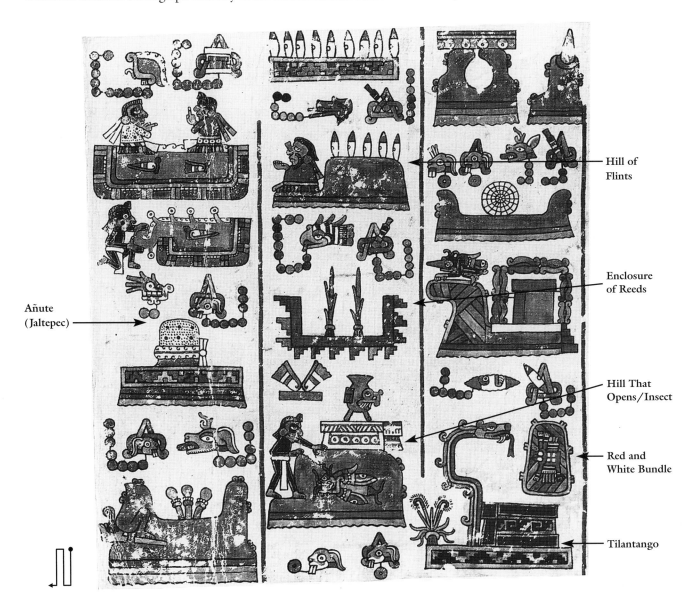

Añute (Jaltepec)

Hill of Flints

Enclosure of Reeds

Hill That Opens/Insect

Red and White Bundle

Tilantango

teca (the volcanoes Popocatepetl and Iztaccihuatl are perhaps included on page 39a, for example). Some communities that lie close to each other appear close to each other in this list, which suggests that the array may be geographically ordered, as one might scan a horizon (Byland and Pohl 1994: 65), but too few of the place signs have been securely identified to say definitively. We do note on page 42bc (Fig. 50) a clustering of Red and White Bundle, Tilantongo (with Ascending Serpent), Hill That Opens/Insect, Enclosure of Reeds, and Hill of Flints, which are the locations of foundation rituals pictured on Zouche-Nuttall 15–19 (Byland and Pohl 1994: 43). Nearby Jaltepec (Añute, Place of Sand) appears in the Vienna on page 42d (Fig. 50). The date accompanying Jaltepec, year 8 Rabbit day 2 Grass, reflects or is reflected by the calendrical names of the pair who founded the Jaltepec dynasty, Lady 8 Rabbit and Lord 2 Grass (Jansen 1982, 1:221; Smith 1994: 128–129 n. 4).

Following the impressive listing of polities, 9 Wind turns his attention to populating this geographic world. A new date (year 13 Rabbit day 2 Deer) signals the beginning of this episode (Fig. 51), where ritual items and the repeated date (13 Rabbit 2 Deer) introduce a conference between the culture hero 9 Wind and twelve anthropomorphic stones and plants (the spirits or forces of the earth and vegetation) and the two black priests (7 Eagle and 7 Rain); most of these earth and plant spirits and the priests appeared earlier with the smaller tree scene on page 50. With this meeting, Lord 9 Wind sets into motion the crucial tree birth event that follows (Fig. 51). There, on page 37b, a large tree rising from a plain of smoking copal balls (identical to the tree and location on Vienna 50) is cut open by the black painted priests (7 Eagle and 7 Rain). From a split between its spreading limbs emerges a male, a female, and 51 other figures, three of whom are known to be lineage ancestors. The place of this tree birth has been identified as Apoala, the small polity important to the Mixtecs as a place of origin. The chroniclers Francisco de Burgoa and Antonio de los Reyes both record that the ancestors of the Mixtec lords were born from a tree or trees at Apoala. A modern Mixtec legend also tells of a man who impregnated a tree that then gave birth to a supernatural hero.[12]

More humans and natural features are created next, the episode introduced by the date year 13 Rabbit day 2 Deer (35a). The important ancestors Lord 1 Flower and Lady 13 Flower (who had been born from the tree) are pictured in a scene of marriage and offering, immediately followed by the appearance of their daughter 9 Crocodile. She marries a Lord 5 Wind (9 Wind serves as a matchmaker), and together the couple makes offerings, still at Apoala. This ritual act produces a series of humans, plants, animals, stones, and human qualities (35b–34d; Furst 1977: 206; Jansen 1982, 1:90–91, 113–119). Although Lord 5 Wind and 9 Lady 9 Crocodile are directly responsible for creating these elements, 9 Wind remains the force that has guided their actions.

Having orchestrated the creation of deities, ancestors, human conditions, and things humans use, 9 Wind turns his attention to the realm of ritual. Now, once again, he participates directly. He makes offerings to the aged couple Lady 1 Eagle and Lord 1 Grass, who sit in the river at Apoala, an act that leads to a gathering of 28 deities (34d–32c). On pages 32d–31 he drills new fire, brandishes sacred plants, and thereby establishes temples and sweatbaths. Then in another ceremony elaborately presented, he and the prototypical priest-shaman 2 Dog pierce each other's ears and the ears of the 44 deities who follow (all wear a distinctive eagle-down ear plug). At this time the deities receive their insignia (Furst 1978c: 176) or personal names (Jansen 1982, 1:168–171), which are painted beside them. Three other ceremonies follow: the first related to rain and the maize crop, the second associated with pulque preparation and drinking (and presided over by 2 Dog), and the third pertaining to the use of mushrooms (presided over by 9 Wind with the assistance of other deities). Then six deities usher in the rising sun (23). The place sign of Apoala (a river enclosing a hand holding feathers), which appears at the onset of these ceremonies, locates them all at Apoala.[13]

These twenty-six pages devoted to the works of 9 Wind thus tell how he descended from the heavens bringing rulership to the Mixteca. He then carried the waters and sky to establish places on the dry land, and he set into motion the birth of royal ancestors and supernaturals. Next, he established sacred architecture, activated the deities with their insignia or names, and, with their assistance, crafted important ceremonies. When all these tasks were completed, the sun rose.

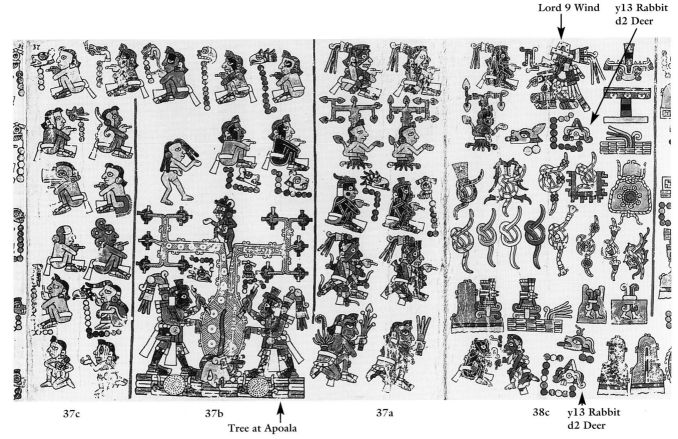

Fig. 51. Codex Vienna Obverse 38c–37abc. After 9 Wind (*upper right*) meets with twelve supernatural entities and spirits, the deities 7 Rain and 7 Eagle cut open the tree at Apoala, out of which are born humans, deities, and human qualities. Photograph courtesy of the Österreichische Nationalbibliothek, Vienna.

Ordering the Mixtec Land. The last 22 pages of the Vienna Obverse explain how the supernaturals organized the territory of the Mixteca into coherent units and established or founded polities. Nine times the painter repeats the same foundation ritual, varying just the details from place to place (Fig. 52).[14] The ritual begins with a symbolic date, followed by the composite glyph of a cradle board, an animal tail, and a platform (which symbolizes the birth or founding of a town), this followed by a named deity who precedes a series of offerings. Next, an A-O year indicator and a single disk (which symbolize the onset of time reckoning) introduce a six-part construction effort, the parts always in the same order: first two men measuring or aligning with a cord pulled tight, a rectangular stone on feet (perhaps either to represent a moving stone or a foot or foundation stone), a stone altar, a stone staircase with bloody stairs, a complete stepped pyramid, and then a man tying fast a block with cord. Four temples then follow immediately, always in the same order, their interiors distinguished by an eye, a bird, a vessel of blood, and two bleeding cacao beans. Another date opens the third section where a named deity drills fire while another holds up a bouquet of three distinctive herbs bound with a paper streamer. The fourth and final part presents a series of places and other temples.

The nine rites vary from each other only in their participants, the number and kind of offerings, and the places being identified. They are rituals of foundation, by which the deities bless and build towns and inaugurate them with the brandished herbs and the drilling of new fire (Boone n.d.). Many of the place signs revealed by 9 Wind and listed much earlier in the Vienna are here integrated into their geographic locations and established as community kingdoms.[15] The last four pages of the Vienna (4–1) picture 16 other polities, their patrons or founders, and the dates of their foundation.

Thus, the full Obverse of the Codex Vienna is dedicated to recording the Mixtec creation. It explains how supernaturals and humans came into being and how the gods and primordial ancestors created and ordered the land. It opens in the heavens before the first gods or cosmic features were born, and before time began. The acts of singing or praying and making offerings start the process in motion. By the time its story ends, the Mixteca has been created, populated, and organized and is ready for human action.

From Origins to Foundations in Local Histories

The cosmogony related in the Vienna Obverse is broadly relevant for all of the Mixteca because its narrative is couched in universal, cosmic terms. Yet many of the story's features also find their place at the beginning of the local histories. Most of the Mixtec genealogical histories begin with episodes of origin (when the ancestors first appear), and they apply some of the same elements found in the universal history of the Vienna Obverse to explain their own polity's origins. These include incidents of descent from the heavens, of birth from the earth or trees or the river at Apoala, as well as primordial marriages. They also employ supernaturals and rituals of foundation.

Heavenly Origins. The heavenly descent of ancestors is a recurring theme in the Codex Zouche-Nuttall, which pictures supernaturals or ancestors coming down to earth from the heavens, bringing with them, figuratively or implicitly, the authority of office. We saw this theme in the early part of the Vienna Obverse (Fig. 49) when 9 Wind descends from the heavens bringing the accouterments of rule to the Mixteca. On Zouche-Nuttall 14 (Fig. 53), dynastic founders Lord 5 Flower and Lady 3 Flint emerge from a heavenly "Chicomoztoc" (Seven Caves), pictured as concentric sky and stone bands breached by a large, mouthlike cave and six smaller caves. A band of footprints leads

Fig. 52. Codex Vienna Obverse 18ab–17a. Foundation ritual overseen by Lord 7 Flower (*lower right, upper right*). Following the date year 1 Reed day 2 Grass (*lower right*), Lord 7 Flower initiates a series of offerings (*right*). The A-O and disk (*center*) introduce the construction effort, followed by the drilling of new fire and presentation of herbs. Places and temples follow on the left. Photograph courtesy of the Österreichische Nationalbibliothek, Vienna.

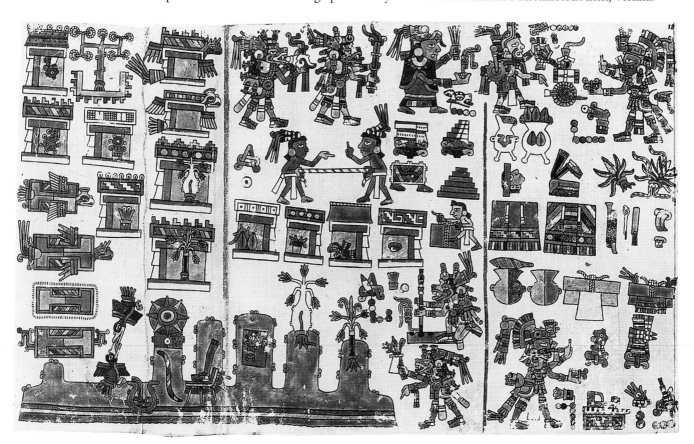

Fig. 53. Codex Zouche-Nuttall 14a. Lord 5 Flower and Lady 3 Flint emerge from the celestial Chicomoztoc (from Anders, Jansen, and Pérez Jiménez 1992b). © 1991, Akademische Druck- u. Verlagsanstalt and Fondo de Cultura Económica.

from heaven to earth, where the couple initiate a new dynasty. On two other occasions, another lord physically brings the implements of rulership from the heavens (Fig. 54), paralleling 9 Wind's actions in the Vienna Obverse. This is Lord 12 Wind, who descends via a sacrificial cord carrying a temple on his back, while his attendants bear the staffs and sacrificial implements he will use to found new dynasties (Zouche-Nuttall 18b, 19). Lord 12 Wind, like the prototypal 9 Wind, brings "rule" from the heavens to establish new polities.

Tree and Earth Births. If rule is brought from the heavens, the Mixtec ancestors themselves are born from the land, water, and plants. The Codex Zouche-Nuttall opens with the emergence of the ancestor Lord 8 Wind (not to be confused with the culture hero 9 Wind) from the earth, followed by his subsequent reemergences from a hill and from the river at Apoala (Zouche-Nuttall 1). The reverse side of the Codex Bodley (40d) opens with the emergence of Lord 1 Flower and Lady 13 Flower from the river at Apoala, followed by the marriage of their daughter 9 Crocodile to Lord 5 Wind at Apoala. A variant rendering of this episode initiates an entirely different sequence in the Codex Zouche-Nuttall (36).[16] We remember 1 Flower and 13 Flower as

the couple in the Vienna (36c) who came from the tree at Apoala, and 9 Crocodile as their daughter whose marriage to 5 Wind was arranged by the culture hero 9 Wind.[17]

Tree births, so prominent in the Vienna, appear in the early pages of the Codices Bodley (1b) and Selden (2a). The first event on the Bodley Obverse (Fig. 55) is the birth of the ancestral Lady 1 Death from a tree; others on this page may have come from trees, too, but the manuscript is too badly damaged to tell.

The opening passages of the Codex Selden combine several of these elements. The Selden history begins when the sun god 1 Death and the Venus god 1 Movement descend from the heavens to shoot darts into the hill of a place sign (Fig. 56). From the resulting crevice is born Lord 11 Water, the grandfather of the woman (8 Rabbit) who will found Jaltepec's dynasty. Page 2 of the Selden (Fig. 57) then features the tree birth of Lord 2 Grass, the male founder of Jaltepec's dynasty (and 8 Rabbit's husband), whose miraculous appearance has been preceded, and probably made possible, by offerings made to the pair Lord 5 Wind and Lady 9 Crocodile in the river of Apoala (1c).

The pair 5 Wind and 9 Crocodile thus play early roles in the dynasties recorded by the Bodley Reverse, Selden, and Zouche-Nuttall. The couple joins the primordial pair Lord and Lady 1 Deer, and others, as supernatural ancestors.

Supernaturals. As Maarten Jansen (1982, 1, esp. 281–288) has persuasively argued, the individuals pictured in the Vienna Obverse are supernaturals rather than mortals. They function as divine ancestors and creators and as representatives of natural forces. Many of them also figure in the dynastic histories, where they continue to serve as creators/ancestors and where some mediate the affairs of the Mixtec rulers.

In particular, three of the primordial creator couples who are active in the Vienna cosmology have early roles in the dynastic histories. We have already seen how the pair 1 Flower and 13 Flower initiates dynasties in the Zouche-Nuttall and Bodley, just as the pair 5 Wind and 8 Crocodile does in the Bodley Obverse, Selden, and Zouche-Nuttall. The ancients Lady 1 Eagle and Lord 1 Grass, who sit in the River of Apoala and receive 9 Wind's offerings in the Vienna (34d–33a), are also visited in the story told on Zouche-Nuttall 14–21; there the first two generations of rulers of Temple of the Feathered Serpent, Hill of the Wasp, and Hill of Flints visit the ancients in their watery domains prior to the rulers' marrying and establishing their sovereignty.[18]

Several supernaturals who appear in the Vienna but are not part of creator pairs also participate in the genealogical histories, some prominently. Lady 9 Grass of Skull Place (Chalcatongo), for example, fights actively in the War of Heaven (Rabin 1979; discussed briefly below) and later is regularly consulted by the rulers of Tilantongo, Jaltepec, and their circle, notably Lord 8 Deer, Lady 6 Monkey, and Lord 4 Wind; she therefore appears in the Bodley, Colombino-Becker, Selden, and Zouche-Nuttall. The sun god 1 Death opens the Selden's history; moreover, his oracle is the object of a pilgrimage by 8 Deer and 4 Jaguar, detailed in the Zouche-Nuttall Reverse, Bodley Obverse, and Colombino-Becker. The priest-shaman Lord 2 Dog is part of a conference following the War of Heaven early in the Zouche-Nuttall Obverse (4c).[19] The lords 7 Deer

Fig. 54. Codex Zouche-Nuttall 18b. Lord 12 Wind descends from the heavens (*right*) via a sacrificial cord, bringing with him the accouterments of rule. In the upper left are placed the quincunx staff and cult bundle. Photograph courtesy of the British Museum.

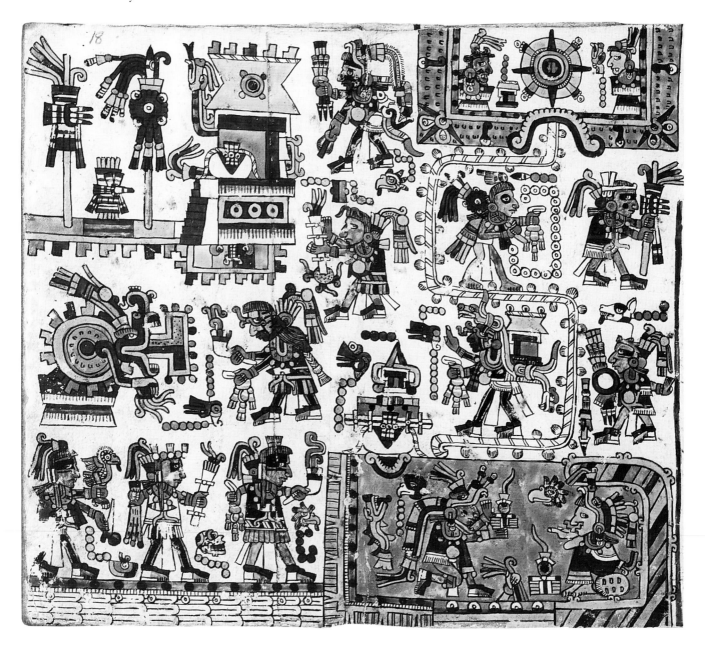

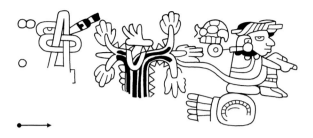

Fig. 55. Codex Bodley 1e. The ancestor Lady 1 Death is born from a tree at Apoala. Drawing by John Montgomery.

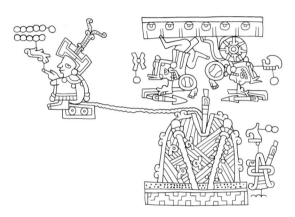

Fig. 56. Codex Selden 1. Lord 11 Water is born from a crevice in the earth, which was opened when the supernatural lords 1 Movement and 1 Death descended from the heavens and shot arrows into the earth. Drawing by John Montgomery.

Fig. 57. Codex Selden 2. Lord 2 Grass is born from a tree. Drawing by John Montgomery.

and 9 Movement, who emerged from the tree at Apoala and have important ceremonial roles in the Vienna Obverse, are invoked at the beginning of the Codex Tulane and appear as cult bundles in the Lienzo of Zacatepec.[20] Other supernaturals who have played a part in the Vienna cosmogony also appear occasionally in the genealogical histories. Usually all these supernaturals play pivotal roles in the early part of the histories, and several continue to function as mediators in royal affairs.

Rituals of Foundation. The foundation rituals that occupy pages 22–25 of the Vienna Obverse (Fig. 52) set the example for the foundation rites in the other histories (Boone n.d.). The Codices Zouche-Nuttall (e.g., 15–19, 21, 22), Bodley (9a), Colombino (5–6), Egerton (3–5), and Selden (3–4), as well as the Mapa de Teozacoalco and several Coixtlahuaca Valley manuscripts discussed in Chapter 6, all include rituals whereby polities are founded or dynastic rule is established at specific locations.[21] Like the Vienna, they emphasize the acts of making offerings and bringing new fire to a site, but they also include the placing of cult bundles, which is not featured in the Vienna. A crucial element in most of these Mixtec rituals is a red "quincunx" staff (sometimes called a Venus Staff) that is brought and placed at the site along with the cult bundle. In the Zouche-Nuttall (Fig. 54), for example, supernaturals or culture heroes carry the emblems of rule and the accouterments of ritual to a dozen or so towns where dynasties are being established. The supernaturals and heroes bring a cult bundle or temple or both to establish the town, a fire-drilling apparatus to drill a new fire, the distinctive red "quincunx" staff to place at the site, and such extras as a conch shell trumpet, a torch, an incense pouch, and a quail for sacrifice, all of which are components of the ritual. The scribe then paints the male and female couple who begin the new dynasty seated together on a platform in the Mixtec convention for marriage.

These ceremonies reflect the universal rituals of foundation described in the Vienna Obverse as they are applied to individual communities. They feature participation by supernaturals who bring the fire and implements of rule to the site. The Vienna ceremonies, however, focus on the gods' activities and the construction effort needed to establish and organize place; they couch the ritual in broad terms. In contrast, the local histories involve human as well as divine actors and focus on placing the cult bundle and the red quincunx staff at a single polity. They tailor a general foundation ritual to fit the particulars of their community kingdom.

Most of the Mixtec histories, thus, begin their narrative in a mythic past, a past that is explained more fully in the Vienna Obverse. The local histories simply select and highlight the features that pertain to their particular stories. Narratives in the Bodley Obverse and Reverse, Selden, Zouche-Nuttall Obverse, and Vienna Reverse all open with origin episodes (sometimes much condensed) and the founding of the relevant dynasties. They then use this primordial and foundational past as the base on which they build the subsequent genealogies.

Genealogies

Genealogies fill most of the content of the dynastic histories. Because parentage and birth order were deciding factors in determining who would rule in the Mixteca, the histories painted for these dynasties give careful reckoning of descent, marriage, and rule. A few extant manuscripts, such as the Reverse of the Codex Vienna, are almost entirely genealogical. The Vienna Reverse opens with a greatly truncated origin episode and moves quickly into the genealogical history of the Tilantongo dynasty. It includes very little nongenealogical information. The Codex Bodley, too, is heavily genealogical in sections. Most of the dynastic histories, however, interlace the genealogies with stories of the rulers' deeds that have shaped their sovereignty. These episodes provide the action of the history, whereas the genealogical sections carry the dynastic line into the future.

Well-understood and broadly applicable conventions guided the painters in depicting genealogical information, but the painters also worked within their own particular preferences. The painter of the Codex Bodley, for example, followed precise rules of sequential order that the painter of the Zouche-Nuttall Obverse did not, and the Bodley painter included more narrative detail. It can therefore help us understand the range and middle ground of these genealogies if we consider examples from both.

The Family of Lord 5 Crocodile in the Zouche-Nuttall

Page 26 of the Zouche-Nuttall presents the marriages and offspring of Lord 5 Crocodile "Raingod Sun," the father of Lord 8 Deer "Jaguar Claw" (Fig. 58). The manuscript reads right to left, beginning in the upper right corner, with red lines guiding the flow of information. There in the upper right Lord 5 Crocodile sits opposite his wife 9 Eagle "Garland of Cacao Flowers" in a marriage statement: they face each other sitting within a palace. Their personal names are worn or attached to them; their calendrical names are below them. The date of this marriage, year 6 Flint day 7 Eagle (A.D. 1044) is between them. Immediately below this scene appear their two sons and daughter: Lord 12 Movement "Bloody Jaguar," the eldest, born in the year 7 House; then the second son 3 Water "Heron," and the daughter 6 Lizard "Jade Ornament." Although these offspring have no umbilical cords to mark their births, we read them as children of the marriage pair because they immediately follow the marriage statement. The Zouche-Nuttall painter does not tell us where the wife 9 Eagle originated, nor does he or she give year dates for the second and third offspring because these data are not important to the story line in this codex. All the individuals have their personal names either attached to them, or as part of their costume, or held in the hands, or painted nearby.

Seventeen years after this first marriage, 5 Crocodile marries again, to Lady 11 Water "Jewel Parrot," who sits alone in the palace at the bottom of the page; the painter has omitted 5 Crocodile (probably for reasons of space), knowing that the reader will correctly interpret this scene as one half of a marriage statement. The date is year 10 House day 6 Deer. Immediately the offspring of this union appear above. Lord 8 Deer "Jaguar Claw," the first son, is born in the year 12 Reed, followed by his younger brother Lord 9 Flower "Copal Ball Arrow" in the year 3 Reed, and Lady 9 Monkey "Smoke Jeweled Quetzal" in the year 13 Flint. We note that Lady 9 Monkey is actually three years older than 9 Flower, having been born the year after her brother

8 Deer. Although the painter has switched their order, he or she was careful to date their births. This ends 5 Crocodile's immediate line.

The story then picks up the marital affairs of the son 8 Deer, who appears in a marriage statement with his first of five wives, 13 Serpent "Flower Serpent," followed by their two sons. The account continues on Zouche-Nuttall 27 with 8 Deer's other wives and their children. Reaching the last of his progeny, the Zouche-Nuttall story returns to 8 Deer's first named son, 4 Dog "Tame Coyote," to follow his line.

This page of the Zouche-Nuttall gives a tight genealogical picture. The story does not stray much from the bare facts of descent, and it keeps its focus on the principal line. Although 8 Deer wears, in his first marriage statement, the distinctive turquoise nose ornament he worked so hard to achieve (discussed below), the painter ignores 8 Deer's exploits in obtaining this symbol of being a lineage head. There is no indication of where the wives originated, nor is there any sense of what happened to the noninheriting offspring. Only the marital and procreative life of the inheriting son is given.

The genealogy adheres to several standard rules. Marriage statements are less depictions of weddings than they are records of marital alliances and are always followed by the offspring. This means that marriage statements usually come late in an individual's biography, for, once all the offspring are mentioned, the story usually continues with them and leaves the parents behind. The genealogy presents the multiple wives and children as a linked sequence and then returns to the inheriting child (the first son unless he did not live) to continue with his or her story. This means that the narrative moves forward in time through all the offspring and then must jump back to pick up the inheritor again. The Bodley and such other dynastic histories as the Selden and Vienna Reverse share these features.

The Family of Lord 5 Crocodile in the Bodley

The Bodley, however, lards its genealogical story with more details than do the other Mixtec histories. It takes care to specify the origins and marital history of the spouses and to indicate what happened to many of the auxiliary offspring. And it breaks its genealogy often to depict the actions of the rulers. This extra detail allows the interpreter to understand the causes and consequences of events, including marriage patterns, better.

The Bodley Obverse reads in a horizontal boustrophedon along five registers that span two pages each, so that one follows a register all the way across two pages before turning back on another register (see Fig. 31).[22] Lord 5 Crocodile's story occupies the right corner of the top register of page 6 and all of pages 7 and 8, but we will concentrate only on the genealogical information in order to compare it with the Zouche-Nuttall.

After presenting Lord 5 Crocodile's exploits (in the first two and one-half registers of 7–8), the Bodley tells of his wives and children (beginning in the third register of page 7; Fig. 59). His genealogical story opens with the date, year 5 Reed day 7 Eagle, when he marries Lady 11 Water "Jewel Parrot"; they sit facing each other on a single woven mat. Behind her, the painter explains her marital history, tied to her by footprints. In a complex and ambiguous scene, the Bodley explains that 11 Water was previously married to Lord 3 Wind "Bat" of Stone Mouth. Two other individuals are linked to this event: Lord 8 Flower "Shining Flint," who is seated behind 11 Water and faces away from her marriage to 3 Wind but is drawn to them by footprints, and Lady 10 House "Stone Quechquemitl," whose name appears above Stone Mouth's place sign. Caso (1960b: 36; 1979: 44, 227, 445) has interpreted Lady 10 House as 3 Wind's first wife, and Lord 8 Flower as the offspring either of that union or of 3 Wind's marriage to 11 Water.

Next 5 Crocodile and 11 Water's first son, 12 Movement "Bloody Jaguar," is born; an umbilical cord from the year 7 House confirms his birth that year (almost all the birth scenes in the Bodley employ umbilical cords). Attached to him is an arrow decorated with a warband, which I believe to be his title (12 Movement was 8 Deer's most trusted companion in arms). He apparently never marries, for none of the Mixtec codices, including the Bodley, shows his marriage. Two years later the daughter 6 Lizard "Jade Ornament" is born (she is linked by her cord to the year 9 Reed); her birth scene conflates with her marriage statement, for she sits on a mat facing her husband Lord 11 Wind "Bloody Jaguar" of Red and White Bundle. A third child, Lord 9 Movement "Bird of Red and White Beak," and then a fourth child, Lord 3 Water, follow connected to the

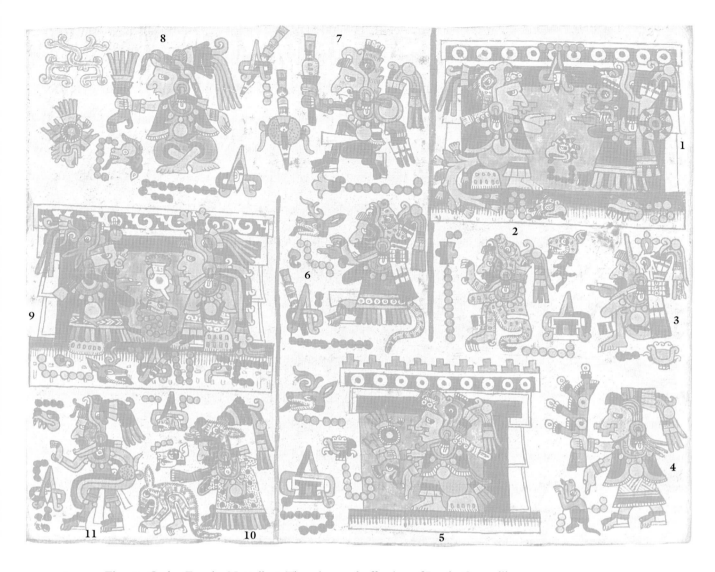

Fig. 58. Codex Zouche-Nuttall 26. The wives and offspring of Lord 5 Crocodile:

1 Lord 5 Crocodile marries Lady 9 Eagle (y6 Flint d7 Eagle).

2 First son, 12 Movement, born (y7 House).

3 Second son, 3 Water, born.

4 Third child, daughter 6 Lizard, born.

5 Lord 5 Crocodile marries second wife, Lady 11 Water (y10 House d6 Deer).

6 Their first son, 8 Deer, born (y12 Reed).

7 Second son, 9 Flower, born (y3 Reed).

8 Daughter 9 Monkey born (y13 Flint).

9 Lord 8 Deer (first son of second wife) marries 13 Serpent (y13 Reed d12 Serpent).

10 Their first son, 4 Dog, born (y7 Rabbit).

11 Their second son, 4 Serpent, born (y9 Flint).

Photograph courtesy of the British Museum.

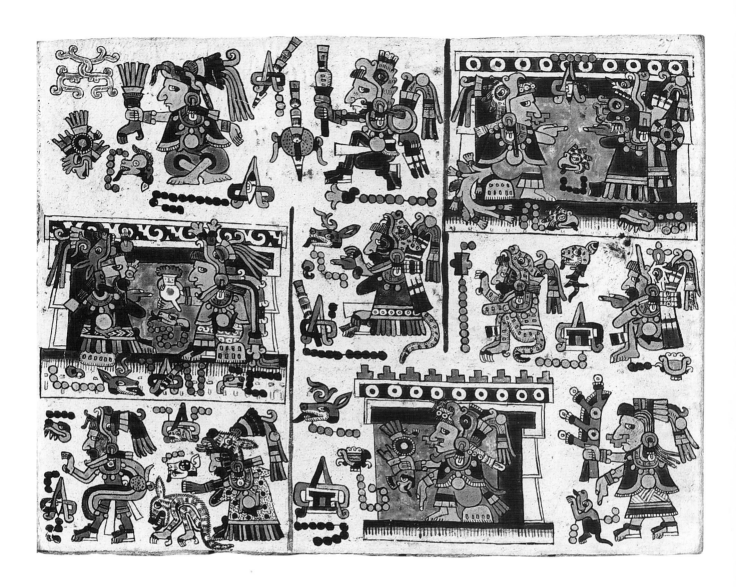

year dates of their birth. They never marry, for the Bodley does not indicate their wives. The next scene explains why. At the Enclosure of the Quetzal, 9 Movement and 3 Water are sacrificed; the date that introduces this scene fixes the event to year 9 (10) Rabbit day 8 Death.[23]

Immediately the reader notices how much the Bodley presentation differs from that in the Zouche-Nuttall. The Bodley puts 5 Crocodile's second wife (11 Water) first, making her the mother of his first group of children,[24] and it adds many more narrative elements to the story. The Bodley informs us about 11 Water's previous union and about her son or stepson 8 Flower, who will figure in the action episodes with 5 Crocodile's sons 8 Deer, 12 Movement, and

9 Flower.[25] The Bodley also follows daughter 6 Wind to her marriage with 11 Wind; this marriage will become important for the story because 6 Wind's husband later married Lady 6 Monkey of Jaltepec (Añute), 8 Deer's rival. The Bodley additionally includes an extra son, 9 Movement, not mentioned in the other codices, and shows how 5 Crocodile's two sons were sacrificed.

A new date, year 10 House day 6 Deer, introduces 5 Crocodile's second marriage, to Lady 9 Eagle "Garland of Cacao Flowers." Behind her, footprints that lead from her parents' names show her to be the daughter of Lord 8 Rain "War Eagle" and Lady 11 Flint "Gray Feathered Ornament," who appear only as calendrical and personal names; their town, Stone Mouth

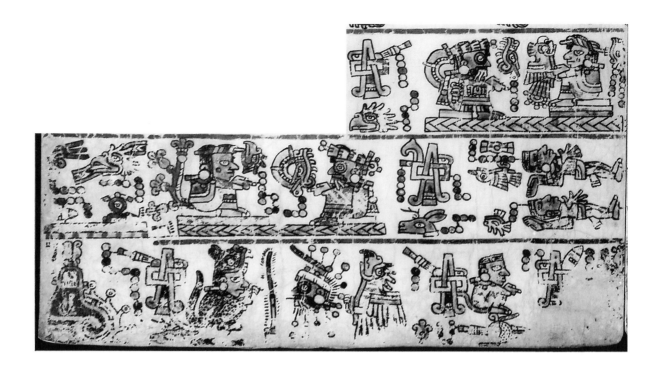

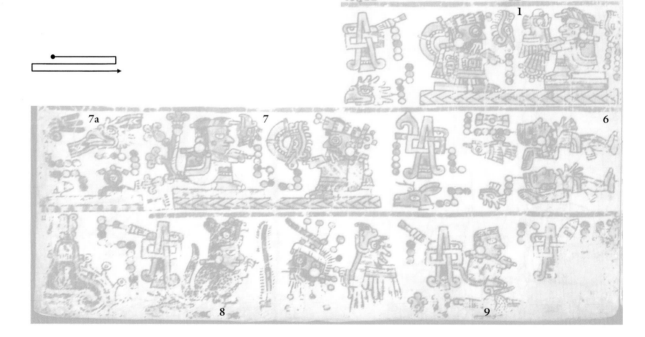

Fig. 59. Codex Bodley 7cde–8cde. The wives and offspring of Lord 5 Crocodile (from Caso 1960b):

1 (y5 Reed d7 Eagle) Lord 5 Crocodile marries Lady 11 Water.

1a Previous marriage of Lady 11 Water to Lord 3 Wind of Stone Mouth.

1a1 3 Wind's previous wife was 10 House.

1a2 Lord 8 Flower was offspring of Lord 3 Wind and either Lady 11 Water or Lady 10 House.

2 First son, 12 Movement, born (y7 House).

3 Daughter 6 Lizard born (y9 Reed); she marries 11 Wind of Red and White Bundle.

4 Second son, 9 Movement, born (y10 Flint).

5 Third son, 3 Water, born (y9 House).

6 (y9 Rabbit d8 Death) Sons 9 Movement and 3 Water sacrificed at Enclosure of Quetzal.

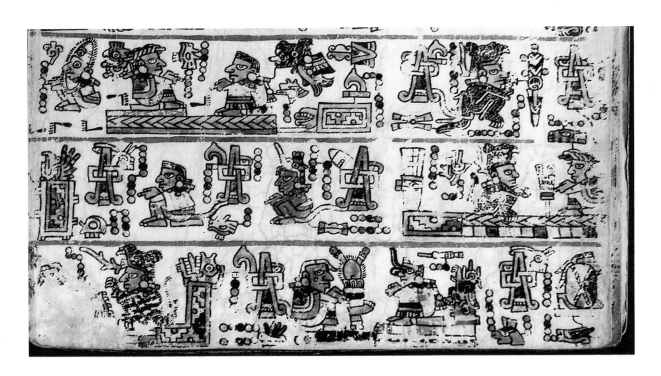

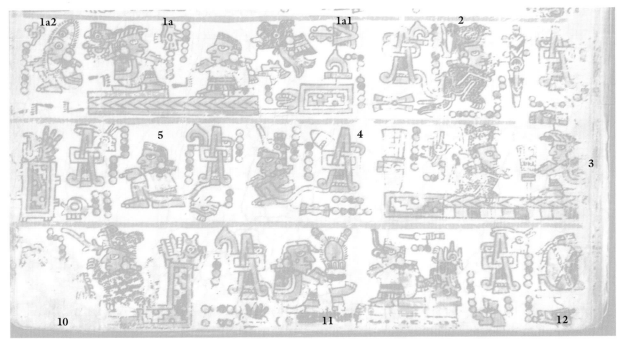

7 (y10 House d6 Deer) 5 Crocodile marries Lady 9 Eagle.

7a She is child of Lord 8 Rain and Lady 11 Flint of Stone Mouth Hill Water.

8 First son, 8 Deer, born (y12 Reed), his titles follow.

9 Second son, 9 Flower, born (y3 Reed).

10 First daughter [9 Monkey] born (y[12] Flint); she marries 8 Crocodile of Skull Frieze.

11 Second daughter, 12 Grass, born (y4 House); she marries 3 Reed of Hill of the Wasp.

12 (y5 Rabbit d9 Dog) Death of Lord 5 Crocodile.

The Bodleian Library, Oxford, MS. Mex. D. 1. Facsimile reproduction courtesy of Sociedad Mexicana de Antropología, Mexico City.

Hill Water is just below in the bottom register. The first child of this union is Lord 8 Deer "Jaguar Claw," tied by his umbilical cord to his birth year, 12 Reed (A.D. 1063). The images that follow—a shining feather, a rain god head surrounded by 18 disks, and an eagle—are his titles.[26] Next the second child, Lord 9 Flower "Copal Ball Arrow," is born, followed by the third child, Lady 9 Monkey "Smoke Jeweled Quetzal" (who is barely visible in the fold between the images); her birth scene is conflated with her marriage scene, for she is pictured married to Lord 8 Crocodile "Bloody Coyote" of Chalcatongo (the skull frieze). The fourth child, Lady 12 Grass "Hand Gold Arrows" is then born; she marries 3 Reed "Smoke Face" of Insect or Hill of the Wasp.

Having described the births and lives of Lord 5 Crocodile's children, the Bodley next represents 5 Crocodile's death. Following the date year 5 Rabbit day 9 Dog, Lord 5 Crocodile is wrapped as a funerary bundle. This is one of the relatively few deaths recorded in the Mixtec dynastic histories, which usually ignore deaths unless the individuals were sacrificed or otherwise killed.[27]

On the next page (9e), the narrative continues with his heir, Lord 8 Deer. The Bodley devotes all of pages 9 and 10 to 8 Deer's exploits (discussed below) and then turns to his marital unions and offspring, which occupy all of pages 11 and 12 as well as the bottom register of pages 13 and 14. The Bodley presents 8 Deer's five wives and many children in the same detail as it did with 5 Crocodile's family, after which it explains the circumstances of 8 Deer's violent death. The story then continues with 8 Deer's firstborn son, 6 House "Jaguar Descending from the Sky," the product of his second marriage.

The Bodley painter clearly does not like to leave loose ends hanging. In the Bodley, all the wives come with their histories, including the identities of their parents and towns, any previous marriages, and any offspring. The marital future of all the rulers' children is recorded. The Bodley is so consistent in showing the marriages of all the rulers' offspring, not just the heir, that the absence of a marriage statement can be taken as a statement that the individual did not marry. In contrast, the Zouche-Nuttall introduces wives without a past or a hometown specified, and it leaves the future of most resulting children untold.

The Bodley adds other extra information: it includes children not mentioned in the other manuscripts, and it reports when and how they were killed (as were 5 Crocodile's sons 9 Movement and 3 Water); it also records the death of 5 Crocodile. Additionally, it assigns titles to the notable half-brothers 12 Movement and 8 Deer, who will figure so prominently in the action episodes that follow.

The Bodley switches 5 Crocodile's first and second wives but does not switch the children accordingly. It presents 11 Water as the mother of 12 Movement, and 9 Eagle as the mother of 8 Deer, when the Zouche-Nuttall (26, 42) and Vienna Reverse (6–7c) agree on the opposite. This may have been a simple error, but other differences between the Zouche-Nuttall and Bodley are attributable to the different story lines the manuscripts are following. After telling 5 Crocodile's and 8 Deer's stories, the Bodley follows the line of 8 Deer's firstborn son, 6 House, the child of 8 Deer's second wife and the son who inherited the throne of Tilantongo. In contrast, the Zouche-Nuttall follows the line of 8 Deer's son by his first wife, Lord 4 Dog, who was to rule Teozacoalco. The Bodley traces the Tilantongo line, whereas the Zouche-Nuttall here traces the line for Teozacoalco.

Each manuscript shows its own biases about its subject matter and the story it intends to tell, and each has its own stylistic features. The Bodley has a tight presentational style and keeps to strict rules. Its low horizontal registers mean that the pictorial information must appear in an unfailing sequence, one feature after another, without pictorial elaboration. Dates generally introduce the events they date. The Zouche-Nuttall, in contrast, has a looser presentational style. The wider, vertical registers allow the painter to achieve a more fluid presentation; within a wide register, there may still be a horizontal back-and-forth boustrophedon reading order to the material, but it is not so clearly indicated as in the Bodley. The Zouche-Nuttall has more space in which the figures function, which allows the painter to set the scene architecturally or geographically. None of the Bodley marriage scenes are located within palaces and qualified by the presentation of chocolate cups. Together the manuscripts illustrate the range of styles for presenting full genealogies. Such major Mixtec screenfolds as the Selden and Vienna Reverse fall within this range.

Ruler Lists

Ruler lists can be considered a subset of genealogies. Where the full genealogy presents all or most of the rulers' offspring as part of the narrative sequence and might include other information to flesh out the genealogical picture, the ruler list omits all these distractions or places them to the side so that the narrative can concentrate on the inheriting child. This yields a sequence of ruling couples, an unbroken sequence that carries with it the understanding that the husband of any succeeding couple is the rightful heir of the preceding couple. The wives usually come from elsewhere, and occasionally their hometown and parentage are given. In the Mixtec screenfolds, these lists take the form of a horizontal row running either left to right or right to left. When ruler lists are painted on lienzos and vertical tiras, as discussed in Chapter 6, they usually appear as a vertical column (usually running bottom to top).

The Becker II, Egerton (or Sánchez Solís), and Muro all have the sequence of couples arranged horizontally.[28] The Muro traces a single sequence from right to left, whereas the Becker II and Egerton read left to right, their stories beginning with one or more mythological origin scenes and continuing with the succession of ruling couples presented in two parallel registers. For example, the Becker II (including the Hamburg Fragment that belongs at the front of it) begins with two ancient ancestors emerging from place signs.[29] It proceeds in two registers with two parallel genealogies and then continues, after the break between the Hamburg Fragment and the Becker II proper, with only one ruling line (in the lower register; Fig. 60). Its line of rulers is presentationally unbroken, because the painter has moved the secondary information to the side and has left it uncolored. The Becker II notes the origin of the wives by drawing their hometowns above or behind them, linked to them by lines and footprints. Ascending footprints inform us about the marital fates of some of the daughters, whose own marriage statements are relegated to the top register. Thus, in Figure 60, we note that Lord 4 Movement "Flaming Sky" married Lady 13 Death "Sun Quetzal Feathers," who came from Warband Hill. Their inheriting son, 3 Death "Jaguar Descending from the Sky," then married another woman named 8 (?) Eagle "Sun Quetzal Feathers," who came from Net-Mouth. In addition to their inheriting son, this couple had a daughter, 12 Dog, who married Lord 2 House of Platform of Tail (?). By placing the extra information (the information not directly germane to the inheriting line) to the side, the painter has kept the line of rule intact.[30]

These horizontal ruler lists in the Becker II, Egerton, and Muro seem to represent a variation from the more typical, and more detailed, presentation of genealogies found in manuscripts like the Bodley and Zouche-Nuttall. Other variations of the horizontal ruler list (e.g., in the Codex Baranda and Lienzo of Tequixtepec) are discussed more fully in Chapter 6, as are the vertical ruler lists included in at least a dozen lienzos and tiras that come from Oaxaca and Puebla.

Dynastic Conflict: The Stories of Lady 6 Monkey and Lord 8 Deer

The flow of genealogical information in many of the Mixtec histories is augmented and interrupted by episodes in the lives of the rulers and their families. These episodes are not merely embellishments on the genealogies; rather, they were included in the histories to explain adjustments in the lines of rule or expansions and contractions in the territories ruled. They are the product of disputes between and among families, and, as such, they include rituals, diplomatic parlays, conquests, and other elements of dynastic intrigue. When, for example, the line of rule of a polity was in danger of failing, the pictorial histories include in their narratives the actions taken by those who effected the shift to a new line. Conflicts about dynastic succession usually arose when the primogeniture inheritance pattern yielded no clear heir. The pictorials show these disputes and their resolution, sometimes briefly and at other times in great detail.

Codices such as the Vienna Reverse hardly mention the fact of a dispute and its resolution. The Vienna Reverse painter gives just enough information to recall the situation and its outcome to the manuscript's interpreters. Other codices, such as the Colombino-Becker and the Zouche-Nuttall Reverse, however, explain the many details in a lengthy presentation, so their stories become more like biographies of individual rulers than dynastic histories.

One principal story, told in part by most of the major screenfolds, concerns the conflict between the families of Tilantongo, Jaltepec, and Red and White Bundle, a conflict that resolved itself by rearranging the earlier alliances and shifting the lines of rule. The story features Lady 6 Monkey "Serpent Quechquemitl" of Jaltepec and her husband 11 Wind "Bloody Jaguar" of Red and White Bundle, whom I have already discussed in Chapter 4 as the rulers of Jaltepec. Its leading protagonist is 8 Deer "Jaguar Claw," the son of the high priest of Tilantongo (5 Crocodile "Raingod Sun"), who was not ordinarily in line for the throne but nevertheless achieved the rule of Tilantongo after the last heir of the first dynasty died suddenly. Lord 8 Deer was aided in his ventures by his brother and especially by his half-brother 12 Movement "Bloody Jaguar," who was to be his companion in arms throughout the latter's life. The ambitious 8 Deer built his domain by conquering lands, vanquishing his foes and rivals, and marrying their wives, sisters, or daughters, their genealogical lines thus continuing through his. Lord 8 Deer eventually met a violent end, killed, so the Colombino (16b) suggests, by or on the orders of 6 Monkey's son 4 Wind "Fire Serpent." Lord 4 Wind then married two of 8 Deer's daughters in order that the conqueror's blood would run through his own children, repeating the pattern 8 Deer had followed. This 8 Deer story takes on the importance it does because the authority of the later rulers of these major polities rested on these events.

Fig. 60. Codex Becker II 1–2. Detail of the ruler list. Descending footprints tell where the wives originated; ascending footprints tell the fate of the daughters (from Nowotny 1964). Reproduced courtesy of Akademische Druck- u. Verlagsanstalt, Graz.

Since no one manuscript tells the whole of the story, I will base my discussion on the sparse but straight-forward version painted on two pages in the Bodley Obverse, amplified by passages from the Selden, Zouche-Nuttall Reverse, Colombino-Becker, and Bodley Reverse. I choose the Bodley over the Colombino-Becker and Zouche-Nuttall Reverse as the base document because the latter two include more detail than is possible to explain in a book of this kind. Additionally, the Zouche-Nuttall, which has already been repro-duced in an inexpensive and readily available facsimile (1975), is a garbled text (Troike n.d.). The Colombino-Becker is a problematic manuscript to use as a base for discussion because it is incomplete and has a compli-cated order and because sometime after it was painted someone scratched out almost all the animal figures, including those that comprise day signs, helmets, and place signs; these losses have made it difficult to iden-tify all the characters and places.[31] I am also motivated by the desire to make the Bodley more easily accessible by publishing two more of its pages.

Preparation for Rule:
Lord 8 Deer's Early Years

The 8 Deer story is set within the larger context of the failure of Tilantongo's first dynasty. Lord 8 Deer of Tilantongo, Lady 6 Monkey of Jaltepec, and her brothers were perhaps all vying with the presumed heir (2 Rain "Ocoñaña" or "20 Jaguar") for the Tilantongo throne.[32] The Codex Selden records a series of strikes against 6 Monkey's family at Jaltepec (discussed in Chapter 4, Figs. 37, 38, 39). First her three older broth-ers were killed and sacrificed (5d–6a); then her father 10 Eagle was attacked by 3 Lizard, who may have been sent by 2 Rain (2 Rain appears in the adjacent scene on 6b); finally 6 Monkey was forced into hiding (6c). Al-though the Selden is not explicit on this point, the at-tacks may have come from 2 Rain and his father in order to preempt any claims 6 Monkey and her broth-ers might advance. Although the Tilantongo and Jalte-pec lines habitually intermarried, 6 Monkey then broke with this tradition and became betrothed to 11 Wind of Red and White Bundle (6d).

Meanwhile, 8 Deer was growing up in Tilantongo. He was not himself in line for rule, because his father,

5 Crocodile, was a priest rather than a ruler.[33] The Zouche-Nuttall Reverse (42–43) begins its account with 8 Deer's family tree (Fig. 58) and several conquests in which the young 8 Deer participated, perhaps assist-ing his half-brother 12 Movement, who was eighteen years his senior. The Bodley does not include these conquests but begins its 8 Deer story with two regis-ters of rituals and other conquests that prepare 8 Deer for the great accomplishments that follow.

Having previously shown 8 Deer's genealogical ties on pages 7 and 8, the Bodley (9e) opens its account of his deeds in the year 3 Flint day 4 Rain (A.D. 1080), when 8 Deer was seventeen (Fig. 61, lower left).[34] It shows Lord 8 Deer emerging from a cave and going di-rectly to another cave, this one characterized by smoke and stars and with a container of jades inside it. Caso (1960b: 38) identified it as the Cave of Smoke and Heaven "where the jade of the god known as 3 Reed was to be found"; the date 3 Reed is painted beside the cave. Footprints then carry 8 Deer to visit the rul-ing couple of Black Top Mountain with Face; they are Lady 4 Rabbit "Quetzal Jewel" (who is the great aunt of the Tilantongo heir and the paternal aunt of Lady 6 Monkey) and her husband, Lord 10 Flower "Bow with Tail." Although we do not know the exact reason for this visit, 8 Deer goes inside the earth at this site and appears sitting before a temple with a cult bundle; a cradle above him seems to hold something like a ser-pent head.[35] Given 8 Deer's dynastic ambitions that follow, I suggest that he is here visiting and perform-ing a ritual at the polity's ancestral temple, probably lo-cated in a cave. The next day (5 Flower), 8 Deer visits the place Caso (1960b: 38) has called Bound Bundles, where he sits before another cult bundle at a temple with stars, to which is attached the calendrical name of the sun god 1 Death. Here he may be paying homage to ancestors again or consulting the oracle 1 Death.[36]

The next year (year 4 House day 6 Serpent) 8 Deer visits the place Mountain with Face and River, pictured in the lower right corner of Figure 61. There he plays the ball game with the Venus deity 1 Movement (pic-tured in register d), whom he apparently convinces to help him attack the River of Precious Stone. That at-tack occurs on the same day (6 Serpent).[37] Another date two years later (year 6 Reed day 13 Flower) introduces two more victories, when 8 Deer conquers Hill of Fe-line/Heaven and Temple of Knot (9–10d). These early

9a

9b

9c

9d

9e

Fig. 61. Codex Bodley 9–10. (See page 112 for key to fig 61.)

achievements—the visits, rituals, ball games, and conquests—establish 8 Deer as a significant political force.
Although we do not understand fully their importance, the episodes are also recorded in the Colombino
(1–2) but not in the Zouche-Nuttall. The following
year, in 5 Rabbit, 8 Deer's father 5 Crocodile dies (his
death is pictured earlier on Bodley 8e [Fig. 59]).

The Meeting with Lady 9 Grass

His father's death may have triggered a meeting that is
pictured in all the 8 Deer accounts (Bodley 9d, Colombino 3abc–4abc, Zouche-Nuttall 46, Selden 6d–7a),
although each source stresses some aspects of the meeting over others. In the year 6 Reed day 6 Serpent, Lord
8 Deer, Lady 6 Monkey of Jaltepec, and Lord 11 Wind
of Red and White Bundle gather at Skull Place before
the supernatural Lady 9 Grass. The Bodley notes only
8 Deer's presence, showing him offering a heart to
9 Grass. In contrast, the Selden omits 8 Deer and in-

10a

10b

10c

10d

10e

stead characterizes the meeting as the moment when Lady 9 Grass blesses the engagement of 6 Monkey to 11 Wind (Figs. 37, 38). The Zouche-Nuttall and Colombino include 8 Deer and 6 Monkey (but not 11 Wind) and add others. In the Zouche-Nuttall (Fig. 62), Lady 9 Grass sits in her Skull temple gesturing before the deceased body of Lord 3 Lizard "Flint Necklace," a distant relative of 8 Deer and 6 Monkey, who is costumed as a *yahui* priest.[38] Present are 6 Monkey (who is called by her second name, "Warband Quechquemitl") and 8 Deer, now twenty-one and dressed as an eagle priest. Lord 3 Lizard's funeral may have occasioned the actual

meeting. The Colombino (3–4a) presentation makes it clear that 8 Deer received objects of rulership from 9 Grass at this time, for 8 Deer will later carry these objects to Tututepec.[39] The meeting thus granted 8 Deer authority to rule, at the same time that it joined the houses of Jaltepec and Red and White Bundle (by betrothing 6 Monkey and 11 Wind).

8 Deer's Rule of Tututepec

This same year (6 Reed) the Bodley shows 8 Deer conquering the place River of the Mouth and Flames and

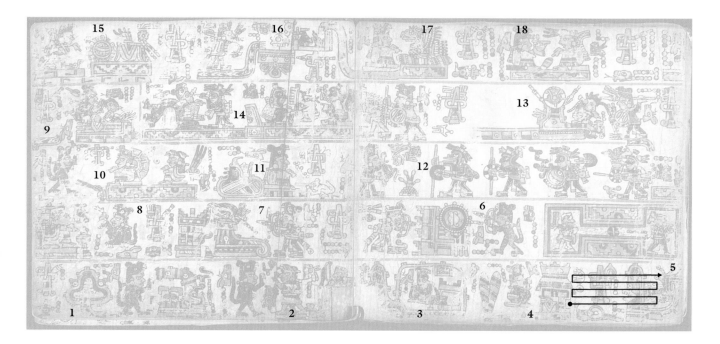

Fig. 61. Codex Bodley 9–10. The deeds of Lord 8 Deer (from Caso 1960b):

1 (y3 Flint d4 Rain) Lord 8 Deer emerges from a cave and goes to Cave of Smoke and Heaven/3 Reed.

2 8 Deer visits Lady 4 Rabbit and Lord 10 Flower of Black Top Mountain with Face.

3 8 Deer is inside earth performing ritual in a cave.

4 8 Deer visits Bound Bundles and sits before celestial temple of Lord 1 Death.

5 (y4 House d6 Serpent) At Mountain with Face and River, 8 Deer plays ball game with 1 Movement (Venus deity).

6 (Same day 6 Serpent) 8 Deer and 1 Movement attack River of Precious Stone.

7 (y6 Reed d13 Flower) 8 Deer conquers Hill of Feline/Heaven and Temple of Knot.

8 (y6 Reed d6 Serpent) 8 Deer makes offering to Lady 9 Grass at Skull Place.

9 (y6 Reed) 8 Deer conquers River of Mouth and Flames.

10 8 Deer visits Lord 1 Death and Lady 11 Serpent of Apoala; they grant him rule of Tututepec.

11 8 Deer seated as ruler of Tututepec.

12 (y[6]Flint, d8 Jaguar) Animal brings word, 8 Deer offers quail in sacrifice, and four travelers, including 4 Jaguar, arrive from Place of Reeds.

13 (y [6 Flint]) 8 Deer conquers Hill of the Moon and takes ruler 3 Lizard captive.

14 (y7 House d1 Wind) 8 Deer brings 3 Lizard to Place of Reeds and presents him to 4 Jaguar for sacrifice, then 8 Deer gets his nose pierced (becomes a *tecuhtli*).

15 8 Deer establishes his rule at Tilantongo.

16 (y8 Rabbit d4 Wind) 8 Deer journeys on warpath to celestial home of the sun god 1 Death (y9 Reed d4 Crocodile); 8 Deer goes into a cradle (?).

17 8 Deer emerges and appears at Bound Bundles.

18 (y12 Rabbit, d7 Flower) 8 Deer makes offering to Lord 13 Rabbit of Bound Bundles.

The Bodleian Library, Oxford, MS. Mex. D. 1. Facsimile reproduction courtesy of Sociedad Mexicana de Antropología, Mexico City.

8 Deer

6 Monkey

3 Lizard dead

9 Grass
at Skull Pace

Fig. 62. Codex Zouche-Nuttall 44abc. The meeting between Lady 9 Grass (*lower right*), Lady 6 Monkey, and Lord 8 Deer at Skull Place (from Anders, Jansen, and Pérez Jiménez 1992b). © 1991, Akademische Druck- u. Verlagsanstalt and Fondo de Cultura Económica.

capturing its ruler 10 Serpent (9b): footprints carry 8 Deer directly from his meeting with 9 Grass in register d to this conquest in register b. Then the Bodley artist drops back to register c to tells us that 8 Deer then paid a visit to the rulers of Apoala, Lord 1 Death "Serpent Sun" and Lady 11 Serpent "Flower Quetzals," who apparently granted him rule of the coastal domain of Tututepec (Bird Hill, represented here by the bird-helmeted head on the stone). This rule, the first of 8 Deer's great achievements, is the culmination of all his earlier preparations: the rituals, visits, conferences, and conquests. Despite his birth (the son of a priest and not a ruler), 8 Deer became a ruler by conquering territories and by gaining the good wishes and assistance of several key Mixtec rulers and such supernaturals as Lord 1 Death and Lady 9 Grass. Although the Bodley does not date this rule, the Colombino notes that 8 Deer established himself in Tututepec in 7 Flint (A.D. 1084), when he was twenty-one years old.[40]

In the next dozen years, while 8 Deer rules and apparently resides in Tututepec, the Selden (7bcd–8abc)

records how Lady 6 Monkey of Jaltepec conquers the rulers of Hill of the Moon and Hill of Bee, who had threatened her and her ambassadors (see Chapter 4, Figs. 38, 39). She marries 11 Wind and soon has the sons 4 Wind and 1 Crocodile (8cd).

8 Deer's Drive to Rule Tilantongo

Then in the year 6 Flint, Lord 2 Rain "Ocoñaña or 20 Jaguar" dies mysteriously. The Bodley (5a–6a) records that this last heir to the throne of Tilantongo committed suicide. From his position at Tututepec, 8 Deer springs into action. Because he has no clear right to the Tilantongo throne according to Mixtec rules of succession, 8 Deer seeks an alternative (a Central Mexican) route to the throne; he has performed on him a ceremony that makes him a lineage head or *tecuhtli* (in Nahuatl) and has his nose pierced as a symbol of this new stature.[41] The Bodley, Colombino (9c–14), and Zouche-Nuttall (50b–53a) all include this episode, which was crucial for 8 Deer's success.

The Bodley (9c) pictures 8 Deer seated as ruler of Tututepec (Fig. 61). The year date 6 Flint (and perhaps the day 8 Jaguar) opens the new episode, when footprints from the right carry a little red striped animal to 8 Deer, the animal seeming to announce something.[42] Lord 8 Deer next rises and decapitates a quail in sacrifice; the head of the quail is carried off by a descending eagle, perhaps the eagle sacrificer. Four strangers approach 8 Deer at Tututepec (10c). All are painted black, have black paint around the eyes and nose, have their hair pulled up in Central Mexican warriors' topknots, and carry the staffs and U-shaped feather fans of merchants. They are differentially accoutered with what are probably personal names (wind god, serpent, smoking shield, and smoking foot, respectively), and the fourth additionally carries in his right hand a frothy bowl with a bird on top (an offering?). The four come from a Place of Cattails or Place of Reeds (Tollan in Nahuatl), on the far right, being representatives of the supernatural or priest Lord 4 Jaguar, whose name sign has speech scrolls rolling from the mouth.[43]

These visitors from the Place of Reeds may be offering 8 Deer the *tecuhtli* ceremony in return for his conquest of Hill of the Moon (Santa María Acatepec in the Mixteca Costa), for this same year a chevron warpath carries 8 Deer to that town (10b). Lord 8 Deer conquers the place and captures its now-humiliated ruler, 3 Crocodile "Curly Hair."[44] The following year, in 7 House on the day 1 Wind, 8 Deer marches the captive 3 Crocodile to the Place of Reeds that is 4 Jaguar's domain. Lord 8 Deer now sports a warband on his shield, while 3 Crocodile has the black stripe painted across his eyes and carries the banner signaling that he is destined to be sacrificed. Footprints direct the pair to the broad platform, identified as Place of Reeds by the small cattail reed plant. There a seated local (identified by his characteristic face paint and topknot) presents the crouching prisoner to 4 Jaguar, who is enthroned opposite. Speech scrolls curling from the presenter's mouth are qualified by the image of a stone, but not the sharp flints that threatened 6 Monkey (see Chapter 3). Apparently the prisoner was a condition for the subsequent ceremony.

The nose piercing occurs on a platform attached to the Place of Reeds (9b). There 8 Deer leans back against a jaguar pelt that itself is draped over a wide upright, the pelt and upright forming an impressive jaguar chair.

One of 4 Jaguar's assistants then pierces 8 Deer's nose with a bone awl and inserts a jeweled nose ornament of the kind worn by Central Mexican rulers.[45] The Bodley artist pictures both the moment before 8 Deer's nose is pierced and the moment after the nose ornament is inserted. The Colombino and Zouche-Nuttall artists chose the dramatic moment of piercing (Figs. 63, 64).

The events leading up to and including 8 Deer's nose piercing are recounted in greater detail in both the Colombino and Zouche-Nuttall. In these accounts, 8 Deer and his companions perform more and varied ceremonies, consult and make offerings to supernaturals, and journey far to reach the Place of Reeds; they also carry with them the red quincunx staff and cult bundle that are 8 Deer's symbols of rule (Figs. 63, 64).[46] All the manuscripts devote much space to this critical event, which they agree occurred on the day 1 Wind in the year 7 House (A.D. 1097).

In the Bodley (Fig. 61), a band of footprints carries 8 Deer from his nose piercing in the second register up to the far left of the first register, where the footprints double back to show him approaching the black stepfret frieze of Tilantongo. He carries the quincunx staff of rule and has smoke curling from his front foot. At Tilantongo, he establishes his authority by placing his symbols of rule on the place sign: a spear embellished with a *ñuhu* face, a shield, the cult bundle, and the quincunx staff. The cognate scene in the Zouche-Nuttall (Fig. 65) also records that 8 Deer took control of Tilantongo by placing his spear and staff there.[47] The Zouche-Nuttall and Colombino explain how 8 Deer then confirms his rule of Tilantongo by meeting with the lords who are his subjects and colleagues. The Zouche-Nuttall devotes fifteen pages (54–68) to this extraordinary meeting, where 8 Deer and 12 Movement face and receive 112 lords.[48] By these actions 8 Deer has successfully gained control of his hometown Tilantongo, following the failure of the first dynastic line. Because he was not the logical successor to the throne, he was compelled to go outside the Mixtec political system and acquire the Central Mexican title *tecuhtli* (or lineage head), symbolized by the nose ornament he would later wear so proudly. Still, 8 Deer obtained the assistance of Mixtec supernaturals in this quest, and he was careful to have his accession to the Tilantongo throne confirmed by his royal colleagues and subjects.

Fig. 63. Codex Colombino 13a. The Colombino-Becker version of Lord 8 Deer's nose piercing locates the ceremony in a coastal place of Cattail Frieze (Tulixtlahuaca of Jicayán). Lord 8 Deer arrives in the lower right and in the upper right makes an offering with 4 Jaguar. CNCA.-INAH.-MEX; reproduced with permission of the Instituto Nacional de Antropología e Historia.

Fig. 64. The Zouche-Nuttall (52bcd–53a) version of Lord 8 Deer's nose piercing. Lords 8 Deer and 4 Jaguar make offerings before and after the piercing (*upper right, upper left*). Lord 9 Flower (8 Deer's brother) carries the conqueror's staff of rule (*lower right;* from Anders, Jansen, and Pérez Jiménez 1992b). © 1991, Akademische Druck- u. Verlagsanstalt and Fondo de Cultura Económica.

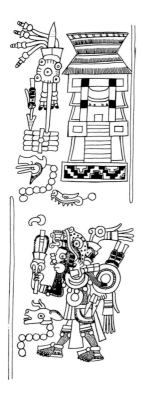

Fig. 65. Codex Zouche-Nuttall 53d. Lord 8 Deer places his quincunx staff at Tilantongo, symbolizing his authority there (from Anders, Jansen, and Pérez Jiménez 1992b). © 1991, Akademische Druck- u. Verlagsanstalt and Fondo de Cultura Económica.

The Journey to the Sun God

Lord 8 Deer's next adventure involves a difficult journey of conquest to the sun god, 1 Death, where he takes part in a ritual or a process (which is still poorly understood) before he returns home. The Zouche-Nuttall and Colombino, as we have come to expect, record fuller versions of this adventure than does the Bodley, but all three codices agree that the adventure began in the year 8 Rabbit, day 4 Wind.[49] On this date, the Bodley (9a) shows 8 Deer traveling on a warpath (and brandishing his weapons) to a celestial place, characterized by small and large star symbols (Fig. 61). It is home of the sun god 1 Death, whose name sign appears there. A figure who is probably 8 Deer is on his back (but with active limbs) in what is probably a cradle. The journey to this celestial place took thirty-nine days, for 8 Deer arrived on the day 4 Crocodile in the new year 9 Reed.[50] A band of footprints then tracks 8 Deer as he emerges from his confinement and goes to a place

characterized by bound bundles and an eagle (10a). If the eagle is here associated with the sun, the place may be the same place 8 Deer visited ritually before his rise to power. That place, pictured in register e of this same Bodley page, has the bound bundles, a celestial temple, and 1 Death's name attached. Back in register a, three years later, in year 12 Rabbit day 7 Flower, 8 Deer sits at Bound Bundles and makes an offering to an otherwise unknown lord named 13 Rabbit "Warband."

The Zouche-Nuttall and Colombino-Becker record a different version of this adventure. The Zouche-Nuttall, which is more complete than the Colombino-Becker, has 8 Deer setting out from Tilantongo with his half-brother 12 Movement and others, who carry his emblems of authority (68b–d). After his brother 9 Flower performs a human sacrifice (69ab), the group travels peacefully past several locations (69bcd) until 8 Deer meets and does battle with 4 Jaguar (70bc). Neither apparently wins, and they later make offerings together (70cd) before launching on a joint journey of conquest (Zouche-Nuttall 71–74, Colombino 18a–19a). The group crosses a great and dangerous body of water (Fig. 66; also Colombino 22–23), followed by more conquests that take them into the vicinity of the sun god. There 8 Deer and companions battle deceased warriors and supernaturals who are the guardians of the sun (some hold banners to signal their sacrificial status), and continue to fight their way to the sun god (Fig. 67, also Becker 1–2). Finally in the supernatural's presence, 8 Deer and 4 Jaguar present offerings of gold and jewels to the sun god (Zouche-Nuttall 78bc). The deity tells them to drill a fire (Zouche-Nuttall 78c, Becker 3b) and then directs them to a celestial platform where they seem to look into an opening (Figs. 68, 69). The two then receive offerings of jewels from the sun god (Zouche-Nuttall 79cd), recross the great body of water (80a), present the offerings in a ball court (80a), and apparently return home.

Regrettably we do not understand the purpose of this extraordinary journey, nor do we know what it did for 8 Deer and 4 Jaguar. The crossing of the great water was apparently a significant accomplishment, because the Zouche-Nuttall dedicates an entire page to it (Fig. 66) and the Colombino fills at least two (22–23).[51] Troike (1974: 276–283) has suggested as a hypothesis that the water crossing carried the companions into a supernatural realm where the sun god

Fig. 66. Codex Zouche-Nuttall 75. Lord 4 Jaguar and 8 Deer (*right, center*) and their companion and guide 9 Water (*left*) cross the great body of water on their journey to the sun god (from Anders, Jansen, and Pérez Jiménez 1992b). © 1991, Akademische Druck- u. Verlagsanstalt and Fondo de Cultura Económica.

Fig. 67. Codex Zouche-Nuttall 77cd–78a. Lords 4 Jaguar, 12 Movement, and 8 Deer approach from the right and battle a coyote warrior (*top left*) and a skeletal warrior (*bottom left*), protectors of the sun god (from Anders, Jansen, and Pérez Jiménez 1992b). © 1991, Akademische Druck- u. Verlagsanstalt and Fondo de Cultura Económica.

resided. She also raises the possibility that the event of looking into the celestial opening could have been, in effect, a looking into the future, as in an oracular prediction. This moment, when 8 Deer and 4 Jaguar seem to peer into the celestial opening, is clearly the climax of the adventure.[52]

The Bodley (Fig. 61) characteristically omits all of 8 Deer's companions and the details of the journey; it suggests that 8 Deer did not simply look into a cavity but actually descended into it, for the Bodley shows a figure, presumably 8 Deer, inside what seems to be a cradle. There 8 Deer holds the same posture he and 4 Jaguar have as they peer into the cavity in the Zouche-Nuttall and Colombino-Becker: legs in a bent-knee pinwheel stance, one hand pointing down and one hand open and up (Figs. 68, 69). The Bodley thus presents a variant of the episode.

The cradle, structure, or piece of furniture that holds 8 Deer in the Bodley (9a) is identical to one seen earlier in the Bodley (10e), where it is located inside the earth at Black Top Mountain with Face. There, we remember that 8 Deer, at the age of seventeen, visited the old relatives Lady 4 Rabbit and Lord 10 Flower and went presumably into their ancestral shrine. In this under-

Fig. 68. Codex Zouche-Nuttall 79abc. The sun god 1 Death (*below*) directs as 8 Deer and 4 Jaguar peer into an opening in a celestial platform (*above;* from Anders, Jansen, and Pérez Jiménez 1992b). © 1991, Akademische Druck- u. Verlagsanstalt and Fondo de Cultura Económica.

Fig. 69. Codex Becker 4. In the Colombino-Becker version of the sun god episode, Lord 1 Death (*seated on left*) directs 8 Deer and 4 Jaguar to peer into an opening in a celestial band, while 12 Movement stands aggressively (*right*). Below are place signs for Place of Reeds, Flints, and Bound Bundles (from Nowotny 1964). Reproduced courtesy of Akademische Druck- u. Verlagsanstalt, Graz.

Fig. 70. Codex Zouche-Nuttall 81a. The murder of 12 Movement in a sweatbath (*below*) and the beginning of his funeral rite (*above;* from Anders, Jansen, and Pérez Jiménez 1992b). © 1991, Akademische Druck- u. Verlagsanstalt and Fondo de Cultura Económica.

ground location, the rectangular object contained what may be a serpent head. After 8 Deer left that place, he visited the celestial temple of the sun god 1 Death at Bound Bundles. Now at the age of thirty-six, when 8 Deer emerges from his cradle in the sky in register a, he again visits Bound Bundles, and he makes an offering to its lord. The Bodley ends its narration of the active life of 8 Deer here, following it with a genealogical reckoning of 8 Deer's many marriages and offspring.

The Murder of Rivals

The Zouche-Nuttall, Colombino-Becker, and Bodley Reverse, however, fill in the rest of his story. Soon after returning from the journey to the sun god, 8 Deer's older half-brother and companion in arms, 12 Movement, is murdered in a sweatbath (Fig. 70, also Becker 5); 12 Movement was fifty-five years old and had never married or ruled.[53] Pohl (1996: 59), building on Caso (1955: 293–295; 1979: 46), sees this event as part of a long-term rivalry between Red and White Bundle (11 Wind's domain) and Tilantongo, and he surmises that Lady 6 Monkey and Lord 11 Wind were to blame for 12 Movement's death. Troike (1978: 556) and Jansen (1982, 1:390), however, have proposed that 8 Deer himself was responsible. Although we may never know who killed 12 Movement, Troike's and Jansen's charge against 8 Deer makes sense in light of the events that follow.

After 12 Movement's funeral rites (Zouche-Nuttall 81–82, Becker 6–7), 8 Deer attacks and conquers Red and White Bundle, the town ruled by 6 Monkey's husband 11 Wind (Fig. 71, also Becker 9c). The Zouche-Nuttall then pictures 8 Deer capturing 6 Monkey's eldest son 4 Wind, taking control of Ball Court Eagle, and sacrificing the two princes of Red and White Bundle, sons of Lord 11 Wind by his first marriage: 10 Dog "Eagle Burning Copal Ball," who dies by gladiatorial sacrifice, and 6 House "Row of Flints," who dies by arrow sacrifice (Fig. 71). The Colombino-

Fig. 71. Codex Zouche-Nuttall 83–84a. After the conquest of Red and White Bundle (*bottom right*), 8 Deer captures 4 Wind (*above right*), takes control of Ball Court Eagle (*bottom center*), and sacrifices 10 Dog (*upper left*) and 6 House (*bottom left;* from Anders, Jansen, and Pérez Jiménez 1992b). © 1991, Akademische Druck- u. Verlagsanstalt and Fondo de Cultura Económica.

Becker (Becker 9c–11) records these same events but adds that Lady 6 Monkey and Lord 11 Wind (the mother and father) were also sacrificed.[54] The Bodley Reverse (33e–34e) places 11 Wind's death before 8 Deer's attack on Red and White Bundle, suggesting that the attack was predicated on the death. All three manuscripts agree that the nine-year-old son 4 Wind was captured but either escaped or was intentionally spared.

We ask why all these members of the Red and White Bundle family were killed while 4 Wind was not. And we ask why 12 Movement was killed after serving 8 Deer so faithfully for so many years. If we interpret 8 Deer's attack on 6 Monkey, 11 Wind, and their family at Red and White Bundle as a retaliation for their murder of 12 Movement (as Pohl suggests), we would expect 8 Deer to have also killed 4 Wind and the other Red and White Bundle son 1 Crocodile. This did not happen. If, however, we suppose (like Troike and Jansen) that 8 Deer was responsible—picturing him as villain rather than hero—these selective killings are logical. The reason, I believe, lies in the genealogical connec-

tions of the individuals and in 8 Deer's desire for undisputed control of Tilantongo: the death of these relatives removes all of the descendants of 5 Crocodile's first marriage, who were 8 Deer's potential competitors to the Tilantongo throne.

Figure 72 shows the genealogy of the descendants of 5 Crocodile as it is presented in the Bodley. We will recall that 5 Crocodile married, as his first wife, 9 Eagle, by whom he had a son (12 Movement), a daughter (6 Lizard), and two other sons (9 Movement and 3 Water) who died early. Lord 12 Movement never married but could have. The daughter 6 Lizard married 11 Wind of Red and White Bundle and by him had two sons (10 Dog and 6 House) and a daughter (13 Serpent). After Lady 6 Lizard died, 8 Deer may have killed her brother 12 Movement and definitely killed her sons 10 Dog and 6 House. Then he took 6 Lizard's daughter, 13 Serpent, as his first wife. Lord 11 Wind and Lady 6 Monkey, the stepparents of 6 Lizard's sons, were probably killed as a by-product of the conquest and also to bring Red and White Bundle under 8 Deer's control. But since 11 Wind and 6 Monkey's natural children (4 Wind and 1 Crocodile) were not descended from 5 Crocodile and were not potential competitors for the Tilantongo throne, they were allowed to live. Eventually they both married two of 8 Deer's daughters (Caso 1979: op. 176).

The Zouche-Nuttall Reverse carries 8 Deer's story up through the sacrifice and funeral rites of the young princes of Red and White Bundle (10 Dog and 6 House); it terminates once 8 Deer has killed and buried the descendants of his father's first marriage. The Colombino-Becker culminates the sacrifice of this group by picturing 8 Deer enthroned and receiving offerings at Tilantongo. As Troike (1974: 341–342) suggests, this must represent 8 Deer's final confirmation as ruler of Tilantongo.

The Zouche-Nuttall, Colombino-Becker, and Bodley Reverse tell us about the deaths of 5 Crocodile's descendants because these manuscripts are interested in this side of the family. The Zouche-Nuttall Obverse follows the descendants of 8 Deer's marriage to 13 Serpent. The Colombino-Becker, after telling about 8 Deer, follows the story of Lord 4 Wind, who eventually married two of 8 Deer's and 13 Serpent's daughters. The Colombino-Becker even indicates that 4 Wind was present when 8 Deer was murdered (Colombino 16b; Troike 1974: 365; 1978: 556; 1980: 414–416). The Bodley Reverse includes 8 Deer more as an in-law and

an interloper, because its story focuses not on 8 Deer but on 4 Wind. Still, it is interested in that side of 5 Crocodile's descendants.

The Bodley Obverse, on the other hand, omits these deaths and conquests. It gives a different version of 8 Deer's demise because its narrative is interested not in 4 Wind but in another side of the family. It follows the line of 8 Deer's second marriage, to Lady 6 Eagle "Jaguar Spiderweb."

8 Deer's Family and His Own Death

After describing the events in 8 Deer's life that it considers pertinent, the Bodley Obverse (10a–14e) reverts to a genealogical reckoning and continues by presenting 8 Deer's five marriages and respective offspring (as it did for his father 5 Crocodile). Lord 8 Deer's first marriage, to 13 Serpent, reinforces his rule of Red and White Bundle (won through conquest) and effectively unites the two sides of 5 Crocodile's descendants. His subsequent wives reaffirm other alliances and expand his domain.

Once 8 Deer has married his fifth and final wife, the Bodley (14e–d) shifts genre again to explain 8 Deer's violent death: a blank space following his last marriage signals a break in the narrative. A date, year 12 Reed day 1 Grass, introduces the scene of 8 Deer shooting an ar-

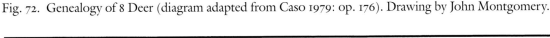

Fig. 72. Genealogy of 8 Deer (diagram adapted from Caso 1979: op. 176). Drawing by John Montgomery.

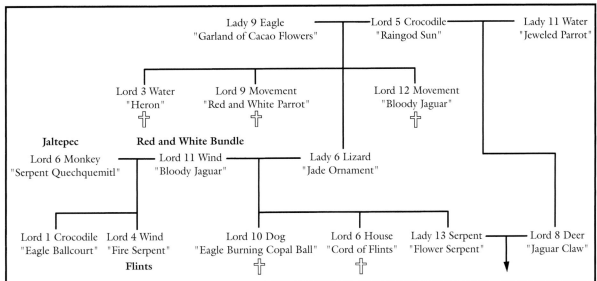

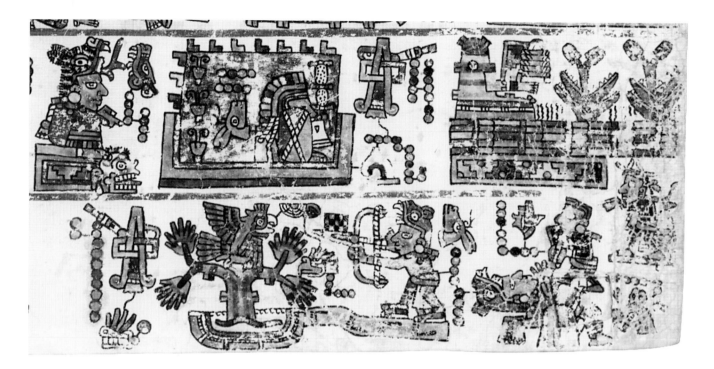

Fig. 73. Codex Bodley 14de. The murder and funeral of 8 Deer. Beginning in the lower register, 8 Deer aims his bow at a parrot linked to the personal and calendrical names of his wife 6 Eagle; in the next scene he is sacrificed at the place identified in the upper register as Hill with Arm and Cacaxtli and Maguey Plain. In the upper left, 8 Deer's father-in-law (8 Crocodile from Skull Frieze, father of 6 Eagle) presides over the placement of 8 Deer's funerary bundle. The Bodleian Library, Oxford, MS. Mex. D. 1.

row at a parrot on a tree in a river (Fig. 73). The Bodley artist has linked the event to 8 Deer's second wife, 6 Eagle "Jaguar Spiderweb," by attaching her personal and calendrical names to the parrot.[55] This may be a simple hunting scene, or it may indicate 8 Deer's attack on a place of that name. If the latter is true, the attack fails, for 8 Deer is immediately sacrificed by two men— 9 Wind and 10 Jaguar "Red Grass"—at the place Hill with Arm and Cacaxtli and Maguey Plain. Eleven days later, 8 Deer's funerary bundle is placed in the darkened enclosure that is his tomb; Lady 6 Eagle's father, Lord 8 Crocodile "Bloody Coyote" of Chalcatongo,[56] presides over the funeral. Lord 8 Deer's life over, the Bodley continues to the next generation, with the marriage of 8 Deer's first son (6 House "Descending Jaguar"), the child of his second marriage (to Lady 6 Eagle). In its selection of events in 8 Deer's life and its genealogical presentation, the Bodley Obverse stresses the primacy of 8 Deer's firstborn son 6 House (the child of 8 Deer's second marriage), who inherited the

Tilantongo throne. The Zouche-Nuttall, in contrast, stresses the primacy of the son of 8 Deer's first wife (4 Dog, the child of 13 Serpent), who inherited the domain of Teozacoalco.

Origins, Lineage, and Deeds of the Ruling Families

Lord 8 Deer's story, and its extensions into the lives of Lady 6 Monkey and Lord 11 Wind, stands out as a central feature of Mixtec recorded history. Events that belong to this story are explained in most of the major Mixtec pictorials, such as the Bodley Obverse and Reverse, the Selden, the Zouche-Nuttall, and the Colombino-Becker. Even the Vienna Reverse, which almost never includes nongenealogical material, interrupts its lineage reckoning to note the deaths of 2 Rain, 5 Crocodile, and 8 Deer and to mention 8 Deer's titles.

The Colombino-Becker and the Zouche-Nuttall Reverse are almost totally devoted to this story. Since the preservation of the story is not likely to be a simple factor of luck, we must recognize it as a fundamentally important narrative in Mixtec royal history.

Jansen (1990: 104) and others have described the 8 Deer story as figuring prominently in the reordering of Mixtec society following the primordial conflict (called by modern writers the "War of Heaven") between the Stone People and the lords from Apoala. In this scenario the Stone People represent the earlier inhabitants of the Mixteca, while the lords of Apoala (functionally equivalent to those who emerged from the tree at Apoala) are the later, Mixtec people, whose history then follows. The War of Heaven is presented, in part, in two early sections of the Zouche-Nuttall Obverse and in the Bodley Reverse.

Building on this approach, Pohl (1994a, 1994b) and Byland and Pohl (1994) link the War of Heaven to the collapse of specific Classic-period sites in the Mixteca, and they tie the 8 Deer story to the readjustment of alliances and marriage patterns that accompanied the rise of the new Post-Classic Mixtec dynasties. Pohl has argued that an old rivalry between Red and White Bundle (the domain of 11 Wind) and Tilantongo (the domain gained by 8 Deer)—a rivalry that began with the War of Heaven—is finally resolved when 8 Deer conquers Red and White Bundle and kills its heirs; then Red and White Bundle drops from the pictorial record. This is very likely the case. But the murder of 8 Deer's rivals also functions to secure him the throne of Tilantongo.

Tilantongo, although not a particularly large polity, had the most prestigious of all the royal lineages. It was the lineage into which the other ruling families wanted to marry, and it seems to have been the lineage that was indeed diffused widely through the Mixtec nobility. Lord 8 Deer killed many of his enemies, married five times (into different families), and fathered a good number of children who themselves came to rule the individual polities that 8 Deer had managed to gather under his control. The result was that at the time of the Spanish conquest, most of the Mixtec rulers were descended in some way from Lord 8 Deer. They looked to the 8 Deer story, and recalled it, in order to explain both their own genealogical situation and their rights to the domains they governed.

Many of these Mixtec rulers also looked to the story of Lord 4 Wind, the son of Lady 6 Monkey whom 8 Deer captured but did not kill. Lord 4 Wind seems to have had a part in 8 Deer's own murder, and as Mary Elizabeth Smith (personal communication 1997) notes, during his long life, he seems to have devoted his energies to dismantling and diluting the holdings of 8 Deer (Troike 1974: 362–364, 474). Lord 4 Wind, like 8 Deer before him, sought the title of *tecuhtli* or lineage head and underwent the ceremony whereby 4 Jaguar pierced his nose for the nose ornament that signaled this status. He also conquered territories, married four times, including unions with two of 8 Deer's daughters, and saw that his brother married two other of 8 Deer's daughters. Smith points out that he was probably responsible for establishing the competing genealogy of Teozacoalco, as well as that of Zacatepec on the coast and a town in the Tlaxiaco area featured in the lost Codex López Ruiz (Smith 1998: 91–92). His story follows 8 Deer's in the Colombino-Becker. His story and that of his paternal ancestors is also featured in great detail in the Bodley Reverse, just as his mother's ancestry is recounted in the Selden.

The Mixtec histories did not only reflect on these tales of heroic and villainous action by early rulers, however; they reached much further, to tell of the primordial origins of Mixtec society. Manuscripts like the Vienna Obverse preserve the features of what must have been a general, pan-Mixtec origin story, probably told in variations by the different polities. Its narrative of creation stresses the sets of primordial ancestors who bring cultural and natural features into being, the birth of gods and ancestors from trees and the earth, the descent from the heavens of culture heroes and ancestors who bring emblems of rule, and the ritual act of organizing the land and bringing "polity" to place. These themes of the Vienna Obverse selectively make their appearance in the dynastic histories. Most of the histories include one or more of the themes to explain how individual dynasties originated and came to control a polity. Manuscripts like the Bodley, Vienna Reverse, Zouche-Nuttall Obverse, and Selden all start their narratives with origin statements, no matter how brief. They explain how the polity and dynasty figure in with "the primordial ordering of time and space" (Jansen 1990: 104). They demonstrate the local origins of the ancestors, and they document the important role of supernatural participation in shaping the dynasties.

Growing out of the origin episodes and the tales of dynastic intrigue, the genealogies carry the stories of the Mixtec royal families forward in time. In doing this they explain, for example, how a ruler living at the time a manuscript was painted is related to the great rulers of the past, and potentially to his or her contemporaries who also trace their lines to the great figures of the past. Although the genealogies do not contain the same kind of action as the episodes of dynastic intrigue and conquest, they are filled with instances of alliance building through marriage, and they record what are, after all, the most critical events for royal power: the unions, offspring, and lines of descent. Genealogically speaking, for example, it does not matter who killed 12 Movement and the others of 8 Deer's rivals; it does not even matter that they were killed at all. What matters is that they left behind no inheriting offspring, which means that rule followed through 8 Deer and his children. The genealogical reckonings track the crucial inheritance patterns of a family, building on the stories of local origin, supernatural patronage, personal achievement, and conquest.

6

Lienzos and Tiras from Oaxaca and Southern Puebla

Lienzos (or sheets) and tiras (or rolls) form a subset of the historical genre from Oaxaca and southern Puebla. They are clearly related to the genealogical histories painted by Mixtec artists on hide screenfolds, for they refer to some of the same places, they include some of the same actors and events, and they are historical expressions of people who share the same general culture. The protagonists in their stories have Mixtec calendrical and personal names, and the artists were generally working in the Mixtec painting style. Moreover, they function, like the screenfolds, to support the claims to land and power of the ruling families of relatively small community kingdoms.

But the lienzos and tiras from southern Mexico are distinct from the screenfold histories discussed in Chapter 5 in being less biographical in their stories, which focus more on the description and inheritance of territory and less on the individual action of an array of nobles. Their dramas are less crowded with auxiliary human players, and they detail fewer events that lead to or resolve interpolity conflicts. Instead, the lienzos and tiras present, more broadly, the history of a polity. They view the polity itself as an entity that is composed of three features: a mythic past and foundation, a line or lines of successively inheriting rulers, and a territory with established geographical limits. As a whole, the ti-ras concentrate on presenting the first two elements—the origin of the polity and the line of rule—whereas the lienzos tie these features to a delineated territory.

The peoples who painted their histories on tiras and lienzos spoke Mixtec, Nahuatl, Popoloca, Chocho, and a host of other languages. Although the extant *res gestae* screenfolds were all painted by Mixtec speakers, the roll and sheet histories clearly had a much wider range in the sixteenth century. Examples come from most parts of central and southern Mexico.

Structurally, too, the lienzos and tiras differ from the screenfold histories. Whereas the screenfolds keep strictly to an event-oriented presentational mode, with the march of successive events held in check by red guidelines, the lienzos and tiras can use both *res gestae* and cartographic presentations. They are also compositionally looser than the screenfolds, with stories that can flow freely across the rolls and sheets. Eschewing the tight and crowded composition of the screenfold histories, their artists emphasize visually the main events, the beginning, and the endings. The lienzos, especially, allow one, and even force one, to view the whole of a story in a single glance.

Structure

Lienzos and tiras are not organized as pages. In the Mixtec screenfolds, the physical fact of the page governs the presentation of information. Red lines divide the pages into registers, and the painter crowds his episodes to fit the confines of the registers and the borders of the pages. Usually figures do not cross the internal folds of facing pages that would be seen together when the screenfold is open; rare is the figure that spans an external page break.[1] The page and the register work together to constrain the reader to follow the succession of scenes in a strict linear order. None of this is the case with tiras or lienzos, which have no preestablished page breaks. The artist of the tira has the whole roll to manipulate as a picture plane; the artist of the lienzo has the whole broad sheet. Information can flow across the sheet and along the roll, occupying, or not, all the space: sometimes the painters span the full width of the roll or fill a large area of the lienzo, and other times they reduce the story to a thin ribbon of events.

The absence of page breaks also encourages the reader to open these documents completely and to view the whole of the presentation at a single moment. The lienzos were obviously unfolded in their entirety to be seen and read, and I suspect the tiras were, too. This means, of course, that the readers had the entire story before them (with the major episodes emphasized visually) while they read the individual episodes that composed this story. Thus they were able simultaneously to note the details of the episodes and to understand how these episodes functioned within the larger picture. The stories told on tiras and lienzos thus have a coherency and a narrative completeness that the purely *res gestae* and annals forms do not; they are also more compositionally pictorial and less indexical or hieroglyphic than the other forms. The lienzo, with its spatial breadth, readily accepts and, indeed, almost calls for a diagrammatic presentation.

Compared with the Mixtec screenfolds, one finds an abundance of empty space in the lienzos and tiras. The compositions are more open, more loosely arranged, and there is more space between the parts and episodes. Where the Mixtec screenfold relies on graphic conventions to distinguish one scene or informational unit from the next, the lienzos and tiras deploy space to separate the parts. All the informational units have a spatial relationship to each other: the space around the events functions to separate them either in time or in location. This abundance of space means that relatively less information is concentrated on the surface of the tira and lienzo than on the *res gestae* screenfold. Because there is less information for the reader to absorb, the reader absorbs it more readily. The reader can then assimilate the full narrative, with its beginning, middle, and end. More so than the screenfolds, many of these lienzos and tiras are structured so that their pictorial stories culminate in a definite ending, an ending that then provides the rationale for the units that comprise it.

Although the tiras usually maintain a loose *res gestae* structure throughout, the lienzos usually shift from a *res gestae* form to a cartographic one. The tiras begin with events leading to the founding of a polity and often then continue to present the line or lines of rule. The lienzos usually also begin this way and embrace the ruler lists, but they end with a map that defines that polity geographically. When the events pertaining to the founding of a polity occur at different places, which they often do, the succession of event to event occasions a move from place to place, so place and time constantly change while the *res gestae* narrative continues. In the lienzos, however, once the map is reached, place becomes stable, and any events must accommodate themselves to the map or ignore it. In the Lienzo of Zacatepec (Fig. 44), as we saw in Chapter 4, they do both: some events are tied to the map while others are independent of it.

Most of the lienzos and tiras also have a specialized kind of *res gestae,* where location does not change at all. This is the ruler list, the linear presentation of the couples who successively rule a polity. Each couple can be understood as an event, and their succession is the figurative string that links the events together. Ruler lists add temporal duration to the foundation events and maps they append.

The map itself is a diagram of the territory on which the events occur or to which the events pertain. Time seems shallow in these cartographs. The geographic features and boundaries of the territory all pertain to the same polity at one point in time, and if events are painted at the various locations, the map figuratively wants to pull them into a vague contemporaneity.

Only by assigning specific dates to the events or by showing a clear linear sequence for the events, can the historian distance these events temporally from each other. The diagram fights with the event sequence over the primacy of space or time. Equally, however, the diagrammatic map projects territory as an entity that endures unchanged through time. The map of Zacatepec thus presents the territory as unchanged from the time its founder entered the area to the time his grandson defeated the last of the enemy neighbors. When the lienzo was brought forth in an 1892 land suit (Smith 1973a: 89), the map still purported the same stable boundaries. The map that dominates most lienzos describes and fixes territory as a spatial entity that existed as one moment in the past, but it also carries this spatial projection into the future, attesting, thereby, to the endurance of that territory.

Stories of Polity in the Tiras

Although the tiras and lienzos share many of the same formal and narrative features, the tiras do not usually include a map or conceptual rendering of territory. Instead, they concentrate, like the screenfolds, on recording the origins of a community kingdom and the duration of its ruling line. These are the two principal elements of most tiras.

The foundational stories often themselves have two parts: the first being the mythic past and the second being the foundation itself. The mythic part of the story can begin in the deep past with the first emergence of supernaturals from rocks, trees, or the sky, and can trace pilgrimages and sacred rites that bring the polity into being. We saw this kind of history in the opening passages of several screenfolds, notably the Bodley Obverse and Reverse, the Zouche-Nuttall Obverse, and the Selden. The mythic past can also be closer at hand, beginning when the polity's soon-to-be founder receives emblems of office and the authority to rule. We saw this kind of history in the opening passages of the Lienzo of Zacatepec. The founding itself is just that. It records the act of founding the polity as a political unit.

The marriage pairs, or ruler lists, bring the founding to the present (when the manuscript was painted). Usually the list is formed of stacked pairs reading from bottom to top (Smith 1973a: 10), but horizontal ar-

rangements are also known. Since inheritance was through primogeniture, the reader understands that the list presents the ruling male and his wife, then the eldest (inheriting) son and his wife, then that son's eldest (inheriting) son and his wife, and so forth (Smith in Smith and Parmenter 1991: 19, 35). These lists figuratively spring from the founding, although the painters do not always render this link pictorially. These ruler lists function to carry the polity through time and to codify the system of land tenure that is based on lineage and inheritance.[2]

The Codex Baranda (Fig. 74), for example, is a horizontal tira (37 cm × 228 cm) that follows two parallel lines of rulers (who appear in rectangular palaces) from their ancient beginnings through into the 1560s, with the last ruler dressed in Spanish attire.[3] The painter placed the auxiliary information, including the coming of the Spaniards, in the space between the two registers.

Vertical ruler lists are more common than horizontal ones, being included in at least a dozen manuscripts (tiras and lienzos both) that come from Oaxaca and Puebla.[4] The Codex Tulane (Fig. 75), for example, is a vertically oriented tira (373.5 cm × 22 cm) that reads from bottom to top along the length of the hide strip. It opens with a series of origin episodes (employing mythological places and ceremonial sites, metaphoric dates, and supernaturals).[5] After the origin scenes, it presents a fifteen-generation ruler list for the town of Chila, the successive rulers stacked one above the other with their wives opposite them. This list gives way for a group scene (dubbed by Donald Robertson [1982] the "campfire scene") in which the first king of Acatlan is confirmed as ruler.[6] There follows another fifteen-generation ruler list, this one for the town of Acatlan (Fig. 75). This ruler list occupies the right side of the roll, while a second column of couples on the left side contains the parents of the Acatlan rulers' brides.

Mary Elizabeth Smith (in Smith and Parmenter 1991: 20, 32) has suggested that vertical ruler lists, such as are found in the Codex Tulane and in many lienzos, represent a native adaptation to a colonial administrative requirement. Noting that the vertical ruler lists are only found in colonial manuscripts, she argues that such documents may have been a conscious effort on the part of the manuscript painters to prove that the last ruler was descended in a direct line, "por línea

Fig. 74. Codex Baranda, which opens with an origin account and continues with parallel lines of rulers. CNCA.-

recta," from the founding ancestors, and that there were no competitors to the throne. The phrase "por línea recta" appears often in colonial litigation, describing a necessary condition for valid rule. Although the implication is that these vertical ruler lists are a colonial invention, they might also be a preconquest form that was emphasized over other presentations to fit colonial needs. The vertical column achieves this admirably, for it presents an unbroken and singular line of rule, with no outside interlopers, and it carefully omits other potential claimants.

Stories of Polity and Territory in the Lienzos

The lienzos ground the narrative content of the tiras to a map of territory. The stories they tell are about land and polity, which is to say, they record how land is territory, and how it becomes polity by being tied to a sacred past, a history, and a chain of human rulers who control it. As Smith (1973a: 169) has pointed out, over and above any specific reason a lienzo was painted, these maps "were prepared for one general purpose: to protect the lands of the community and of the native nobility." These manuscripts achieve this purpose by naming features of the landscape and organizing them in such a way as to demarcate a specific territory. They join this territory to a past that can be both mythic and secular, one that usually begins when ancient ancestors or supernaturals emerge into the living world or when they assign rulership to royal mortals. Then the manuscripts channel this past through the descent line of the rulers. This union of place, history, and rule thus formed a kind of community charter, such that many towns in Oaxaca and southern Puebla relied on their lienzos to function as community land titles throughout the colonial period and into the nineteenth century (Smith 1973a: 162), some even into the twentieth century (Parmenter 1982: 46–48).

Thus, there are usually three main parts to the histories recorded in the lienzos: the story of divine or human action that brings a polity into being, the listing of successive rulers, and the map that defines the territory in question. These represent the social and geographic elements—the shared past founded in the sacred, the line of rule, and the land—that compose a community kingdom. Since the first two parts also characterize the tiras, it is the lienzos' cartographic component that most distinguishes them from other genres.

The map graphically organizes and presents knowledge about the territory. It represents pictorially or conventionally not what is seen but what is understood to be. It emphasizes certain features and not others, and by so doing it signals to the reader what the historian considered important. Usually a circuit of place signs delineates the boundary of the territory. As we saw with the Lienzo of Zacatepec (Fig. 44), these place signs may be sites of habitation or geographic features.

INAH.-MEX; reproduced with permission of the Instituto Nacional de Antropología e Historia.

They can be major places or locations barely notice-able on the ground, but they are all presented equally. Sometimes the place signs face outward, sometimes in-ward, and sometimes the bases of the place signs are all oriented in one direction defining a top and bottom for the lienzo. A line often joins them at their bases, form-ing a cartographic rectangle that outlines the territory. The boundary thus formed is more conceptual than ac-tual, for the boundaries on the map often correspond only roughly to a circuit that can be walked on the ground. Within the territory, rivers, lakes, springs, sometime roads, and other major features are located roughly according to their actual geographic situation. Toward the center of the map is the town whose terri-tory is being presented. Often subject towns are scat-tered around it.

Lienzos physically unite this map with foundation events and ruler lists in different ways. The foundation events and ruler lists can be located beside the map and largely separate from it, as in the Mapa de Teozacoalco. Or these narrative elements can be placed fully within the map, as in the Lienzo of Ihuitlan. The ruler list and the representation of place can also be blended, to-gether forming a historical presentation that is less car-tographic or *res gestae* than it is diagrammatic. Such is

Fig. 75. Detail of the Codex Tulane ruler list for Aca-tlan (*right column*) with the parents of the wives pre-sented (*left column*). Photograph courtesy of the Latin American Library, Tulane University.

the Lienzo of Philadelphia, where the place signs assigned to the ruler lists and descent lines may or may not form a map. These three documents are discussed here in some detail as representatives of the different ways lienzo painters brought together the foundation events, ruler lists, and spatial projections or maps.

Mapa de Teozacoalco

The Mapa de Teozacoalco (Fig. 76) is one of the maps painted by native artists in response to the Relaciones Geográficas questionnaire circulated by the viceregal government to the towns in New Spain in the late sixteenth century. Specifically the *mapa* responded to question 10, which called for a map of the town, but it also provided information for questions 9 and 14, which asked about the town's founding and rulers.[7] Although this document was prepared in 1580 expressly for the Spanish government and was painted on pieces of European paper that had been glued together to

form a vast paper sheet (142 cm × 177 cm), it replicates the features of a historical lienzo.

The Map. The map of the territory (Fig. 77) is painted as a circle circumscribed by a line that joins the base of forty-six place signs; these signs are Teozacoalco's boundaries.[8] Smith (1973a: 166) has suggested that the circular shape of this territory owes more to the European tradition of circular *mappa mundi* than it does to the indigenous tradition of cartographic rectangles. The appearance of a European-style sun at the upper edge of the sheet orients east at the top, as is the case in European maps of the day. Inside the circle, the natural and human-made features of Teozacoalco are painted in a blend of indigenous and European styles. Ranges of hills are pictured as shaded and undulating fields of green, with clusters of trees signaling forests in the European manner. Rivers and streams are presented according to indigenous conventions as blue bands of flowing water, carried along by the wavy lines of the current and punctuated by liquid fingers that end in jade or turquoise disks and shells. We note that

Fig. 76.   Mapa de Teozacoalco. Photograph courtesy of the Benson Latin American Collection, University of Texas at Austin.

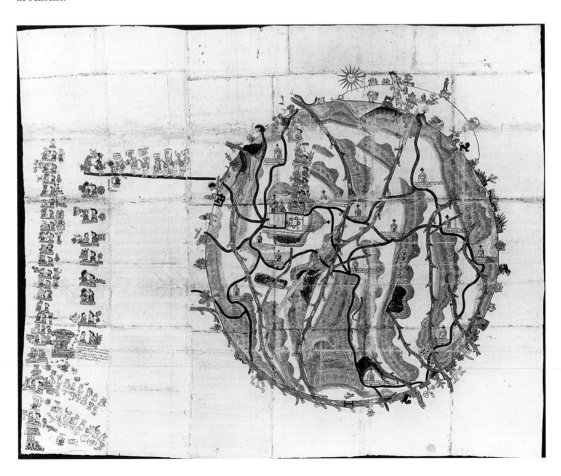

the waters consistently flow from east to west; on the southern (right) side of the map, they originate in the hills. Cutting irregularly through the land of Teozacoalco, roads are conventionally depicted as brown ribbons marked by footprints and, now that horses have arrived, with hoofprints. Most of these roads lead to and from Teozacoalco proper, represented in the center left of the circle by its square plaza flanked on its eastern side by a tall church and shorter bell tower and on its southern side by a building and courtyard complex that the Spanish gloss identifies as the ruler's palace.

In Teozacoalco's hinterlands, thirteen small build-

ings, with arched doorways and crosses on the top, conventionally locate Teozacoalco's *sujetos* or subject towns.[9] A shallow bulge at the top of the cartographic circle represents the territory of Elotepec, a town formerly subject to Teozacoalco. Mundy (1996: 112) suggests that the *mapa* artist was copying here an old map that had originally embraced Elotepec but was since revised to omit the former *sujeto;* the painter simply copied both boundaries.

Ruler Lists. Three ruler lists are associated with this territorial map, two in columns that rise along the left side of the sheet (Fig. 78) and one that grows from Teozacoalco's civic center inside the map (Fig. 79).

Fig. 77. Map of the polity of Teozacoalco on the Mapa de Teozacoalco. Photograph courtesy of the Benson Latin American Collection, University of Texas at Austin.

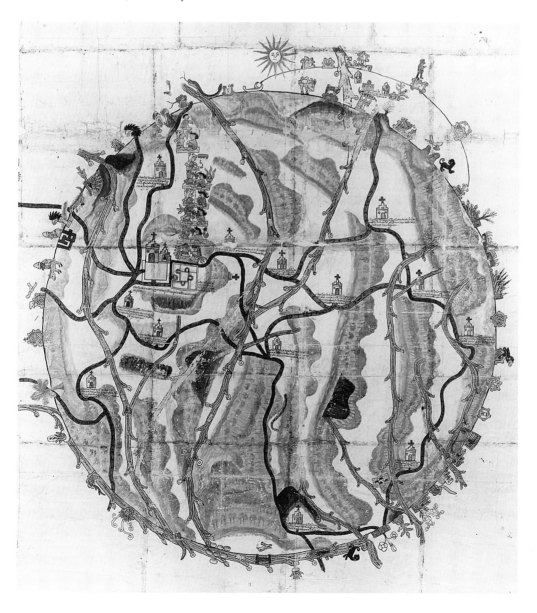

Fig. 78. The ruler lists for Tilantongo (*left*) and Teozacoalco (*right*) on the Mapa de Teozacoalco

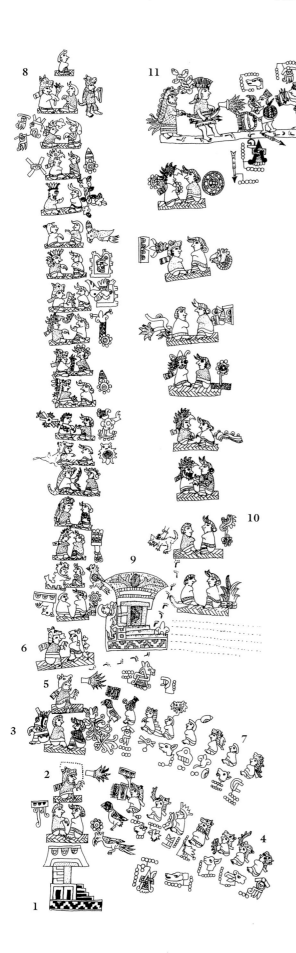

1 Tilantongo.

2 Lord 2 Rain "20 Jaguar"; died without an heir.

3 Lord 5 Crocodile "Raingod Sun" and wife 9 Eagle "Garland of Cacao Flowers."

4 Ceremony to confirm rule; should be for 5 Crocodile.

5 Lord 12 Movement "Bloody Jaguar"; died without an heir.

6 Lord 8 Deer "Jaguar Claw" and wife 13 Serpent "Flower Serpent."

7 Ceremony to confirm rule; should be for 8 Deer.

8 Last marriage pair; man's brother "Coyote/Stick in Hand" (standing on right) went to rule Teozacoalco; pair's daughter (seated above) ruled Tilantongo until 1576.

9 Teozacoalco.

10 8 Deer's son, 4 Dog "Tame Coyote," marries 4 Death "Jewel Crocodile" of the Teozacoalco line and assumes rule there.

11 Lord 2 Dog "Cord of Flints" with wife 6 Reed "Feathered Serpent."

12 Ceremony to confirm rule of 2 Dog "Cord of Flints."

Photograph courtesy of the Benson Latin American Collection, University of Texas at Austin; drawing from Anders and Jansen 1988: 137, courtesy Akademische Druck- u. Verlagsanstalt, Graz.

In each column, the ruling pairs sit facing each other on a woven mat, in the conventional marriage statement of rulers; the man is on the left, and the columns read bottom to top. What at first seems like a straightforward listing of rulers yields a more complicated story.

Fig. 79.   The latest rulers of Teozacoalco, rising upward from the palace of Teozacoalco inside the territorial map on the Mapa de Teozacoalco:

1 Lord 2 Dog "Cord of Flints" and wife 6 Reed "Feathered Serpent."
2 Lord "Coyote/Stick in Hand" from Tilantongo marries a woman of the Teozacoalco lines and assumes rule there.

Photograph courtesy of the Benson Latin American Collection, University of Texas at Austin.

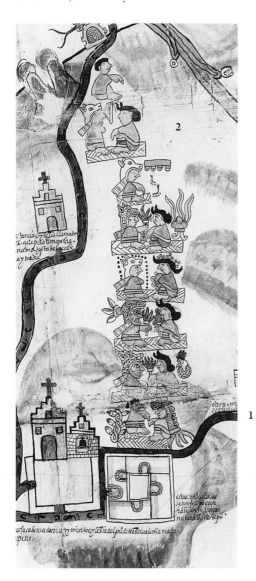

The narrative of these rulers begins in the far lower left corner with a list of the successive rulers not of Teozacoalco but of the prestigious line of Tilantongo, which rises above the place sign of that polity (Fig. 78); Tilantongo is represented here by a Temple of Heaven on a black and white platform (signaling Tilantongo's other name, Black Town). The first ruling pair shown—Lord 5 Movement "Smoking Sky" and Lady 2 Grass "Jewel Quetzal"—are identified not by their day names but only by their personal names, as are all the other rulers. They are not Tilantongo's first rulers, only the first ones represented here. Above them is their inheriting son, 2 Rain "20 Jaguar," without a mate. Since we know from other sources (Bodley 5ab, Vienna Reverse 5a) that this man never married or actually ruled Tilantongo, his presence here in a list of rulers is a deviation from the norm; here he apparently signals the end of Tilantongo's first dynasty. Next, Lord 5 Crocodile "Raingod Sun" (whose descendants are discussed in Chapter 5) is shown with his wife, 9 Eagle "Garland of Cacao Flowers," followed by their eldest son, 12 Movement "Bloody Jaguar," who also never married or actually ruled Tilantongo. The inclusion of 5 Crocodile and 12 Movement in this list caused Caso (1949) to believe that 5 Crocodile founded Tilantongo's second dynasty, and it took Rabin's revised chronology to show that 5 Crocodile actually died before 2 Rain did and thus could not have succeeded him (Jansen 1982, 1:374–380). Regardless of the story as recounted in the other histories, the Mapa de Teozacoalco here credits 2 Rain, 5 Crocodile, and 12 Movement with rule. Lord 8 Deer "Jaguar Claw," who did found the second Tilantongo dynasty, appears with his first wife 13 Serpent "Flower Serpent" as the fifth in line. Thereafter, the rule of Tilantongo rises through seventeen successions until it reaches the last marriage pair. Above them sits their single daughter on the mat of rulership, the last in the Tilantongo line presented here; she ruled until 1576.[10] To their right stands the man's brother, "Coyote/Stick in Hand," who faces in the direction of Teozacoalco, where he went to assume rule.

To the right of the column at the bottom, near where the single males 2 Rain "20 Jaguar" and 12 Movement "Bloody Jaguar" sit, are two rows of seven seated men, who have both personal names and calendrical names (below them). Enacting a ceremony that Caso (1949: 160) called the "offering of rulership," the nobles present offerings in the form of a quail, a fiery torch, and a configuration of two rectangles that seems to combine a handful of quetzal feathers, a string of three beads, and perhaps a fringed tunic. Although the *mapa* artist has angled these rituals as if to join them to the single males who did not rule, this is clearly an error. The proper recipients of the ceremonies should be 5 Crocodile and 8 Deer, men who were not born in line for the throne and who are shown in the screenfold histories conducting ceremonies toward that end.[11] The date below the first ceremony, year 12 Flint day 10 Serpent, is the year after 2 Rain was born; although this date is not specifically mentioned in the other pictorials, it was generally the time when 5 Crocodile is shown in the Bodley (8b) making offerings at various places. I suggest it dates the first "offering of rulership."[12] The date above the second rulership ceremony, which is year 8 Rabbit day 4 Wind, probably dates that event as well. In the Zouche-Nuttall (68b), Bodley (9a), and Colombino (18c), it is the date on which Lord 8 Deer sets out on his journey to the sun god following his installation as ruler of Tilantongo. Some historical slippage has occurred between the preconquest screenfolds and this late-sixteenth-century reckoning of Tilantongo's early rulers.

Teozacoalco's line of rule is just to the right of Tilantongo's (Fig. 78); it begins next to the large place sign of Teozacoalco, a sign that combines several features of the town's name: a man shown bending the platform as a phonetic reference to "great," the temple itself large in scale with a bleeding cacao pod on top, and the trefoil flower (Smith 1973a: 57–58). The first lord and his wife sit together to the right of the place sign. Since they died without a male successor, rule passed to their daughter 4 Death "Jewel Crocodile." She sits above them facing her husband, 4 Dog "Tame Coyote," whom we know from other sources (Bodley 11c, Vienna Reverse 8a, Zouche-Nuttall 26c) to be Lord 8 Deer's first son by his first marriage. Footprints from 8 Deer in the Tilantongo line to 4 Dog in the Teozacoalco line show how this son of Tilantongo married into the Teozacoalco royal family when their line of succession was in peril. Six more seated rulers of Teozacoalco are stacked above.

The uppermost ruler, Lord 2 Dog "Cord of Flints," and his wife 6 Reed "Feathered Serpent" are pictured standing, facing another group of seven named nobles who present them with gifts in another rulership ceremony; the date just below sets the rite in year 10 House day 6 Reed. As explained in the Zouche-Nuttall (31–34), the previous ruling couple had no male heirs. One of their daughters, however, married a Zaachila ruler and gave birth to the son 2 Dog, who then inherited the Teozacoalco throne from his maternal grandparents. Lord 2 Dog's wife herself was the daughter of Tilantongo rulers. None of this detail is included in the Mapa de Teozacoalco, which takes pains to present the line of rule as untroubled and unbroken. At those dynastic moments when the strict succession of male heirs failed, the artist recorded the ceremony that officially conferred rulership on the next male ruler.

After this installation, footprints along the road to Teozacoalco visually carry Lord 2 Dog "Cord of Flints" and Lady 6 Reed "Feathered Serpent" into the map and to Teozacoalco proper, where they appear as ruling marrieds just above the ruler's palace (Fig. 79). Four successively ruling couples are stacked above them until the line of male inheritance falters again, noted by the appearance of a single lord named "Coyote/ Descending from the Sky" (his calendrical name is not known). The line of ruling marrieds resumes when Lord "Coyote/Stick in Hand" appears with a woman who is probably an inheriting daughter. We remember "Coyote/Stick in Hand" as the brother of the last male ruler pictured in the Tilantongo line on the far left. Thus, once again, a prince from Tilantongo has assumed the rule of Teozacoalco. Finally, their son, who is unnamed pictorially, appears; he is still single and not yet seated on the woven mat of rule. In 1580, when the map was drawn up, "Coyote/Stick in Hand" still ruled Teozacoalco.[13]

Thus the Mapa de Teozacoalco combines a map with ruler lists. There is no hint of a sacred past, and even the ruler lists, extensive as they are, begin well after the towns' foundings. The only events actually shown, other than the marriage pairs, are the movement of a Tilantongo prince to Teozacoalco and the three rituals that confer rule. The map projects Teozacoalco forward and backward in time and presents it as a durable, stable entity. Ruler lists are given for both Teozacoalco and Tilantongo because the former drew on the latter for male rulers when its own succession was in danger, and the artist perhaps wanted to make clear that the prestigious lineage of Tilantongo flowed through Teozacoalco's own ruling family.

The columns of rulers demonstrate very clearly that the last rulers are descended directly from the earlier ones, "por línea recta" (Smith 1973a: 10). The lists smooth over any difficulties in royal succession. Extraneous children or potential claimants to the throne are omitted, and potentially questionable successions are shown to be validated by appropriate ritual. One sees clearly that Teozacoalco's royal line is complete and relatively uncomplicated, and that it springs from the celebrated line at Tilantongo.

As specialized kinds of *res gestae* forms, the ruler lists are locked to specific locations. The ruler list of Tilantongo springs from the place sign of that town, and we read its rulers as all residing there. We likewise read the ruler list of Teozacoalco as occupying that place, a fact that is made even more explicit when the ruler list shifts spatially to inside the map. Although the history painter had plenty of space at the top of the sheet to finish the original column of Teozacoalco rulers, he chose to transfer the line to the town proper after the coronation of 2 Dog "Cord of Flints" (Fig. 79). It may be that the original map had a ruler list beginning with 2 Dog and his wife, or the painter may have moved the line to reinforce its presence at Teozacoalco. Once the ruler list moves inside the map, it initially subsumes itself to the ambient cartographic space by locating 2 Dog and his wife just above their palace. Thereafter, however, the ruler list ignores the cartography of the map entirely as the succession rises to the last ruler at the top.

Several other lienzos follow this format of locating the ruler list on the side. Such is the Lienzo de Guevea, from the Zapotec-speaking town of Santiago Guevea in the Isthmus of Tehuantepec; its ruler list, which includes only males, pertains to the lords of Zaachila (Whitecotton 1990: 108–121). The Lienzo of Tequixtepec I (Fig. 89) and the Lienzo of Tlapiltepec (Fig. 90) also have the ruler lists separate from their maps, although the Tlapiltepec lienzo has additional ruler lists within its map. These lienzos all recognize the complementary relationship between the ruler list and the map; they distinguish the two by locating them side by side, but they join them when the ruler list flows into the map.

Lienzo of Ihuitlan

The union of the ruler list, with its temporal depth, and the map, with its spatial breadth, is more complete in the Lienzo of Ihuitlan (Fig. 80). The Ihuitlan lienzo is a great sheet of cotton (248.5 cm × 157.5 cm) that overlays ruler lists for several towns in the Coixtlahuaca Valley directly on a topographic map of the larger region. Painted sometime in the sixteenth century, it presents the founding of a number of polities, explains genealogical relationships between several royal lines in the valley, and laces both the map and the ruler lists with references to other sacred and secular events.[14] The map occupies all of the lienzo's surface, which forces the painter to fit the ruler lists and historical data within the confines of the cartograph rather than adjacent to it, as we saw in the Mapa de Teozacoalco. The Ihuitlan lienzo looks familiar as a Mixtec-style document, for Mixtec calendrical names and dates are employed, and almost all the graphic conventions are Mixtec. The only Aztec stylistic element is the pose of the women, who are seated with their legs beneath them in the "Aztec woman's pose," a feature that appears in other Coixtlahuaca Valley manuscripts.

The Map. The lienzo's map spans the entire cotton sheet. Instead of a tight cartographic rectangle or circle inscribing the community, the place signs of fifteen towns and hamlets are more irregularly located around the edge of the map. Most are *sujetos* of Ihuitlan, but Coixtlahuaca in the lower left and a cluster of four polities in the upper left (Coxcatlan, Tehuacan, Acatlan, Tlacotepec) tie the region of Ihuitlan to the larger world of the Coixtlahuaca Valley and southern Puebla (Figs. 80–82). Another eight sites are represented inside this area, along with six groups of fields or plots of land. Most of the signs, especially those on the left side of the lienzo, are also accompanied by seated ruling couples. Almost all are identified by glosses that give the Nahuatl name of the place.

Three of the places—Tlapiltepec and Coixtlahuaca (Fig. 83), both in the lower left corner, and Ihuitlan, in the lower center of the map (Fig. 84)—are pictured with cult images and sacred bundles inside the hill glyphs or, in the case of Ihuitlan, on top of the hill sign within and in front of the temple. These cult figures— one at each site is actually a round bundle—have the round "death" eyes and fanged teeth of supernaturals,

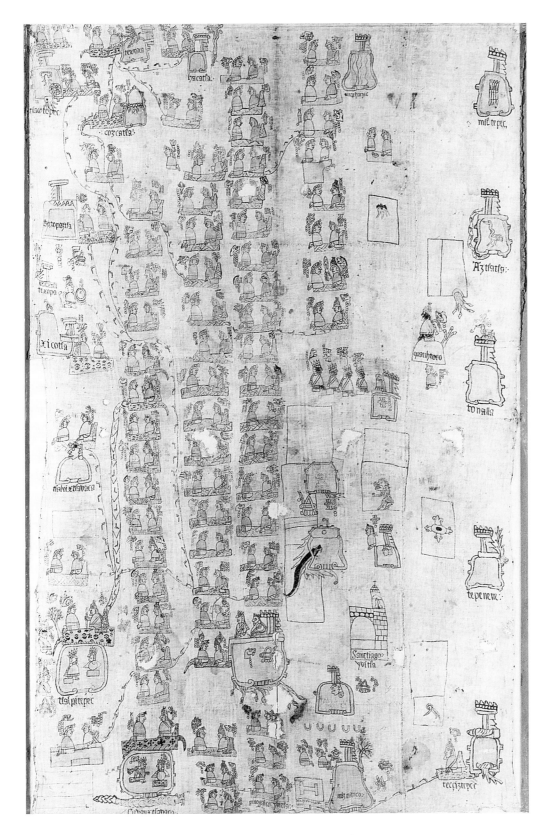

Fig. 80. Lienzo of Ihuitlan. Reproduced courtesy of the Brooklyn Museum.

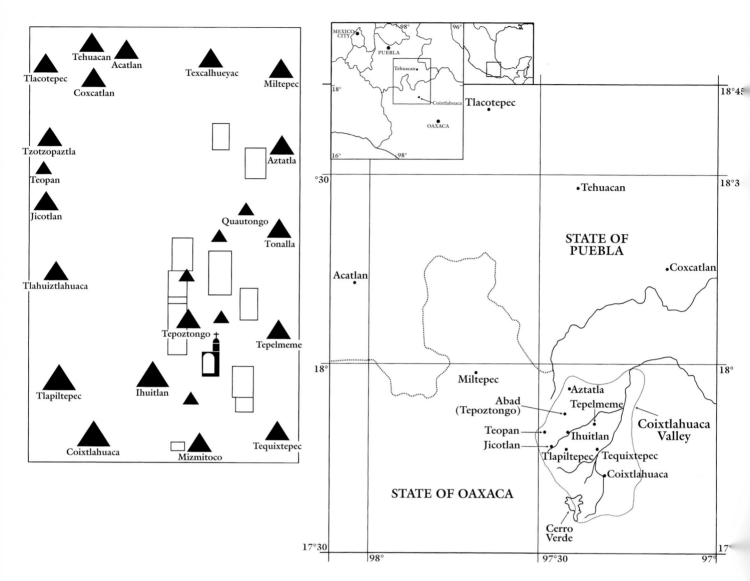

Fig. 81. Diagram of the map on the Lienzo of Ihuitlan. Drawing by John Montgomery.

Fig. 82. Area referenced by the map on the Lienzo of
Ihuitlan. Drawing by John Montgomery.

and they wear sawtoothed crowns that Parmenter
(1982: 41; 1993: 35) suggests are composed of amate or
woven cane. Those at Coixtlahuaca are named 1 Lizard
and 9 Wind, the latter being the supernatural featured
in the Vienna Obverse as a creator of lands and humans
(the Mixtec equivalent of Quetzalcoatl). As is discussed
more fully below, Caso (1954) suggested that several
Coixtlahuaca pictorials describe the 9 Wind cult being
introduced into the area. Here the figures and bundles
are presented as the gods, perhaps also supernatural ancestors, of the towns.

In the center of the lower half of the map is the

polity to which the lienzo pertains, Santiago Ihuitlan
Plumas (Fig. 84). It is represented both by a colonial
church with bell tower, glossed Santiago Ihuitlan—the
only church (and the only colonial image) in the
map—and by the site's indigenous place sign. This sign
combines the circular shape of a swollen hill sign with
the element of water, signaling, perhaps, the community kingdom as a "water hill" (*altepetl* in Nahuatl).[15]
No civic center is formally outlined on this map, as
there is in the Mapa de Teozacoalco; instead the polity
is indexed by its sign and the colonial church.

The map also lacks topographic and landscape fea-

Fig. 83. The place sign of Coixtlahuaca on the Lienzo of Ihuitlan. The founding rulers are seated above on the jaguar skin platform and the cult images are embraced within the place sign. Reproduced courtesy of the Brooklyn Museum.

tures, such as forests, ranges of hills, watercourses, and roads, which were painted for Teozacoalco. Less a visual picture of the land, the map is a conceptual diagram of territory defined by the location of settled places. Only the rectangular fields, which cluster on the right side of the lienzo around Ihuitlan itself, betray the need to depict actual physical space, and they, too, are named glyphically. It is a map created fully within the representational framework of the indigenous people, not one that embraces European stylistic features in order to make it more suitable and readable by Spanish audiences. Only the glosses suggest a potential European readership.

The map generally agrees well with the geography of the Coixtlahuaca Valley and southern Puebla, if we think of this geography in experiential rather than in universal terms (Fig. 82). This is not a map of the area as seen or imagined from the air, with cartographically correct spacing of its features: for example, Tlapiltepec, shown on the map in the lower left corner as being close to Coixtlahuaca, is actually much closer to Ihuitlan. Instead, it is a map of locations as these are un-

derstood and referenced from the ground at a particular point. The top of the map is oriented toward the northwest. As Parmenter (1982: 10–11) explains, the map is configured as if one were standing in the town of Ihuitlan, looking around, and pointing in the direction of the surrounding towns. Although some towns are farther away from Ihuitlan than others, and a circuit connecting them would undulate considerably, their sight lines from a point in Ihuitlan are accurately presented on the map. Exceptions are the four distant towns in southern Puebla—Tlacotepec, Tehuacan, Coxcatlan, and Acatlan—which are clustered together in the upper left corner of the lienzo. Within the Coixtlahuaca Valley, however, the geography conceptualized and presented here is the earthly equivalent of naked-eye, horizontal astronomy, as practiced throughout Mesoamerica (Aveni 1980: 48–98).

Ruler Lists. On this map, inside the loose frame of the surrounding place signs and between the cartographic space of the interior ones, the artist presents several ruler lists (Fig. 85). Three long lists (which I call columns 1–3) rise from near the bottom of the map to nearly the top, a fourth (column 4) begins halfway up on the right side, and two shorter lists (columns A and B) start near the middle of the very bottom edge. In all the lists, females sit on the left and males on the right. The men are on thrones that have backs, and many have their hair pulled up in a style often sported by Coixtlahuaca Valley warriors and priests (or those par-

Fig. 84. The place sign and colonial church identifying Ihuitlan on the Lienzo of Ihuitlan. Rising to the left and on top of Ihuitlan's place sign are the two lineages of the polity. Reproduced courtesy of the Brooklyn Museum.

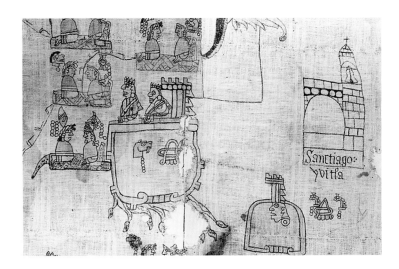

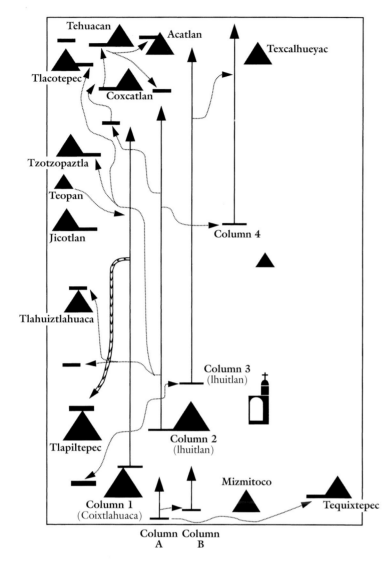

Fig. 85.   Diagram of the ruler lists on the Lienzo of
Ihuitlan. Drawing by John Montgomery.

gathered here on Ihuitlan's lienzo to explain how the
Ihuitlan royal line is connected genealogically to other
ruling lines in the valley and beyond. The ruler lists
show how Ihuitlan's ancestors came from the same ancient lines as Coixtlahuaca's and how Ihuitlan later contributed wives and husbands to polities near and far.

The ruler list of column 1 pertains to the polity of
Coixtlahuaca, which is identified by the large serpent
under its hill glyph (Fig. 83). The first couple, Lord
8 Wind and Lady 4 Reed, sit prominently on an elaborate jaguar-skin platform. They are presented here,
emphasized and slightly enlarged, as Coixtlahuaca's
founders. To the right, a short list of three couples (column A) identifies their ancestors. These three pairs in
column A seem to me to have been added after the
main ruler list was begun, because they become smaller
toward the lower edge and seem crowded. Two sets of
footprints leave the lowermost pair, Lord 9 Crocodile
and Lady 12 Eagle, and go to the first female in column
B and to the male enthroned on the far right at Tequixtepec. This first, ancestral couple thus contributed a
daughter, 8 Death, to the first couple in column B and
installed a son, 3 Lizard, as lord of Tequixtepec. The
three couples of column A, rulers of Yucucuy (Cerro
Verde, south of Coixtlahuaca), must have been added
to the lienzo in order to explain this relationship.

Rulers of the Coixtlahuaca line are stacked sixteen
high above the place sign, ending near the top of the
page (column 1). Halfway up, a path marked by footprints and chevrons drops from Lord 10 Serpent and
Lady 13 Serpent down to the place sign of Tlapiltepec
in the lower left corner. The artist is telling us that their
son, 3 Rain, conquered Tlapiltepec, probably defeating
the two dead men seated to the left of the place sign,
and married the Tlapiltepec princess 6 Deer. Behind
6 Deer's name may be the name of another wife,
6 Monkey (Caso 1979: 263). The year sign 10 Reed below and to the left of Tlapiltepec's place sign, or the
year 11 House day 12 Wind to the right of the couple,
may signal the date of 3 Rain's conquest and assumption of rule.

The Coixtlahuaca line is itself amended only once.
Just above Lord 10 Serpent and his wife, a line of footprints leads from the seated warrior in front of Teopan on the left edge of the sheet to Lord 6 Water.
Although other lienzos from the Coixtlahuaca Valley
identify 6 Water as the regular successor to 10 Serpent

ticipating in rituals).[16] None are pictured with arms,
and all but three are identified by their calendrical
names.[17] Together the pairs face each other on platforms that are usually of woven reed but sometimes,
especially for the line of Coixtlahuaca, are of jaguar
skin, complete with a tail (Fig. 83). Lines of footprints
from one list to another show how the offspring of one
family marry into others. The history and lineages presented here are also featured in the Lienzos Coixtlahuaca I, Meixueiro, Seler II (Coixtlahuaca II; Fig. 86),
Tlapiltepec (Fig. 90), and Tulancingo, although the
ruler lists here are more complete. These lineages are

(Caso 1979: 221), Caso (1961: 242) suggested the Ihuitlan lienzo was indicating that he came from Teopan (which Caso identified as Texupan, to the south) and married into the Coixtlahuaca line. An alternative presents itself, however, for this 6 Water was the lord Atonaltzin whom the Aztec emperor Moctezuma Ilhuicamina captured during the latter's conquest of Coixtlahuaca in the mid-fifteenth century (Parmenter 1993: 54); Moctezuma may have approached Coixtlahuaca through Teopan, which, as Parmenter (personal communication 1997) points out, is an entrance into the valley. The seated, enthroned warrior who is near but not actually at Teopan lacks a Mixtec calendrical name. Caso read the smoking shield just in front of him as his personal name. His warrior's topknot is more fully in the Aztec style than the similarly bound hair of the Coixtlahuaca rulers, and he is the only male on the lienzo wearing a white cloak bordered by a plain band. Moreover, he and Teopan's place sign seem to have been squeezed into the space left between Tzotzopaztla and Jicotlan as a later addition. This Teopan male might even be Moctezuma himself as the captor of 6 Water Atonaltzin, for only rulers, priests, and supernaturals are included on the lienzo.[18] If so, this would be the one time in the lienzo that footprints indicate only travel rather than travel and descent.

Column 2, attached to the left side of Ihuitlan's place sign, and column 3, which rises just above it, both pertain to Ihuitlan (van Doesburg n.d.; Fig. 85). Both lines stem from the short list of rulers in column B below, a royal line assigned by a gloss to Pinoyalco Ihuitlan, perhaps the ancient name of Ihuitlan (Caso 1961: 245). This earlier royal line opens with Lord 13 Vulture and the Lady 8 Death, the wife who comes from the early Yucucuy line (in column A), and runs for only three couples to Lord 4 Rain and Lady 3 Grass just beneath Ihuitlan's place sign. Although the Ihuitlan artist does not specify how this line is connected to those above it, the Lienzo of Tlapiltepec shows the couple as the predecessors of Lord 6 Rain and Lady 10 Flint, the first rulers pictured for Ihuitlan in column 2. Ihuitlan's founding is given here and in the Lienzo of Tulancingo as year 12 Flint day 5 Serpent (Parmenter 1993: 23).

This Ihuitlan line (column 2) rises for fifteen successions. Lines of footprints from Ihuitlan couples to other royal lines and places indicate that eight times Ihuitlan offspring moved to other towns or entered other lineages as rulers or marriage partners. The second couple, Lord 6 Movement and Lady 1 Monkey, sent a son (12 Crocodile) to the unidentified place in the lower left corner of the lienzo and sent a daughter (9 Wind) to marry into the second Ihuitlan line (column 3). The next couple contributed four males who settled at an unidentified place on the lower left edge of the lienzo, at Tlahuiztlahuaca above it, and at Tzotzopaztla and Tlacotepec along the upper left edge. Just over halfway up, the couple Lord 4 Water and Lady 3 House provided a male to begin a new line to the right (column 4). Their successors then sent a son to marry a woman in the upper left, a union that yielded a daughter who married the lord of Coxcatlan in the state of Puebla; that marriage then contributed a son for Tehuacan and grandchildren for two other locations.[19] The lienzo emphasizes Ihuitlan's role as a source of royal sons and daughters for other polities in both the Coixtlahuaca Valley and Puebla.

In comparison, the second Ihuitlan line (column 3) appears parochial. This line begins just above Ihuitlan's place sign, with Lord 11 Deer and Lady 9 Wind, who follow Lord 6 Rain and Lady 10 Flint (the first couple shown in column 2) in other related lienzos (e.g., Tlapiltepec). Toward the top of its seventeen-couple list, Lord 5 Death and Lady 5 Wind send a daughter to wed Lord 8 Dog in column 4, but she is the only royal in this line to be shown leaving home.

Column 4 is not well understood. Although Caso (1961: 248) assigned it to Texcalhueyac at the top of the lienzo, Parmenter (1993: 39–41) has suggested instead that it pertains to the unglossed town below that is identified by the date 6 Movement, where four priests gather. The four men wear black face paint, "sawtooth crowns," and tunics that characterize some of the priests in Coixtlahuaca Valley documents (discussed below). As Parmenter says, this is very probably a religious place, as yet unidentified.[20]

One might ask why these particular ruler lists are presented here together. I do not know why the fourth column of rulers appears here, but Coixtlahuaca (column 1) was the largest and strongest city-state in the area, and during Aztec times it was the capital of the province. Too, Coixtlahuaca contributed a son to Tlapiltepec, a town closely allied with Ihuitlan and near it geographically, and its ancestral line (column A) had earlier sent both a son to Tequixtepec and a daughter to the ancient line of Pinoyalco Ihuitlan (column B). The two Ihuitlan lineages (columns 2, 3) in turn sprang from this ancient line and contributed to other lineages; Ihuitlan's first lineage (column 2) especially was the source of many brides and grooms for other polities. These ruler lists, together with the footprints of genealogical connection, show how the ruling families of the Coixtlahuaca Valley and beyond are related to each other. Visually and conceptually, they form a web of genealogical connections that unifies the map of the area, one that pulls the near and distant towns together into a single political organism.

History is encoded throughout the map and the lists. Most of it is genealogical history and the succession of rulers, although the dates may recall foundings and other events. If I am right about the male at Teopan referring to Moctezuma Ilhuicamina, the lienzo also shows the Aztec conquest of Coixtlahuaca, which was an event of considerable significance. The map presents all the features of this large geographic area as being roughly contemporaneous. The ruler lists create their own artificial spaces as sequences of unspecified temporal duration, but they are necessarily tied at various points to real places on the map. The dates, too, link their events to real places. The cartographic format of the Ihuitlan lienzo thus forces time and events to fit within the spatial confines of the map.

Most of the other lienzos from the Coixtlahuaca Valley follow the format of Ihuitlan's. Usually a cartographic rectangle studded with place signs defines the territory, which fills most of the available space (Fig. 86). The ruler lists, if any, run upward within the territory thus defined, and other events of a historical nature (including sacred occurrences and foundings) fill voids between places or are themselves attached to places. Such are the Codex Meixueiro (or Tulane's Lienzo A, a tracing of a lost lienzo for Coixtlahuaca), Lienzo Coixtlahuaca I, Seler II or Lienzo Coixtlahuaca II (Fig. 86), Lienzo of Tulancingo, Lienzo of Nativitas, and Lienzo of Tlapiltepec (Fig. 90).[21] These lienzos embrace the sequences of action and the ruler lists within the territory to which they pertain, thereby grounding the foundation events and the ruling families to the lands they control.

Lienzo of Philadelphia

This cotton sheet from the Mixteca Baja favors the genealogical or historical over the cartographic (Fig. 87). Instead of a frame of enclosing place signs that outlines a specific territory, nine place signs set the geographic stage, but until these locations are securely identified, we cannot tell whether this is a conceptual presentation of real space or simply a diagram of related events involving the nine places. In the upper half of the lienzo the places can be called (reading from left to right) Hill of a Dead Man with Blond Hair, Serpent Hill, and Corn Plant Place, the latter with a twenty-four-generation genealogy rising from it. In the bottom half, the signs are (clockwise from left) Red and White Platform, Stones and Checkered Stone, Cobweb Valley, Valley, 1 Reed Plain, and Red Circle Hill. The prominent place signs Red and White Platform, Rattlesnake Hill, and Corn Plant Place also appear as central features of the Codex Abraham Castellanos, which led Parmenter (1966: 20–21) to suggest that the lienzo comes from near San Esteban Atlatlauhca, south of Tlaxiaco. Until Corn Plant Place is identified, however, the lienzo cannot be definitely assigned to a specific location (see Smith 1998: 165–172).

On the surface, the narrative appears to be a simple one: lords from Red and White Platform and Hill of a Dead Man with Blond Hair (on the left) journey to the other places where they are seated together as ruling couples, as if they are founding the new towns.[22] The lords on the left, all male, face to the right. Lines of footprints carry them in pairs to the places on the right, where one of each pair becomes or is replaced by a female of the same or a similar name who now sits facing the companion as in marriage.[23] The five small polities in the lower half of the sheet all come directly from Red and White Platform; they apparently left in year 9 Flint day 9 Serpent. In the upper half of the lienzo, the pair from Hill of a Dead Man with Blond Hair initiate the ruler list at Corn Plant Place; this happened in year 4+ (?) day 6 Death (the year date is cut off). Although Caso (1964) and Parmenter (1966: 22) have interpreted the ensuing list of twenty-four rulers as reading up column 1 on the far right, down column 2, up column 3, down column 4, and finally up column 5 in a boustrophedon manner, Smith (1998:

Fig. 86. Lienzo Seler II. Within a cartographic rectangle that defines territory, ruler lists rise upward from place signs; the principal event of foundation is pictured in the lower center, surrounded by the circle of place signs. Photograph courtesy of the Staatliche Museen zu Berlin–Preussischer Kulturbesitz, Museum für Völkerkunde.

172) suggests that all the columns read bottom to top in the usual manner.

Several of the places in the lower half of the lienzo are identical to those that appear in the Vienna Obverse when the Mixteca is being created. Specifically, Caso (1964b) identified Stones and Checkered Stones with the Checkerboard Hill in the Vienna Obverse (45a, 21) and Cobweb Valley with the same place sign in the Vienna Obverse (42b, 7b).[24] He also likened Lord 1 Grass and Lady 1 Eagle in the lienzo to the same pair who appear as ancestral founders at Apoala in the Zouche-Nuttall (16b) and Vienna Obverse (34d–33a, 16a). This suggests to Smith (1998: 165) that the lower half of the lienzo is devoted to the actions of ancient ancestors and the upper half to the ruling dynasty of Corn Plant Place. The other people in the lienzo are not known to be mentioned in extant Mixtec pictorials, which shows the document to have a local perspective.

The Lienzo of Philadelphia may be less a cartographic history than a diagrammatic one, and, indeed, Smith does not see it as a map at all. If the place signs, once they are securely identified, are found not to have a cartographic relation with each other, we will have only a diagram of events rather than a diagram that is also a map. All the places save Serpent Hill are sites of events. The painter has gathered the points of origin on the left and has placed the new polities on the right, with clear lines linking them. The Lienzo of Yolotepec (Caso 1958b) is another diagrammatic history, where people, events, and time flow from point to point across the face of the sheet.

Uniting Lineage with Place

The Mapa de Teozacoalco, the Lienzo of Ihuitlan, and the Lienzo of Philadelphia represent three different solutions to the problem faced by history painters who wanted to unite lineages with place. These solutions also reflect different views, on the part of the painters, about what kinds of documents these were. The Teozacoalco painter runs his columns of rulers beside his map, keeping the two independent until toward the end when he relocates the ruler list to Teozacoalco proper. He sees the map and the ruler list as essentially separate entities. The Ihuitlan painter fills the entire

Fig. 87. Lienzo of Philadelphia. Individuals leave the place signs on the left and travel to those on the right; at Corn Plant Place, twenty-four generations of rulers rise upward from the place sign. Photograph courtesy of the University of Pennsylvania Museum (neg. #58-19821).

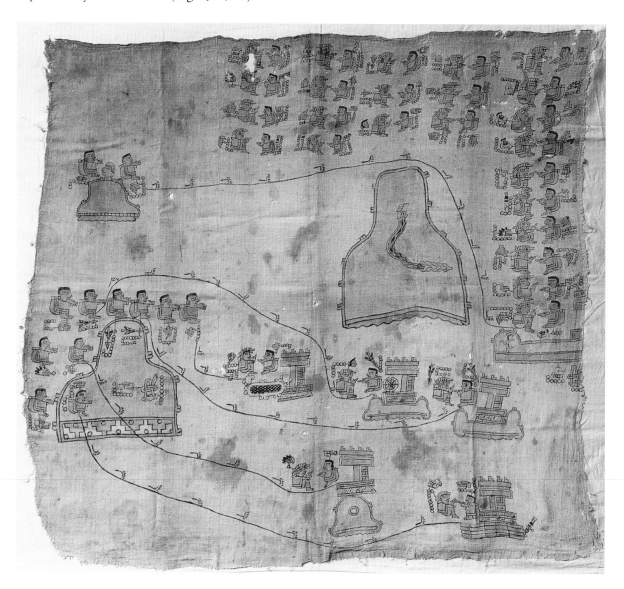

sheet with his map, and then fits the ruler lists and historical events inside it and within the space left between the place signs. This tells us that he sees these ruler lists as inseparable from the map and governed by its spatial framework. He attaches the ruler lists to individual place signs at strategic points, these points being the moments when dynasties began or were renewed or when individuals abandoned their own royal lines to join the lines of different polities. The purpose of this document is to explain precisely how the rulers of many of the towns in the region came from the same two dynasties. For both the Mapa de Teozacoalco and the Lienzo of Ihuitlan, the map is the very reason for the ruler lists; the ruler lists explain the dynastic politics behind the maps. The Teozacoalco map, however, can stand alone without the ruler lists, whereas the Ihuitlan map cannot. Most of the Coixtlahuaca Valley documents and many of the lienzos from elsewhere follow the Ihuitlan format in embedding history within the territorial map.

The painter of the Lienzo of Philadelphia joins place and ruler list together differently. He eschews the frame of place signs that defines territory in the Teozacoalco map and Ihuitlan lienzo and instead includes only those place signs that come with events (excepting Serpent Hill, the largest place sign in the lienzo). Instead of thinking in territorial terms, he concentrates on explaining that supernaturals and lords from two places journey to found other polities. His explanation comes less as a map than as a diagram, one less historically dense and therefore visually looser than the fuller Ihuitlan. He sees his document first as a history and only perhaps secondarily as a map. Relatively fewer lienzos follow this diagrammatic approach.

Lienzos are first and foremost spatial projections. Most project a specific territory as it exists cartographically, usually defining the lands of a community kingdom. To this territory are attached the foundation stories and royal lineages. These three elements—territory, a shared foundation history, and a continuing line of rulers—were the fundamentals by which these people defined their communities and polities.

Supernatural Origins and Rituals of Foundation in Seven Coixtlahuaca Valley Pictorials

A number of documents from the Coixtlahuaca Valley, seven so far, contain nearly identical accounts of the origin of a lineage and kingdom. As Parmenter (1982: 38–44, 62) has pointed out, there are two different stories, two distinct narratives that trace the origins of cults, royal lineages, and community kingdoms in the area.[25] One tells how ancestors emerged out of sacred waters to establish a royal lineage. The other tells how a group of men brought a cult bundle and the accouterments of rulership to a place, where they drilled a new fire and founded a polity. Both stories recall episodes of origin and rites of foundation that we saw in the Vienna Obverse and the Zouche-Nuttall. The documents usually either juxtapose or braid these two stories together, which tells us that the historians understood both to be necessary parts of their cosmogony. They may represent the origins of two lines of descent or the fusion of two methods of reckoning political power.

Four of the manuscripts that record these stories are lienzos, and three are tiras. Although their formats differ, they generally organize the narrative as a *res gestae,* which then sometimes ends as a map. Most follow the origin stories with ruler lists for one or more polities. The manuscripts are as follows:

Codex Baranda (Figs. 74, 104): A hide tira (37 cm × 228 cm) that reads left to right, it opens with a cluster of visual references to both stories, after which it presents two parallel rows of rulers, ending with a single couple who may unite the two lines. The historical events between the rows are unrelated to the opening sacred history (Caso 1958a; Acuña 1989).

Codex Gómez de Orozco: A fragmentary hide tira (21.4 cm × 69.5 cm) painted on both sides, reading left to right, it includes the opening parts of both stories, one on each side of the tira (Caso 1954).

Selden Roll (Fig. 88): A tira of paper (38 cm × 350 cm) that reads from left to right, it begins as a *res ges-*

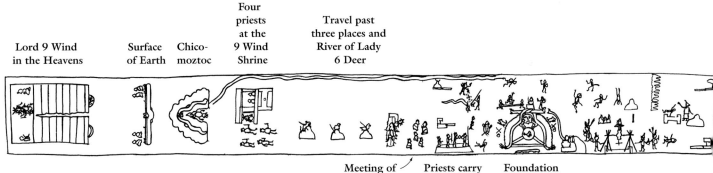

Fig. 88.   Diagram of the Selden Roll. Drawing by John Montgomery.

tae narrative that converts to a map to present the actual founding. It concentrates on the bringing of rulership and a cult to a polity and the ritual of foundation (Burland 1955; Corona-Núñez 1964–1967, 2:101–113; König 1979: esp. 38–44).

Lienzo Seler II (Coixtlahuaca II; Fig. 86): A cloth lienzo (375 cm × 425 cm) whose surface is almost entirely occupied by a cartographic rectangle, with a variety of events recorded at different places. In the lower middle, a circle of place signs defines the space wherein the foundation ritual occurs. Three ruler lists rise from this circle; two other ruler lists (pertaining to Coixtlahuaca) rise on the left, and one short one appears in the lower left (König 1984).

Lienzo of Tequixtepec I (Fig. 89): The cloth lienzo (330 cm × 250 cm) opens in the lower left corner with a *res gestae* narrative in panels that read from left to right across the bottom of the sheet; it presents only the story of the emergence of the ancestors. Thereafter a single ruler list, also in panels, continues in a horizontal boustrophedon (right-left and left-right). Finally a cartographic rectangle, which occupies the upper three-fourths of the lienzo, defines the territory of Tequixtepec and presents the ruling couples (Parmenter 1982).[26]

Lienzo of Tequixtepec II: A relatively narrow cloth lienzo (279 cm × 70 cm), reading from bottom to top vertically, it begins with the ritual of founda-

tion and continues with a vertical ruler list of over fifteen couples (Parmenter 1982: 47, 56–59).

Lienzo of Tlapiltepec (Figs. 90, 91): A cloth lienzo (397 cm × 169 cm), it reads as a *res gestae* narrative from the lower left corner up to the middle left, where it presents foundation scenes. It includes both stories. Then it offers parallel ruler lists for Yucucuy (Cerro Verde) and Miltepec. The right side is a map dotted with towns, ritual and secular events, and short ruler lists (Caso 1961; Parmenter 1982, 1993; Johnson 1994, 1997).

The Dynasty That Emerged from the River

The first story parallels many Mixtec origin stories, where the first ancestors emerge from the earth or waters and give birth to descendants who found polities. This story begins when two ancient forebears, Lord 7 Reed and Lady 4 Movement, emerge from the River of Quetzal Feathers and Jade.[27] Their successors, Lord 7 Jaguar and Lady 1 or 8 Jaguar, are in turn followed by Lord 12 Flint and Lady 12 Flint of a place whose sign combines a hill and a tree that holds a nest or bowl of many curved elements. The 12 Flints' children then found distinguished dynasties.

The Lienzo of Tequixtepec (Fig. 92) and the reverse of the Codex Gómez de Orozco both open with this story. In both, the presentation is in three registers, which are meant to be read simultaneously left to right. The middle register contains the narrative proper.

There on the left, Lord 7 Reed rises unclothed, or relatively so, out of a river characterized by long green feathers and a single large green oval: the River of Quetzal Feathers and Jade. He faces the woman 4 Movement in a marriage statement. Next, to the right, their successors, Lord 7 Jaguar and Lady 1 Jaguar, face each other in a marriage statement. At this point, the Gómez de Orozco manuscript breaks off, but the Tequixtepec lienzo continues the story by presenting the next pair, Lord and Lady 12 Flint, seated facing each other on top of a large place sign. This tall hill, or double mountain with snow-capped peaks, has a distinctive tree growing from its valley, one that bears a bowl containing many U-shaped elements.[28] As the home of the 12 Flints, it is an important sacred/ancestral place, somehow connected to the otherwise unknown Hill

Fig. 89. Lienzo of Tequixtepec I. Origin stories occupy the bottom panels, and twenty-two ruling couples follow sequentially beginning in the lower right. Within the cartographic rectangle that is Tequixtepec's boundaries, two ruling couples are enthroned on the place sign of Tequixtepec. Photograph courtesy of Ross Parmenter.

Ruler lists for
Yucucuy (Cerro Verde)
(left) and
Mitlepec (right)

Map of the
Coixtlahuaca
Valley

Foundation
scene

Places in
Puebla and beyond

Origin
stories

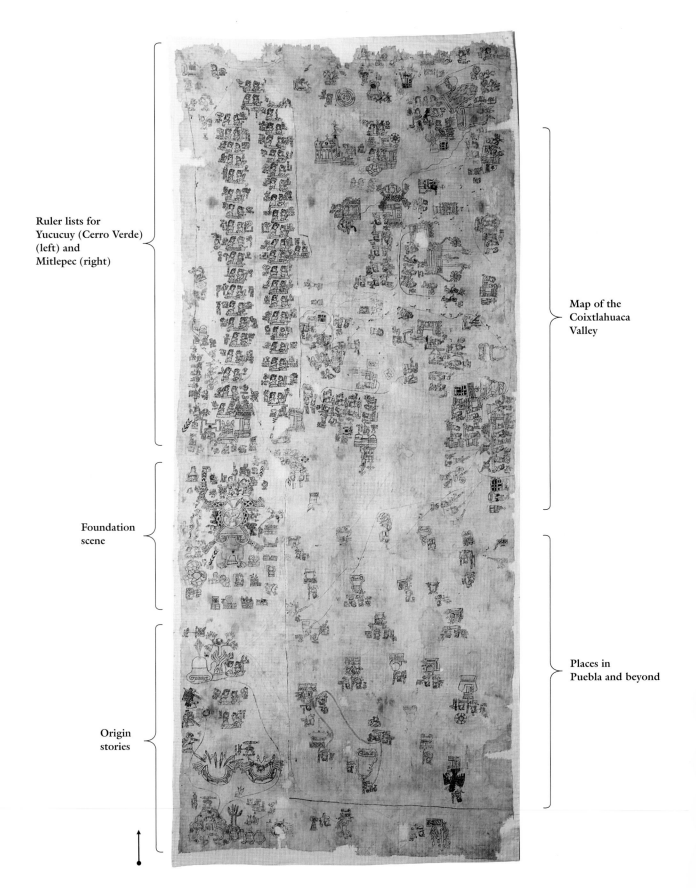

Fig. 90. Lienzo of Tlapiltepec. Reproduced with permission of the Royal Ontario Museum, Toronto, Canada.

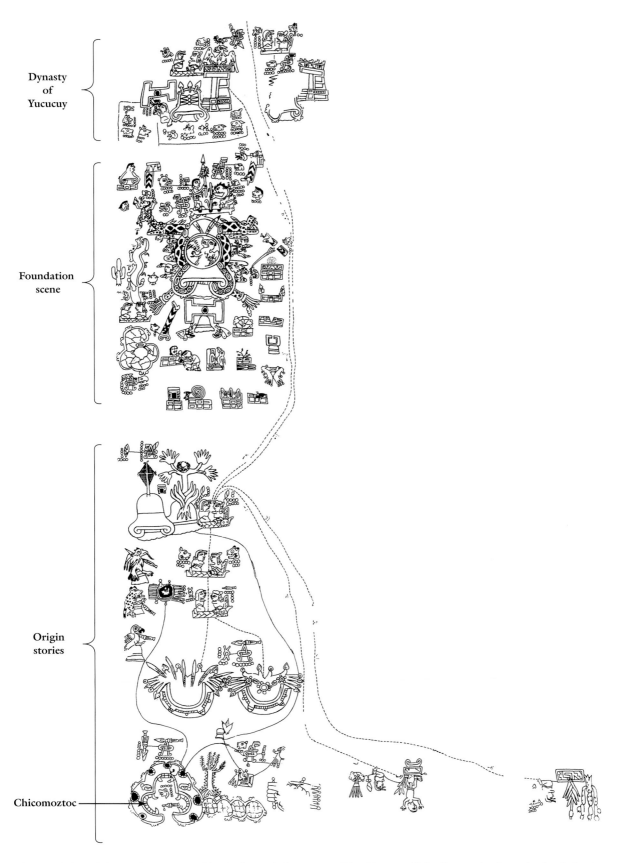

Fig. 91.   The origin stories presented in the lower left quarter of the Lienzo of Tlapiltepec; both stories begin in the lower left corner. Drawing by Nicholas Johnson.

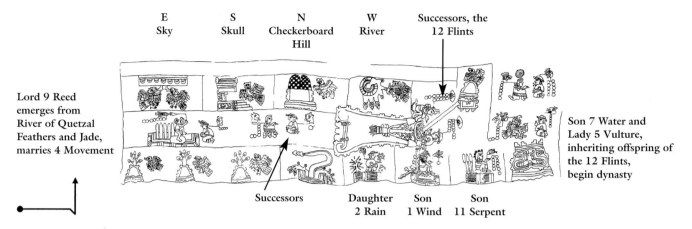

Fig. 92.   The lower section of the Lienzo of Tequixtepec showing the predynastic story in three concurrently running registers (from Parmenter 1982: fig. 33). Reproduced with permission of Ross Parmenter and Dumbarton Oaks.

of Bird and Enclosure. In the lienzo's upper register (Fig. 92), conventional representations of the four cardinal directions (associated here with birds) frame this story of emergence and establishment and perhaps situate it in cosmological terms. The directions are Sky (east) with eagles eating blood, Skull (south) with an owl, Checkerboard Hill (north) with a black and white eagle, and River (west) with another owl.[29] The Gómez de Orozco includes both River (west) and Checkerboard Hill (south) with their birds. In the Tequixtepec lienzo's lower register, the three hills with trees and birds are not understood, nor is the next scene, a river with a serpent's tail.

The three individuals who follow, however, are known. They are the "non-inheriting children of the 12 Flints," to quote Parmenter (1982: 63), offspring of Lord and Lady 12 Flint, who moved elsewhere to join other lineages and did not remain to found the main lineage that follows. Here they are pictured on the place signs of their new homes: Lady 2 Rain "Jeweled Fan" went to Plain of Plant/Running Man, Lord 1 Wind "Flowered Serpent" went to Curved Hill/Water, and Lord 11 Serpent "Jeweled Diadem" went to Place of Rushes (a Tollan).[30] The Gómez de Orozco codex includes only 11 Serpent and 1 Wind before it breaks off. A cave and rampart place sign in the Tequixtepec lienzo then introduces the inheriting line of the 12 Flints' children, beginning with Lord 7 Water and Lady 5 Vulture, who found the dynasty that follows. The Tequixtepec lienzo continues this ruler list through twenty-two successions. Its eleventh and twelfth ruling couples

(3 Lizard and 11 Lizard and their wives) then reappear together on jaguar thrones as rulers of Tequixtepec in the middle of the lienzo's map.[31]

The Lienzo of Tlapiltepec tells this same story slightly differently (Fig. 93). It pictures the River of Quetzal Feathers and Jade as two distinct rivers side by side. Red lines from these rivers extend upward to the couple Lord 7 Reed and Lady 4 Movement, who have emerged. Then a line continues through their successors to the 12 Flints, who are seated beside their place sign; dates mark the events of emerging and founding. From here four other red lines run from the 12 Flints to their four children. Two lines extend to the far lower edge of the lienzo, locating Lady 2 Flint and Lady 11 Serpent (here she is a female) at their new homes;[32] one rises upward, continues between the two columns of rulers, and finally locates the third child, 1 Wind (here also as a female) at a place of a curved hill and a river at the top of the lienzo. The inheriting line rises, too, but leads to the place Caso (1961: 251) identified as Yucucuy (Cerro Verde), the place sign characterized by three pointed leaves (Fig. 94). There the inheriting son 7 Water and his wife 5 Vulture begin the Yucucuy dynasty that rises above. This founding, like so many other Mixtec beginnings, is dated to year 1 Reed day 1 Crocodile.

In its outlines, the story is a simple one. An ancestral couple emerges from a river, has children, and then has grandchildren whose offspring marry into distant lineages and found an important local dynasty.

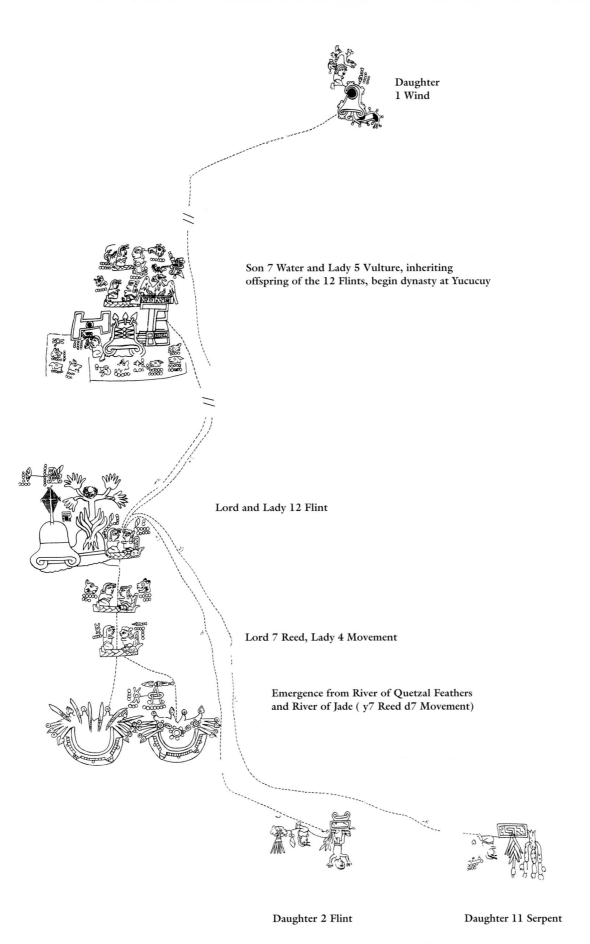

Daughter
1 Wind

Son 7 Water and Lady 5 Vulture, inheriting
offspring of the 12 Flints, begin dynasty at Yucucuy

Lord and Lady 12 Flint

Lord 7 Reed, Lady 4 Movement

Emergence from River of Quetzal Feathers
and River of Jade (y7 Reed d7 Movement)

Daughter 2 Flint   Daughter 11 Serpent

Fig. 93. The story of the dynasty that emerged from the river in the Lienzo of Tlapiltepec. Diagram based on the
drawing by Nicholas Johnson.

Ruler list continues

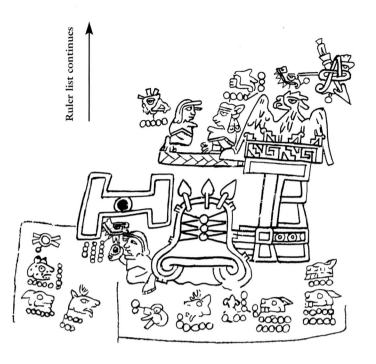

Fig. 94. Lord 7 Water and Lady 5 Vulture begin the dynasty of Yucucuy in the Lienzo of Tlapiltepec. Drawing by Nicholas Johnson.

Bringing and Establishing Sacrality and Rulership

The second story also parallels Mixtec accounts, ones that tell how polities are established through ritual action. The story explains how sacrality and rulership are brought physically to the area. It features the descent of the culture hero 9 Wind (who is so active in the Vienna Obverse) from the heavens and through the earth, to emerge via Chicomoztoc (Seven Caves) into the mundane world. Priests carry his cult bundle and implements of rule past several places until they arrive at a still-unidentified but important location. While others bring rain and groundwater to the area, the priests place 9 Wind's cult bundle, drill a new fire, and found a polity. This tale of divine descent, cave emergence, and the bringing of rulership to a place parallels in a general way the cosmogony of the Vienna Obverse. It is told most completely in the Selden Roll.

The Selden Roll begins with Lord 9 Wind seated at the top of a nine-layered heaven (Fig. 95 left). He is flanked by the ancients Lord and Lady 1 Deer (who also

Fig. 95. The descent of Lord 9 Wind from the heavens and through the earth, emerging via Chicomoztoc in the Selden Roll (from the 1955 edition). The Bodleian Library, Oxford, MS. Arch. Selden. A. 72. Facsimile reproduction © 1955 Gebr. Mann Verlag, Berlin.

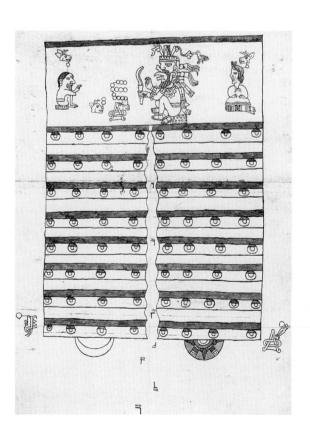

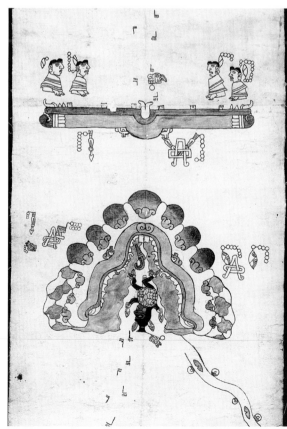

appear in the opening pages of the Vienna Obverse [51a; Fig. 47] seated in the heavens wearing 9 Wind's wind-god mask and headdress). The date in the Selden Roll is a ritual one of origin, year 13 Rabbit day 2 Deer. Another date of origin, year 1 Reed day 1 Crocodile, is recorded on either side of a sun and moon at the base of the heavens. Footprints carry 9 Wind down from the heavens to the earth, presented as the splayed mouth of the earth monster and appropriately named 1 Rabbit. Four men—1 Flint, 7 Flint, 5 Flint, and 12 Flint—sit above the earth. The date is given as year 7 Reed day 7 Reed, another metaphoric creation date (e.g., Vienna Obverse 47b, 45d, etc.). These same scenes are replicated in the opening pages of the obverse of the Codex Gómez de Orozco before that manuscript breaks off, except that the individuals themselves have been erased from the Gómez de Orozco, leaving only their traces and day names.

The Selden Roll narrative passes next to a cave of origin, conceptualized by a large open mouth in the earth and flanked by the metaphoric dates year 8 House days 3 Reed and 4 Jaguar and year 7 Flint day 7 Flint. Within

is one of 9 Wind's curved ear ornaments, evidence of his presence. More prominent is a *yahui* sacrificer named 1 Jaguar, identified by his turtle carapace and the flints on his feet, head, and hands. He emerges from the cave, and the implication is that he carries 9 Wind's cult into the mundane world.

The narrative branches here. One branch follows a path of flints and stars across the top of the roll to the location of the foundation ritual, where the priest 13 Lizard arrives with a cult figure wearing a sawtooth crown (Fig. 100). The main branch, however, follows four priests, all of whom have dark gray body paint, have black face paint around the eyes like a mask, wear sawtooth crowns, and are draped in fasting cords; they are named 13 Lizard, 10 House, 4 Monkey, and 9 Vulture (Fig. 96). In the Selden Roll, they face a cult bundle of 9 Wind at his shrine; perhaps they obtained the bundle from this place, if they did not themselves bring it here.

The opening scene of the Lienzo of Tlapiltepec, in the lower left corner of that great sheet, recounts these episodes but focuses on the cave (Fig. 97). There the

Fig. 96.   The four priests at the 9 Wind shrine in the Selden Roll. The Bodleian Library, Oxford, MS. Arch. Selden. A. 72.

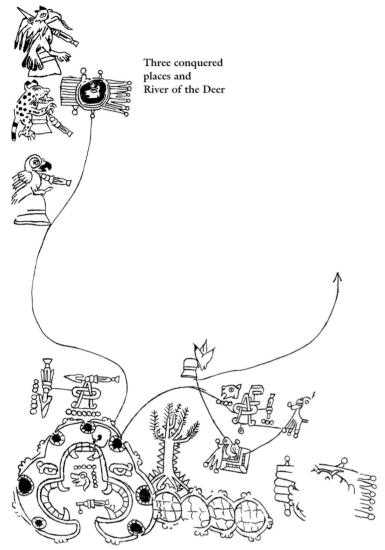

Three conquered
places and
River of the Deer

Chicomoztoc with day dates (personal names) 9 Wind and 1 Reed
inside (y7 Reed d7 Reed)

Fig. 97.   The coming of 9 Wind as told in the Lienzo
of Tlapiltepec. Drawing by Nicholas Johnson.

large open mouth of the earth is embellished with
seven smaller cave openings around it. Inside are the
day names 9 Wind and 1 Reed (9 Wind's Aztec name)
to signal 9 Wind's presence in the cave. The date, year
7 Reed day 7 Reed, associated in the Selden Roll with
9 Wind's passage through the earth, appears here
as well, as do the days 3 Reed and 4 Jaguar year
1/8 House,[33] associated with Chicomoztoc.

The Lienzo of Tlapiltepec and the Selden Roll both
show travel past three conquered places—Hill of the
Jaguar, Hill of the Eagle, and Hill of the Macaw—and

River of Deer/Woman (?), identified by a deer's head
in the lienzo and by a nude woman named 6 Deer in
the roll (Figs. 97, 98). The adjacent scene in the Selden
Roll has all four priests in conference with the archetypal priest-shaman 2 Dog, a supernatural companion
of 9 Wind who performs many rituals in the Vienna
Obverse. The priests are holding thin strips of something, the uppermost inclines his head slightly, and all
have speech scrolls.

This conversation with 2 Dog may well be the opening episode in the entire narrative. Although footprints
carry 9 Wind and the narrative from the heavens to this
meeting, other footprints, closer to the bottom in the
Selden Roll, carry the story from 2 Dog to the heavens. This suggests that 2 Dog may have instructed
the priests wearing the sawtooth crowns to obtain
9 Wind's cult from the heavens, which they then did. If
so, this would explain why the Lienzo of Tlapiltepec
(Fig. 97) has two lines connected to Chicomoztoc: the
line on the left may begin rather than end at the River
of the Deer; the one on the right then leaves Chicomoztoc, on the days 3 Reed and 4 Jaguar in the year
1/8 House. In the Selden Roll, immediately after their
conversation with 2 Dog, the priests appear for the first
time actually carrying the cult bundle of 9 Wind, along
with implements to be used in founding a town
(Fig. 99). They emerge from an opening in the earth.
The first carries the cult bundle and staff and an incense pouch; the second and third carry herbs, a shield,
and a great arrow or spear; the fourth bears the fire-
drilling board, a long-handled incense pan, and a
conch shell trumpet. These are the same implements
usually brought to locations for foundation rituals in
the Vienna Obverse and Zouche-Nuttall (Boone n.d.;
see Chapter 5).

This bringing of the cult objects now culminates in
the large foundation scene that occupies the rest of the
Selden Roll and the equally prominent scene that dominates the left side of the Tlapiltepec lienzo (Figs. 100,
101). The location's place sign is a large hill crossed by
great serpents, one of flints and one of curls (perhaps
representing smoke or clouds); the Selden Roll shows
two of each type of serpent. In the middle of the hill
sign, a circular cartouche frames a parrot or quetzal.
The Selden Roll also features the monumental frontal
face and arms of a human who has fanged teeth and
black paint around its eyes similar to the face paint of

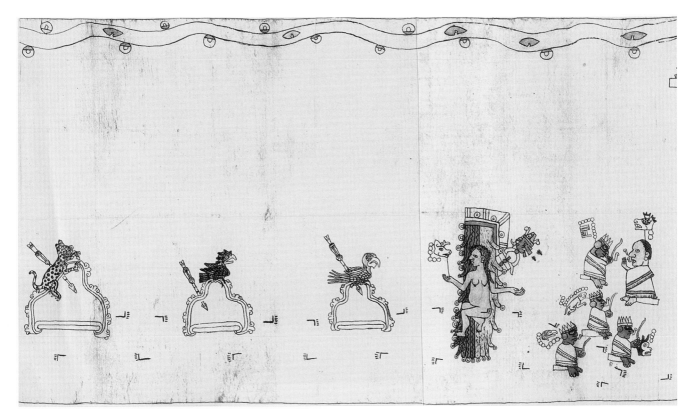

Fig. 98. Travel past three conquered places and the meeting of four priests with Lord 2 Dog in the Selden Roll (from 1955 edition). The Bodleian Library, Oxford, MS. Arch. Selden. A. 72. Facsimile reproduction © 1955 Gebr. Mann Verlag, Berlin.

the priests; on either side, springing jaguars, shields, and crossed arrows or spears signal war. The place sign in the Lienzo of Tlapiltepec lacks the frontal face and jaguars but adds eagle and *yahui* sacrificers flying out of the sides of the place sign. Parmenter (1993: 35; also reported in Jansen and Gaxiola 1978: 14) has proposed the location may be Ñaate, a prominent hill near Tlapiltepec.

In both representations, the actual ritual takes place on top of the place sign. The Selden Roll shows the cult bundle of 9 Wind, now holding the arrow or spear that one of the priests has brought, firmly situated on a platform. Immediately to the left, the priests 9 Vulture and 4 Monkey hold the drilling board while 10 House drills a new fire. The fourth priest, 13 Lizard, arrives at the top of the scene carrying another cult bundle. The date is year 10 House day 4 Lizard. The same participants drill fire in the Lienzo of Tlapiltepec: priest 10 House raises the staff prior to setting it in the ground (here the staff is like the red quincunx staffs

Fig. 99. The four priests carrying the cult bundle of 9 Wind and the implements of rule in the Selden Roll. The Bodleian Library, Oxford, MS. Arch. Selden. A. 72.

Fig. 100.   The foundation scene in the Selden Roll. Above the elaborate place sign is the cult bundle of 9 Wind (year 10 House day 4 Lizard); three priests participate in the fire drilling (*to the left*), while the fourth (*upper left*) brings another cult bundle. The Bodleian Library, Oxford, MS. Arch. Selden. A. 72.

that mark foundation rituals in the Zouche-Nuttall [15–19, 21–22]), while priest 13 Lizard actually drills the fire. Priests 9 Vulture and 4 Monkey are represented only by their day names on either side of the drilling; the date above them is the same year 10 House day 4 Lizard of the Selden Roll.

Around this climactic scene in both manuscripts are other elements that contribute to the foundation. The Selden Roll presents what I suggest is the act of bring-

ing life-sustaining waters to the area (Fig. 102). To the left of the fire drilling, a Raingod priest or supernatural named 7 House shakes the severed head of another rain god until water sprinkles out of the neck. Below this a man named 4 Crocodile—characterized by a beard, turquoise diadem, and warrior's topknot—has cut in half a great serpent, from which water now flows. The males appear to be bringing rain and groundwater respectively to the area. Although the Tlapiltepec lienzo

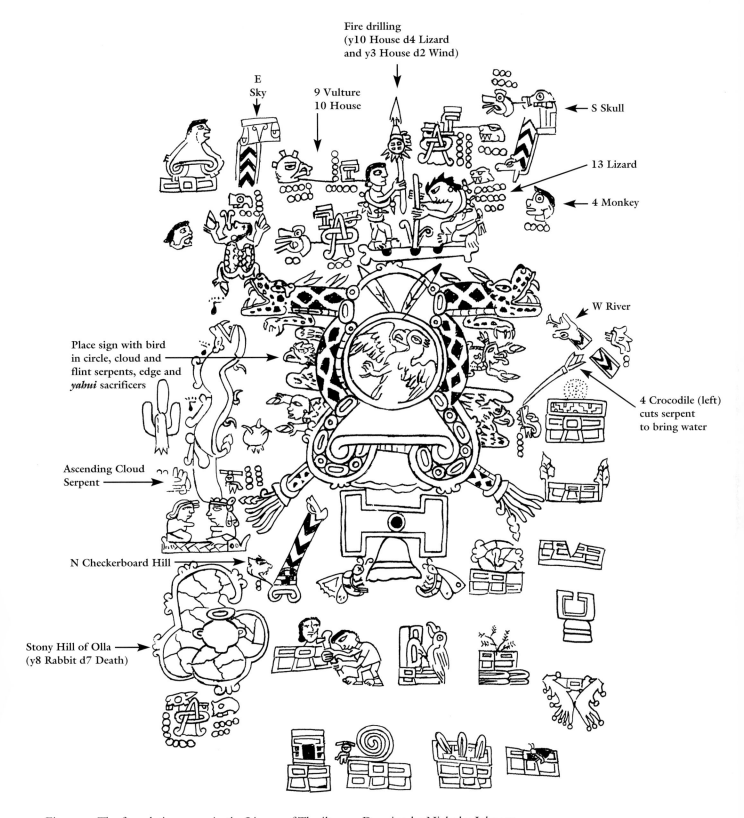

Fire drilling
(y10 House d4 Lizard
and y3 House d2 Wind)

E
Sky

9 Vulture
10 House

S Skull

13 Lizard

4 Monkey

W River

Place sign with bird
in circle, cloud and
flint serpents, edge and
yahui sacrificers

4 Crocodile (left)
cuts serpent
to bring water

Ascending Cloud
Serpent

N Checkerboard Hill

Stony Hill of Olla
(y8 Rabbit d7 Death)

Fig. 101. The foundation scene in the Lienzo of Tlapiltepec. Drawing by Nicholas Johnson.

Fig. 102. The bringing of waters to the land in the Selden Roll; 4 Crocodile cuts a serpent to release water, while 7 House drips liquid from a Raingod head. The Bodleian Library, Oxford, MS. Arch. Selden. A. 72.

does not detail these acts, it does include, to the right of the place sign, the severed serpent, the long shovel or digging stick, and 4 Crocodile's name (Fig. 101). The Selden Roll also shows how 4 Crocodile's companions participate in the conquest and pacification of the area.

Place signs and flora around the central scene reveal more about the area. Cacti pictured to the left of the scene in both manuscripts suggest an arid climate. A ball court is on the right in the Selden Roll and just below in the lienzo. A distinctive place or nearby places is the Stony Hill of the Olla and the Ascending Cloud (?) Serpent, which are separate in the lienzo but conflated in the roll, where the serpent rises out of the open mouth of a man in the olla. The metaphoric date asso-

ciated with this place or places in both documents is year 1/8 Rabbit day 7 Death. Around the edges of the larger foundation scene, and at the four corners in the Selden Roll, are place signs representing the cardinal directions (Figs. 101, 103). In both manuscripts, they have chevron bands attached, symbolizing not conquests but that this founding takes place in an area with enemies all around. Sky and Skull are easily recognizable at the top edge in the lienzo and at the right edge on the roll. Opposite, the Tlapiltepec lienzo has Checkerboard Hill (attached to the day/name 2 Dog) and River (conflated with the act of cutting the serpent to draw water). The Selden Roll presents a Hill with Knots (instead of Checkerboard Hill) and River. These cardinal directions add an air of universality to the foundation ritual, for they suggest that this arid land extends to the four quarters.

Both the Lienzo Seler II and the Codex Baranda contain parts of both stories. The Lienzo Seler II (Fig. 86) begins the first story outside its cartographic rectangle in the lower right corner of the sheet. There the 12 Flints and their predecessors appear near Chicomoztoc at the River of Quetzal Feathers and River of Jade; lines of footprints then locate the noninheriting children at their new homes elsewhere on the sheet. The inheriting son, 7 Water, and his wife, 5 Vulture, begin the central genealogy in the middle of the sheet. The foundation ritual takes place in the middle of the sheet just below this ruler list, where the four priests drill the new fire above the large place sign of the intertwined serpents; a shield and spear speak of conquests. To the lower left of this foundation, a short ruler list is presented for the Stony Hill of the Olla, whose founda-

Fig. 103. The place signs of the cardinal directions in the Selden Roll. Drawing by John Montgomery.

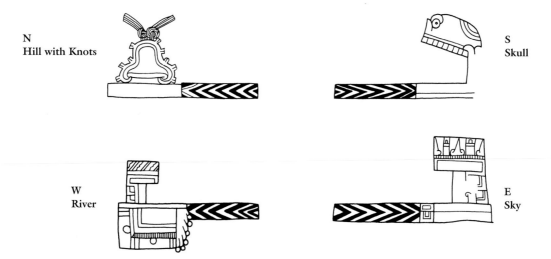

N
Hill with Knots

S
Skull

W
River

E
Sky

tion is dated, like it is in the others, to year 1 Rabbit day 7 Death.

The Codex Baranda contains less a pictorial telling of the stories than a cluster of visual, shorthand references to them (Figs. 74, 104). The first story is recalled by the day names for Lord 7 Reed and 4 Movement who emerged from the rivers (these rivers perhaps symbolized by the two place signs at the upper left), by the distinctive tree at which the 12 Flints reside, and by the tower with three arrows (which Johnson [personal communication 1997] identifies as Miltepec or Arrow Hill). More elements pertain to the second story, which opens with the dates 1 Reed 1 Crocodile in the upper left next to the sun and 13 Rabbit 2 Deer below

the sun, which signal 9 Wind's descent from the heavens. The two 1 Flint dates may refer to the Flint men along the earth band in the Selden Roll, or, more probably, as Johnson suggests, to the 8 Flint 8 Flint date of the primordial 12 Flint couple (Lienzo of Tlapiltepec). Immediately the Baranda jumps to the founding itself, represented by the hill with crossed serpents, topped by a face, with rampant jaguars and *yahui* priests (in their turtle guise) on either side. Beside it sit the four priests themselves, who are named slightly differently than in the other manuscripts. The Stony Hill of the Olla appears above them. The episode whereby water is brought to the land is emphasized in the Baranda by the great serpent whose body is severed to release water.

Fig. 104. The stories of origin in the Codex Baranda. CNCA.-INAH.-MEX; reproduced with permission of the Instituto Nacional de Antropología e Historia.

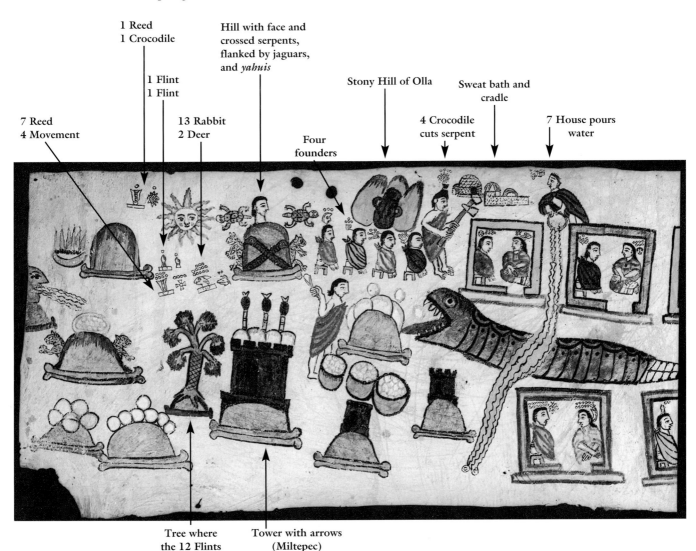

Above the serpent's head stands the man 4 Crocodile, holding his weapon aloft (here a long ax), while the man 7 House pours water from a bowl. The Baranda artist adds a sweatbath and cradle to this story of origins and foundation; these are both appropriate embellishments symbolizing birth, for new mothers take sweatbaths after giving birth.

The foundation story included in these manuscripts thus details how four priests physically brought the cult of 9 Wind and established it at this place of the intertwined serpents. After rain and groundwater are brought forth, a new fire is drilled to inaugurate the place as a polity. This story essentially parallels the accounts of foundation told in the Vienna Obverse and several times in the Zouche-Nuttall. It represents a widespread understanding in the Mixteca and southern Puebla that places become polities when sacrality (in the form of a cult bundle) and rulership (in the form of implements of rule) are brought to a location, a ritual is accomplished, and a new fire is drilled to begin the new era (Boone n.d.). Life-sustaining water must also be brought by supernaturals (or their agents), who are crucial participants in this entire process.

Two Stories of Origin

These Coixtlahuaca Valley documents, like the Mixtec historical screenfolds, explain the origins of rulership and political power. They do so by presenting two stories, each different in the nature of its participants and the kind of events it details, which were shared as cosmogonies by many polities in the valley. Although not all the manuscripts recount both stories, both stories seem to have figured in the legendary pasts of the valley towns. One speaks of rulers, and the other speaks of sacrality and polity.

The first story focuses on the rulers themselves, telling how ancient forebears emerged from a sacred river. It traces these ancestors to Lord and Lady 12 Flint, residents of an important place, whose offspring go near and far to found or join major dynasties. Their principal heir founds the dynasty of Yucucuy (Cerro Verde in the southwestern corner of the Coixtlahuaca Valley), a lineage that is featured prominently in the Lienzo of Tlapiltepec and Lienzo Seler II (among others) and that leads into the Coixtlahuaca lineage in the Ihuitlan lienzo (Fig. 85, column 1). This story of ances-

tral emergence is not unlike those told briefly in the opening pages of the Codex Selden, Codex Bodley, and Codex Zouche-Nuttall.

The second story is more territorially based, focusing on the bringing of a cult and government or polity to a specific place. The story may actually begin, if we can trust the footprints in the Selden Roll, when the supernatural Lord 2 Dog bids four priests to seek the cult of 9 Wind. They journey to the heavens and cause 9 Wind to descend from the celestial realm, passing through the earth to emerge through Chicomoztoc, a legendary origin point. The story then details how they carry 9 Wind's bundle and implements of rule to a place of interlocked serpents, which seems to represent the origin point for many polities in the area. They bring forth waters, establish the cult, drill a new fire, and defeat supernatural and human enemies, thereby establishing polity as a religious and governmental institution. This is essentially the same story that is told in the Vienna Obverse, when 9 Wind descends to create and order the lands of the Mixteca, and in the Zouche-Nuttall when other supernaturals descend to bring the implements of rule to new polities.

The two stories work together to provide the elements necessary for rulership. One contributes the fact of lineage from divine ancestors who emerged from the earth. The other contributes the cult of a principal supernatural, the bringing of waters, and the ritual of foundation. On the legendary foundation provided by these stories, the history painters can then build the lists of subsequent rulers and can define their lands.

The three elements of sacred history, ruling lineage, and territory are the subject focus of the lienzos from Oaxaca and southern Puebla. These lienzos present the origin stories and the foundation events of a community, either by picturing them in some detail or by recording a date, personage (supernatural or otherwise), or event that signals the fuller story. They recount the continuing line of rule by picturing the successively ruling couples usually stacked one above the other on top of the polity's place sign in lists that can rise through dozens of successions; these lists pronounce that the ruling lineages figuratively grow from that place. Ultimately, the lienzos tie these events and people to the lands of their community, which are usually described cartographically as a conceptual map of the territory; this map makes clear the extent of the community's holdings. Some lienzos (e.g., Tequixtepec) begin with origin stories and ruler lists that are distinct from and prior to the map of the territory. Others (e.g., Ihuitlan), however, embrace the events and rulers within the map itself, effectively grounding these narrative elements at specific locations. Regardless of the format, the lienzos unite the three elements that defined polity and community for their people.

The tiras feature the same elements of foundation history, ruling lineage, and land, except that the land they define is usually represented by its place sign rather than by a map of its territorial extent. Both the tiras and lienzos functioned as community charters for their polities, locating their communities in space and time by tying the town in question to its sacred past and its continuing line of rulers.

7

Stories of Migration, Conquest, and Consolidation in the Central Valleys

The cartographic histories from the central valleys of Mexico and Puebla share many features of form, structure, and content with the lienzos from Oaxaca and southern Puebla. Like their counterparts to the southeast, they are founded on a broad cartographic presentation of land, sometimes delineated as a territory by a circuit of place signs. The histories join this spatial projection with a *res gestae* narrative that can lead up to the cartograph, can track through it, or can merge completely with it and thereby define it. One sees in these histories the union of a map with a sequence or sequences of events. Too, the Central Mexican cartographic histories focus, like the lienzos, on the founding of polities.

Similarities between the two genres tend to fall away after this, however, for the Central Mexican documents pertain more to the Aztec sphere and address particularly Aztec historical concerns, whereas the lienzos of Oaxaca and southern Puebla are more culturally Mixtec. The Aztec map-based histories tend also to be painted on native paper, or occasionally hide, rather than the cloth preferred in Oaxaca. The Aztec documents discussed in this chapter do not feature long columns of couples who rule carefully circumscribed territories. Rather, in telling stories about the migration, conquest, and consolidation of their *altepetl*, they

focus on the movement of people through legendary and real space and on their actions within this space. The protagonists of these Aztec histories are the people themselves rather than their gods or supernatural ancestors (as is more the case in the Mixtec stories). Patron deities may be the driving force behind a move, and priests may appear as bearers of cult images, but the gods themselves keep in the background. These stories concern themselves with the physical actions of clan and tribal leaders and their followers—heroic humans who may be led by divine guidance. The purpose of these histories is to describe the migrations of people from idealized and sacred points of origin to their final homelands and then usually to explain how the people settle, define their territory, and create an independent *altepetl*.

The migrations in these pictorial accounts originate in a sacred earthly place, either a place of departure where the people actually emerge from the earth or an ancestral homeland. Many stories told pictorially and in prose identify the point of departure as Chicomoztoc (Seven Caves), a legendary and in many ways metaphoric place of origin from which the tribal leaders emerged. Chicomoztoc figures prominently in such migration accounts as a great, multipocketed opening into the earth, usually pictured as the maw of the earth monster. At the same time, the Mexica Aztecs and others who migrated into the Valley of Mexico also specified Aztlan as their ancestral homeland, characterizing Aztlan as an island city in the middle of a lake, a place of abundance, a home of reeds and herons. Although several Aztec prose sources speak of Chicomoztoc as a place of origin, the pictorials and the prose sources that actually detail the migration of the Mexica of Tenochtitlan all begin with these people's departure from Aztlan. From Aztlan, the Mexica migration accounts tell us, also came the Xochimilca, Chalca, Tepaneca, Acolhua, Cuitlahuaca, Huexotzinca, Matlatzinca, and Malinalca, among others.[1] Chicomoztoc, when it is featured in these Aztlan migration stories, then appears as a later stage of the journey.

Two complementary truths are operating concurrently here. The first is the general understanding of the Central Mexicans that their ancestors emerged from Chicomoztoc. The second is the Aztec understanding that they specifically came from Aztlan. The rationale for these migrations is the peoples' understanding that they came from elsewhere and journeyed long and hard to reach their present homeland. This perspective is very different from that of the Mixtecs, whose towns of origin are within the Mixteca and whose histories explain how the ancient ancestors emerged from the land, waters, and trees of the very locale where they live. As Mary Elizabeth Smith has said conversationally, the Aztec story is "We walked a long way to get here," whereas the Mixtec story is "We have lived here all the time."

Once the people have arrived at their general destination, the Aztec cartographic histories then show the founding of polities, and in this respect they are similar to the lienzos of Chapter 6. Usually they picture and name the founders seated near the place sign of the new *altepetl* and describe the conquest of any competing peoples in the area. Then sometimes they encircle these actions with a circuit of boundaries joined by lines of footprints. This circuit effectively defines the territory geographically at the same time that it records the act of delimiting it.

These cartographic histories and migration stories cater to the documentary needs of the Central Mexican *altepetl*, and, as Pohl (1994b: 93, 109–111) has pointed out, these needs were different from those of the equivalent Mixtec community kingdoms. Whereas the Mix-

tec rulers claimed authority through a reckoning of divine descent and according to a strict pattern of inheritance, the Nahua rulers of Central Mexico made no such claims. They ruled because their ancestors had emerged from Chicomoztoc or departed from Aztlan and migrated to the new land where they conquered and settled.

Nahua ideas of royal succession also differed from those of their contemporaries in Oaxaca (Spores 1984: 302–303). Among the Nahuas, rulership could, and often did, pass from brother to brother rather than strictly from father to eldest son. On the death of a *tlatoani,* the council of elders elected a new ruler from a group of equally eligible family members, including uncles, brothers, and sons. Thus when Chimalpopoca (the third Mexica *tlatoani*) died, his uncle Itzcoatl was elected, followed by Chimalpopoca's brother Moctezuma Ilhuicamina and then Itzcoatl's son Axayacatl (Carrasco 1971: 350). For the Mexica, it was not even necessary that both parents be royals; Durán (1994: 71) notes, for example, that Itzcoatl was born of a slave woman from Azcapotzalco. Although rulers were usually chosen from the same royal family, succession was based more on accomplishment and suitability for office than on primogeniture. The histories reflect this situation, for they focus more on the deeds of the rulers than on their bloodlines. Detailed genealogies and long ruler lists of the kind that were so fundamental to the Mixtec screenfolds and lienzos are not a central feature of Aztec histories.[2]

This is not to say that the Aztecs ignored bloodlines. To the contrary, claiming Chichimec origins as former hunter-gatherers, they considered it important that their rulers also have Toltec ancestry. This blood heritage from the fabled Toltecs ran through the royal families of older, more established cities such as Culhuacan (Place of Those with Ancestors), and the Aztec rulers married into this line many times. For example, Acamapichtli, the first Mexica *tlatoani,* was the son of the Culhua ruler's daughter, who had married a Mexica warrior. Acamapichtli himself married another Culhua princess.[3] This pattern of newcomers marrying into the old Toltec lines is also a feature of the Texcocan histories. For the Aztecs, it was important to be both Chichimec and Toltec. A number of pictorial and alphabetic histories speak to this point, although they do not digress much into family genealogies.

One sees the cultural shift to the Nahua-speaking world of the Aztecs from the Mixtec-, Zapotec-, and Chocho-speaking world of their southern neighbors by the simple shift in naming practices. Whereas the southerners used their calendrical names, the Aztecs always used their personal names. Only for a very few Nahuas (e.g., Nezahualcoyotl [Fig. 26d]) do we even know the individual's calendrical name.

The migration was a crucial feature of all the Nahua accounts of the past, and there were multiple migrations, not simply one. Each people had its own distinct migration and arrival, and each historical account stresses the separateness of these journeys. The accounts of the Mexica migration often identify the other groups who left Aztlan, but these accounts are careful to differentiate each group and explain that they departed at different times and followed different routes, the Mexica departing last. Each polity, then, celebrated its own migration. As Schroeder (1991: 123–124) has pointed out, the fact of having arrived separately was an important factor in achieving or retaining independent *altepetl* status in the early colonial period. The Chalcan historian Chimalpahin, Schroeder's source, tells how Viceroy Mendoza asked a Xochimilcan notable to investigate the disorganized political situation of Amaquemecan in the 1540s. Schroeder says, "One important item on the judge's agenda was to determine if the five altepetl had separate 'arrivals'" (p. 123). The legitimacy of one *altepetl* was suspect because it lacked a separate migration.[4] By stressing separate migrations in their histories, the *altepetl* are asserting original and continual autonomy. Such histories carry the claim that these polities have always, from the point of origin, been independent and self-reliant.

The Combination of Circuit and Map

The cartographic histories from the central valleys place great emphasis on place. Geography, whether it is Cartesian or conceptual, governs the presentations. Places are arranged on the sheet in a spatial relationship to each other. Then events are attached to the places where they occur. The reader thus understands the spatial relationships between places and their events. There is no event without a place, although there may be places without events, which add to the physical or ideological description of the area. Events in these histories are subsumed by location, because what happens is less important than where it happens. The emphasis is less on the uniqueness of the event itself and the details of its action than on the fact that it occurred in a certain location.

In many ways the places in the cartographic histories become mnemonic cues to the events that occurred there. In this sense, the places are "sites of memory," to use Leibsohn's (1993: 182) phrase, places that have absorbed the power of the people who have been there and the events that have happened there. Throughout Mesoamerica, certain places carried meaning as homes of ancestral or tutelary gods, as openings to the earth lord, or as locales of crucial action or ritual (e.g., Vogt 1981: 119–126; Broda, Carrasco, and Matos 1987: 89). This, of course, is not a solely Mesoamerican perspective. Cultural anthropologists studying the Western Apache (Basso 1984: 22–23, 45), the Arunda of Australia (Tuan 1990: 99–100), and the Melanesians of Papua New Guinea (Rodman 1992: 650–651), for example, have noted how these people use locations in their cultural landscape as codes for important legendary events; journeys through the landscape or views of it call up the stories of the sites. The Apache landscape is thus "a repository of distilled wisdom," a keeper of historical tradition, where stories are irrevocably tied to individual locations (Basso 1984: 45). Even those of us who are no longer close to the land and who have been educated to view places as coordinates on a map automatically link some places with specific events in the collectively learned past. For people educated in U.S. history, the sites of Pearl Harbor and Appomattox are mentally inseparable from the Japanese air strike and Lee's surrender to Grant; Gettysburg resonates both with the devastating Civil War battle and Lincoln's address, which itself consciously drew upon the older attachment. For a great many people, places call up the significant events that have occurred there.

This unity of event and place also works the other way. Locations become marked and differentiated from the land around them because something happened there, and they are organized together in a history because this history tells of these happenings (Bruner 1984: 5). As Leibsohn (1995: 269) argues for one of the Cuauhtinchan maps included in the Historia Tolteca-Chichimeca, "terrain [represented by a sequence of place signs] unfolds because a suite of significant events calls these particular sites together." She proposes that "history is a pretext for geography" in these maps because the painted "landscapes are produced by narratives that disclose events that transpire at the feet of certain mountains, along the banks of specific rivers, and within the boundaries of individual communities." In these instances, the point is not that the place recalls the event, but that the event requires the place to be identified.

The spatial compositions created by this unity of event and place are not geometrically accurate as in the modern sense of a map. Instead, places and actions are put into an abstract and conventional spatial relation to each other. These arrangements may be cognitive maps, approximating to greater or lesser degrees the actual geography of a territory, as in the Mapa de Teozacoalco or the Lienzo of Ihuitlan (Figs. 76, 80), or they can take the form of a sequence of locations, virtually a listing of places that traces a route, as in the first part of the Selden Roll (Figs. 95, 98). Leibsohn (1995: 269), in discussing the migration histories in the Historia Tolteca-Chichimeca, has invoked Michele de Certeau's (1984: 115–130) distinction between a tableau and a tour to highlight these two types of cartographic presentations. Certeau's tableau is a preexisting spatial abstraction, like a map in the modern sense, through which one's movement can be charted from location to location. His notion of tour is the sequence of locations through which one actually travels, which reveal themselves only when they are reached. Robertson (1959: 180) earlier compared this sequence of places, this itinerary, to a railroad map, where "the stations are in a sequence, but the distances on the map are not representative of the distances between the stations." As Robertson points out, the tour, itinerary, or circuit presents a path that is "always more regular and direct than the actual path," one that regularizes the irregularity of nature. In a tour, place signs are presented as equals, regularly spaced and evenly sized regardless of the size and complexity of the actual location. As Leibsohn (1995: 269) points out, the tour or itinerary yields toponomy rather than topography.

The findings of the anthropologist Vishvajit Pandya about the cultural construction of space by the Ongees, hunter-gatherers of Little Andaman in the Bay of Bengal, may be relevant here. Pandya (1990: 777, 793) notes that the Ongees "define space through the practice of movement," so their maps are "not of places in space but of movements in space." He explains:

> There is a fundamental difference between the way we map places in a space and the way the Ongees do. When we draw maps to show a pattern of movement or for navigation, we first plot space and then mark the route through it. . . . The Ongees do just the reverse when they draw maps. . . . [A]n Ongee will first plot out movement. The types of lines he or she uses to plot movement index the places through which the lines pass. Finally, the combination of lines will lead him or her to demarcate various places, the sum total of which paradigmatically constitutes space. An Ongee . . . first plots a route and then marks the space. (p. 784)

The itinerary or circuit maps of the cartographic histories do the same.

The temporal element of sequence enters these two kinds of cartographic presentations because events usually occur at one place before the others. Sequence is usually very clear in an itinerary presentation where a road marked by footprints links the place signs and events as coming before or after the ones next to them. It is much less clear in map or tableau presentations, where many competing paths and sequences can weave a web of contemporaneity. Duration, so difficult to achieve in a cartographic history, can be conveyed by the addition of dates or blue disks that signal the years that have passed.

These tour and tableau formats can take their places in a cartographic history as separate entities that do not overlap appreciably. Such is the situation with the Selden Roll, where the tour leads directly to the tableau (Fig. 88). The two formats can also be combined or blended, with circuits running through the geographically arranged map, generating a tension between one and the other. In these compositional and formal respects, the cartographic histories of the central valleys are not unlike the lienzos from the Mixteca and Puebla. They tell only slightly different stories.

A major feature of the cartographic histories is that they present the beginning and the end of a story within the same visual composition. They treat the story as a single entity that is divisible into parts, and they diagram these parts as a single presentation. This allows the reader to see the story's shape, to note the opening, middle, and closing. The stories told by the cartographic histories have conclusions. Their narratives do not simply cease, as is the case with so many *res gestae* and annals presentations. Rather the onset of the action and everything that follows lead directly to a culminating event or cluster of events. The diagrammatic nature of the cartographic histories gives all this information simultaneously to the reader, who interprets it and digests it at his or her own pace. The reader, not the painter, chooses the order of reading.

The seven cartographic histories discussed below represent the range—in terms of both content and structure—of this Aztec historical genre. Most are migration histories, although some use the migration more as a prelude to the *altepetl*'s history after its founding. Several of these documents are also included here because they have been little studied and only poorly reproduced, yet are important for understanding Aztec history and historiography. The Mapa Sigüenza is highlighted both because it is the only cartographic account of the Mexica migration from Aztlan and because its structure provided me with the key to understanding the narrative structure of several other manuscripts. The three cartographic histories from the *altepetl* of Cuauhtinchan in the Puebla Valley near Cholula are among the half-dozen pictorial histories that have survived from this town; although Cuauhtinchan Map 2, the Mapa Pintado, and the Map of Cuauhtinchan's Founding all tell of the founding of Cuauhtinchan, they show how easy it was for the ancient historians to emphasize different aspects of this past and to format their stories differently. The three Texcocan cartographs—Codex Xolotl, Mapa Tlotzin, and Mapa Quinatzin—also form their own subgenre; as complementary documents, they each highlight a different part of Texcoco's past by tracking *res gestae* narratives and locating diagrams on spatial projections of territory. There is less uniformity among the corpus of Aztec cartographic histories than there is among the Oaxacan and Pueblan lienzos.

The Mapa Sigüenza

The Mapa Sigüenza begins as a circuit and ends as a map (Fig. 105). Painted on a single sheet of fine native paper (54.5 cm × 77.5 cm) with a delicate hand, it covers the Mexica migration from Aztlan to Tenochtitlan. Over 400 years of migration history are presented here, if one judges time by the eight bundles of reeds marking the binding of the years at the close of the 52-year cycle, which are attached to various places. The right half of the sheet and the top of the left half are occupied by the departure from Aztlan and the itinerary of the journey, whereas the middle and lower area of the left half gives itself over to a map of the southern region of Lake Texcoco, through which the action moves. The Mapa's story has many elements in common with other pictorial accounts of the Mexica migration, but it varies from the others by naming different places along the route and different representatives for the group.[5] Because it has not been adequately published and lacks a full commentary, I will discuss it in some detail.

The story opens in the upper right quadrant, where the Aztecs leave their mythical island homeland (Fig. 106). Aztlan is rendered as a hill sign topped by a plant with feathery foliage and surrounded by the watery square of a lake. Just outside the upper right corner of the lake sits the curved hill sign of Culhuacan, in this case an ancestral or sacred Culhuacan named in the prose sources Teoculhuacan (e.g., Durán 1994: 10; Chimalpahin 1965: 65). This ancient Culhuacan is linked to Aztlan in a number of accounts (e.g., Anales de Tlatelolco 1948: 31; Historia de los Mexicanos por Sus Pinturas 1979: 39; Codex Boturini 1, see Chapter 8), and Durán even says that Teoculhuacan was also called Aztlan. Attached to the lake below this is one of the bundles of reeds, pictured here as a full plant with its roots and root ball and with the foliage bound by a knotted rope, which signals the binding of years at the close of a cycle. Within the lake, the heads and attached name signs of a man (on the left) and a woman (on the right) represent the residents of Aztlan.[6] The migration itself begins with the act of canoeing across the lake, represented by a human lying in a canoe below Aztlan's hill sign.

Then, disguised as a large white bird, the tribal deity Huitzilopochtli perches atop the plant of Aztlan's place

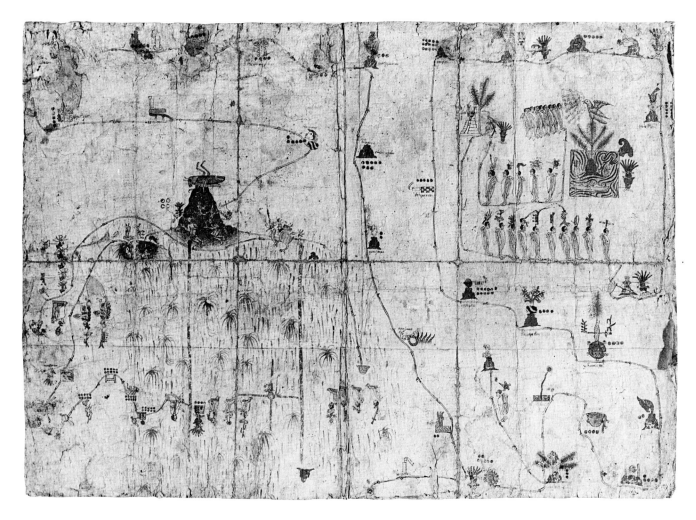

Fig. 105. Mapa Sigüenza. CNCA.-INAH.-MEX; reproduced with permission of the Instituto Nacional de Antropología e Historia.

sign and commands a crowd of Aztecs to go forth, its fulsome speech carried by the waves of speech scrolls that roll from its mouth. The migratory path begins there as a narrow ribbon punctuated by footprints. As the leaders of the tribe actually set off on the journey, they are individually identified by name glyphs. The amount of space available on the line of the journey allows the artist to present five men first and then ten more below that.[7] The first stop along the migration recorded here is Aztacoalco (the place sign combines a water bird, olla, and water), where the painter records that the Aztecs constructed a temple and bound the years once more (Orozco y Berra 1960, 3:122). The large tree at this place may refer to an episode where

the people were forced to move when a great tree broke in two (see Chapter 8).

After the migrating leaders are named, the migration proceeds anonymously along the footprinted path from site to site, each site identified by its place sign. The footprints establish the direction of the path and, in the absence of walking figures, also provide the action. The reader knows to assume that all the Aztecs and their leaders are following this path. Most sites are accompanied by a number of small blue disks, which indicate the number of years the Aztecs paused in each place. Year bundles at some sites signal the closing of other fifty-two-year cycles. The migratory path leads around the upper right quadrant in a roughly counterclockwise direction to the lower right; then it doubles back and undulates along the bottom of the sheet before it rises to the top of the sheet and crosses to the far upper left, where it doubles back again and drops down to Chapultepec (Grasshopper Hill), situated prominently in the left side of the sheet.

Few eventful moments occur along this path to relieve the monotony of movement from place to place. At the top of the right side, a funerary bundle records one leader's death at Mizquiyahuayla (Round Forest of Mesquites), where the Aztecs also celebrated the close of another cycle (Orozco y Berra 1960, 3 : 126). The migratory path diverges only once, at the bottom of the right side, where Huitzilihuitl leaves Cuauhtepec ([?] Eagle Tree) along a path that leads up to Cuauhmatla (Eagle Hunting Net). Chicomoztoc (Seven Caves) appears along the route in the upper midpoint of the sheet as a hill with a dark circular cave inside and seven disks above; there the Aztecs pass eight years.

When the Aztecs finally arrive at Chapultepec on the left side of the sheet, they have entered the lakeside around Lake Texcoco (Fig. 107). There is a fundamental shift in the pictorial account here. Their story takes on more detail, the presentation of information becomes less purely toponymic and more geographic and pictorial, and most of the figures appear upside down, which means that the reader is required either to turn the sheet around or to move to the other side in order to follow the story easily. The singular route of the migration also now diverges into three separate paths. Tribal leaders again make their presence known by being named and shown in action.

Below Chapultepec, the lake itself is not toponymically named but is pictorially described as a marshy swamp, dotted with reeds and rushes and cut by straight blue canals. One large canal drops down from the base of Chapultepec; another runs parallel to it on the right,

Fig. 106. The Aztecs' departure from Aztlan on the Mapa Sigüenza. CNCA.-INAH.-MEX; reproduced with permission of the Instituto Nacional de Antropología e Historia.

Fig. 107. Chapultepec and the area of Lake Texcoco on the Mapa Sigüenza. Tlatelolco is on the right, Tenochtitlan lower center (at the junction of two canals), Culhuacan middle left. CNCA.-INAH.-MEX; reproduced with permission of the Instituto Nacional de Antropología e Historia.

extending downward to a tallish hill that may be Texcoco at the bottom edge of the sheet. Tenochtitlan is located between these two wide canals, represented by the smallish nopal cactus growing from the juncture of two smaller, perpendicular canals. To the right of Tenochtitlan, a conventionalized mound of earth locates Tlatelolco, and along the far left edge of the sheet a curved hill represents Culhuacan. The artist has hereby created a rough map of the southern lake area, with west at the top. From the vantage point of

Tenochtitlan in the middle of the swamp, Chapultepec lies to the west, Tlatelolco to the north, Texcoco to the east, and Culhuacan to the south. The lacustrine vegetation and all the place signs, except Chapultepec and Tenochtitlan, are upside down, as are most of the humans.

Although this is a history of the Mexica migration that ends in Tenochtitlan, Chapultepec is the largest place sign on the entire Mapa, which suggests that the author is stressing Chapultepec's role in the history

Fig. 108. Chapultepec on the Mapa Sigüenza. CNCA.-INAH.-MEX; reproduced with permission of the Instituto Nacional de Antropología e Historia.

(Fig. 108). The details of the narrative affirm this bias. Two paths lead from Chapultepec. To the right, one passes by the place of the cut-up man and deer, perhaps Mazatlan mentioned in other accounts (Durán 1994: 34). From here, one path continues to the right and down to Tlatelolco, while another doubles back past the base of Chapultepec to end at Culhuacan on the left edge. A third path leads from Chapultepec to a swampy nest just to the left of Chapultepec where the three Aztec leaders are named. This is the path that carries the Mexica past ten other sites to the founding of Tenochtitlan.

The story elaborated here includes several episodes that are known from other pictorial and alphabetic sources. The Aztecs settle in Chapultepec but are evicted after a hard-fought battle that forces them into the marshes at a watery place.[8] During this conflict the Aztec ruler Huitzilihuitl and others are brought as prisoners before Cocoxtli, the lord of Culhuacan, and executed. Eventually the Aztecs journey to Culhuacan, where they beg the Culhua lord for a place to stay; he allows them to stay in Tizapan.

The Mapa Sigüenza presents this story in several scenes. At the foot of Chapultepec's enlarged hill (Fig. 108) are the collapsed and bloodied bodies of two dead Aztec leaders, clearly killed in the battle of Chapultepec. The short path to the watery patch just to the left of Chapultepec records the Aztec's eviction; three other leaders are named here.[9] The part of the story that concerns Culhuacan directly is placed near that city's place sign and inverted on the Mapa (Fig. 109). In front of Culhuacan, the artist paints the Culhua ruler Cocoxtli enthroned. In a vertical row next to his feet are the bloodied severed heads of other defeated Aztecs, who were probably prisoners brought before Cocoxtli. They include Huitzilihuitl and four other named warriors.[10] Facing Cocoxtli are two Aztec warriors wearing animal skins that signal hunter-gatherer or Chichimec status, which is suitable to their reduced circumstances; they come bearing offerings for the lord.[11] This appears to be a scene of supplication, whereby the stricken Aztecs beg the Culhua ruler for land. We know from other sources that he grants them land, and the migratory path then continues to a watery square that may be Tizapan, where they celebrate the end of a cycle.

From here the Aztecs' path continues past several more place signs, two of which have symbols of war (the shield and club) attached. The last few places agree with those in the other histories: after Iztacalco (Place of the Salt House), the daughter of one leader gives birth at a place thereafter named Mixiuhcan (Place of Childbirth), and a sweatbath is built at the place then known as Temazcaltitlan (Sweatbath; Durán 1994: 40–41). When the Aztecs finally reach Tenochtitlan (Fig. 110), the event of foundation is pictured without the elaboration of ceremony described in the Selden Roll. The momentous occasion is signaled simply by the appearance of seven leaders seated on woven reed mats (but not full thrones) on either side of Tenochtitlan's place sign.[12]

All but one of the founders carry the same names as the men who left Aztlan some 400 years earlier. Two were previously reported to have died at Chapultepec. This suggests that these personal names identify clan or family groups rather than individual mortals, or that the migratory leaders have a structural, narrative function in the story that transcends ordinary life spans.

The Mapa Sigüenza covers the entire migration but concentrates its detail on the crucial periods: the beginning when the Aztecs leave Aztlan, their disastrous defeat and eviction from Chapultepec, and the founding itself. Three kinds of space are combined on the map to enable it to present this range of material clearly on such a relatively small painting surface. There is itinerary space, geographic space, and what I call experiential space. Along the main route of the migratory journey, space is used conventionally. It functions at regular intervals to separate the stops along the journey but does not otherwise define territory or represent actual distance. When the story reaches the shores of Lake Texcoco, however, geographic or cartographic space assumes control of the presentation. The account becomes a map-based history. The artist locates sites around the lake in a geographic relationship to each other, and he gives the reader an idea of the topography of the lake, because territory and geography have finally become important for the migration history. The location of Tenochtitlan vis-à-vis the other lakeside cities is central to the Aztec story.

Displacing or intruding into the itinerary space and the cartographic space is experiential space, the picto-

Fig. 109. The Culhua ruler Cocoxtli (*seated*) receiving the new arrivals on the Mapa Sigüenza (inverted for clarity). The severed heads of five migrants appear below. CNCA.-INAH.-MEX; reproduced with permission of the Instituto Nacional de Antropología e Historia.

rial space of individual scenes, which allows the artist to present important events in greater detail. Around Aztlan, experiential space accommodates Huitzilopochtli's speech to the assembled Aztecs by unifying the bird atop the tree with the group of men in a single composition; its use then allows the artist to picture and identify the travelers (whether they be families or individual men). This kind of space also unites Cocoxtli at Culhuacan with the two Aztec warriors who come before him with offerings, and, to culminate the story, it brings together the seven founders in a single scene around the place sign of Tenochtitlan. By utilizing itinerary and geographic space (the tour and the

Fig. 110. The founding of Tenochtitlan on the Mapa Sigüenza (inverted for clarity). CNCA.-INAH.-MEX; reproduced with permission of the Instituto Nacional de Antropología e Historia.

tableau), the artist is able to summarize and condense much of the history so that he can expand the pictorial narrative in experiential space when more detail should be included.

By using two different spatial systems, one itinerary and the other geographic, as the foundation of the pictorial history, the painter is differentiating what is important in the two parts of the migration story. In the first half of the story, it was important to tell that the Aztecs left Aztlan and traveled from one place to another. The geographic location of Aztlan is unimportant to the painted story, as are the locations of the stops along the migration. What is necessary to the history painter is the sequence of the towns on the route. Once the Aztecs arrive in the Valley of Mexico, however, geography becomes a real factor, because the geographic situation of the various lakeside towns was an integral part of the story about the Aztec rise to power. As Tenochtitlan grew to greatness in the years to come,

its position in the middle of Lake Texcoco would also prove to be one of its chief advantages in commerce and in war. The history painter of the Mapa Sigüenza wanted his readers to understand just where Tenochtitlan was with respect to its neighbors, so he positions the second half of the migration story in geographic space.

Several other Aztec cartographic histories use this combination of itinerary and geographic space, as do such Mixtec and Coixtlahuaca documents as the Lienzo of Zacatepec, Lienzo of Tlapiltepec, and Selden Roll. All these histories record the journey of their protagonists from some origin point to the territory in question, which is then graphically described. In the first part of these stories, geography is less important than the sequence of places, so the itinerary format efficiently addresses the needs of the narrative. When geography does become important in the second part of these stories, the narrative requires a cartographic expression of the territory. The narratives thus begin by moving in *res gestae* fashion through undefined space and then, when the homeland is reached, move from one specific location to another on the map.

The Cartographic Histories of Cuauhtinchan

This same juxtaposition of itinerary and map is seen in some of the Cuauhtinchan pictorials. A group of six cartographic histories have come down to us from the *altepetl* of Cuauhtinchan, located just south of the modern city of Puebla and just southeast of the ancient city of Cholula.[13] The *altepetl* was ethnically diverse, but Nahuatl was the dominant language, and its people were politically and culturally affiliated with the Aztecs, who conquered Cuauhtinchan in the fifteenth century. Three of the Cuauhtinchan pictorials (Cuauhtinchan Maps 1, 2, and 3) are large sheets of native paper that exist as independent entities. A fourth document is a sheet of European paper backed by native paper, called the Mapa Pintado en Papel Europeo e Aforrado en el Indiano; it is now bound in the same volume with the Historia Tolteca-Chichimeca, although it was painted prior to the Historia earlier in the sixteenth century. The fifth and sixth of Cuauhtinchan's cartographic histories were painted as part of the Historia Tolteca-Chichimeca (c. 1545–1565), where they provide cartographic relief to the annals structure of the volume; the Historia in which these maps are embedded blends pictorial segments and alphabetic texts to tell the history of Cuauhtinchan from its migratory origins through its founding and up to 1544, where it breaks off.

All of the six cartographic histories focus on the early period of Cuauhtinchan's history, the time when the people were migrating to the area and founding their polity. They yield special insights when studied as a group because they all pertain to the same polity and people and they are thus all part of the same historical tradition. There is a fair amount of overlap in their narratives, but each document still tells a slightly different part of Cuauhtinchan's larger history and from a slightly different perspective. I will focus on Cuauhtinchan Map 2, the Mapa Pintado, and the map of Cuauhtinchan's founding and boundaries that spans pages 32v–33r of the Historia Tolteca-Chichimeca. Cuauhtinchan Map 2 echoes the Mapa Sigüenza, whereas the two smaller maps may be related as prototype to copy.

Cuauhtinchan Map 2

This great panel of native paper (c. 109 cm × 204 cm) is topically parallel and structurally similar to the Mapa Sigüenza (Figs. 111, 112). By this I mean that it tells the story of the migration of the Cuahtinchantlaca (the people of Cuauhtinchan) from their point of origin to the founding of Cuauhtinchan. In this case, the point of origin is Chicomoztoc, and the journey takes the people to the important civic and religious center of Cholula (functioning as a narrative equivalent to Chapultepec) and then on to Cuauhtinchan. Like the Mapa Sigüenza, Cuauhtinchan Map 2 begins as an itinerary but ends as a map. The journey from Chicomoztoc to Cholula follows along an undulating path past a series of places. Then, once the people reach Cholula and approach the territory around Cuauhtinchan, the account shifts to a map-based format where Cuauhtinchan's foundation is presented in the middle of a cartographic rectangle framed by a circuit of boundaries. In its structure and the overall outlines of the story, the map is a Cuauhtinchan equivalent of the Mixtec Lienzo of Zacatepec, the Coixtlahuaca Valley Selden Roll, and the Mexica Mapa Sigüenza. It is a migration-to-foundation story where the tour format of the journey yields to a tableau presentation of the founding.

The Cuauhtinchan migration begins in the upper left corner at Chicomoztoc where Chichimec leaders emerge to follow a winding route—almost a horizontal boustrophedon—down to the bottom of the sheet, then back up, then down and up again until Cholula is reached in the middle of the map. The yellow footprinted path bifurcates about a third of the way into the journey, so that two paths eventually reach Cholula. The *altepetl* of Cholula is represented by the architecture of its palace, presented here as four one-story structures and a central temple-pyramid around a courtyard, flanked on the sides by two auxiliary buildings (Fig. 113). The right of the sheet is given over to the map of the Cuauhtinchan-Tepeaca area delimited by the same yellow footprinted path that winds its way counterclockwise around the territory, beginning and ending at Cholula.

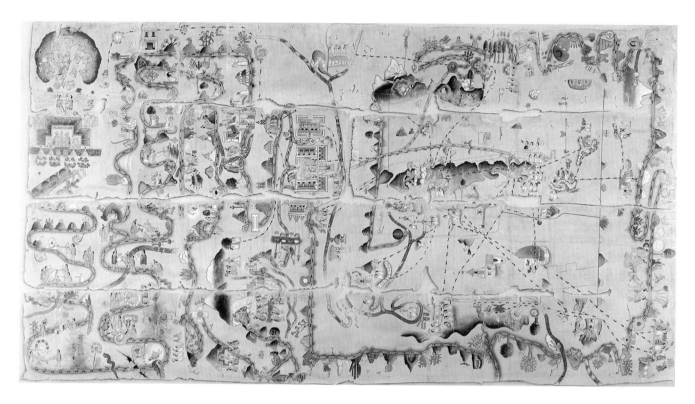

Fig. 111. Cuauhtinchan Map 2. Photograph of the 1892 copy. CNCA.-INAH.-MEX; reproduced with permission of the Instituto Nacional de Antropología e Historia.

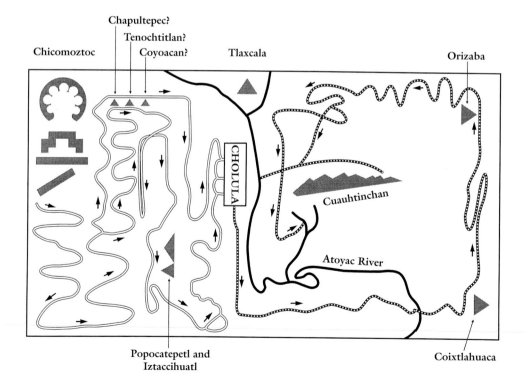

Fig. 112. Diagram of Cuauhtinchan Map 2. Drawing by John Montgomery.

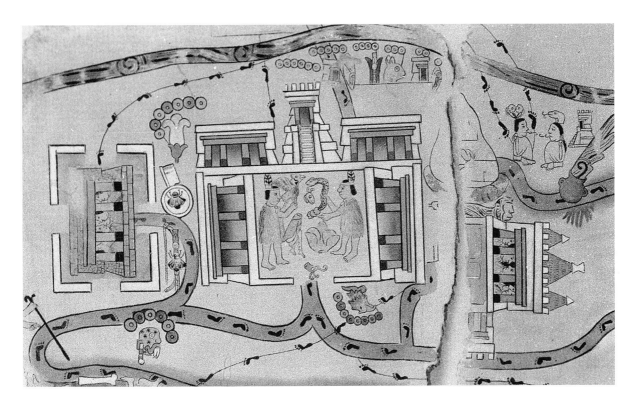

Fig. 113. The city of Cholula on Cuauhtinchan Map 2. Photograph of the 1892 copy. CNCA.-INAH.-MEX; reproduced with permission of the Instituto Nacional de Antropología e Historia.

Although Chicomoztoc seems the logical starting point for the narrative—and it does mark the onset of the migration—the story actually begins in the middle at Cholula. The narrative presented here is roughly parallel to the alphabetic and pictorial account in the Historia Tolteca-Chichimeca. The Historia thus becomes important to analysis of the map because it fills in narrative details that are pictorially represented. The Historia account tells how the Toltecs had come to Cholula in the year 1 Flint and remained there six years (in the map, we see the years 1 Flint to 6 House painted just above Cholula's palace [Fig. 113]). The two Toltec lords Icxicohuatl (Serpent Foot) and Quetzalteueyac (Quetzal Plume from Lips) decide to seek out the Chichimecs in Chicomoztoc and beg their help in defeating the Toltecs' enemies in Cholula. They set out on the day 8 Eagle and arrive at Chicomoztoc five days later. In the Cuauhtinchan map, we see this journey represented by the thin black line punctuated with footprints that leads from the base of Cholula up to the top of the map and over to Chicomoztoc. The day signs

from 8 Eagle to 13 Flower show the progress of the journey.

The Historia then tells how Icxicohuatl (Serpent Foot) and Quetzalteueyac (Quetzal Plume from Lips) beckon the Chichimecs to leave the caves, which they do (Fig. 114). The Historia's text conflates Chicomoztoc with Culhuacan (calling it Colhuacatepec), and it specifies that eight tribes left, naming them (Leibsohn 1993: 328). After emerging, the Chichimec rulers fast prior to undergoing a rite that confers *tlatoani* status on them; then there are several episodes and other rituals before the journey actually begins. The Historia recalls the emergence and onset of the migration in some detail, but only its outlines are necessary here, because most of the details do not match those in the map.

In the map, Chicomoztoc is a seven-pocketed cave from whose recesses men dressed as Chichimecs emerge (Fig. 114). Each lobe is marked with a pictorial element that identifies the tribe (Simons 1968: 52).[14] Their weapons are the bow and arrow characteristic of Chichimecs, although two hold fire serpent staffs and

Fig. 114. Chichimec emergence from Chicomoztoc on Cuauhtinchan Map 2; the dates are 1 Crocodile and 2 Wind. Photograph of the 1892 copy. CNCA.-INAH.-MEX; reproduced with permission of the Instituto Nacional de Antropología e Historia.

four also bear on their back the tobacco pouches of priests. The one female warrior in their midst wears an elaborate back device and carries a shield and a baton in the form of a severed leg.[15] Fourteen Chichimecs are pictured coming forth.[16] The first, shown seated, is the only one with a name sign; he is Coatzin (Serpent), de-

scribed in the Historia as the interpreter and mediator between the Toltecs and Chichimecs. The two Toltecs who have come to draw out the Chichimecs stand below the cave. Icxicohuatl's name sign has been lost, but Quetzalteueyac is readily identifiable by the quetzal feather that rises from his lips. Both are dressed in the cotton cloaks of civilized Toltecs. The emergence of the Chichimecs has taken two days, 1 Crocodile and 2 Wind, which are pictured just to the right of the cave's opening. A sun appears on the left of the cave's opening. These latter features recall the opening scenes in the Selden Roll where Lord 9 Wind, flanked by the sun and the moon, descends from the heavens on the day 1 Crocodile to pass through Chicomoztoc (Fig. 95). The Anales de Tlatelolco (1948: 31) also recount an emergence from Chicomoztoc in the day 1 Crocodile. What follows in the Cuauhtinchan map is a poorly understood series of scenes, described in detail by Simons (1968: 52–53), that mark the postemergence activity during the days 3 House through 5 Serpent.

The migration itself starts on the day 6 Death, where the road begins to wind past a series of places. Most of the locations along the route have not been securely identified, although Simons (1968: 61–62) has proposed that Chapultepec, Tenochtitlan, and Coyoacan are pictured along the second path from the top of the map as Grasshopper Hill, Nopal Cactus, and Coyote Hill; and the two volcanoes Popocatepetl and Iztaccihuatl are clearly included near the bottom. Progress along the route is signaled both by the footprints and by the successive day signs. At various points, the Chichimecs engage in different activities: they sacrifice an eagle and later a human, kill a deer, encounter locals, do battle, and so forth. None of these small episodes is described in prose or pictures in the Historia, and almost none of the place signs appears in the Historia either. The Map and the Historia are two different tellings of the Cuauhtinchan migration.

In the map, the road bifurcates on the day 2 Eagle, where one group leaves the other. The shorter road, which splits off to the left, goes more directly to Cholula; it is the road that continues to carry the day signs. It enters Cholula from the top just after the day 6 Rain, arriving on 7 Flower. The other road is the more circuitous; it is the road that leads past Chapultepec and Tenochtitlan and the two volcanoes, winding back on itself several times. It is the road that enters Cholula coming up from the bottom of the map.[17]

By the time the Chichimecs arrive at Cholula, twenty days have passed since they were first called forth at Chicomoztoc. The emergence and journey has occupied a full suite of the twenty day signs, beginning with Crocodile and ending with Flower. I stress this because I believe this twenty-day count is functioning metaphorically here to represent a full and complete amount of time. The migratory action begins on the first day of the day count, 1 Crocodile, the day that marks so many other supernatural births, descents, and emergences. This is not to say that the Chichimecs, taking the shorter route, could not have actually reached Cholula in twenty days, but that the twenty days that run from 1 Crocodile to 7 Flower are highly symbolic. They represent the initial run of the day count as well as the complete cycle of the day signs, and they metaphorically signal the beginning and completion of the most fundamental unit of time. Too, the emergence from Chicomoztoc and the ensuing rituals are symbolic as events that initiate the process of Cuauhtinchan's creation.

Once the Chichimecs arrive at Cholula, the Historia Tolteca-Chichimeca tells how they help the Toltecs handily defeat their enemies, for which the Toltecs grant the Chichimecs the right to found new *altepetl* in the area. The battle is represented in the Cuauhtinchan map by the bow and arrow and the shield and sacrificial banner painted near the day sign 7 Flower (Fig. 113). In the plaza of Cholula's palace, the sacrifice by two Chichimecs of a quail, serpent, grasshopper, and butterfly is probably related to their founding of new towns.[18]

Cuauhtinchan Map 2 then turns to a cartographic rendering of the area east of Cholula, oriented with north at the top (Fig. 115). The itinerary space of the migration gives way to a map of the region, where the major features of the land are now fixed geographically. From this point forward the events are pictured as taking place in an actual landscape, and the focus is on the site of Cuauhtinchan, situated just to the right of the center of the sheet (and secondarily to the founding of other polities). The geography of the area encompasses Cholula on the western edge, then Tlaxcala and the mountain of Malinche to the north (above Cholula), the peak of snow-capped Orizaba (in the upper right corner), the city of Coixtlahuaca (the hill of serpents

in the lower right corner), and the Tentzon mountain range along the lower border. The great Atoyac river system runs down from Tlaxcala, past Cholula, and then along the base of the Tentzon range to flow off the bottom edge of the sheet.[19] On the left, the volcanoes Popocatepetl and Iztaccihuatl are part of the ambiguous space of the itinerary, but they are still placed on the sheet as if they were part of the geographic setting of the Cholula-Cuauhtinchan area.

The range of hills that runs left to right in the center of the cartograph embraces the new town of Cuauhtinchan, whose place sign is rendered here as an eagle and a jaguar facing each other inside a cave. Although the Cuauhtinchan map is badly damaged here, one can still see some of the seated men and women gathering at the founding. Around this large territory, a meandering path links a great number of place signs (most as yet unidentified) like a circuit, one that begins at Cholula and ends there as well. This is not Cuauhtinchan's boundary line. Instead, traces of a cartographic rectangle inside the undulating frame suggest the polity's borders. Footprints and black lines dotted with footprints describe paths of movement within the area as well as political and family connections.

Cuauhtinchan Map 2 is quintessentially a migration-to-foundation history, sharing narrative elements and its structure with other such pictorials. The founders emerge from a place of origin—here it is Chicomoztoc, whereas elsewhere it is Aztlan (Mapa Sigüenza) or the heavens and Chicomoztoc (Selden Roll and related manuscripts)—to follow an itinerary, moving from site to site through ambiguous space to the founding. As in the Selden Roll and others, the emergence begins on the metaphoric day 1 Crocodile; in Cuauhtinchan Map 2, it culminates nineteen days later once all the twenty day signs have run their course. As in the Selden Roll, too, individuals have traveled to the point of origin in order to draw out the migrants. Then when the travelers near their new territory and real space becomes important for the narrative, the historian shifts the format to a cartograph to describe the founding events as occurring in geographic space. This is also the case in such other founding documents as the Mapa Sigüenza, Selden Roll, and even the Lienzo of Zacatepec.

In the Cuauhtinchan map, Cholula functions as the pivot of the story, the link between the tour of the journey and the tableau of the founding, and it is the place

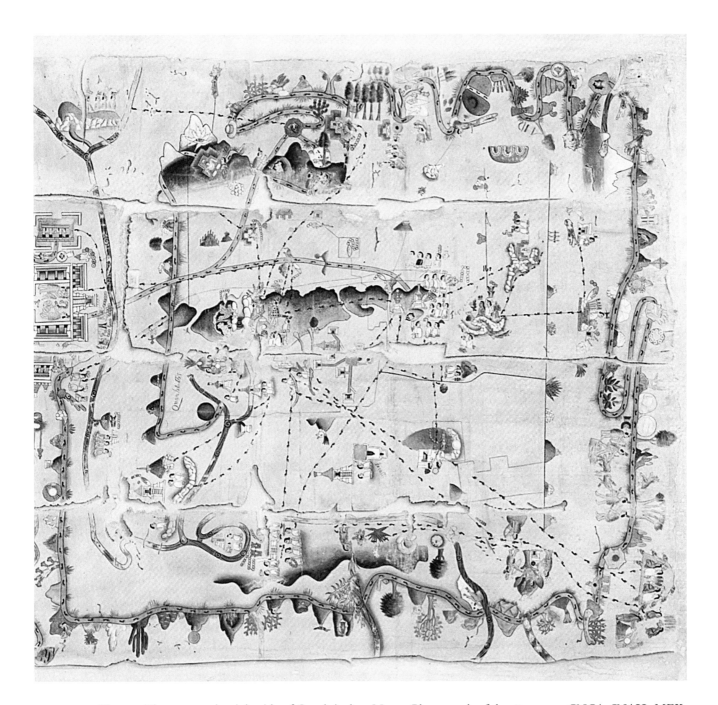

Fig. 115. The map on the right side of Cuauhtinchan Map 2. Photograph of the 1892 copy. CNCA.-INAH.-MEX; reproduced with permission of the Instituto Nacional de Antropología e Historia.

where the Chichimecs are given permission to found new *altepetl*. In this way, it functions visually like Chapultepec in the Mapa Sigüenza but thematically like Culhuacan. Both Cholula and Culhuacan are places long invested with political authority. For the newcomers, both are also sites of political transformation, where the wanderers arrive from their journeys, serve the earlier settled people who live there, and are repaid by being granted their own lands to settle.

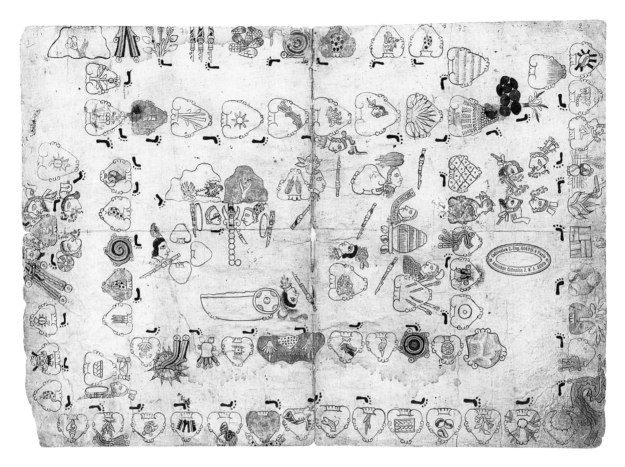

Fig. 116. Mapa Pintado en Papel Europeo e Aforrado en el Indiano. Photograph courtesy of the Bibliothèque Nationale de France, Paris.

The Mapa Pintado and the Map of Cuauhtinchan's Founding

The acts of defining and settling these lands are the focus of two smaller cartographic histories, both painted on European paper (c. 30 cm × 44 cm) and bound in the pages of the Historia Tolteca-Chichimeca. These are the Mapa Pintado en Papel Europeo e Aforrado en el Indiano (Mapa Pintado), painted prior to the Historia and later inserted at the front of it (Figs. 116, 117), and the Map of Cuauhtinchan's Founding, which is painted on facing pages 32v–33r as an integral part of the Historia (Figs. 118, 119). The two are related as prototype to copy, for the Historia map seems to be a loose and selective revision of the Mapa Pintado; it keeps the same format as the earlier document and

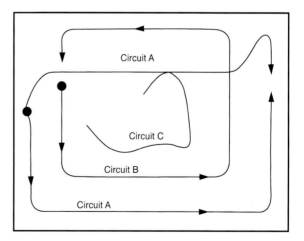

Fig. 117. Diagram of the circuits on the Mapa Pintado. Drawing by John Montgomery.

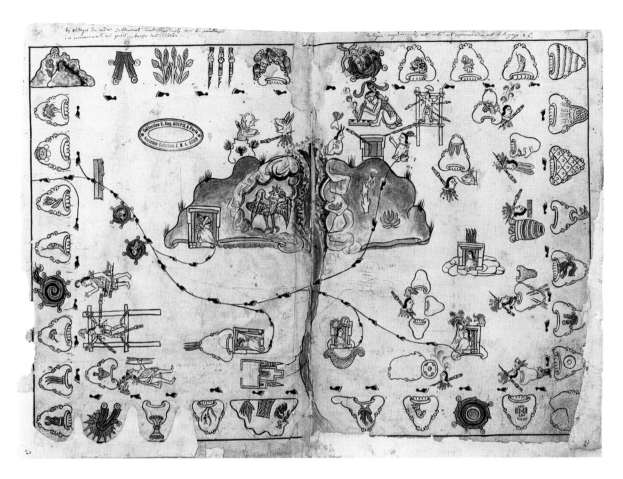

Fig. 118. Map of Cuauhtinchan's Founding, Historia Tolteca-Chichimeca 32v–33r. Photograph courtesy of the Bibliothèque Nationale de France, Paris.

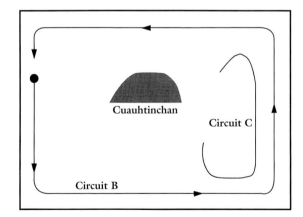

Fig. 119. Diagram of the Map of Cuauhtinchan's Founding. Drawing by John Montgomery.

repeats about two-thirds of the content, but it adds other data.[20] Both documents treat the second half of Cuauhtinchan's migration-to-foundation story, taking up the narrative once the Chichimecs and their Toltec allies have actually entered the immediate area of Cuauhtinchan and directing their lenses on the actual process of founding. Thus, Cholula is omitted, and the geography pertains to the local area of Cuauhtinchan. The two histories present the Chichimecs' arrival in the area, their establishment of boundaries, their conquests of competing polities, and their founding of Cuauhtinchan. Both differ from the itinerary-to-map format of Cuauhtinchan Map 2 because they employ the itinerary itself to define territory.

The Mapa Pintado diagrams three interlocking circuits of toponyms (Fig. 117). Circuit A is a route of travel, which begins on the left of the map, immediately bifurcates, and continues at the top and bottom to the right side of the page. Circuit B is a set of boundaries for Cuauhtinchan beginning in the upper left corner and running counterclockwise, and Circuit C is a loose series of conquered places (less a true circuit than a collection of places that appear in the same relative position). In the center of these circuits is the place sign of Cuauhtinchan presented at the moment of its founding. Although the Mapa Pintado (Fig. 117) contains all three circuits, the Map of Cuauhtinchan's Founding (Fig. 119) omits the initial route of travel that is Circuit A.

The story, told more completely by the Mapa Pintado, begins on the left side of the page (Figs. 116, 117). There the two Toltec heroes Quetzalteueyac (Quetzal Plume from Lips) and Icxicohuatl (Serpent Foot) converse in a meeting with two lords (described as Chichimecs in the Historia). The group separates, one traveling the top route and the other the bottom route until the paths of Circuit A meet again on the right side of the page, where the two Toltecs meet in conversation with two other Chichimecs: one is a Cuauhtinchantlaca (pictured on the top, with the cactus name sign), and the other is from Totomihuacan (pictured below, with a banners name sign).[21] Not only has this route brought the Chichimecs into the area, but it has also delimited part of the boundaries of the neighboring polity of Totomihuacan, for the lower route of Circuit A duplicates one side of Totomihuacan's border. The founding of Totomihuacan is pictured as an aside in the lower left corner of the map where the founder appears with a cult bundle and a bow and arrow next to the Totomihuacan's place sign (the hill with the basket).

The rest of the narrative concentrates on Cuauhtinchan and is replicated in the Map of Cuauhtinchan's Founding. Footprints that begin near the upper left corner of Circuit B and continue in a counterclockwise direction define the boundaries of Cuauhtinchan as a cartographic rectangle. Other footprints carry the Cuauhtinchantlaca into the interior of this territory, where the founders Moquiuix (with black stripe across cheek) and Teuhctlecozauhqui (the serpent head) are pictured just below Cuauhtinchan (Fig. 116). Cuauhtinchan's place sign is elaborated here to include several of the polity's appellatives: Home of the Eagle (Cuauhtinchan), Place Where the Hill Is Broken, Place

of Maguey Cactus, and Place of Unripe Corn, represented by the eagle, the split hill, the maguey cactus, and the corn stalk with tender ear (Leibsohn 1993: 347, 387 n. 88; 1994: 177, 184). The foundation date is the year 8 Reed. Below and to the right, the seven polities of Circuit C are shown in defeat: arrows fly, and the named rulers appear as bloody severed heads.

The Map of Cuauhtinchan's Founding in the Historia (Figs. 118, 119) tells the same founding story but adds details. To describe the ritual, it shows Moquihuix seated in a house/palace on the left of Cuauhtinchan's place sign and also drilling a new fire above the right, while Teuhctlecozauhqui sits below facing his new Toltec wife. Footprints from the left have brought these two founders here, just as other footprints have brought three other Chichimec lords to settle three other polities below Cuauhtinchan.[22]

In both of these pictorial accounts of Cuauhtinchan's founding, and especially in the Mapa Pintado, the reading order and thus the historical sequence of the narrative is ambiguous. It is impossible to tell solely from the cartographic presentations which circuits and routes, and which actions, are to be read before the others. The alphabetic text of the Historia Tolteca-Chichimeca, which follows the Map of Cuauhtinchan's Founding, lists the boundaries first, then tells how the founders entered their altepetl and laid waste to the land (Leibsohn 1993: 347–349). The order of reality, however, might well have been different, for the people could logically have drilled the fire and established the town before they defined their boundaries. Colonial prose accounts of foundation rituals usually put the walking of the boundaries last, just before the celebratory feast (Boone n.d.). The point here is that the historian, by not specifying the reading order, has left it up to the reader. This creates a competition between the several circuits and actions that ask to be read first, or at least not last. One feels this especially in the Mapa Pintado, where an extra circuit is crowded on the sheet and where the footprints and place signs are so ambiguously spaced that the paths of movement are difficult to follow. Here the place signs and routes come equally to the fore and vie for prominence.

Leibsohn (1994: 166–170) points out that cartographic histories "simultaneously deploy itinerary and tableau [and] . . . hold the two systems in tension, making no attempt to reconcile the incongruities." This observation is particularly apt for the Mapa Pintado and the Map of Cuauhtinchan's Founding, which blend the circuit and map formats even more so than do Cuauhtinchan Map 2 and some of the others. In these foundation histories, toponyms alone describe the physical region, and their placement is based less on geography than on the requirements of design that put them in sequential order, regularly spaced, together on the sheet (Robertson 1959: 180). The place signs do not so much form a map as they create a set of itineraries. There is no sense of a preexisting geography into which the Chichimecs stepped, as there is on the right side of Cuauhtinchan Map 2. Instead, as Leibsohn (1995: 269) has noted, the toponyms exist only because the Chichimecs came to these places. In these two cartographic histories, more than most others, the actions of the protagonists cause the land to be revealed.

Of these three cartographic histories from Cuauhtinchan, Cuauhtinchan Map 2 is the most extensive both in its narrative and in the area it covers geographically. It and the Historia Tolteca-Chichimeca are the only Cuauhtinchan histories to relate the Chichimecs' emergence from Chicomoztoc and subsequent journey to Cholula prior to coming to Cuauhtinchan. The area it represents stretches from Chapultepec and Tenochtitlan in the Valley of Mexico, to Tlaxcala in the north, the distant Peak of Orizaba in the east, and Coixtlahuaca toward the southeast. The Mapa Pintado and the Map of Cuauhtinchan's Founding in the Historia are much more subscribed. As local documents, they concentrate on the Chichimec arrival in the immediate vicinity of Cuauhtinchan, the establishment of boundaries, conquests of nearby competitors, and the founding of *altepetl*.

The Texcocan Map-based Histories

On the other side of the mountain range, in the Valley of Mexico, Texcocan historians were painting equivalent stories about the Acolhuaque (the people of the Acolhua domain, whose *altepetl* ultimately paid tribute to Texcoco). Three of these cartographic histories have survived to preserve Texcoco's pictorial image of its past. This image extends later in time than does the past recorded in Cuauhtinchan's maps, and it is structured differently, for the Texcocan maps prize the spa-

tial projection of territory as the a priori foundation for the narrative. The Codex Xolotl, Mapa Tlotzin, and Mapa Quinatzin are named for the first three Texcocan rulers. The Codex Xolotl is a group of ten *amatl* sheets that together form nine sequential segments of Texcocan history (sheets 9 and 10 are joined to create a single large map). The Mapa Tlotzin is a relatively short hide tira, and the Mapa Quinatzin is three *amatl* sheets, two still connected to each other.

The documents cover Texcocan history from the time when the earliest founders, as wandering Chichimecs, entered the Valley of Mexico, and they carry the stories up into the fifteenth and mid-sixteenth centuries.[23] There is no recounting of a long migration from Chicomoztoc or Aztlan, however. The narratives might refer obliquely to the migration, but they all begin once this journey is largely behind and the people near their destination. Nor do the stories culminate with the founding of the *altepetl*, as do the maps pertaining to Cuauhtinchan. The foundation of Texcoco is included, to be sure, but it serves as a stage in the political development of the polity, a point from which the histories progress. The Codex Xolotl recounts Texcocan history up to Nezahualcoyotl (Fasting Coyote) in the early fifteenth century. The Mapa Quinatzin takes Texcoco up to the rule of Nezahualpilli (Fasting Lord), Nezahualcoyotl's son, and the Mapa Tlotzin records the continuous rule of Texcocan *tlatoque* past the Spanish conquest and into the 1530s.

The narratives in these three cartographic histories are founded on geographic maps. Whereas Cuauhtinchan Map 2, the Selden Roll, and the Lienzo of Tlapiltepec open with a distinct itinerary sequence that precedes and leads to a map (which the narrative then enters), the Texcocan pictorials begin with the map itself; in this they are similar to the Mapa Pintado and the Map of Cuauhtinchan's Founding in the Historia Tolteca-Chichimeca. But unlike the latter two, the Texcocan pictorials do not rely on regularized circuits of toponyms to define territory or signal the movement of people across the land (except when Xolotl walks Tenayuca's boundaries). Instead, geographically founded cartographs cover the full surface of the Codex Xolotl and Mapa Tlotzin and part of the Mapa Quinatzin, and the narrative is then fit onto the preexisting features of the land. In this respect, the Texcocan maps are similar to the Lienzo of Ihuitlan and the right side of Cuauhtinchan Map 2. The presentation of history accommodates itself largely to the requirements of the map. The Texcocan documents are also more diagrammatic than the others, in that some situations or relationships are presented more as diagrams than as scenes, because their authors fit genealogies or ruler lists and a considerable amount of action between the geographic locations.

Codex Xolotl

The Codex Xolotl is a case in point. It is the fullest of the Texcocan pictorial histories, covering events that occurred in a dozen or more polities in and around the Valley of Mexico.[24] And it treats the genealogical and political situation of this wide network of sites in detail, crowding the spaces between the geographic features and toponyms with action and short genealogies. Its ten leaves of amate (c. 42 cm × 48 cm) form a series of eight maps on which historical episodes are painted; sheet 8 is a cluster of interwoven vignettes without a cartographic foundation, and leaves 9 and 10 are covered by a single map.[25]

The geographic presentation is fairly consistent from map to map (Figs. 42, 120). Toponyms of the principal sites and descriptive images of the major natural features are arranged roughly as they are on the ground, and the maps are oriented with east at the top. Run-

Fig. 120. Map 2 of the Codex Xolotl. Photograph courtesy of the Bibliothèque Nationale de France, Paris.

ning parallel to the top is the long line of undulating mountains that delimits the eastern edge of the Valley of Mexico. Below this and running parallel to the mountains is the great system of lakes: Lake Xaltocan as the loop to the left, Lake Texcoco as the broad body in the middle, and Lakes Xochimilco and Chalco forming the upward curve on the right. The physical reality of these topographic features is abstracted pictorially on the map to preserve the shape of the lake and the slopes of the hills. Individual polities, however, are represented by their toponyms.[26] In the lower right, for example, the curved hill marks Culhuacan, and the Grasshopper Hill identifies Chapultepec. Sites might appear or disappear as their importance for the story grows or wanes, but the basic features of the land endure. The maps provide a stable ground on which the Acolhua play out their roles in the story.

The story follows the rise of Texcocan authority in the valley from the arrival of the first Chichimecs under the leader Xolotl up to the onset of the Tepanec war in 1427, when Texcoco and Tenochtitlan revolted against the imperialist maneuvers of the Tepanecs of Azcapotzalco. Of all the Texcocan pictorials, the Codex Xolotl covers the broadest expanse of territory. Although it focuses on Texcoco, it is also concerned with the activities of polities like Cholula across the mountains, Culhuacan and Chalco in the south, and Tenochtitlan across the lake. The affairs of these cities appear as sub-narratives in the larger story that revolves around Texcoco. As Susan Spitler (n.d.b) has pointed out, the purpose of the Codex Xolotl was to legitimize the claims of Nezahualcoyotl to the Texcocan throne after the Tepanecs forced him into exile. The codex does this by showing that it was the Texcocan Chichimecs who occupied and first took control of the entire Valley of Mexico, who intermarried with important Toltec families and took up the mantle of civilization, and whose affairs have always been central to valley politics. The underlying theme of the codex is that the Texcocans were the people who originally dominated the valley and allowed others to settle there, and that Texcocan royal blood flows in the veins of the other rulers. It presents Texcoco as the center of the political history of the valley. More so than other pictorial histories, its story is told biographically, with emphasis placed on the specific actions of individual rulers and their families.

As explained in Chapter 4, map 1 of the codex (Fig. 42) describes the Chichimec entrance into the valley, under the leadership of Xolotl (the beast Xolotl) and his son Nopaltzin (Nopal Cactus). After reconnoitering the land, Xolotl founds his polity at Tenayuca and ritually takes control of the territory by walking its boundaries. The narrative of map 1 closes with Xolotl enthroned at Tenayuca, surrounded by his son, wife, and six vassals. Map 2 resumes the narrative with Xolotl still seated at Tenayuca, his wife behind him (Fig. 121). They and all the other Chichimecs still wear the animal skin clothes of the nomads they have been, and the men consistently wear their hair long and carry the Chichimec bow and arrow. This costume distinguishes them from the already civilized Toltec people living in the valley, who wear white cotton clothes and whose males cut their hair below the ear.

The historian uses several methods to present the different kinds of information needed by the narrative. Events are depicted as individual scenes or vignettes, which are usually located near their geographic location on the sheet but otherwise exist in experiential rather than geographic space. Marriage unions and lines of descent (forming short genealogies) are specialized events that have their own spatial requirements and are presented as diagrams, where a husband and wife sit together, usually facing each other, with lines joining them to their offspring who are shown below. These brief genealogical presentations use a space that is neither experiential nor geographic, but rather diagrammatic. Like experiential space, it serves to remove the presentations from the geographic constraints of the map. Dotted lines, solid black lines, footprints, and speech scrolls link people and tie different scenes together, conveying information about association, descent, and travel.

When map 2 opens, genealogies illustrate the unions and descendants of several of the already civilized people in the area, most of whom live in the south (on the right side of the map).[27] These families are important to the story because they marry into the Chichimec lines and thus become part of the civilizing process. Xolotl and his wife are seated at Tenayuca, just below the lake (Fig. 121); lines of descent connect them to their two daughters below, while their son Nopaltzin appears to the left of Tenayuca in a marriage and progeny statement with his own wife.

Fig. 121. Detail of the central area of the Codex Xolotl map 2, showing Xolotl's meeting with the three recent arrivals, his and Nopaltzin's meeting with Itzmitl (*upper left*), Nopaltzin's battle with Nauhyotl (*upper center*), and Xolotl's meeting with Achitometl (*upper right*). Photograph courtesy of the Bibliothèque Nationale de France, Paris.

Xolotl does not face his wife because he is in conversation with three newly arrived Chichimecs, who request and are granted lands. This scene occupies most of the western edge of Lake Texcoco, although we read it as occurring at Xolotl's headquarters in Tenayuca. The first Chichimec, Acolhua (Water Bent Arm), is given Azcapotzalco (Ant Heap) and appears there at the bottom center of the map with his new wife (Xolotl's second daughter) and children (Fig. 121). The second Chichimec, Chicomecuauh (Seven Eagle), is given Xaltocan (Sand Spider) and appears there in the lower left with his new wife (Xolotl's other daughter) and children (Fig. 120). The third Chichimec, Tzontecomatl (Hair Jar), is given Acolman (Water Bent Arm), which is pictured as a cave in the upper center of the sheet, where he appears with his new wife, who is descended (so the black line tells us) from the ruling family at Quechollan (Large Beaked Bird) in the upper

right of the map (Fig. 120). This division of land and these three newly founded dynasties are metaphorically dated to the year 1 Flint, the Aztec year of beginnings. Three other newly founded polities and dynasties on the sheet are also dated to 1 Flint.

Another conference scene, just above Tenayuca, brings Tzontecomatl's son Itzmitl (Obsidian Arrow) from Acolman to ask Xolotl and Nopaltzin that tribute lands be granted to his own infant son Huetzin (upper left of Fig. 121). The subject of this conversation is conveyed by the speech scrolls, Huetzin's (Kettle Drum) name glyph, and the glyph of a little nude infant, which appear between the speakers. The lands that Xolotl gives are represented along the left side of the sheet where five Chichimec rulers are seated in front of their towns, with skewered rabbits (their tribute) before them. They are all connected by dotted lines to Xolotl's lips and also to Huetzin, who is seated below Acolman in the upper middle of the map.

In the upper left of the sheet, Xolotl and Nopaltzin appear again on either side of a rectangular preserve that is situated just east of (above) Texcoco; Texcoco, the eventual capital, is represented by the hill sign embellished with a stone and a vase. At this meeting lands are conveyed to Nopaltzin's three sons, who are seated directly above. The two younger sons are given lands to the northeast, and a line carries them to sites in the far upper left corner of the sheet. The eldest son Tlotzin (Falcon), however, founds a new dynasty in the upper middle right of the map, where he appears at a cave in the year 1 Flint with his wife and children.

Not everyone accepts Xolotl's largess, however, particularly Nauhyotl (Four Nose), the lord of Culhuacan, who refuses to recognize Chichimec supremacy. A bloody war erupts, represented in the middle of the map by the scene of Nopaltzin and Nauhyotl doing battle, their figures visually overlapping but effectively ignoring the geography of the lake (Fig. 121). At Nauhyotl's feet, the blood flowing from the stepped pyramid signals his defeat; the event is dated to the year 13 House, inserted between them. Immediately to the right, another scene explains how Xolotl meets with Achitometl (Water Chia Maguey), Nauhyotl's grandson, and seats the latter on the Culhua throne. Achitometl's genealogical relationship to his grandfather is presented to the right, just above Culhuacan's place sign.

The story told in the Codex Xolotl is largely a web of related biographies and genealogies. Multiple narratives and family trees pertaining to the rulers of different polities run through the document and intersect with each other. This codex is the closest of all the Aztec pictorials to recording the kind of personalized account of the lives, unions, and progeny of the *altepetl* rulers that characterizes the Mixtec screenfolds. But whereas the Mixtec screenfolds organize their dynastic records as *res gestae,* with their strong sequences of events, the Xolotl codex organizes the past geographically and diagrammatically over a series of maps. The map-based format prohibits long sequences of events and denies narrative continuity, but it excels in charting the spatial relationships between actions and the political ties between the polities.

Time is exceedingly ambiguous in the Codex Xolotl,

despite occasional year dates that lock events to one of the fifty-two-year cycles when they are not functioning metaphorically. The stability of the land and its features brings an implicit contemporaneity to the action arranged on its surface, but the narrative requirements of the story push some events earlier or later. Some events capture a moment, while others stretch over a long time, and all may occupy different layers of time. Time is longest in the genealogies, which present a union and progeny, which themselves will have other unions and progeny. Xolotl, for example, appears on the map in a marriage and progeny statement, as does his son Nopaltzin, his grandson Tlotzin, and his great-granddaughter Azcaxochitl (Ant Flower), who marries the lord in the upper middle fold; thus Xolotl and his great-great-grandsons all exist within the time span of map 2. It is left up to the reader to note that Xolotl's marriage and progeny statement must predate those of his offspring, which necessarily float later in time as the generations progress. The shallowest time comes when individuals meet in conference, as when Xolotl receives the three newly arrived Chichimecs who request land, a meeting that would not have lasted longer than a day or two.

Mapa Tlotzin

Time is slightly less ambiguous in the Mapa Tlotzin, only because less information is crowded onto the tira (Figs. 122, 123). In the most general sense the Mapa Tlotzin covers the same material as the Codex Xolotl but in much less detail.[28] Its hide strip (31.5 cm × 127.5 cm) concentrates on the Chichimecs' arrival, the process by which they learn Toltec ways and become civilized, the founding of three polities, and the succession of Texcocan rulers from Tlotzin to Don Pedro Tetlahuehuetzquitzin, the sixth Texcocan lord after the Spanish invasion (Aubin 1886b: 316–317; Spitler n.d.a, n.d.b). Structurally the narrative is told over one great map, which is bracketed on the left and right by scenes that are somewhat independent of the map.

The presentation of territory in the *mapa* approaches a spaceless landscape where flora and fauna describe the ecology of the area and people move within this natural environment (Robertson 1959: 136). The land is punctuated by six caves, whose slopes are covered with desert vegetation. All but the one on the far right are named glyphically. They follow a generally north-south line, creating a conceptual map of the Valley of Mexico with east at the top, like a vertically compressed version of one of the maps in the Codex Xolotl (compare Fig. 122 with Figs. 42, 120). Reading left to right (north to south), the caves are Tzinacanoztoc (Bat Cave), Quauhyacac (Where the Trees Begin [a tree with a nose]), Texcoco (the hill with a rock),[29] Huexotla (Willow), Coatlichan (Home of the Serpent), and the unnamed place on the far right identified as Tlatzallan-Tlallanoztoc (Between Two Mountains, Underground Cave; Aubin 1886b: 305–307; Spitler n.d.a, n.d.b). Below and upside down are the three major cities on the other side of the lake, reading left to right, Azcapotzalco, Tenochtitlan, and Culhuacan, the latter two pictured with their ruling couples. The author presents a compressed map of the cultural situation of the valley, one that ignores the lake in the middle.

Into this world the Chichimecs come walking on the far left, moving easily through a desert ecology among cacti, deer, a rabbit, a bird, and serpents. They wear the characteristic hide clothes, have long loose hair, and carry bows and arrows and hunting baskets. Three couples enter this northern part of the valley. The first is Amacui (Paper ?) and his wife (Twisted Flower) below him; this is thought to be Xolotl and his spouse by other names (Aubin 1886b: 304). The second is Nopaltzin, Xolotl's son, and his wife (Eagle Woman) below him; the third is Tlotzin (Falcon), Xolotl's grandson, and his wife (Crown of Flowers) below him (Aubin 1886b: 313). Their travels end with the three couples seated together in the cave at Quauhyacac: Amacui/Xolotl and his wife facing each other at the top, Tlotzin and his wife below on the left, and Nopaltzin and his wife below on the right. This short series of scenes on the left effectively establishes that the family of Texcocan Chichimecs has arrived in the valley.

The next part of the story is told in the far upper right corner where vignettes explain how Tlotzin and his wife were taught the skills of sedentary people. Small scenes show a man (identified by the Nahuatl gloss as a Chalcan noble) teaching the Chichimec lord how to roast game over a fire, plant corn, grind corn on metates and cook it on a griddle, and drink *atole* (corn gruel). On the very far right, Tlotzin's wife is pictured in a cave giving birth to Quinatzin, while Tlotzin waits below, calling out Quinatzin's name.

The rest of the pictorial is given over to representing the founding of three major Acolhua *altepetl*: Texcoco, Huexotla, and Coatlichan. The events themselves are signaled by the appearance of the founding couples seated facing each other inside caves. These are not actual scenes of moments when couples sit together inside caves, however, because the three locations are not particularly characterized by caves. Instead, the artist is presenting what is in effect the Texcocan icon for the foundation of *altepetl*, one that is equivalent to the Coixtlahuaca practice of seating the founders on jaguar thrones. On the right, the Coatlichan ruler Tlacoxin/Itzmitl and his wife are followed by their eldest son Huetzin and his wife, with their seven children behind her; all are named (Aubin 1886b: 318–320). At Huexotla the author pictures Tochtzin (Rabbit) and his wife, followed by the three ruling couples who succeed them; all of the men, but only the founding wife, are named (Aubin 1886b: 317–318). The focus of the Mapa is clearly on Texcoco, where the artist paints the longest ruler list.

At Texcoco, Tlotzin and his wife are pictured at the top of the cave with an infant in a carrying basket between them. Then follows their heir Quinatzin and his wife and another infant in a basket. This is not to be read as a gathering of people but as the beginning of a ruler list, with the successive rulers pictured below.[30] Four ruling couples follow below the cave, after which a succession of only the male rulers continues on the left. The wives' names drop away after the first four, and then the wives themselves. One notes that Nezahualcoyotl (Fasting Coyote) is the first Texcocan ruler to wear a cloak of white cotton, to bind his hair, and to sit on an *icpalli* (a woven mat throne with a back rest). This tells the reader that he is the first *tlatoani* of Texcoco as an independent Nahuatl *altepetl* in the fullest sense, and we know from other sources that it was Nezahualcoyotl who, with Itzcoatl's help, threw off the yoke of Tepanec oppression. Behind his wife appear seven artisans plying their crafts (Fig. 124): a manuscript painter, pigment grinder, mosaic worker, goldsmith, featherworker, lapidary, and wood-carver. The historian employs these images to explain how Nezahualcoyotl brought the fine artisans to Texcoco and transformed it into a cultural showplace.

Thus in several parts of the Mapa Tlotzin the historian emphasizes the process by which the Texcocan

Fig. 122. Mapa Tlotzin (First Section, featuring the arriving Chichimecs). Photograph courtesy of the Bibliothèque Nationale de France, Paris.

Fig. 123. Diagram of the Mapa Tlotzin. Drawing by John Montgomery.

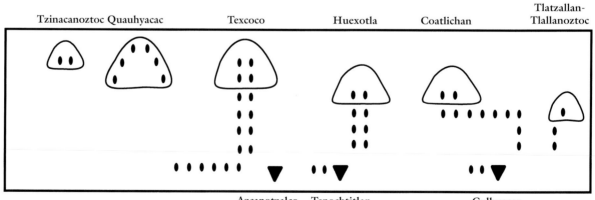

Fig. 122. Mapa Tlotzin (Second Section, featuring the ruler list of Texcoco).

Fig. 124. Seven artisans are shown behind Nezahualcoyotl's wife in the Mapa Tlotzin. They represent the crafts of manuscript painting, pigment grinding, mosaic working, gold working, feather working, precious-stone carving, and wood working. Photograph courtesy of the Bibliothèque Nationale de France, Paris.

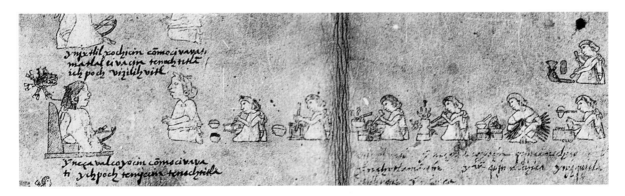

Fig. 122. Mapa Tlotzin (Third Section, featuring the rulers of Huexotla).

Chichimecs are civilized and bring culture to their realm, a theme that also plays itself out in the Codex Xolotl. The Texcocan line of rule is another point of pride. Texcoco is the only polity whose ruler list is complete and brought up to the present. The other polities are frozen in the past. If we are to go solely by the Mapa Tlotzin, Huexotla had four successions only, and Coatlichan but two before their royal lines dropped from notice. Tenochtitlan and Culhuacan are likewise presented here in a single historical moment, when Huitzilihuitl was ruling Tenochtitlan and Cocoxtli ruled Culhuacan. The artist presents only Texcoco's history as continuous and ongoing.

The narrative in the Mapa Tlotzin achieves three goals. It establishes the arrival of the Chichimecs and the founding of the three major *altepetl*. It recounts the civilizing process: both the initial lessons about growing corn and preparing food in the Mesoamerican manner and the later cultivation of the arts. By virtue of the extended Texcocan ruler list, it then carries the unbroken line of Texcocan rulers to the present.

Mapa Quinatzin

Similar themes are pursued in the Mapa Quinatzin, although this document is less a history per se than a combination of history and exposition about the

Fig. 122. Mapa Tlotzin (Fourth Section, featuring learned skills and the rulers of Coatlichan).

political and social features of Texcoco (Fig. 125).[31] The Mapa exists as three distinct *amatl* pages (c. 35–38 cm × 44 cm), the first two still joined, which are generally ordered top to bottom. Only the first is a cartographic history in any sense, telling of Texcoco's Chichimec past. The second page is a diagram of the *altepetl*'s political system, figuratively set in the royal palace, and the third is a pictorial arrangement of crimes and punishments under the wise watch of Texcocan judges. Like the Mapa Tlotzin, the Mapa Quinatzin functions to document Texcoco's Chichimec past and adoption of Mesoamerican ways (page 1), and it too holds Texcoco as a model *altepetl*. Whereas the Mapa Tlotzin boasted that Texcoco was a home for artisans and en-

joyed a distinguished and unbroken *tlatoani* line since its founding, the Mapa Quinatzin (pages 2 and 3) celebrates Texcoco's political and legal system.

Page 1 is a spaceless landscape (Robertson 1959: 136) where in the top two-thirds of the page unnamed Chichimecs hunt, enjoy a campfire, and bury their dead amid the flora and fauna of an arid region. In the upper center, a Chichimec couple and child—virtually the same image that is repeated several times in the Mapa Tlotzin—sit together in a cave to signal their arrival and establishment of a new home (Fig. 126). This settling process closely parallels the opening scenes of the Mapa Tlotzin.

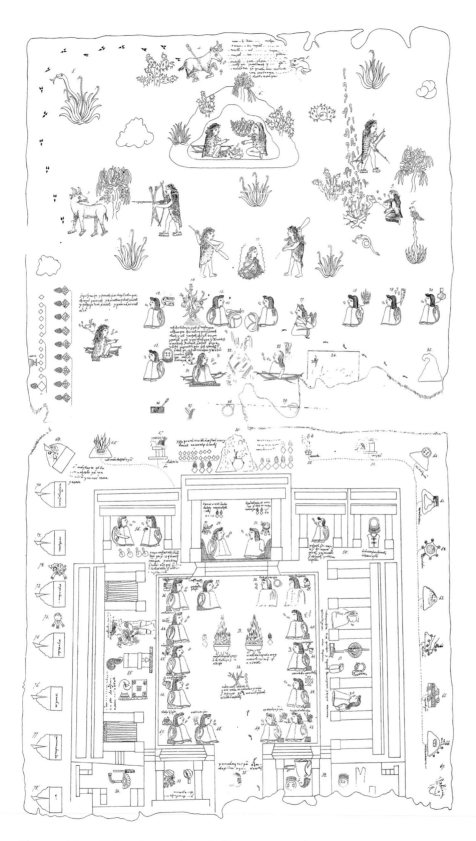

Fig. 125. Mapa Quinatzin 1–2 (from Aubin c. 1849–1851).

Fig. 126. Mapa Quinatzin 1, showing a Chichimec couple in a cave. Photograph courtesy of the Bibliothèque Nationale de France, Paris.

The bottom third of the page shows the Chichimecs adopting Mesoamerican ways. Quinatzin on the left receives two Toltec arrivals, one identified in other sources as a manuscript painter. In the lower center, nearly obliterated by wear, Quinatzin's two successors, Techotlalatzin and Ixtlilxochitl sit facing each other across a burning funerary bundle; this may be a scene of Quinatzin's death, but the main point being made is that the Texcocans (now wearing cloth cloaks) have adopted the custom of cremating their dead. Just above them two seated men have brought Toltec weapons (the atlatl) and the cult bundles of new deities to Texcoco, while the woman to their right has brought what appears to be domesticated corn. Footprints have carried them from the ancient polity of Culhuacan, rendered by its curved hill sign in the lower right corner. Three other men, representing other ethnicities, arrive on the right. This bottom third of the page parallels the

scenes of cultural instruction in the upper right corner of the Mapa Tlotzin.[32]

Page 2 has no parallel in other pictorial documents. Architecturally, it presents an ideal palace, with a principal receiving hall (top center) and side halls arranged around a central courtyard. The side rooms are here occupied by individuals, pictorial elements, and objects that identify the bureaucratic function of these rooms as an armory, treasury, house of song, and so forth. The successive Texcocan rulers Nezahualcoyotl (left) and Nezahualpilli (right) sit together in the audience hall while fourteen noble vassals gather in the courtyard below. Around the outside of the palace, twenty place signs are arranged almost as a circuit; they represent the towns subject to Texcoco, the urban centers on the right and top and the rural towns on the left (marked by digging sticks). Texcoco's place sign, a hill with a stone and vase, appears just above the palace. This page has advanced in time from page 1 to highlight the political organization of Texcoco's extensive realm under the rules of Nezahualcoyotl and his son Nezahualpilli. The page holds an organizational chart for the polity.

Page 3 is also without parallel, for it is a pictorial explanation of the Texcocan legal code, presented as scenes in a loose grid. Along the top row are the lords of Tenochtitlan and Tlacopan, Texcoco's allies, and a series of seven cities defeated by their combined forces.[33] The legal system itself is below, with Nezahualcoyotl's and Nezahualpilli's judges sitting on the right and the individual crimes and punishments presented in rectangular panels to their left. This is not the only document to speak of Texcoco's legal code, which was touted by the chroniclers as being particularly just, but it is the only one to present it pictorially. Like the diagram of Texcoco's political situation, the artist here celebrates the *altepetl*'s advanced legal system.

The Mapa Quinatzin, like the Codex Xolotl and the Mapa Tlotzin, is a pictorial testimony to Texcoco's political and cultural accomplishments. Although it focuses on different aspects of Texcoco's past, it agrees with the other pictorials about the basis of Texcocan greatness. All three documents focus on the foundation of the *altepetl* (first Tenayuca and later Texcoco) by the Chichimecs under Xolotl or his successors and on Texcoco's central position as the source from which the other Acolhua polities draw their political power. Then the three pictorials describe the process by which the Texcocan Chichimecs became acculturated and civilized in the ways of the Toltecs. The manuscripts are most similar when they treat these aspects of Texcoco's early history, for they diverge thereafter. The Codex Xolotl proceeds to elaborate the genealogical ties that bound the Texcocan royal family to those of other *altepetl* and to support Nezahualcoyotl's right to rule. The Mapa Tlotzin affirms Texcoco's unbroken ruler list, and the Mapa Quinatzin concentrates on Texcoco's political and legal achievements. Together they provide a multifaceted picture of Texcoco as a polity.

Stories of the Old, Old Past

The cartographic histories from the central valleys, like their counterparts in southern Puebla and Oaxaca, tell about the early history of their polities. They treat the times prior to and surrounding the *altepetl*'s founding, and almost all promote the founding as their story's central event. A number of documents concentrate on the activities prior to the founding, when the people migrated into their new homelands from distant places, conquered their rivals, and defined their new polities. Such are the Mapa Sigüenza and the three Cuauhtinchan pictorials, whose narratives open with the migration and culminate in the founding. The Mapa Sigüenza and Cuauhtinchan Map 2 even begin their stories at the very points of origin, when the people emerge from or leave idealized places (Aztlan and Chicomoztoc), whereas the others begin their histories once the migrants are already near their new homes.

The Texcocan pictorials stand apart from the others here, for they highlight the founding and refer back to the migration but use the foundation event as a springboard for the rest of the story. Although opening in the deep past, they carry the story farther into the present than do the others. In this respect, the Texcocan cartographic histories are similar to the lienzos of Ihuitlan and Philadelphia (Figs. 80, 87), which also carry the *altepetl* stories ahead from the foundations. The Texcocan Mapa Tlotzin (Fig. 122) is particularly like them in grafting ruler lists onto the foundations.

Caves in the Central Mexican pictorials take on a greater importance than they do in the lienzos and tiras from Puebla and Oaxaca. Although Chicomoztoc makes its appearance as a point of origin in the Selden Roll and Lienzo of Tlapiltepec (Figs. 95, 97), the place of Seven Caves is more closely associated with the people of the central valleys who saw it as the place from which their ancestors emerged. Its presence in the Coixtlahuaca manuscripts demonstrates how the historians of the Coixtlahuaca Valley shared the Central Mexican tradition. In the Texcocan pictorials, caves also function as icons for the founding of polities, where the convention has the founding couple, dressed as Chichimecs, sitting inside a cave facing each other with a child in between. The three cartographic histories from Texcoco (Codex Xolotl, Mapa Tlotzin, and Mapa Quinatzin) all employ this icon; the Codex Xolotl adds to it the year date 1 Flint, the metaphoric founding date among the Nahuas.

Almost all the founding moments require that the husband and wife both be present, because it is the couple, not just the man, who founds the polity. This is true also for the lienzos and tiras in southern Puebla and Oaxaca and for the Mixtec genealogical histories, which cannot afford to ignore one side of these important unions. An exception to this is the Mapa Sigüenza (Fig. 110), which, like all the other Mexica pictorial histories, ignores the females almost entirely. Leibsohn (personal communication, 1997) notes that the Cuauhtinchan paintings also tend to omit the women. In the Mapa Tlotzin (Fig. 122), we see the females begin to fade from the ruling couples, first losing their names and then disappearing altogether. My sense is that the females fall away when genealogy ceases to be so important and perhaps also because the colonial environment in which most of these manuscripts were painted undervalued the female contribution to a union.[34]

Another feature that stands out in these pictorials is the people's Chichimec past. The manuscripts all explain or suggest the hardships the migrating people endured to find their new homelands, and many specify that the migrants were the vigorous desert nomads known as Chichimecs. The historians assign them this label by picturing them dressed in skins with long flowing hair and carrying bows and arrows or hunting baskets, a marked contrast to the white cotton cloaks, sandals, cut hair, and obsidian clubs of the settled people. The Texcocan pictorials focus particularly on the process of acculturation, the "civilizing [of] the Chichimecs," to borrow Paul Kirchhoff's (1948) phrase, whereby the arriving nomads learned civilized, Toltec ways.

As cartographic histories, their narratives are intertwined with maps. Either their stories are arranged on maps, or their stories themselves form maps by the telling, or both. Several documents employ both the tour and the tableau (to use Certeau's terms) in creating their narratives. They begin with an itinerary and switch to a map.

The itineraries record a series of events that occur at different places in an otherwise undefined territory, so as the narrative moves from event to event, it also moves from place to place. Because they are migration histories, their stories are themselves about the movement of people, and the geographic actuality of the space through which they move is not as important as the fact of moving sequentially from point to point. In this way the first parts of the Mapa Sigüenza and Cuauhtinchan Map 2 (Figs. 105, 111) respectively carry

the Mexica and the Cuauhtinchantlaca from their legendary points of origin to their new homelands across lands that are only figuratively present. In the Mapa Pintado and the Map of Cuauhtinchan's Founding (Figs. 116, 118), however, the itinerary from place to place also establishes the actual boundaries of the polity; here the circuit of places defines real territory.

The other cartographic histories rely on maps of preexisting lands as the foundations for their stories. In these, the features of the land are arranged on the sheet in approximate correspondence to their relative location on the ground. Geographic features, such as lakes, rivers, and mountain ranges, are generally described pictorially, whereas the cultural features—the cities and named sites—are represented by their place signs. We see this clearly on the right side of Cuauhtinchan Map 2 (Fig. 115), where the place signs locate polities among the rolling hills and system of rivers of the Puebla Valley east of Cholula. This blending of pictorial depiction and conventional signage creates a geographic foundation to which the events in the stories can then be tied.

When the artist places events on this map, he relies on the geographic messages of the map at the same time that he is forced to violate some of these messages. Because events in the past took place at specific locations, the historian assigns them to those locations on the map, relying on the geographic meaning of the map's space to distinguish events at Tenayuca from events at Culhuacan, for example. But in order to picture an event near Tenayuca, the artist must carve space for that pictorial information out of the map, creating a pocket of nongeographic space within the geographic plane. When this pocket holds a scene of an event, such as a meeting, I refer to it as experiential space, because it represents a space that is actively occupied by the painted participants. Such is the large space just below Lake Texcoco on map 2 of the Codex Xolotl (Fig. 121) where Xolotl grants lands to three new arrivals; such also is the space on the right side of Cuauhtinchan's Mapa Pintado (Fig. 116) where the two Toltecs meet two Chichimecs.

When this pocket of pictorial information holds elements that have a logical but not a physical association with each other, as in a marriage and progeny statement or a ruler list, I refer to it as diagrammatic space. It is less a pictorial reproduction of an event or events than a diagram of an association. The short genealogies in the Codex Xolotl are essentially graphic visualizations of marital union and descent, just as the ruler lists in the Mapa Tlotzin present royal succession. The graphic explanations of Texcoco's political and legal system on pages 2 and 3 of the Mapa Quinatzin also employ diagrammatic space. In these, a change in placement signals a change in social meaning but not necessarily a change in either physical location or time.

Time is the least pronounced element in the cartographic histories. Most rely on sequential time, conveyed by directional movement, sequences of events, and defined paths of travel. Duration can be recorded by disks or other symbols that stand for the passage of years, and hard dates can be added to individual events, but time still remains somewhat ambiguous. The Mapa Sigüenza (Fig. 105), for example, uses two kinds of temporal markers: it employs groups of blue disks to mark years of duration, and it pictures year bundles to signal the close of 52-year cycles. The two systems fail to correspond, however, for the year bundles suggest that the migration took over 400 years, while the disks give it less than 200. In either case, these temporal guides influence the narrative very little. Most of the events in the Cuauhtinchan documents remain undated, and the Mapa Tlotzin is without dates entirely. Cuauhtinchan Map 2 does assign specific day dates to various parts of the migratory route, but I believe these days are functioning metaphorically. Hard dates sometimes mark the year *altepetl* are founded.

The Codex Xolotl (Figs. 42, 120) employs the greatest range of temporal markers, and perhaps for this reason its time is the most ambiguous of all the cartographic histories. Lines and footprints that tie genealogies together or track physical movement through space provide sequential time. Thus in map 1 footprints trace Xolotl and his son while they reconnoiter the valley, and in map 2 lines link daughters with the wives they later become. Implied sequences are also established by the juxtaposition of related events, although there might be no painted line to connect them explicitly. Thus in map 2 Nauhyotl's defeat is followed on the right by Xolotl's negotiations with his successor. Groups of blue disks convey duration, measured in units of a year, and precise year dates tie some events to the fifty-two-year cycle. Other events, such as foundings of *altepetl* and dynasties, however, seem to be dated metaphorically. Ultimately, the sequence of the

separate maps is yet another device to place people and events in time. Even by combining all these various strategies to record time, however, it would be extremely difficult to lock the events in the Codex Xolotl into a single clock. Events on each sheet float in a vague contemporaneity, with some sinking deeper into the past and others rising as later; time is clearly not the issue. At issue is the land on which these events take place and the relative spatiality of concurrent events in different locations. The Codex Xolotl, like the other cartographic histories from the central valleys, views history as a cluster of related actions that take place on the land.

All the cartographic histories, including the lienzos from Oaxaca and Puebla, focus first on the geographic identity of the community kingdoms whose histories they relate. They use the spatial projection of territory as the ground on which their narratives play out, which means that their narratives are securely located at specific sites. Although time markers are implicitly and explicitly embraced in the narratives, spatial relations take precedence over temporal ones. Just the opposite is true, however, with the Aztec annals histories, which privilege time over space.

8

Aztec *Altepetl* Annals

Time, so relatively unimportant for the cartographic histories, is the central and governing feature of annals histories. Time, as measured by a continuous and sequential count of the years, is the armature that supports the record of events. Events are painted beside the count, often tied specifically to the appropriate year with a line. Even the Nahuatl terms for annals focus on the element of time. Chimalpahin, whom James Lockhart calls the greatest annalist of the early colonial period, used the term *xiuhpolhualli* (year count, year relation), but the genre was also referred to as *xiuhtlacuilolli* (year writing) and *(ce)xiuhamatl* (year paper or year book; Lockhart 1992: 376). Motolinía used the term *xiuhtonalamatl* (year day book) when he characterized the annals history as the only Aztec book that recounted the truth, distinguishing it from divinatory and religious manuscripts. These terms all begin with the word for year (*xihuitl*), and they describe the structural basis of the genre rather than its content. By including the term *amatl* (paper), they also reflect the physicality of the annals as books (tiras or screenfolds) of paper rather than hide. Molina (1970: 30) translates *coronista* as "altepetlacuilo, xiuhtlacuilo" (*altepetl* writer, year writer; Lockhart 1992: 587 n. 8), which fuses the *altepetl* focus of the documents with their structure.

Physically the annals exist as histories painted on amate paper rather than hide. The preconquest form, which is preserved in the least acculturated of the colonial annals, was usually a long, narrow strip along which the year count would run. With the introduction of European paper after the Spanish invasion, indigenous annals came also to be painted across or down the pages of this "new" paper, now bound as a book.

The content of these annals embraces both the migratory and imperial past. A number of annals trace the Aztec story from its very origins at Aztlan through to the founding of Tenochtitlan and beyond. Many continue their record past the coming of the Spaniards and into the second half of the sixteenth century. The migratory accounts focus on a succession of place signs that signal subsequent stops along the journey. The imperial records include a range of events that would have been of interest to the *altepetl* as a corporate body: deaths and successions of rulers, the ending/beginning of fifty-two-year cycles, conquests, major building programs, great celebrations, and natural and climactic phenomena, usually dire, such as earthquakes, eclipses, droughts, and pestilence. Lockhart (1992: 378) has characterized these events as "the sort of thing the populace would tend to become excited or concerned about and long remember." Enrique Florescano (1994: 51) has described the content of the annals as "the avatars and experiences undergone by the [ethnic] group from the beginnings of its migration to the present."

The annals preserve a very different view of the past than do the Mixtec *res gestae* and the cartographic histories. These are *altepetl* stories, concerned with events pertinent to the community at large, and they view the world as the people of the *altepetl* viewed it. In contrast to the Mixtec *res gestae* histories that focus on the genealogy, family history, and personal exploits of the ruling lords, and thus seem to be family-owned histories, the annals have very little that is genealogical or personal in them. Almost never do they include statements of marriage and progeny; wives, siblings, and offspring are not ordinarily part of the story.[1] There may be the occasional birth event, usually for the rulers of Texcoco (such as Nezahualcoyotl and Nezahual-pilli),[2] but it is characterized as an isolated occurrence, independent of mother and father. Rulers usually appear in the annals only when they succeed to the throne and when they die, and in these cases they are rendered conventionally as seated rulers and funerary bundles (Fig. 34). Conquests are also presented conventionally, by a place sign with a burning roof or a shield and spear, or occasionally by two humans fighting; there is rarely a sense of personal victory by one ruler over another. These are not personal or family stories but stories of the *altepetl* as a corporate body.

Land, too, is virtually ignored, for the annals are not about territory as such. Usually the location of most events in an annals account is left unmarked, because it is assumed to be the place where the document was painted. When location is given, it comes in the form of the place sign. Events do not happen in geographic space but in temporal space; they are not assigned to one place or another, but to one time or another. The reader may not always be sure where an event took place, but he or she always knows when it did. As Leibsohn (1993: 163) has pointed out, annals are essentially unsuited for showing the establishing of polities and setting of boundaries. She notes that in the Historia Tolteca-Chichimeca (an annals history that interweaves pictures and prose), the artist had to insert maps into the account in order to present this kind of information. A chief benefit of the annals history is its chronological structure, for it organizes all recorded history into a single sequence and thereby avoids the confusion caused by multiple competing sequences. Thus,

Bruce Byland and John Pohl (1994: 233–264), following Emily Rabin, adopted an annals format to organize and clarify the events of Mixtec history represented in the *res gestae* screenfolds. Indeed, prose sources often have a chronological table at the front or back of a prose history. The annals format, by focusing on time, can draw together a multitude of events in different places into a coherent statement.

The annals history is a particularly Aztec genre of painted history. Elites in near and distant parts of the Triple Alliance empire—from Tenochtitlan and Texcoco in the Valley of Mexico to Tlapan in Guerrero—had annals painted. The Mixtecs, however, did not, nor did the people of southern Puebla and the Coixtlahuaca Valley who were heavily Mixtec-influenced. Clearly the annals are Aztec to the same extent that the *res gestae* screenfolds are Mixtec. Elsewhere I have argued that the annals history is a form developed by the Mexica to accommodate their official history, one that was then adopted by other elites in the empire wishing to emulate or bind themselves to those in power at Tenochtitlan (Boone 1996). Although it is impossible to prove this point definitively, we can note that almost all the annals that are primarily pictorial either focus exclusively on the Mexica or concern themselves with Mexica history along with their own (Boone 1996: 201).[3] Those that are dedicated to Tenochtitlan history include the Codices Aubin (and cognates Fonds Mexicain 40 and 85), Azcatitlan, Boturini, Mendoza, and Mexicanus.[4] Annals from the Acolhua domain—Codex en Cruz and Tira de Tepechpan—cover Mexica as well as Acolhua events, as do the annals in the Codex Telleriano-Remensis and its copy, the Codex Vaticanus A/Ríos.[5] The Codices Moctezuma and Saville combine Tenochtitlan history with events in locations that are as yet unidentified (Glass 1975a: 170–171; Cuevas 1929). From Hidalgo to the north, the Codex Huichiapan intersperses Tenochca events with local occurrences, as do the Nahuatl glosses in the Anales de Tula (which carry almost all the historical information).[6] Even in distant Tlapan in Guerrero, the Codex Azoyu I (24) features Tenochtitlan's place sign, perhaps recording the coming of Aztec dominion over the area (Vega Sosa 1991: 83–84). The painters of these manuscripts were, moreover, working within the Aztec painting style (Boone 1996: 182–192); they were clearly thinking about Tenochtitlan and considered themselves culturally or politically tied to the capital.

This tradition of painted annals continued after the conquest and into the seventeenth century. In fact, all extant annals postdate the conquest. Beginning in the sixteenth century, the tradition also became alphabetic and continued in this manner as an important indigenous prose genre into the eighteenth century (Lockhart 1992: 376–392). A number of mid-sixteenth-century texts in Nahuatl and Spanish are essentially transcriptions or readings of pictorial annals covering preconquest history. Such are parts of the Historia de los Mexicanos por Sus Pinturas, the Relación de la Genealogía y Linaje de los Señores, and the Origen de los Mexicanos (known collectively as the Juan Cano Relaciones), the Anales de Cuauhtitlan, and the Anales Históricas de la Nación Mexicana (Anales de Tlatelolco), as well as Alvarado Tezozomoc's Crónica Mexicayotl and Chimalpahin's Relaciones, to name some of the best known.[7]

There are also prose annals that use the preconquest past as background for their principal topical focus on the colonial period (e.g., Anales de Tecamachalco [1992]), and others that concern themselves solely with the colonial era (e.g., Anales de Tepeaca, Anales de Tlaxcala [Gibson and Glass 1975: 373–374]). In these later prose annals especially, Lockhart notes a difference between the treatment of the distant past (the period before the annalist began) and the near past (when the annalist was writing). Prior to the date when the prose annalist actually begins, the entries are sparse and brief, but once the account reaches the then present, the entries are more detailed, vivid, and personal. Lockhart (1992: 381) notes that the annalists "seem to have recorded current events as they occurred, year in, year out, using their own observations and public knowledge as the source." Although such late-sixteenth- and early-seventeenth-century pictorial annals as the Codex Mexicanus and Codex Aubin may not have been pictorially updated year to year (their painting styles do not change this often), they do become increasingly partisan and crowded with details toward the end; new hands also add pictorial and alphabetic information.

Although most extant annals are documents unto themselves, several late-sixteenth-century examples are part of more comprehensive or diverse documents. The Codices Mexicanus, Telleriano-Remensis, and Huichiapan all preface their annals with calendrical and religious information. The Telleriano-Remensis opens with the eighteen monthly feasts and a fragmentary *tonalamatl,* and the Codex Huichiapan correlates the Otomi and Christian calendars and includes an alphabetic history of the Otomi town of Jilotepec before it begins its Huichiapan annals. The Codex Mexicanus contains dominical calendars, calendrical correlations, the zodiac, a diagram of humors, a partial *tonalamatl,* and a genealogy before its annals, and ends with another fragmentary *tonalamatl.* The Codex Aubin retains a consistent historical focus, but it appends a ruler list for Tenochtitlan to the end of its annals. In the Telleriano-Remensis, the annals history is included as one part of a cultural encyclopedia, a compendium of information on indigenous life, usually created to inform a Spanish readership. Such compendia of diverse genres, functioning like anthologies of indigenous intellectual culture, form a distinctly colonial genre.

Structure, Time, and Space

All annals by definition are organized around the continuing count of years, but these years can be configured in several different ways.[8] The simplest form is a single strip of sequent years placed side by side or bottom to top. Most extant annals are variations, however. Their ribbons of years are either broken into shorter segments to fit on a page of native or European paper, are bent to follow the edges of a page, or are pieced and stacked into neat clusters. Several annals even employ two or more configurations, either because their parts were copied from different sources or because the annalists were responding to different narrative needs. Many of the annals are painted on pages of European paper, bound as a book. In this situation, the artists had to adjust the ribbon of the year count to fit the relatively limited space of individual pages.

Unbroken Year Count

The original annals form seems to have structured the year count as an unbroken ribbon of time that runs across or up a long strip. Such is the Tira de Tepechpan (Fig. 127), which runs left to right, as well as the Codex Saville (Fig. 128; Cuevas 1929) and the first part of the

Codex Moctezuma, both of which run bottom to top. The Tira de Tepechpan and the Codex Saville, coincidentally, describe the years as circles rather than the usual rectangles.[9] Although the Codex Mexicanus (Fig. 34) is painted on pages of native paper bound as a book, it is structurally identical to these annals because it has a virtually unbroken year count that fully spans the width of facing pages. I believe this unbroken annals form to be prototypal because it takes advantage of the spatial features of the preconquest tira, and all the other forms begin with the strip of years and either bend it or break it.

Clearly derived from this form are annals that are painted on pages of European paper and divide the ribbon of time artificially into sections that fit, with margins, on each page. The Codex Aubin, in the imperial section (Fig. 129), for example, arranges the year count in short strips of five years that read top to bottom on each page. The migratory section of the Codex Telleriano-Remensis runs strips of ten years left to right across its pages.[10] In both these cases, the breaks in the year count carry no meaning themselves; they simply accommodate the limits of the European page. The time lines remain conceptually intact.

Another form of preconquest annals organizes the years around the fifty-two-year cycle. Acosta (1979: 282, 289) describes it as a history arranged as a cross. An example survives as the Codex en Cruz (Fig. 130), an amate strip that features three configurations of fifty-two years, which are each divided into four thirteen-year strips that are arranged like four spokes radiating from a central point (see diagram in Fig. 131). In each configuration, the years read from the center outward, first the spoke on the left, then the one on the bottom, on the right, and on the top, in a generally counterclockwise rotation (Dibble 1981: 4–5). The reader would presumably rotate the document as he or she read each thirteen-year section, for all the imagery is oriented to be viewed this way. In the Codex en Cruz, the artist has also ruled space for the imagery that would pertain to each year so that events occurring in each year could be stacked in the narrow column above the year sign. This dividing of the space for each year is not characteristic of any other annals and may not have been a feature of the usual preconquest form.

The Placement of Events in Temporal Space. In these annals with unbroken, straight year counts there is relatively little space beside the time line for events. This

---

Fig. 127. Tira de Tepechpan 12–13, covering the reign of Axayacatl from 2 Flint (1468) to 2 House (1481). Photograph courtesy of the Bibliothèque Nationale de France, Paris.

requires that events be reduced to their epitome, their simplest and most telling form. Thus, events in the annals are almost always conventions or symbols, and they are almost always drawn at about the same scale, which sets up equivalencies between them, intentional or not. We see this in the Codex Mexicanus (Fig. 34) and Codex en Cruz (Fig. 130) where the images presented side by side suggest events of the same magnitude. This is even more apparent in the Codex Aubin (Fig. 129), where the artist records a series of six events for the five years of 9 House through 13 House: the quarrying of stone at Malinalco and the death of the Mexican ruler Ahuitzotl, the seating of his successor Moctezuma Xocoyotzin, again the quarrying of stone at Malinalco, the beginning of trade in cacao, and finally the appearance of the Tzitzimitl, a celestial demon that descends to devour humankind when the sun fails, as during an eclipse (Lehmann and Kutscher 1981: 25–26, 153–155). Although we know from other sources that the quarrying of stone did not carry the same import as the change in the Mexica monarch, the annals form does not tell us this. It brings the events together as elements that carry the same historical weight.

Time governs the placement of these events along the year count. By this I mean that the placement of an event beside the time line carries temporal meaning. The area next to one year must logically pertain to that year and not another, and a change in location along the year count means a change in time. Although the painters usually record only one event (or none) for each year, when they must have two or more, they place them as much as possible within the space of the relevant year. The Codex Aubin historian grouped the work of the Malinalco stone cutters and the death of Ahuitzotl in the space next to the year 9 Flint in order to date them then (Fig. 129). He located the seating of Moctezuma next to its year of 10 Rabbit. The Tzitzimitl's visage at the bottom of the page is located there only because the demon appears in the year 13 House; a move to the middle of the page would signal that it appeared in 11 Reed. Just as in cartographic histories, where geographic space is the foundation for the presentation, in annals temporal space is the underlying ground on which events are recorded.

The Use of Experiential and Diagrammatic Space. Like cartographic histories, annals often interrupt this foundation space (be it geographic or temporal) to accom-

Fig. 128. Codex Saville, covering the reign of Axayacatl from 1 Reed to 2 House. The years 1 Reed (1467), 1 Flint (1480), and 2 House (1481) are named with date signs inside the circles. On the right side of the count appear Moctezuma's death and Axayacatl's accession in 1 Reed (*bottom*) and Axayacatl's death and Tizoc's accession in 2 House (*top*). On the left is a larger, unidentified ruler whose name sign is a reclining human within a cave. Photograph courtesy of the National Museum of the American Indian, Smithsonian Institution (N9653).

modate the needs of a more complex presentation. In the Tira de Tepechpan (Fig. 132), for example, the artist carves a scene out of the temporal space next to the year count in order to present an important episode that was part of the Tepanec war (when the Tepanecs of Azcapotzalco sought to overthrow the Acolhua and Tenochca rulers). The Tira is like a double annals, for it presents events pertaining to Tepechpan above the ribbon of the years and presents Tenochtitlan information below (Noguez 1978). When the Tepechpan rulers change, the circular frames around the year signs change color. Below the count we note the death of the Tenochca ruler Chimalpopoca (Smoking Shield) in 12 Rabbit, followed two years later in 1 Flint by the accession of his successor Itzcoatl (Obsidian Serpent). Three years later, we note the conquest of Azcapotzalco (Ant Heap) in the year 4 Reed, this event tied to Itzcoatl's speech scroll by a dotted line that tells us Itzcoatl ordered or was responsible for the conquest.

Below the conquest, the defeated Azcapotzalco ruler Maxtla (Loincloth) is pictured enthroned but with his eyes closed in death. Footprints extending from him back in time to the large scene above the line at 12 Rabbit signal that he was responsible for the actions there.

This earlier event is the murder of the Tepechpan ruler Tencoyotzin (Coyote Lips), who is graphically pictured being clubbed to death by four priests, who carry the priestly tobacco gourds on their backs, wear headdresses of the Tepanec god Otontecuhtli, and have name glyphs (Noguez 1978: 73, 79–80). The footprints tell us that they are Tepanecs from Azcapotzalco (as the Nahuatl gloss confirms), or that they come under the orders of Maxtla, or both, which is surely the case. Usually the deaths of rulers are indicated conventionally, as with Chimalpopoca below, whose murder Maxtla likewise ordered. Indeed the Tepechpan artist initially did draw Tencoyotzin simply as a similar funerary bundle, but he later changed his mind and decided

Fig. 129. Codex Aubin 39v–40r, imperial annals for 4 Flint (1496) through 13 House (1505). Events on 40r are as follows: 9 House, quarrying stone, death of Ahuitzotl; 10 Rabbit, accession of Moctezuma; 11 Reed, quarrying stone; 12 Flint, cacao trade; 13 House, descent of Tzitzimitl. Photograph courtesy of the British Museum.

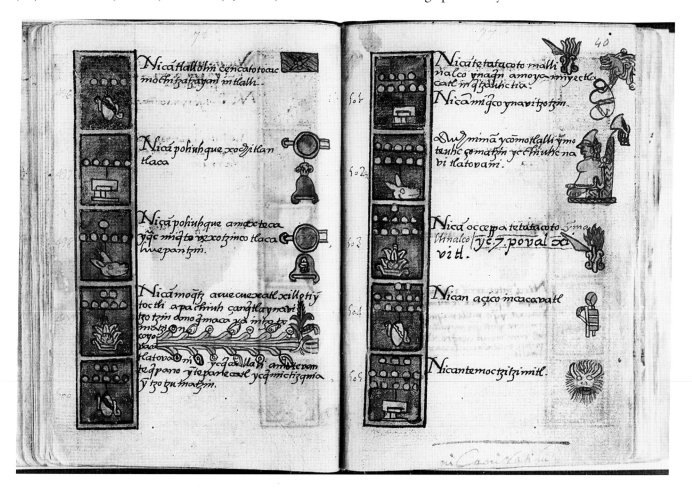

to provide more of the violent detail. He painted over Tencoyotzin's funerary bundle with white paint and covered it with the scene of the ruler being clubbed.

Immediately thereafter the lord Cuacuauhtzin (Strong [wooden] Staff) is represented walking away (Noguez 1978: 83–84). Footprints carry him to an unidentified place represented by a hill with flints (?) and the symbol for jade, where he may have stayed for the duration of the Tepanec war; footprints carry him back to the year count on 4 Reed, the year of Azcapotzalco's defeat, which suggests that he returned home then.[11] Nine years later (in 13 Rabbit) Cuacuahtzin is finally installed as ruler of Tepechpan.

This complex presentation of the deaths of the Tepechpan and Tenochtitlan rulers, the Tepanec war and eventual defeat of Azcapotzalco, and Cuacuahtzin's abandonment of Tepechpan and return requires several different kinds of space. Temporal space easily locates

Fig. 130. Central section of the Codex en Cruz, covering the years 1 Rabbit (1454) through 13 House (1505). Events pertaining to each year are fit in the strip just above the year (from Dibble 1981, atlas). Reproduced courtesy of the University of Utah Press.

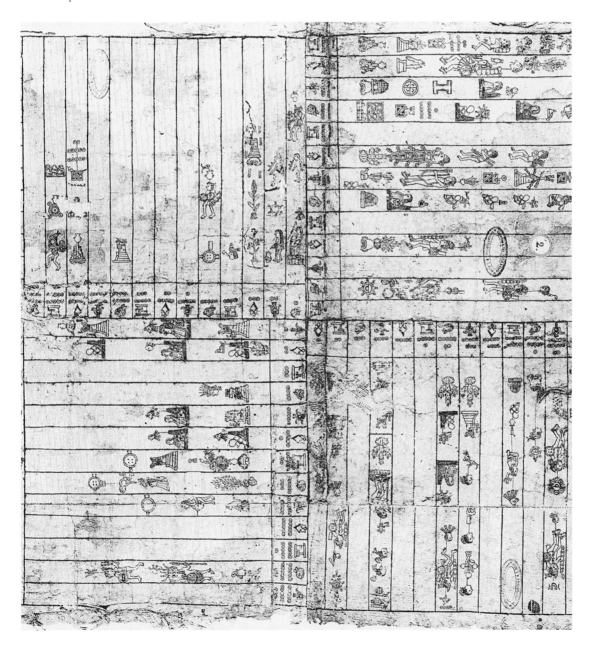

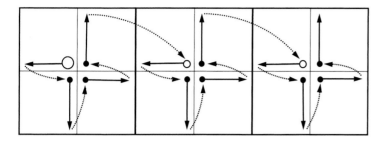

Fig. 131. Diagram of the reading order of the Codex en Cruz. The years read from the center outward in four blocks of thirteen, beginning with the upper left block. Drawing by John Montgomery.

several of the events securely in time. The placement of Chimalpopoca's death, Itzcoatl's accession, and the defeat of Azcapotzalco tells the reader when they occurred, and the three images marking Azcapotzalco's defeat (the place sign, shield and club, and Maxtla's death) are ordered nicely in line with the relevant year.

The scene of Tencoyotzin's murder, however, occupies more than the vertical space next to its year. The four assassins occupy the space of three more years, and the footprints that lead from Maxtla to them cross the space of another four. In order to explain how the ruler was killed and by whom, the artist has had to override the temporal space of the annals. He uses experiential

space to group the four assassins and victim in a single scene, and he uses a cross between itinerary and diagrammatic space to show how these men came from Azcapotzalco under Maxtla's orders. Then he links the temporally ambiguous scene to a fixed year with a line from Tencoyotzin's knee to the circle of 12 Rabbit. When Cuacuauhtzin leaves Tepechpan for the Hill of the Jade Disk and returns home five years later, another blend of itinerary and diagrammatic space accommodates his travels, the beginning and ending of which are also tied to the year count with lines (of dots and footprints, respectively).

In many other places in other annals, temporal space gives way to experiential space and diagrammatic space when the narrative requires that relationships other than strictly temporal ones be explained. Dotted lines, straight lines, and lines of footprints help to convey these other relationships, just as they do in the cartographic histories. Lines also serve to tie events to specific years when their dates might be unclear.

Regularly Bent and Spaced Year Counts

The unbroken year count has two mutations. One increases the temporal space around the years, and the other shrinks and commingles it. Colonial annalists, looking to give each year more space, simply spaced

Fig. 132. Tira de Tepechpan 9–10, reporting events related to the Tepanec war, including the deaths of Tencoyotzin and Chimalpopoca in 12 Rabbit (1426), the accession of Itzcoatl in 1 Flint (1428), and the conquest of Azcapotzalco in 4 Reed (1431). Photograph courtesy of the Bibliothèque Nationale de France, Paris.

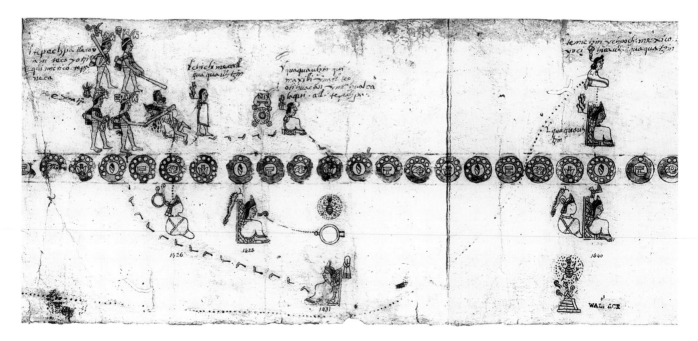

Fig. 133. Codex Azoyu I, p. 11, covering the years 8 Deer (1370) through 13 Movement (1376). CNCA.-INAH.-MEX; reproduced with permission of the Instituto Nacional de Antropología e Historia.

out the individual years across the page. We see this stretched time line throughout the annals of the Codex Huichiapan (which features two years to a page) and at the ends of the Codex Aubin (one year per page for fols. 48v–67v) and Codex Telleriano-Remensis (two to four years per page for fols. 32v–49r; see Fig. 151). This stretching out of the unbroken year count seems to have been a colonial response to the desire to add more information to the annals, for it appears at the ends of colonial annals that earlier followed tighter time lines. It does not represent a change in the conceptual structure of the annals, however; it only accords the years more space for the events assigned to them.

The other mutation takes the continuing year count and bends it to conform to and follow the edges of a page. In a tira format, we see this in the annals section of the Codex Borbonicus, where the years 4 House to 13 Rabbit run left to right across the top of the strip, only to turn back (where the strip is lost) and run right to left from 7 Reed to 2 Reed along the lower edge of the strip. In other examples, the bent year count ac-

commodates the shape of a page, rather than a tira. We see this on several pages of the Telleriano-Remensis annals (fols. 29r–31r) and throughout the Codex Azoyu I (Fig. 133).[12] In the Azoyu I, the Tlapan historian uses a regional variant of the year count—one that employs the numbers 2 through 14 and year signs Deer, Malinalli, Movement, and Wind—and he runs the count around two sides of each amate page, from the lower right to upper left. This act of framing the page with the year count unifies the space next to the years into a single panel, one that then may pertain to all the years that make up the frame. This provides the artist with a full panel to fill with one elaborate or several simple images, but it means that the exact timing of the events is often unclear. This page frame arrangement may be a colonial adjustment of the preconquest annals form, because it clearly accommodates the page format well.[13]

I consider these regularly spaced and bent forms mutations of the otherwise unbroken year count, for the spacing and bending seem not themselves to carry meaning. Other configurations of the year count do

Fig. 134. Codex Mendoza 2r, depicting the foundation of Tenochtitlan, surrounded by the year count from 2 House (1325, *upper left*) through 13 House (1349, *upper center*). Tenoch and nine other clan leaders encircle Tenochtitlan's place sign; below are recorded the conquest of Culhuacan and Tenayuca. The Bodleian Library, Oxford, MS. Arch. Selden. A. 1, fol. 2r.

carry meaning, however. In these, the artist intentionally alters the year count in order to emphasize or accommodate the story's narrative.

Intentionally Broken and Clustered Year Counts

A number of annalists addressed the occasional need for more pictorial space by halting the year count at specific moments in the story and by clustering the years into more compact packages. In these cases, the annalists break up the year count into historically meaningful sections or periods. The difference between these irregularly broken year counts and the regularly broken ones just discussed is that the cuts here carry narrative information.

The first part of the Codex Mendoza, for example, is an annals history that opens with the founding and development of Tenochtitlan and then continues with the reigns and victories of the Mexica rulers. The individual pages or facing pages of European paper are dedicated to different periods in Tenochtitlan's history. The first concentrates on Tenochtitlan's founding (Fig. 134); here the year count begins in the upper left corner in 2 House and runs for fifty-one years as a counterclockwise border around the page to end in 13 Reed at the top. This is not an arbitrary grouping of the years that simply frames the page; rather the fifty-one years represent the *altepetl*'s early, pre-imperial period. The Mendoza then continues on subsequent pages to present the successive years of each ruler, from Acamapichtli to Moctezuma Xocoyotzin, as individual strips (Fig. 135). Beside the strips are painted the installation of the ruler, the convention for war, and the towns each

Fig. 135. Codex Mendoza 10r–10v, covering the reign of Axayacatl from 4 Rabbit (1470) through 2 House (1481). The largest place sign documents the conquest of Tlatelolco and Moquiuix's fatal fall. Reproduced with permission from *The Codex Mendoza* by Frances F. Berdan and Patricia Rieff Anawalt (Berkeley: University of California Press, 1992), vol. 4.

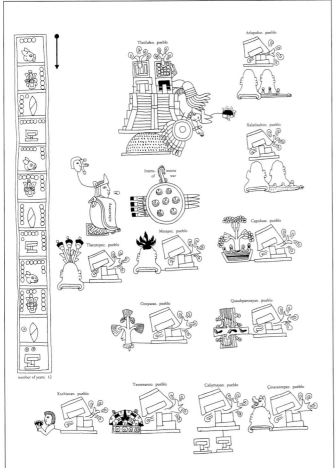

Fig. 136. Codex Azcatitlan 36–37, covering the reign of Axayacatl. Axayacatl's accession (*far left*) and death (*far right*) bracket the events, including eight conquests (*below*), the battle at Tlatelolco's temple

claimed to have conquered. This is indeed a continuous-year-count annals because all the years are presented, but it is one where the year count is subservient to larger events, these events being Tenochtitlan's founding and the reigns of the Mexica rulers. Within each reign, the victories are not separately dated; the paintings tell us only that they occurred during these years. Nor are the installation and the (assumed) death of the ruler dated precisely. The strip of years gives us either the inaugural year and last full year in office or the first full year in office and death year; the accompanying Spanish text tells us it is the latter (Boone 1992: 51). The year count strips tell about time, but they also function here as events in themselves; they define the reigns of the rulers.[14]

A mutation of the Codex Mendoza's structure, one further removed from the annals form, appears in the Codex Azcatitlan, where, after the founding of Tenoch-

titlan, the successive reigns of the Mexica rulers span facing pages (Fig. 136). The ruler's enthronement on the left opens each reign, and events in each reign are gathered in what seems to be roughly chronological order, but no hard dates are added. Like the Codex Mendoza, it is a history organized by reigns, except that the Codex Azcatitlan includes a broader range of events (paralleling the range of events pictured in the annals) and omits the years entirely. It is hard to say whether this organization of Mexica history reflects a preconquest form.

Clustered and Stacked Years. The liability of year counts that stretch the full length of tiras and pages (i.e., Tira de Tepechpan, Codex Mexicanus) is that the insistent listing of years as a straight line occupies so much space. Especially in early periods in an *altepetl*'s history, there were long stretches when nothing noteworthy happened; the annalist is still obligated to paint

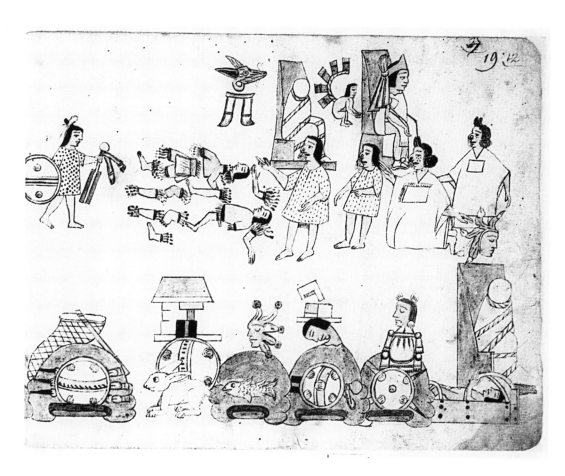

where Moquiuix died (*left*), and the death of Nezahualcoyotl and accession of Nezahualpilli (*upper right*). Photographs courtesy of the Bibliothèque Nationale de France, Paris.

all the years. One way around this was to cluster the years in rows or columns. Several annals do this effectively: all are migration histories, where the principal events are the movements and settlements along the journey. They are the Codex Boturini, the migratory portions of the Codex Azcatitlan and Codex Aubin, and two annals cognate with the Aubin (Fonds Mexicain 40 and 85).

The Codex Boturini, for example, alternates events with clusters of years, which it organizes in a boustrophedon. In Figure 137, footprints bring the Aztecs to settle at Tollan (Place of Rushes), this settlement marked by the place sign and the four seated Aztec men. Then follow the nineteen years of residence at Tollan—4 House through 9 Reed, after which footprints carry them to the next location. The Codex Aubin (Fig. 138) also alternates settlements with clusters of years, but it differs from the Boturini in two re-

spects: it orders the years left to right in rows stacked top to bottom (so that one follows the years in the same pattern that one follows the lines of an alphabetic text), and it places the years of residence before the place. Thus in Figure 138, the years of residence begin in the upper left and run from 3 Flint to 9 Reed, after which the artist paints Tollan's place sign. If one were to translate the pictorial texts, the Boturini would say "and the Mexica went to Tollan and remained for nineteen years from 4 House to 9 Reed," whereas the Aubin would say "and for twenty years, from 3 Flint to 9 Reed, the Mexica settled at Tollan." The two Fonds Mexicain annals (40 and 85) are very similar to the Aubin, except that they, too, put the place signs before the years of residence.

By clustering the years in blocks, the annalists free space for larger or more elaborate presentations of some events. The Codex Boturini takes advantage of

Fig. 137. Codex Boturini 7–8, covering the stay in Tollan over the years 4 House through 9 Reed and the stay in Atlitlalaquian (Where the Water Disappears) over the years 10 Flint through 6 House. CNCA.-

this especially later in the migratory story, when it follows a cluster of years with a *res gestae* explanation of how the Mexica were driven from Chapultepec and their ruler sacrificed at Culhuacan (Fig. 145), discussed more thoroughly below.

The Codex Azcatitlan likewise blends the annals form with a loosely flowing *res gestae* (Fig. 139). In fact, its blocks of years are placed very much to the sides and corners of the pages in order to leave as much space as possible for what is essentially a loose boustrophedon itinerary. Undulating left to right across the pages of European paper, the migratory path carries the Aztecs past a series of places; Tollan is in the upper right. The whole presentation is more pictorial and cartographic than those in the Boturini and Aubin. The artist depicts the Mexica traveling through space, from place sign to place sign but also over mountains and across rivers. This presentation is more like the migration

itineraries of the Mapa Sigüenza and Cuauhtinchan Map 2 than it is like a traditional annals history. Even though it includes all the sequent years, it is not always clear which years pertain to which event.

Mixed Formats

Several annals change the way they present the year counts. They begin using one form and shift to another. This is partially because the colonial documents that have come down to us were themselves redactions of several earlier sources that used different structures. It is also true that some annalists themselves chose to vary the structure in order to accommodate more narrative detail. Annals with mixed formats include the Codex Aubin (and cognates Fonds Mexicain 40 and 85), the Codex Telleriano-Remensis (and the Codex Vaticanus A/Ríos copy), and the Codex Moctezuma.

INAH.-MEX; reproduced with permission of the Instituto Nacional de Antropología e Historia.

The Codex Aubin, for example, shifts several times. It begins by employing an intentionally broken and clustered count of years interspersed with events to present the migration (Fig. 138). Then after the founding of Tenochtitlan, its years appear as regular strips, five to a page, emulating an unbroken year count but adapted to the European page (Fig. 129). The years of the Spanish invasion (1 Reed through 2 Flint) are intentionally spaced over several pages to accommodate the many events of those extraordinary times, after which the years return to the earlier pattern of five to a page. After 8 Flint (1552), however, the annalist accords each year its own page, which he fills with as many as ten different images; then the annalist pairs his last two years (12 Reed and 13 Flint [1595 and 1596]) on the same page. Thereafter, the original artist ceases work, and the annals history continues as a Nahuatl text, from 1597 to 1603, when a new painter picks up the old system and paints five years (8 Flint to 12 Flint) in a series down the page. The annals history finally ends with 12 Flint (1608), for which no event is recorded.[15]

Several other colonial annals become looser and lose their original structure toward the end. They also become increasingly alphabetic. We see this particularly at the end of the Codex Telleriano-Remensis, where the polychrome year signs and images eventually give way to boxes drawn in black ink with Spanish notations and then to alphabetic texts entirely.

The annals form, with its emphasis on time, is an ideal one for showing continuity. Because its narrative is usually based in one locale, its story is geographically stable, and the year count can carry the community's history forward endlessly in time. All the events are assumed to take place in the same *altepetl* unless otherwise indicated. The polity's place sign is not usually

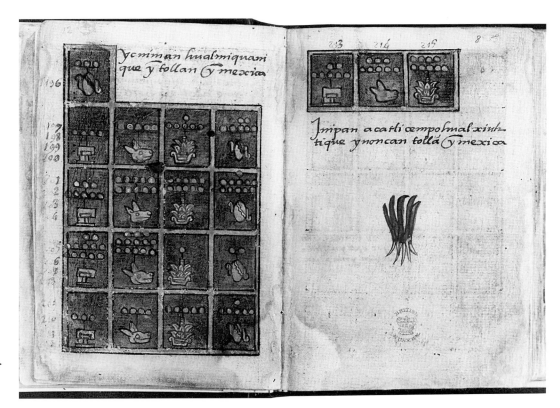

Fig. 138. Codex Aubin 7v–8r, covering the stay in Tollan over the years 3 Flint through 9 Reed. Photograph courtesy of the British Museum.

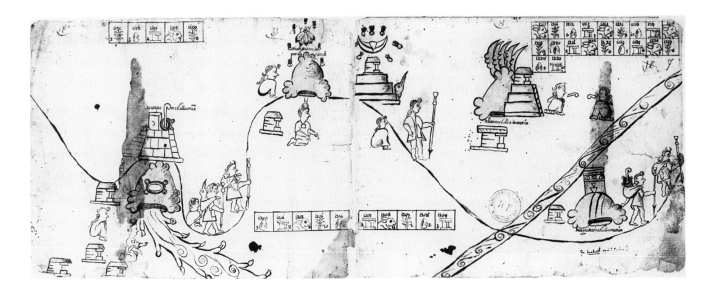

Fig. 139. Codex Azcatitlan 12–13, covering the migration past several sites in the years 2 Reed through 10 House; Tollan is in the upper right. Photograph courtesy of the Bibliothèque Nationale de France, Paris.

given, except in annals like the Codex en Cruz that present the histories of several *altepetl* simultaneously and must therefore employ place signs to keep the stories separate. The *altepetl* manifests itself in the presentation of its founding, but is otherwise implied rather than stated. When events, such as conquests, occur in another location, the place sign is given, more to qualify the event than to move the narrative to that location. Place is never the changing feature in the annals that time is.

Because place is so relatively unpronounced in annals, this narrative form is fundamentally unsuited to presenting migrations, where the narrative is the movement of people across the land. This is why so few extant annals (only the Codex Mexicanus and Tira de Tepechpan) present the migration along an unbroken, straight year count. The Aztec annalists addressed this basic incompatibility by breaking the year counts into shorter segments, which they could cluster on the tira or page and alternate with presentations of the migratory stops and activities. In order to accommodate the migratory story, they fused the annals and *res gestae* structures to achieve a dated itinerary, a tour of the places and events along the journey.

Annals Stories

There are hints that the Aztecs once painted cosmogonic annals, for part of the Historia de los Mexicanos por Sus Pinturas seems to derive from one. All existing pictorial annals, however, begin when the Aztecs leave Aztlan or later. Collectively their stories cover the migration, the imperial period after the founding of various *altepetl,* and the changing cultural situation after the arrival of the Spanish up to the seventeenth century. Although the colonial years follow the preconquest ones in an easy continuity, the migration stories and the imperial stories are usually actualized as distinct accounts, with different formats and entirely different kinds of events included in them. Thus, they are best analyzed as separate narratives. Table 1 summarizes the periods covered by thirteen annals.

Stories of the Mexica Migration

The migration story recounted in the annals is the story of the Mexica migration. Its features are sufficiently standardized to suggest that there existed a principal narrative that was circulated in several versions. The migration accounts in the Azcatitlan, Boturini, and Aubin seem to belong to one version of the narrative, as does Torquemada's (1975–1979, 1:113–135) alphabetic rendering. The Boturini and Aubin manuscripts are so close that they may well derive from the same (perhaps distant) prototype. The cartographic redaction in the Mapa Sigüenza seems to belong to another version, and the Codex Mexicanus, Tira de Tepechpan, and foundation scene in the Codex Mendoza fit somewhere in the middle, although the situation is far from clear. The migration account preserved incompletely in the Codex Telleriano-Remensis and Vaticanus A/Ríos seems to be from another tradition entirely. A separate study of the different versions is needed.

As the pictorial annals present it, the migration always begins in Aztlan, from where a group of tribes, usually eight, leaves for the journey to the Valley of Mexico.[16] They travel to a series of places, punctuated by Teoculhuacan, Coatepec, and Tollan, and reach the Valley of Mexico, where the Mexica are expelled from Chapultepec and their ruler sacrificed at Culhuacan. After living for a time under Culhua control, the Mexica eventually make their way to Tenochtitlan, where they found the capital. At the beginning of the story the annals usually name the migrating tribes; at the end, they sometimes name the Mexica tribal leaders.

The pictorial annals' insistence on an Aztlan departure might seem to be at odds with several prose accounts that name Chicomoztoc as the place of origin (e.g., Sahagún 1959–1982, bk. 10:195, 197; Torquemada 1975–1979, 1:47) and the well-known illustrations in Durán's history that show tribal couples seated in seven caves, followed by the migratory leaders moving forth out of a cave (Durán 1994: pls. 1–3).[17] The first page of the migration story in the Codex Vaticanus A/Ríos (66v) also pictures seven tribes coming from seven caves and does not mention Aztlan (Fig. 144; Quiñones Keber 1995: 197). These sources seem to be saying that the migration began at Chicomoztoc rather than Aztlan, but the situation is not that divisive. True,

Table 1. CONTENT OF THE AZTEC ANNALS

DOCUMENT	MIGRATION	IMPERIAL	COLONIAL
Aubin	Aztlan to founding	yes	to 1608
Azcatitlan	Aztlan to founding	yes	undated, but includes Bishop Zumárraga (1528+)
Azoyu	no	begins 3 Movement (1300)	to 8 Wind (1565)
Boturini	Aztlan to Culhuacan	no	no
Cruz	no	begins 1 Rabbit (1402)	to 12 House (1569)
Huichiapan	no	begins 2 Reed (1403)	to 10 Flint (1528)
Mendoza	foundation only	to death of Moctezuma (1521)	no
Mexicanus	Aztlan to founding	yes	last painted year is 7 Rabbit (1590)
Moctezuma	no	begins 1419?	to 5 Reed (1523)
Saville	no	begins 1407	years break off at 1535
Telleriano-Remensis and Vaticanus A/Ríos	from Chicomoztoc to founding	yes	last painted year is 5 Rabbit (1562)
Tepechpan	end of journey to founding	yes	breaks off at 1590
Tula	no	12 House (1361) to 3 House (1521)	no

the Aztecs understood Chicomoztoc generally as a place of origin, but they claimed Aztlan as their own homeland. Many prose sources reconcile any difference simply by equating the two places;[18] Durán (1994: 10–11, 213) himself explains that the seven caves were in Aztlan. A few prose annals differentiate the two but indicate that the Aztecs left Aztlan and then emerged from Chicomoztoc some years later (Historia de los Mexicanos por Sus Pinturas 1979: 42–43; Chimalpahin 1997: 105). This latter scenario may be what is pictured in the Codex Vaticanus A/Ríos, as explained below.

Departing Aztlan. In the pictorial annals, Aztlan itself is always an island in the middle of a rectangular lake. Usually it features a large hill sign, from one to nine buildings (including one that is larger and presumably the temple), and one or more of the people who reside there. The Codex Azcatitlan and Codex Boturini are stylistically different but iconographically very close here (Figs. 140, 141). They both feature a pyramidal platform with Aztlan's place sign (a vertical reed and the symbol for water) and picture a priest canoeing across the lake in the direction of Teoculhuacan (the bent hill).[19] Teoculhuacan is always pictured just on the shore opposite Aztlan, as if the two were conceptually linked; indeed, the prose sources often give Teoculhuacan as a variant name of Aztlan (e.g., Durán 1994: 10–11, 213). At Teoculhuacan the Azcatitlan and Boturini depict Huitzilopochtli as a hummingbird in a cave giving instructions to the Aztec people. The Codex Mexicanus (Fig. 142) offers a slightly different version of Aztlan's reed and water place sign, and it agrees with the Mapa Sigüenza (Fig. 106) in including a crowd of people being instructed by Huitzilopochtli, who speaks from the top of a tall tree. The hill sign at the top of its page is likely the place sign of Teoculhua-can. The year of leaving, and the first year of the Aztec annals, is always 1 Flint.[20]

Three of the pictorials (Aubin, Azcatitlan, and Boturini) immediately specify the eight tribes who left (Fig. 141); they list the same tribes in the same order, representing them by a house and their place signs (although the Aubin, which names them alphabetically, reverses the order). According to the place signs (confirmed by the glosses in the Aubin and Azcatitlan), the tribes are the Matlatzinca (hunting net), Tepaneca (stone), Chichimeca (bow and arrow), Malinalca (malinalli grass), Cuitlahuaca (dung [square and water]), Xochimilca (flower field), Chalca (jade disk), and Huexotzinca (little [rump] tree).[21] The Mexica are curiously absent from this list, and we must assume that the list is meant to name the *additional* groups who left with the Mexica.

Also pictured and named at this time are some of the individual leaders. Again the Aubin and Boturini agree (as does Torquemada) in presenting just four *teomama* (god bearers) who carry the image and accouterments of Huitzilopochtli's cult as bundles on their backs (Fig. 141): they are the priestess Chimalma (Shield), and the men Apanecatl (Water Banner), Cuauhcoatl (Eagle Serpent), and Tezcacoatl (Mirror Serpent), shown moving off on the journey. The Azcatitlan includes these four among its larger crowd of eleven. The Mapa Sigüenza, however, pictures and names an entirely different group of fifteen (Fig. 106), a group that includes individuals who appear at Tenochtitlan's founding in the Codex Mendoza.

Following this listing, the Aubin and Boturini both recount an episode that separates the Mexica from the eight other groups and sends them off alone. The pictorials explain how the resting migrants are disturbed by the breaking of a great tree, an augury, so Huitzilopochtli tells them, that the Mexica must leave the eight additional groups and journey alone. Torquemada (1975–1979, 1:113–114) also recounts this episode, which is particular to the Aubin-Boturini narrative tradition.

This separation behind them, the Mexica continue on the journey. The Codex Aubin and Boturini include the same sequence of places and the same years, whereas the others show variant routes and timings.

Three pictorials feature Chicomoztoc as a significant site along the migration. The Codex Azcatitlan and Codex Mexicanus (Fig. 143) both show the Mexica going to and leaving Chicomoztoc after the Aztlan departure, whereas the Codex Vaticanus A/Ríos (Fig. 144) begins its account here. In each case, the place is visually described as a seven-pocketed cave; in the Codex Mexicanus, it has a great tree growing up from its center and leafing out behind the year count. The Codex Mexicanus chooses this moment, not earlier, to name the migrating tribes; their seven place signs are attached to the seven pockets by lines that record their emergence.[22] Although the cave occupies the space next to three years (12 Flint to 1 Rabbit), 1 Rabbit is probably the date of emergence because it is the last of the three years, it falls twenty-six years (half a cycle) after Aztlan, and it is metaphorically linked to the earth. The next year, 2 Reed, is marked by tied cords or reeds signaling the binding of the years.

I suggest that the Vaticanus A/Ríos (Fig. 144) is recording a similar episode. As a copy of the Telleriano-Remensis, it preserves the painting and texts that are now missing from its prototype. The painting in the Vaticanus A/Ríos depicts seven men dressed as Chichimecs, one in each cave, and it follows this emergence with the year sign 2 Reed, which means that the caves date either to 1 Rabbit or 2 Reed. Moreover, this 2 Reed is the same date in absolute terms (A.D. 1195) as in the Codex Mexicanus. The glosses in the Vaticanus A/Ríos (which were also copied from the Telleriano-Remensis), however, identify the men with ethnic groups associated more with Puebla than the Valley of Mexico; this suggests, as Quiñones Keber (1995: 204–205) insightfully notes, that the original writer was following a Pueblan source rather than a Basin of Mexico source.[23] If this is the case, the writer (Pedro de los Ríos) took a fragmentary pictorial of the Mexica migration (Codex Telleriano-Remensis) and annotated it to pertain to another area (Puebla) with which he was familiar.

All the pictorials except the atypical Telleriano-Remensis (and its Vaticanus A/Ríos copy) include Tollan and Coatepec (where the Azcatitlan records Huitzilopochtli's birth). All also present in some detail the chain of events when the Mexica were expelled from Chapultepec, their ruler was sacrificed, and they became servants to the Culhua.

Fig. 140. Codex Azcatitlan 2–3, showing the Aztecs leaving Aztlan. Photograph courtesy of

Fig. 141. Codex Boturini 1–2, showing the Aztecs leaving Aztlan in the year 1 Flint (p. 1) along with eight other tribes led by four god bearers (p. 2). CNCA.-

the Bibliothèque Nationale de France, Paris.

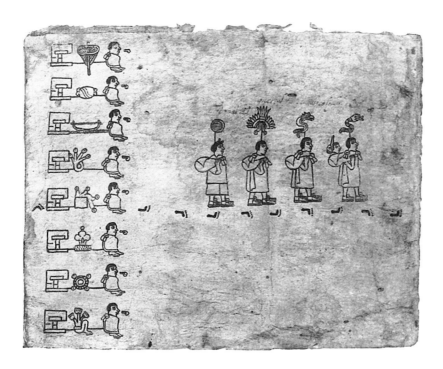

INAH.-MEX; reproduced with permission of the Instituto Nacional de Antropología e Historia.

Fig. 142. Codex Mexicanus 18, showing the Aztecs leaving Aztlan in the year 1 Flint. Photograph courtesy of the Bibliothèque Nationale de France, Paris.

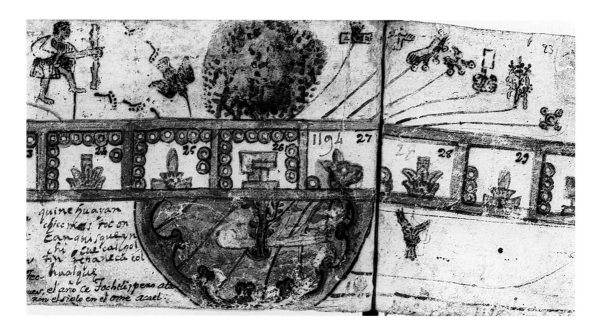

Fig. 143. Codex Mexicanus 22–23. The Aztecs are journeying to Chicomoztoc, where seven tribes emerge in 1 Rabbit (1194). Photograph courtesy of the Bibliothèque Nationale de France, Paris.

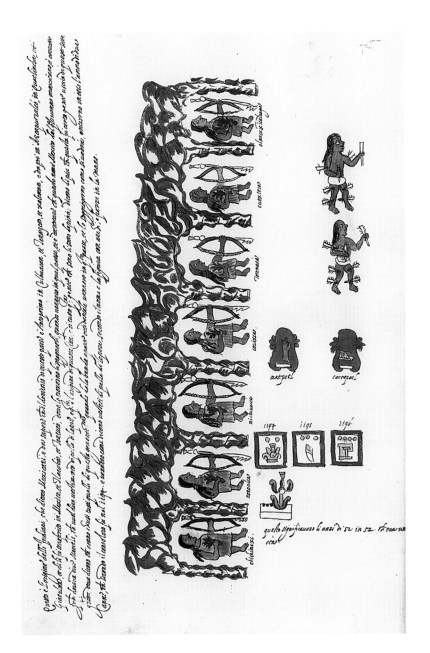

Fig. 144. Codex Vaticanus A/Ríos 66v. The Chichimecs are shown leaving Chicomoztoc, followed by the year 2 Reed (119[5]). Photograph courtesy of the Biblioteca Apostolica Vaticana.

The Culhuacan Captivity. This ignominious episode in their migratory past was clearly very important to the Mexica, for it is covered more thoroughly than any other in all the pictorial annals (including the Tira de Tepechpan and the Telleriano-Remensis and Vaticanus A/Ríos). The Codex Boturini (Fig. 145), for example, pictures the Mexica being forcibly expelled from Chapultepec in the year 2 Reed, after they had drawn their new fire. Prior to this, the migration in the Boturini had been relatively uneventful. The historian describes how the Mexica flee to the marshes of Acocolco (Twisting Water) where we see them weeping, now in miserable animal-hide clothes. Two warriors then bring the Mexica leader Huitzilihuitl (Hummingbird Feather) and his daughter Chimalaxochitl (Shield Flower) as captives before Coxcoxtli, the lord of Culhuacan, where

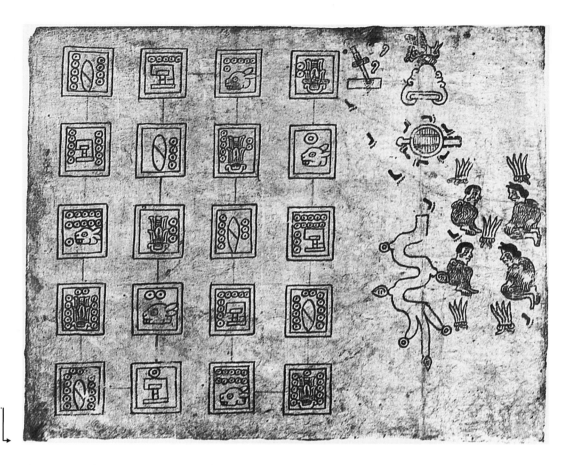

Fig. 145. Codex Boturini 19–20. After the Aztecs are defeated at Chapultepec and driven into the marshes (p. 19), they enter Culhua service when their leaders are brought before Cocoxtli (p. 20).

the two will be sacrificed.[24] The Mexica remain in Culhua servitude for several years. The last one and a half pages of the Codex Boturini explain how the Mexica assist their Culhua overlords in defeating the Xochimilca, including the extraordinary detail that the Mexica cut off the ears of every Xochimilca they captured or killed and presented these in bags to Coxcoxtli.

The painted annals agree that the migration then proceeds from Culhuacan to several locations—including the sequence Iztacalco (Place of the Salt House), Mixiuhcan (Place of Childbirth), and Temazcaltitlan (Sweatbath)—before reaching Tenochtitlan.

Founding of Tenochtitlan. Representations of the foundation itself are as standardized as images of the departure from Aztlan. Although there are a number of variations, they all draw on the same repertory of elements, which the artists could choose to add or not (Figs. 110, 134, 146–148). These elements include Tenochtitlan's place sign of a rock and nopal cactus, the

eagle perched on top of the cactus (with or without a bird or snake in its mouth), the named founders, the principal ruler Tenoch, early buildings, and a pictorial description of the lake. All the pictorials include Tenochtitlan's place sign; five of them include five or more founders (Mapa Sigüenza, C. Mendoza, Tira de Tepechpan, C. Mexicanus, C. Azcatitlan; Figs. 110, 134, 147, 146).[25] Five also describe the flora and fauna of the lake (Mapa Sigüenza, C. Mendoza, C. Aubin, C. Azcatitlan, C. Vaticanus A/Ríos; Figs. 110, 134, 148). Three add early buildings to the scene (C. Mendoza, C. Aubin, C. Azcatitlan; Figs. 134, 148), and three add the eagle (C. Mendoza, Tira de Tepechpan, C. Aubin; Figs. 134, 147, 148).

The foundation of Tenochtitlan brings the migration to a close. Usually this event occupies more space than any other event in the journey, except for the departure from Aztlan. In those manuscripts with unbroken year counts (e.g., C. Mexicanus and Tira de Te-

CNCA.-INAH.-MEX; reproduced with permission of the Instituto Nacional de Antropología e Historia.

pechpan), the founding occupies a large area of experiential or diagrammatic space next to the year count (Figs. 146, 147), but in those annals that break up the year count to accommodate events (e.g., C. Aubin, C. Azcatitlan), the founding usually fills a page or two (Fig. 148). It and the departure from Aztlan are the great events that bracket the migration, sitting like equivalents on either side of the journey that has transformed the Mexica from a humble tribe to the people destined to control much of Mesoamerica. Both events stress place; they ground the journey at the beginning and the end to these two specific sites, which are physically so similar.[26] These are the sites, too, that the annalists often choose to describe pictorially rather than represent glyphically.

Most annals that record the migration continue past the foundation to record the story of the *altepetl*. In these annals the foundation event is the base from which the imperial account proceeds. It identifies the *altepetl* and grounds the following narrative there. In the Tira de Tepechpan, for example, the founding of Tepechpan (in the register above the year count) and the founding of Tenochtitlan (below the year count and occurring later in time [Fig. 147]) initiate the *tlatoani* lines for these polities. In the Codex Mendoza (Fig. 134), the foundation is the event that establishes Tenochtitlan both as an *altepetl* and as the historical subject of the account. In annals that cover both the migration and the imperial story, the founding serves as a fulcrum for the two, culminating the migratory past and initiating the drive to imperial greatness.

Imperial Annals

Under this term "imperial" are the continuing stories of the *altepetl* after their foundation, both before the Triple Alliance empire came into being and after. The establishment of the empire is not itself marked in

Fig. 146. Codex Mexicanus 44. Tenochtitlan is founded in the year 2 House; eight clan leaders are named. Photograph courtesy of the Bibliothèque Nationale de France, Paris.

Fig. 147. Tira de Tepechpan 5. Tenochtitlan is founded in the year 7 House (1369); five named clan leaders appear with their wives. Photograph courtesy of the Bibliothèque Nationale de France, Paris.

Fig. 148. Codex Aubin 25v, showing the founding of Tenochtitlan. Photograph courtesy of the British Museum.

the annals, except under the guise of the conquest of Azcapotzalco, which is sometimes signaled (e.g., C. Azcatitlan 32, C. Mexicanus 61, C. Telleriano-Remensis 31r). The Aztecs, who did not themselves have a term for empire, based their political system on the *altepetl* and expanded from there (Gibson 1971: 378–379). I call the Aztec accounts imperial histories to distinguish them from the migration stories (and from the dynastic histories of the Mixtecs) and to reflect their emphasis on the conquest of other polities. The two major themes that run through the imperial annals are the continuing line of Mexica rulers and the many conquests they achieve.

Coverage of Altepetl. Most painted imperial annals, like the migration accounts, are Mexica stories, concerning themselves with events relevant to Tenochtitlan, but several cover more than one *altepetl* and are less Tenochtitlan-focused. The Codex Mendoza, which concentrates on conquests, treats the Mexica exclusively, as does the wider spectrum of events in the Codex Aubin. Other annals, namely the Codices Azcatitlan, Mexicanus, and Telleriano-Remensis, focus largely on the Mexica and are soundly Mexica-based, but they also include a few events pertinent to their important neighbors in the Valley of Mexico—for example, the accessions of Tezozomoc of Azcapotzalco and Nezahualcoyotl of Texcoco. In the Codex Azcatitlan (whose imperial part is not technically an annals account but probably derives from one), the artist places notices of Texcoco's affairs off to the side of the principal stream of Tenochtitlan events. The Codex Telleriano-Remensis is the broadest of all the extant painted annals in its subject focus. As Quiñones Keber (1984: 99; 1995: 198, tables 14 and 15) points out, it records events in the Valley of Mexico from a Mexica point of view, but it also pictures the seating of the two principal Texcocan rulers (Nezahualcoyotl and Nezahualpilli) as well as rulers and events of several other polities (some unidentified). The only full sequence of successive rulers, however, is for Tenochtitlan; Tlatelolco's rulers appear, but only when they do battle (twice against the Mexica; i.e., 31r, 33v, 36v; Quiñones Keber 1995: table 14).[27] Despite these inclusions, these five annals look at the world from the perspective of Tenochtitlan.

Two annals take a decidedly Acolhua perspective. Although the Tira de Tepechpan covers Tepechpan and

Tenochtitlan history almost equally, its point of view is the relatively small *altepetl* of Tepechpan in the Acolhua realm; Tenochtitlan seems to be included to elevate Tepechpan visually to a status paralleling that of Tenochtitlan (Boone 1997: 186–187) and also because at least one Tepechpan lord married into the Mexica royal family. The Codex en Cruz covers slightly more Texcocan events than Tenochtitlan ones; it also treats political and kinship relations between the Texcocan court and the small polities of Tepetlaoztoc and Chiauhtla and selects events that are important to these towns (Dibble 1981: 5, 59). Because the Codex en Cruz concentrates on land assignments in Chiauhtla toward the end of its history, Dibble favors Chiauhtla as its place of origin. These Acolhua annals, like the Mexica ones, choose to present some events and omit others according to the interests of their own *altepetl*.

Annals from other polities likewise juxtapose or blend Tenochca rulers and events with their local ones. The Codex Huichiapan (from Huichiapan near Tula) and the Codices Saville (Fig. 128) and Moctezuma (perhaps both from the Valley of Mexico) are incompletely studied and remain poorly understood, but one can see that they present the succession of Tenochtitlan rulers even while they concentrate on the native rulers and events pertinent to their own *altepetl* (Caso 1992; Cuevas 1929; Glass 1975a: 170–171). Only the Codex Azoyu I from distant Tlapan shuns the rulers of Tenochtitlan (Vega Sosa 1991).

Coverage of Events. Events in the imperial annals are fairly standardized, although some annals include more or fewer and slant them one way or another.[28] They are the kind of occurrence likely to be of interest to the people of a community. The most basic elements, after the year count, are the sequent rulers and the binding of the years or the New Fire ceremony at the turn of the fifty-two-year cycle. Even the simplest annals, such as the Tira de Tepechpan and Codex Saville, include these.[29] The fifty-two-year cycle can be marked in several ways: as a fire drill (C. Telleriano Remensis, C. Mendoza [Fig. 134]), as a knot of reeds or cord next to the year count (C. Saville, C. Mexicanus [Fig. 143]), or most simply as a knot around the Reed of the year sign (C. Mendoza, C. Boturini, Tira de Tepechpan [Figs. 134, 145]). The Codex en Cruz records the ceremony in 1502 by picturing people on a rooftop looking for the new fire to be drawn (Dibble 1981: 39–40;

Quiñones Keber 1984: 101). Royal succession comes with the pictured funerary bundle of one ruler immediately followed by the seating of the next, although deaths are often omitted for brevity.

Conquests are the elements next in importance. They are included in every extant annals and, overall, are the most numerous events recorded. This should not surprise us, because the Aztec empire was created and maintained by conquests (either diplomatic or military) over neighbors and distant peoples, and Mexica *tlatoque* had to prove themselves with a victory on the battlefield before their accession to the throne was fully valid. Since most of the annals pertain to the Mexica, the conquests are largely Mexica ones, but local victories take their places in the local stories. Conquests dominate all the other events in the Codices Azcatitlan (Fig. 136) and Telleriano-Remensis. In the Codex Mendoza (Fig. 135) historical reportage is limited to the accession of the Mexica rulers and their claimed conquests, for the codex was commissioned as a report to Charles V on the Mexica lords, their successes in war, and thus their territories (Boone 1997: 157).

Other cultural phenomena included in many of the annals are significant building programs and their dedicatory ceremonies, the occasional sacrifice, and the establishment of trade or tribute relations. Several annals record the impressive dedicatory ceremony that accompanied Ahuitzotl's renovation of the Templo Mayor in 8 Reed (1487), preceded by Tizoc's renovation a few years earlier (C. Aubin 38rv, C. Azcatitlan 39, 41; C. Mexicanus 71, C. Telleriano-Remensis 38v–39r); the Telleriano-Remensis also includes the dedication of a temple in Tlacopan as well as the sacrifice of important war captives on other occasions (40r–42v). The Codex en Cruz records the principal Templo Mayor dedication as well as the completion of temples in Texcoco and Chiauhtla (2b, 2c; Dibble 1981: 20–21, 26–27, 29–30). The Codices Aubin and Telleriano-Remensis mention when certain trade routes are opened or new sources of tribute are established, these being for such luxuries as cacao (Fig. 129) and jewelry (C. Telleriano-Remensis 33r, 33v, 43r). These kinds of cultural events are occasionally recorded in the Mixtec screenfolds, but the next category is not.

The annals as a historical genre is distinctive in recording astronomical events and climatic or ecological phenomena. Noteworthy celestial events include solar eclipses, a comet, columns of fire, and the like. Events on the ground range from earthquakes, droughts, devastating storms, and floods to plagues of mice and grasshoppers. These climatic and ecological events share the feature that they are potentially harmful to people and the subsistence base; the earthquakes must particularly have frightened people who understood that the present world would disintegrate in an earthquake. The disastrous drought and famine of 1 Rabbit (1454), when so many people in the Valley of Mexico starved and died, is noted in most of the annals. Astronomical phenomena are mentioned principally in the Telleriano-Remensis, which counts four eclipses, one comet, a light in the sky, and a column of smoke to the heavens. The Telleriano-Remensis also records the most natural disasters, followed by the Codices Mexicanus and Aubin. In contrast, the Codex Azcatitlan and Tira de Tepechpan omit the natural and climatic phenomena altogether (Quiñones Keber 1984: 100). Clearly, different annalists had different opinions about which events should be recorded and which ones should be passed over.

The Reign of Axayacatl. The nature of the annals genre and the variety within it are apparent when their perspectives on the same period of time are compared. The reign of the Mexica ruler Axayacatl (Water Face), for example, is reported in nearly forty pictorial and alphabetic sources. I have chosen to focus on its pictorial telling because Axayacatl's rule was rich with a full range of events, and his recorded life also features several personal episodes, events of a biographical nature that are not usually recorded in the annals. I concentrate here on seven pictorial versions of his reign: the Tira de Tepechpan and the Codices Azcatitlan, Mendoza, Aubin, Mexicanus, Telleriano-Remensis, and en Cruz. Although these annals differ in their coverage and dating of events, most agree on several basic ones, summarized in Table 2. Axayacatl's reign began in 2 Flint–5 Reed (1468–1471) following Moctezuma Ilhuicamina's death and ended with his own death in 2 House–4 Reed (1481–1483).[30] The two major events reported during this time are his conquest of neighboring Tlatelolco and his being badly wounded in the battle of Xiquipilco (Incense Bag) during the Matlatzinca campaign, which most of the annals cover more elaborately than they do other events. The other conquests usually reported are of Cuetlaxtlan (Tanned

Table 2.

THE COVERAGE OF MAJOR EVENTS IN AXAYACATL'S REIGN IN SEVEN ANNALS

DOCUMENT	ACCESSION	DEATH OF NEZAHUALCOYOTL AND ACCESSION OF NEZAHUALPILLI	CONQUEST OF TLATELOLCO
Aubin	5 Reed (1471)	—	7 House (1473)
Azcatitlan	day 1 Water	yes	day 5 Rain
Cruz	2 Flint (1468)	6 Flint (1472)	7 House
Mendoza	4 Rabbit (1470)*	—	yes
Mexicanus	4 Rabbit	—	7 House
Telleriano-Remensis	3 House (1469)	6 Flint	7 House
Tepechpan	2 Flint	—	—

DOCUMENT	BATTLE OF XIQUIPILCO	EARTHQUAKE	ECLIPSE	DEATH OF AXAYACATL
Aubin	12 Rabbit (1480)	9 Reed (1475)	13 Reed (1479)	1 Flint (1480)
Azcatitlan	yes	—	—	yes
Cruz	12 Rabbit	—	—	2 House (1481)
Mendoza	yes	—	—	2 House
Mexicanus	12 Rabbit	9 Reed	13 Reed	4 Reed (1483)
Telleriano-Remensis	12 Rabbit	1 Flint (1480)	10 Flint (1476)	4 Reed
Tepechpan	—	—	—	2 House

*The C. Mendoza records the first full year in office.

Leather), Ocuillan (Caterpillar), and Matlatzinco (Hunting Net). During this time, Nezahualpilli succeeded Nezahualcoyotl as lord of Texcoco, and there was an earthquake and an eclipse.

Typically, the Tira de Tepechpan is the most terse (Fig. 127). It notes only Axayacatl's accession the same year his predecessor died and his own death when Tizoc became lord.[31] The Codices Mendoza and Azcatitlan offer more information, concentrating on Mexica conquests during his reign. In the Codex Mendoza (Fig. 135), Axayacatl's reign length runs along the left

side of the page, beginning with the ruler's first full year in office and ending with his death year (Boone 1992: 36; Berdan and Anawalt 1992, 4:24–26). His actual seating is stated by the image of Axayacatl enthroned, whereas his death is signaled only by the end of the count. In front of the *tlatoani,* a shield and spears introduce the reader to the thirty-seven conquests that fill this page and the next, in no presently understood order. These conquests, and the accession and death of the ruler, are the only events recorded, although the conquest of Tlatelolco is presented more elaborately than the rest. It was a major event in Mexica history when Axayacatl declared war on his brother-in-law and brought Tlatelolco fully under Mexica control. The alphabetic chroniclers explain how Moquiuix (Drunken Lord) retreated to the top of his own temple, from where he either was thrown alive or dead, or jumped (as the accompanying text states).[32] His death fall is what the artist reports here; Moquiuix's name sign is here an iconographic referent to his name—the face of a pulque god with hair of foam.

Sharing the same structure but lacking the year count, the Codex Azcatitlan (Fig. 136) also concentrates on Mexica conquests and elaborates the Tlatelolco victory (Barlow and Graulich 1995: 116–119). It begins with Axayacatl's seating on the left, dated here to the day 1 Rain in the lower left corner, and it ends with the ruler's death on the far right.[33] Between these points, the conquests run as a straight line left to right, the hill signs slightly overlapping in an implied chronological order.[34] The conquest of Tlatelolco is the second one pictured, where Tlatelolco's place sign is embellished with what I suggest is Moquiuix's name sign (Drunken One, appearing as a vomiting face) and the day of victory, 5 Rain. The pictorial elaboration of this conquest is presented above as a scene that spans the width of the facing pages in what is, in effect, a second register. Around Tlatelolco's great pyramid, Axayacatl and other Mexica warriors in quilted cotton armor (on the left) defeat the Tlatelolcans, who are shown killed and cut into pieces. The dismembered body tumbling down the pyramid is identified as Moquiuix by his turquoise diadem among the scattered weapons. On the right, captives wait with bloodied noses, the women also crying. In the upper right corner, a third register above and behind the Tlatelolcan losers records the death of Nezahualcoyotl (Fasting Coyote) and the subsequent accession of Nezahualpilli (Fasting Prince), lords of Texcoco. The Codices Mendoza and Azcatitlan stand out from the other annals, because both group all of the events in Axayacatl's reign together without establishing their precise dates. They also focus on conquests, and they elaborate the defeat of Tlatelolco.

In contrast, the Codices Aubin, Mexicanus, Telleriano-Remensis, and en Cruz are more typically annalistic in that they assign each event to a specific year and they concentrate less on the conquests. The Aubin

(Fig. 149) is the most succinct of the four, for it represents all the events conventionally and without any pictorial elaboration (Lehmann and Kutscher 1981: 23–24, 150–152). It reports the death of Moctezuma and seating of Axayacatl in 5 Reed, followed by the conquest of Xochitlan, the conquest of Tlatelolco, an earthquake, the conquests of three other polities,[35] and an eclipse. Axayacatl's death is not pictured (although the gloss mentions it), but it is implied by the seating of Tizoc in the year 1 Flint.

The Mexicanus (Fig. 150) is similar in that it glyphically records both the death and accession of the relevant rulers and, in between, the conquests of six polities as well as the earthquake and eclipse (Mengin 1952: 452–455).[36] Twice, however, it pictures Axayacatl actually in battle. The ruler is unnamed but wears his distinctive Xipe costume when he attacks the Tlatelolco temple in 7 House (the temple drawn with a diminutive Moquiuix on top) and in 12 Rabbit when he is badly wounded in the leg by the ruler/warrior Tlilcuetzpal (Black Lizard) during the conquest of Xiquipilco in the Matlatzinca campaign.

The Telleriano-Remensis (Fig. 151) likewise employs conventions for the deaths and accessions of rulers and for the earthquake and eclipse, but it becomes more pictorial with the conquests (Quiñones Keber 1995: 220–224). For most conquests, the annalist paints the shield and spears and adds a pictorial description of men fighting. Generally a Mexica warrior (identified ethnically by Tenochtitlan's place sign) fights a named or unnamed enemy who is standing on his place sign.[37] The annalist further elaborated the battle of Tlatelolco, however, by picturing Moquiuix at the base of his great temple and adding Tlatelolco's three allies around it (the named lords of Coyoacan [Coyote], Culhuacan [Bent Hill], and Tenayuca [Ramparts]; Fig. 151). Moquiuix is named by the sign of a pulque bowl.

The Codex en Cruz (Fig. 152) stands apart from the others because it is an Acolhua document and naturally focuses more on the affairs of Texcoco than of Tenochtitlan (Dibble 1981: 13, 20–26). The thirteen-year period beginning in 1 Reed opens with the dedication of temple pyramids in Texcoco (below) and Tlatelolco (above), the latter marked by Tlatelolco's place sign (here a pot, mound of earth, teeth). Mexica events are usually accompanied by Tenochtitlan's place signs when they are included. In 2 Flint the annalist presents the death of Moctezuma and the accession of Axayacatl above Tenochtitlan's place sign. Texcocan events follow in the next several years, including the dedication of two temple pyramids and, in 6 Flint, Nezahualcoyotl's death and Nezahualpilli's accession. Because it is understood that these events occurred in Texcoco, no place sign is added. In 7 House, the conquest of Tlatelolco is signaled by Tlatelolco's place sign, temple, and the shield and club war sign. Moquiuix is also present; he is pictured during his fall, identified by a name sign that renders his name phonetically as a mouse trap (*mon*) and an eye (*ix;* Dibble 1981: 22–23).[38] In 12 Rabbit, the annalist records the battle of Xiquipilco by picturing Axayacatl full figured and dressed in his Xipe battle costume, and above him the warrior Tlilcuetzpal (Black Lizard) who wounded him. Three years later, after the annalist records Huastec participation at the dedication of a temple pyramid in Tenochtitlan, he records Axayacatl's death and Tizoc's succession in 2 House.

These seven painted annals agree on the major features of Axayacatl's reign, and they agree on many of the dates (Table 2). They vary most widely in dating Axayacatl's accession and death, which suggests that slippage may have occurred when the annals were copied from their earlier sources or when these sources were themselves made. A slippage of a year or two can easily happen because one source may note the accession year, whereas another source notes the first full year in office, or the death year as opposed to the last full year in office; copyists may then compound the errors (Glass 1974: 14–15). Given the four-year range of accession and death dates summarized in Table 2, it is surprising that all the annals agree on the dates of the battles of Tlatelolco and Xiquipilco, but, of course, there is less room for movement with these singular events. Three annals report an earthquake and eclipse, but in different years, and we have to question whether these are the same events dated differently or are multiple events dated correctly. An investigation of this,

Fig. 149. Codex Aubin 37r–37v. The reign of Axayacatl from 5 Reed (1471) through 1 Flint (1480). Photograph courtesy of the British Museum.

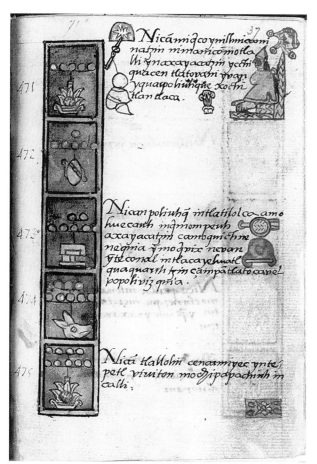

Fig. 150. Codex Mexicanus 68–71. The reign of Axayacatl from 4 Rabbit (1470) to 4 Reed (1483). Photograph cour-

which is outside the scope of this study, would need to consider whether the annalists were dating these phenomena relative to other events and not simply according to the year count.

Three of the annals also note the change in rule at Texcoco. It is natural for the Acolhua Codex en Cruz to do so, but the Azcatitlan and Telleriano-Remensis also do so because they are more inclusive than other Mexica-based annals. They do not add Texcoco's place signs because the Texcocan rulers were sufficiently well known. The death of Nezahualcoyotl (who carried independent Texcoco to cultural greatness after the Tepanec war) and the succession of Nezahualpilli (who died shortly before the Spanish invasion after a rule of over forty years) would have been events of major importance in the valley.

This comparison of reportage in seven Aztec annals reveals that individual annalists were relatively free to choose what they considered noteworthy. The only events during this period noted in all these annals are the accession and death of Axayacatl. After that, the perspectives of the annalists governed their choices. Most probably chose to represent the major battles of Tlatelolco and Xiquipilco because these were extraordinary incidents in which *tlatoque* were killed or badly wounded, and they must have been the subject of

much discussion among the people. This brings up the point that the episodes recorded in these imperial annals are as much community focused as they are elite focused, which is in contrast to the other historical genres. The imperial annals, more than any other genre, record events that affect the community at large.

The imperial annals, more so than other historical forms, also present the stream of these events as ongoing and relatively indivisible; the accounts do not form themselves into coherent chapters or sections. If there is any periodicity to the imperial annals, it comes in the forms of the reigns of the rulers, usually Mexica rulers. These reigns and the year count are the foundation on which other information is put.

King Lists. A genre related to the imperial annals is the king list. Pictorial lists of the *tlatoque* of Tenochtitlan, Texcoco, and Huexotla are found in Sahagún's Primeros Memoriales (1993: RAH 51r–53v; 1997: 185–196) and Codex Florentine (1959–1982, bk. 10:1–5), where accompanying alphabetic texts note the reign lengths and tell of conquests and other events during the reigns. A number of prose sources likewise include this kind of descriptive list of *tlatoani* reigns, which are alphabetic versions of the Mendoza and Azcatitlan (e.g., Anales de Tlatelolco [1948: 3–12, 15–18] and Codex Chimalpopoca [Bierhorst 1992: 134–138]; see also

tesy of the Bibliothèque Nationale de France, Paris.

Nicholson 1971: 52). Even sparer is the painted list of Mexica rulers that follows the annals history in the Codex Aubin (70r–79r), where the artist shows the ruler seated in office and paints turquoise disks to note the duration of his reign but adds no other information. These pictorial and alphabetic listings of the rulers and their reigns represent distant and stripped-down variants on the annals theme. They differ from the Mixtec and Coixtlahuaca Valley ruler lists in omitting the female half of the couples.

Then the Spaniards Came

Annals remained a viable historical form through the sixteenth century and into the seventeenth. The traditional structure keeps fundamentally steady: unbroken year counts remain unbroken, and regularly broken ones often retain the same pattern. The iconography changes, to be sure, with the introduction of European objects, persons, and forms, and sometimes the figural style becomes less sure, but the indigenous pictography remains largely intact. These are, after all, documents painted mostly for native use rather than Spanish use. Postconquest annals still record accessions and deaths of rulers, conquests, astronomical events, natural disasters (now more epidemiological than cli-

matic), building programs, and other *altepetl* events, but they expand on this repertory to include the activities of important Spaniards. They continue to address the concerns of the *altepetl* by bringing the Spaniards into their ongoing story.

The annals show how the Aztecs viewed the Spaniards first as aliens and invading conquerors and then as collaborators and leaders. Their accounts of the conquest tell us what elements and episodes the Aztecs themselves considered the most important. The annals also record events that alter and shape the systems of government and religion, just as they did in preconquest times, and they are careful to include the acts whereby indigenous rulers retained or enhanced their power.

The features that characterize the Spaniards as a distinct people for the Aztecs—the first things the Aztecs noticed and mentioned—are those things that the Spaniards had or used that the Aztecs did not. These are, principally, their clothes and beards, their steel weapons, their ships, their horses, and their religion. The first image of the Spaniards, in the temporal framework of the annals, comes on 13 Rabbit (1518) in the Codex en Cruz, when an indigenous merchant spies the Spaniards at sea (Fig. 153; Dibble 1981: 45). The merchant's cape, fan, and walking stick identify him;

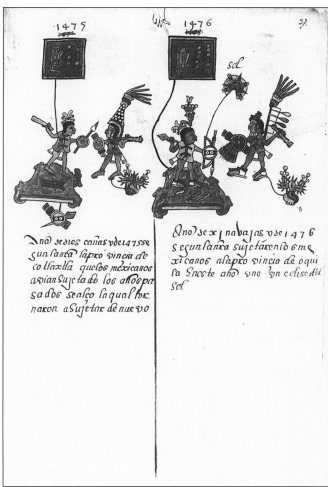

Fig. 151. Codex Telleriano-Remensis 36v–37r. Part of the reign of Axayacatl. Tlatelolco is conquered in 6 House; in other years, polities are defeated as part of the Matlatzinca campaign. Photograph courtesy of the Bibliothèque Nationale de France, Paris.

the symbols of eyes convey the action of his looking. His gaze is directed at two bearded Spaniards with brimmed hats and steel-tipped lances, who are cupped by a lunette (implicitly their ship) floating in water that is conventionally rendered. The annalist brings attention to the Spaniards' distinctive pointed banner (so different from Aztec banners) and the cross between them, respectively symbolizing the Spanish government and the Catholic church. The year is 1518, when Moctezuma's merchants observed Juan de Grijalva's expedition off the coast of the Yucatan Peninsula. In the next year, 1 Reed (1519), the annalist characterizes the Spaniards as men on horseback, again with steel lances, who arrive in Tenochtitlan. In other painted annals,

too, the Spaniards are consistently bearded, they carry the distinctive steel lance or sometimes a sword, and they wear either the brimmed hat or a helmet. Most annals show them mounted. According to the Aztec annalists, the Spaniards are characteristically equestrian.

Most of the painted annals describe the conquest as a complex series of events that occur over several years. Except in the Codex en Cruz, these events begin with the arrival of the Spaniards in 1 Reed (1519) and continue through the fall of Tenochtitlan in 3 House (1521) to the death of Cuauhtemoc, the last independent Mexica *tlatoani,* in 6 Flint (1524). A comparison of two versions of this story—in the Tira de Tepechpan and the Codex Mexicanus—illustrates the usual features.

In the Tira de Tepechpan (Fig. 154), the annalist locates Spanish events both above and below the year count, blending to some extent the Tepechpan/Tenochtitlan division (Noguez 1978: 105–119). In the year 1 Reed the annalist pictures Cortés below the count; we note the characteristic lance, hat, beard, long-sleeved tunic, and tall boots (painted red probably to symbolize tanned leather). Above the year count, the cross and the dove of the Holy Spirit symbolize the simultaneous arrival of Christianity. In 2 Flint the smallpox epidemic that devastated Mexico-Tenochtitlan and surrounding polities is represented by a spotted seated man. Above him the woman Ome-

tochtli (Lady 2 Rabbit), regent of Tepechpan, has died of the disease, for her funerary bundle is attached to the stricken man with a dotted line.[39] Below, in Tenochtitlan, the artist reports the burning of the Templo Mayor, the death of Moctezuma Xocoyotzin (Angry Lord), the accession of Cuitlahuac (Dung), and then his death eighty days later (the eighty days represented by the four disks and banners). Cuauhtemoc's (Descending Eagle) accession is reported the next year, 3 House. The Tira does not actually record Cuauhtemoc's surrender and the fall of Tenochtitlan to the Spanish. It does report that Cuauhtemoc died in 6 Flint (1524), where his funerary bundle is pictured. The de-

Fig. 152. Codex en Cruz 2b–c. The reign of Axayacatl from 2 Flint (1468) through 2 House (1481; from Dibble 1981, atlas). Reproduced courtesy of the University of Utah Press.

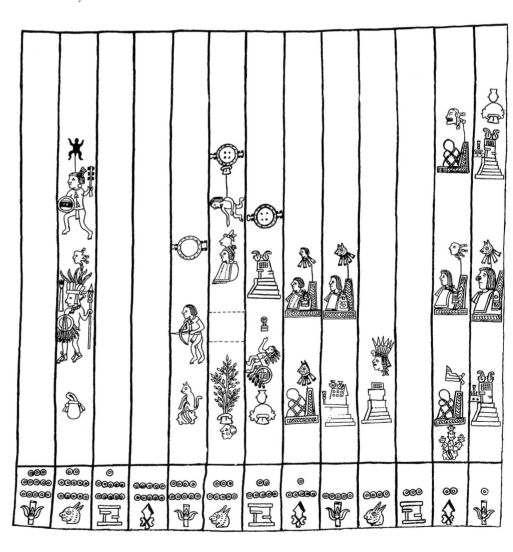

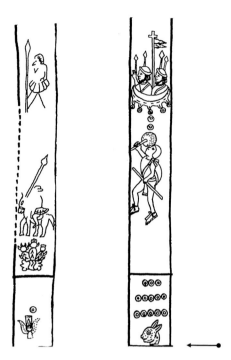

Fig. 153. Codex en Cruz 3a–b. The first sighting of a Spanish caravel in 13 Rabbit (1518) and Cortés' landing in 1 Reed (1519; from Dibble 1981, atlas). Reproduced courtesy of the University of Utah Press.

tails of his death are given just below: he was hanged by Cortés during the march to Honduras, and the annalist pictures a stripped man hanging head down from a tree (the prose sources say it was ceiba).[40] Later, in 5 Flint (1536), the Tira will show the installation of the next *tlatoani,* Panitl, skipping the intervening place holders appointed by Cortés who were not of the royal family.[41]

Above the year count, in the formerly designated Tepechpan sphere, the annalist shows a meeting between Cortés and an Acolhua elite (Fig. 154). Cortés is seated on a distinctive armchair whose curved frame becomes the symbol of Spanish authority throughout the colonial annals.[42] The conqueror is also painted black (ordinarily an Aztec sign of priestly status) and holds the steel lance. He speaks to an Acolhua elite, whom the Nahuatl gloss names Ixtlilxochitl; perhaps he is Don Hernando Cortés Pimentel Ixtlilxochitl, son of Nezahualpilli and *tlatoani* of Texcoco beginning in either 1522 or 1526 (Noguez 1978, 1:112). If so, he is the first Texcocan ruler to be mentioned in the Tira de Tepechpan. Since he was not *tlatoani* of Tepechpan, he is not

pictured here in the same manner as the newly seated Tepechpan lords. Instead, he stands wearing a turquoise cloak and an eagle helmet (?) and holding a long native spear. The Nahuatl gloss above Cortés says that the conqueror gave towns to the Acolhua. Since this meeting between Cortés and a non-Tepechpan lord was important enough to be included here, it is likely that the glosses are correct and that the annalist is recording the fact that Cortés reconfirmed the rights and territories of the Acolhua lord(s).

Two years later, 6 Flint (1524) is marked by the arrival of the twelve Franciscans, here symbolized by a monk (his body a priestly black) holding a cross. Two more years later, in 8 Reed (1526), the larger image of a bishop—complete with miter, crosier, and black body paint—signals the arrival of Juan de Zumárraga, the first bishop of Mexico.[43]

The Tira de Tepechpan thus reports the conquest and its effects on the *tlatoani* line. It records the deaths of Tepechpan's regent and all three of Tenochtitlan's rulers, but it also documents the critical fact that the Spaniards confirmed the status and rights of the Acolhua lords. The annalist, attuned to the religious changes of the century, records three of the most important events in the Christianization of Mexico: the arrival of the faith, of the twelve Franciscans, and of the influential Zumárraga.

The Codex Mexicanus (Mengin 1952: 463–472) includes many of these same events in its coverage of the conquest and aftermath, but it presents the conquest itself more as a series of diplomatic and military episodes (Fig. 155). The events for 1 Reed are so numerous that they occupy the space next to the three previous years, although lines often tie them to 1 Reed. The first element pictured is a Spanish caravel—here described at anchor with its tall masts, lookout perches, rope ladders, and sails furled—followed by a scene of Cortés giving gifts to an envoy of Moctezuma. The place sign between Cortés and the ship identifies the location as Tecpan-tlayacac on the Gulf Coast (Mengin 1952: 463). Cortés is dressed characteristically as a Spaniard and sits in the chair of authority. Here he offers to the envoy a pair of European shoes, a steel-tipped lance, and a beaded necklace. Moctezuma's gifts to Cortés are represented below the year count; they are part of the costume of the deity Quetzalcoatl, which Moctezuma sent to Cortés, gifts that Cortés donned when

Fig. 154. Tira de Tepechpan 15, covering the arrival of the Spaniards in 1 Reed (1519) through the arrival of Bishop Zumárraga in 8 Rabbit (1526). Photograph courtesy of the Bibliothèque Nationale de France, Paris.

Aztec ambassadors boarded his ship off the Veracruz coast. The gifts include, generally from left to right, a beaded cape, two feather headdresses, two feather cloaks, five disks of turquoise mosaic (below), a tunic, and two shields. Although the Codex Vaticanus A/Ríos (87r) conventionally records Moctezuma presenting a gold and jade necklace to Cortés, the Codex Mexicanus is alone in picturing this first exchange of gifts on both sides.

Above the year 1 Reed, the military conflict begins in earnest, signaled by the Spanish soldier in steel helmet, with shield, sword, lance, and banner. The next year, 2 Flint, is marked by a prone smallpox victim and the burning of the Templo Mayor. Below, the annalist records the death of Moctezuma, with a spear stabbing into the back of his funerary bundle to explain how he was killed, and, just to the right, the accession of Cuitlahuac. Cuitlahuac's actual death is not pictured, but the (nineteen) circles attached to his name sign and to the year 3 House may be an attempt to note the short duration of his (eighty-day) reign. Above 3 House, the annalist records the actual conquest of Tenochtitlan, and he does so by using the Aztec convention of a shield and weapons, except that it is a Spanish victory signaled by a Spanish shield, a Spanish sword and lance, and a Spanish helmet. The artist has taken Spanish ele-

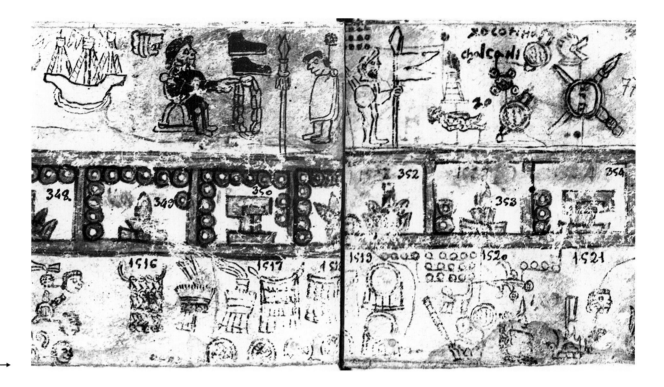

Fig. 155. Codex Mexicanus 76–77, covering the arrival of the Spaniards in 1 Reed (1519) through the conquest of Tenochtitlan in 3 House (1521). Photograph courtesy of the Bibliothèque Nationale de France, Paris.

ments and used them meaningfully in the traditional iconographic system. Later conquests, where the Spaniards and Nahuas have joined forces, are marked by an Aztec shield backed by the Spanish steel sword and the Aztec obsidian-edged sword (e.g., in 6 Flint [1524]).

Although the Tepechpan and Mexicanus emphasize slightly different aspects of the Spanish invasion and conquest, they and the other painted annals tend to agree on certain features that characterize the catastrophic encounter. There is the initial arrival, the coming of Christianity, the destruction of the Templo Mayor, smallpox, the death of Moctezuma, the quick succession of Cuitlahuac and Cuauhtemoc, and finally Cuauhtemoc's death. Several annals present the burning of the Templo Mayor or the siege of Tenochtitlan more pictorially as a relatively large scene of battle (i.e., Aubin, Azcatitlan, Huichiapan, Moctezuma, Vaticanus A/Ríos). One sees the violent struggle in the Codex Moctezuma (Fig. 156), for example, where an Aztec and a Spanish warrior clash against the flaming backdrop of the Templo Mayor. Tenochtitlan's place sign is to the right of the pyramid's base, and the spotted head below the Aztec warrior's feet records the quieter devastation of smallpox.

After the conquest, the annals continue to report selected events that affected religious and political life. On the spiritual side, these are principally the arrival of the Franciscans, the arrival of Bishop Zumárraga, the institution of marriage and baptism, and Zumárraga's death, although other actions of the friars and secular clergy are included occasionally. In the political and social realm, the annals report the evacuation of Tenochtitlan, Cortés' appointment of interim governors for Tenochtitlan, sometimes the arrival of members of the first and second Audiencia, and almost always the arrival of the first viceroy, Antonio de Mendoza. Other secular events are also reported in one annals account or another.

The annalists incorporated the Spanish world into their records by drawing on images from that world to represent the alien data and by integrating the images into their traditional system of native pictography. They took Spanish forms and codified them into iconic conventions and glyphs that were subjected to the same formal grammar as their own conventions and glyphs. Thus a human with spots becomes in effect the glyph for the devastating plague of smallpox in 1520. A Spanish shield and crossed sword becomes the symbol for the Spanish conquest. Spaniards are identified as foreigners by an iconographic assemblage that includes a beard, brimmed hat, tunic, lance, sword, and horse. Accouterments of Spanish life also become symbols of different aspects of Spanish colonial culture. For example, the curved chair and the European crown become the signs of authority and rule, the Spanish equivalent of the reed mat, speech scroll, and turquoise diadem of native *tlatoque*. The cross and the dove, already European conventions for Christianity, readily transfer to the Aztec annals as icons of the Catholic Church. The European banner with two points almost always marries the cross to represent Spanish political and religious authority. Likewise, the bishop's miter becomes a symbol of the bishop, as for example, in the Codex Mexicanus where a bishop's miter and indigenous-style footprints leading to the year count in 10 Flint (1528) signal Bishop Zumárraga's arrival.

Even pictorial naming practices carry over from Aztecs to Spaniards in the colonial annals. When Aztec artists need to identify specific Spaniards, they create name signs for them. A few of these name signs are iconic. For example, the conqueror Pedro de Alvarado, who was known as Tonatiuh (Sun) because of his golden hair, has the sun as his name sign (Fig. 11a). The name signs of the saints often derive from their attributes: for example, a key for St. Peter and arrows for St. Sebastian (Galarza 1966; Boornazian 1996: 84–86; Diel n.d.c). For most Spanish names, however, the artists depict them phonetically, not spelling them completely but referring to their main sounds. There is considerable variation in this, as one might expect, when every painter is making his or her own way with the new, strange names. Thus Viceroy Antonio de Mendoza's name (Fig. 11d–h) is rendered variously as a gopher (*toza*) and either a stone (*te*) or a maguey leaf (*me*) to yield *te-toza* or *me-toza* (Mendoza), sometimes with the addition of a bird (*toto*) to approximate "Antonio" or "Don," and with an eye (*ix*) and a bean (*e*) to yield *ix-e* (Virrey; Boornazian 1996: 90–91). In this process of naming and recording the Spaniards and their actions pictorially, the annalists effectively Mexicanize them.

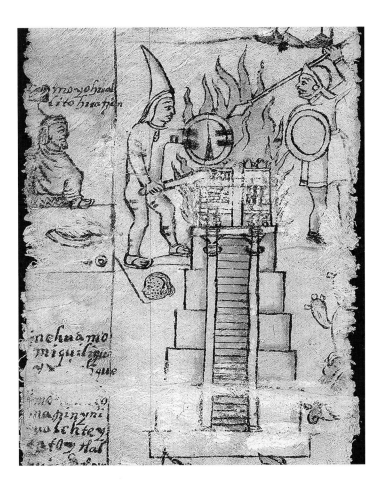

Fig. 156. The battle of the Templo Mayor in 2 Flint (1520) in the Codex Moctezuma. CNCA.-INAH.-MEX; reproduced with permission of the Instituto Nacional de Antropología e Historia.

Concurrently, the annalists report how the Mexicans are Hispanized. They show indigenous baptisms and marriages and native warriors fighting with steel swords alongside Spaniards (during the Mixton war). After some initial disruption of *tlatoani* rule following the conquest, the annals resume their reporting of the traditional system of royal succession as long as it lasts. The line dissipated earlier in Tenochtitlan, but in Tepechpan it held on at least until the 1580s. The iconography of rulership changes, however, as indigenous rulers come to understand that Spanish traditions of authority are increasingly important for them (Barnes n.d.; Diel n.d.a, n.d.b). In the Tira de Tepechpan, they come to sit in the Spanish chair and wear European crowns, and when they die their funerary bundles are laid prone, in accord with European burial practices

Fig. 157. Tira de Tepechpan 17, reporting the death of Water Stone (Don Cristóbal de Maldonado) and the accession of Flowers House (Don Bartolomé de Santiago) in 1 House (1545). Photograph courtesy of the Bibliothèque Nationale de France, Paris.

(Fig. 157). The Tepechpan account presents the tradition of indigenous rule as ongoing, but it illustrates how new seats and new articles of dress now symbolize authority in the mid-sixteenth century.

In short, the colonial annals draw the Spanish world into their tradition of conceptualizing and recording history. Just as the Aztec empire brought new *altepetl* and gods into its political and religious systems before the conquest, the Aztec annalists fold the events, ideas, and objects brought from Europe into their iconographic system. Spaniards are now playing major, controlling roles in Aztec political, economic, and social life, but the basic structure of the annals and the Aztec concept of history continues.

Reflections on *Altepetl* Time

The Aztec annals, like almost all Mexican histories, have a very narrow historical focus. They view all people and all events from the perspective of the *altepetl,* from the origin of its people to the present, and they usually include only those that impinge directly on the *altepetl.* As Charles Dibble (1981: 5) points out, "There is no codex or written source that gives a general history of the Valley of Mexico. The codices and subsequent [alphabetic] *anales* were the product of individual cities . . . , and each interpreted and recorded events with a local bias or each recorded events that were absent in other sources." The annals track one people and one place through time. The painting surface of the annals with unbroken year counts records temporal space rather than geographic space, and time always goes forward. Except in the migrations, the narrative does not move around from place to place.

Tenochtitlan's place sign does not usually appear in the Mexica annals, except at the founding of the *altepetl,* and there it functions more as an event than a location. It is also used in the Telleriano-Remensis as an ethnic marker for Tenochca warriors (Fig. 151). The island city's place sign is not generally needed because all the events in the Mexica annals are assumed to take place in Tenochtitlan unless otherwise stated. When the place signs of other polities appear, they identify people, such as Moquiuix's allies in the Telleriano-Remensis, or they locate conquests or other events in polities outside the capital. The Codex en Cruz stands apart in this respect because it juxtaposes events pertinent to four valley polities, and thus employs place signs to distinguish between them.

Although I have been discussing the annals as traditional indigenous documents, all existing ones postdate the conquest. Most were painted toward the middle and end of the sixteenth century with the express purpose of carrying Aztec history to that time. Most have also been edited: images have been scratched out or covered over, other images have been inserted to modify or continue the story, and glosses in Nahuatl, Otomi, and Spanish have been added to amplify or repeat the painted record. The last painted year in the Codex Aubin, for example, is 12 Flint, 1608; it is the last of a group of years that was added along with alphabetic texts after the first annalist stopped painting with 1596. This tells us that this document still held considerable value for its Nahuatl-speaking owners at the opening of the new century; it was still a record of the past worth augmenting.

From the perspective of the postconquest sixteenth century, the Aztec migration story has a nearly legendary aura belonging to the deep past. The annalists conceptualize the migration as the origin and developmental history of the people, a shared history that prepares the Mexica for imperial greatness. The migration is the only story in the annals to have a coherent narrative plot, a constructed story line with a well-defined beginning, middle, climax, and culmination (as per Chatman [1978, 1981a: 262] and Ricoeur [1981: 174]). By the time the migration histories were painted, the personae and episodes of the migration had already been structured and shaped into an integrated story by countless repaintings and retellings. The migration is thus a story that is complete and can be viewed and judged accordingly. It begins at Aztlan and culminates with the founding of Tenochtitlan.

This narrative closure is not reached in the imperial accounts of the postfoundational past. The imperial stories remain open ended and essentially unfinished, for the Spanish invasion and conquest are hardly the culminating moments of Tenochtitlan's expanding program of conquests. For the annalists, the fall of Tenochtitlan neither signals the end of the Aztec world nor stands as the goal of its history, in the same way that the founding of Tenochtitlan does for the migration. Instead, the Aztec imperial annals are reflections on a past that has not been completed and is not over at the time of the telling.

This, I believe is the essential feature of the Aztec annals. They convey more than anything else the message of continuity. In those annals that begin at the beginning in Aztlan, such as the Codex Mexicanus and Codex Aubin, time literally starts its count when the Aztecs go forth from their ancient homeland, and it continues through the foundation of Tenochtitlan, through the conquests marking imperial expansion, and beyond to the then present. After the conquest, the Spaniards and their cultural equipment become part of the story. The story these annals tell is that the Aztec world began with time at Aztlan and continues to the present, with the promise that it will run for as long as the year count (and time) runs.

One sees in the pictorial annals, perhaps even more clearly than in the alphabetic ones, how indigenous life persisted after the conquest. There was not the wholesale destruction of indigenous society and the total substitution of one social order for another that European historians so often describe. In scholarly and popular writing, much has been made about how the Aztecs and their neighbors entered European history with the Spanish conquest, with the implication that they abandoned their own, but, as Walter Mignolo (1995a) points out, this is because Europeans and the medium of alphabetic writing have shaped colonial discourse. The Aztec histories of the colonial period are less widely known and used than the Spanish ones, and the pictorial annals of the sixteenth and early seventeenth century even less so. They have been all but ignored as documents that convey the understandings and aspirations of the indigenous colonial elites. As windows into the intellectual culture of the colonial Nahuas, however, the painted annals show clearly that the Spaniards entered Aztec history.

9

Histories with a Purpose

The Mexican pictorial histories are documents that call up and organize memory of the past. Their intent is to select from the innumerable days, people, things, places, and occurrences of previous times a relatively minute corpus of individuals and actions that have meaning for their creators and then to structure and shape these elements into a singular past that serves as the foundation for the present. Each document does this. Each painted history charts its own version of the past, whether or not it relies on other sources, and each constructs the past from the perspective of the present moment when it was painted.

This past, like the present that created it, belongs to the indigenous Mexican elite. The histories all revolve around the rulers and their families or the rulers and their polities. They are largely silent about the commoners who actually inhabit these community kingdoms, just as they ignore the minor nobility, in order to concentrate on those actually in power. Since the people who commissioned the histories are the rulers and their circle, they required histories that are more diplomatic than social.

Throughout the preceding chapters, I have presented these histories as examples of the preconquest tradition of manuscript painting. Several of the extant pictorial histories actually do predate the conquest:

the Codices Colombino-Becker, Bodley, Vienna, and Zouche-Nuttall, for example, are considered to have been painted before the Spanish arrived (Smith 1973a: 16–19; Glass 1975a: 12–13).[1] But, by far, most of the histories postdate the conquest and are therefore as colonial as they are precolonial. They belong to that world of manuscript painting that survived and flourished for a time in a Mexico newly brought under Spanish control.

These manuscripts then are part of two universes. In a large sense they reveal to us the preconquest tradition and should be analyzed in this light, which is what I have done with this volume. But the postconquest manuscripts are also specifically colonial documents, painted by historians looking back on a past that is purer and less complicated than the cultural chaos and demographic collapse of the mid- and late sixteenth century. They reflect the perspectives and aspirations of the colonial elites as surely as their preconquest counterparts did for the preconquest elites. This dual citizenship impinges on the questions we might have about their purpose, voice, and audience, for which there are two answers, one preconquest and one postconquest. The Codices Mendoza and Telleriano-Remensis, for example, have sections that belong to the universe of Aztec annals, but these manuscripts were specifically painted as cultural reports on the Aztecs intended for Spanish readers. The Codex Mexicanus and Codex Aubin are indigenous histories painted for indigenous colonial elites. We must recognize these documents both as preconquest and as colonial. If we are to understand them as colonial documents, we must first understand the preconquest tradition they represent, and this has been my goal in this volume. Other studies can and should concentrate on their colonial nature.

Shared Themes

The pictorial histories, vastly more so than the alphabetic histories penned by indigenous writers, are direct and relatively unfiltered expressions of the Mexicans' historical consciousness. People, places, and events appear in the pictorials because these are the features of the past that mattered to the authors. Despite differing cultural perspectives from Oaxaca to the Valley of Mexico, the historians agree on the importance of three overarching themes, which persist throughout the range of pictorial histories. The historians emphasize the people's origins, the founding of their *altepetl,* and the continuity of the family, polity, or line of rule. It is the material between these points and the details of the presenting that create narrative variation.

Origins

Most of the painted histories open with the origin of the people of the *altepetl.* This origin can be couched in various ways but manifests itself in the first appearance of the people themselves—their human, legendary, or supernatural ancestors. In every case, the line of humanity relevant for the story begins at this point. The first individuals do not simply appear ontologically as a statement painted on the page, strip, or sheet, however; they come from somewhere. Usually the ancestors emerge from a feature of the natural world: a tree, or a crag, cleft, or cave in the earth, or an opening in the heavens. They are figuratively born from the physical environment in which humankind lives. If the ancestors are supernatural, those who emerge are supernaturals, and if the ancestors are humans, humans emerge.

In the Mixteca, where rulers are descended from su-

pernatural ancestors, these supernaturals emerge from trees, clefts, flint knives, and openings in the earth, or they descend from the heavens. Thus the initial scenes in the Mixtec Codices Bodley, Selden, and Zouche-Nuttall record the emergence of the ancestors of the royal lines: in the Bodley Lady 1 Eagle is born from a tree (Fig. 55); in the Selden (1–2) the first male ruler of Jaltepec and his wife's grandfather respectively rise up out of a tree and a cleft cut into the earth (Figs. 57, 56); and in the Zouche-Nuttall (1–2) Lord 8 Wind emerges from clefts. The famous "tree birth scene" in the Vienna Obverse shows the Mixtec ancestors rising from a cleft cut into a great tree at Apoala (Fig. 51). Mixtec ancestors also descend from the heavens, as pictured in the Vienna Obverse, Zouche-Nuttall, and Selden Roll (Figs. 46, 53, 54, 95). When the culture hero 9 Wind first appears in the Vienna Obverse, he is born of a flint knife; later he descends from the heavens with the accouterments of rule (Figs. 48, 49).

In the Aztec pictorials, the tribal leaders themselves emerge from the earth. They come out of the seven-pocketed cave called Chicomoztoc, the metaphoric point of origin of all Central Mexican people. Although the Mexica specify Aztlan as their place of origin, they blend it with Chicomoztoc. Their alphabetic histories locate Chicomoztoc at Aztlan. Their pictorials sometimes blend the two by picturing, for example, seven houses or buildings on the island (Fig. 141), or, more often, they place Chicomoztoc as a separate stop along the migration (Fig. 143). Not being descended from supernaturals, the Central Mexicans carry their gods with them.

Chicomoztoc, as a point of origin, is particularly associated with Aztecs and their immediate neighbors, but it is not exclusively a Central Mexican construct. The metaphor of Chicomoztoc, over and above the metaphor of a cave, has a wider range. In the Selden Roll a Chicomoztoc is the point of emergence into the world for Lord 9 Wind after he descends from the heavens (Fig. 95); in the Lienzo of Tlapiltepec 9 Wind's Chicomoztoc emergence opens the story (Fig. 97). Although these Coixtlahuaca Valley documents draw from both Mixtec and Central Mexican traditions, the Mixtecs also shared some sense of Chicomoztoc. The Codex Zouche-Nuttall, for example, initiates the dynastic line for a polity variously identified as Place of the Ascending Serpent (Furst 1986) and Wind Temple

(Byland and Pohl 1994: 76–80) by picturing Lord 5 Flower's descent from a celestial cave with seven pockets (Fig. 53). The point of agreement for all these origin episodes is that the first ancestors came from somewhere or something.

A few manuscripts do not focus on the earliest origins, for they pick up the story later, but still prior to the polity's founding. Such are the lienzos of Zacatepec and Ihuitlan, the Mapas Tlotzin and Quinatzin, and the Codex Xolotl. The Zacatepec lienzo opens when the ancestral founder receives the title and accouterments of rule from the Mixtec Lord 4 Wind, and the Ihuitlan sheet begins with the common ancestral couple to several lines. The Tlotzin and Quinatzin maps, as with the Codex Xolotl, begin when the migrants approach or enter their new homelands. Their stories all begin with the staging process for the foundation.

Founding of Community Kingdoms

From the moment of origin to the founding of the community kingdoms, the histories picture the emergent ones engaged in a wide range of activities. Although the mix of marriages, pilgrimages, migrations, battles, and such differs greatly from the Mixtec to the Aztec spheres (and varies from manuscript to manuscript), the episodes all eventuate in, and prepare the protagonists for, the foundation of the *altepetl*. The Mixtec and Aztec manuscripts come together again to agree on the importance and basic features of the founding. The moment of the founding is one of the most prominent events recorded in the pictorials, usually presented as a large scene that culminates a series of events immediately preceding it (Boone 1997, n.d.; Figs. 100, 134).

Several histories detail the ritual itself and the preparation for it. From the Codex Vienna, Codex Zouche-Nuttall, Selden Roll, and Map of Cuauhtinchan's Founding, in particular, we are told that the foundation rituals have shared features (Boone n.d.; Figs. 52, 54, 100, 118). The ritual itself involves identifying and naming the territory, establishing the cult of the patron deity, constructing a temple or altar, lighting a new fire, and defeating any opposing neighbors. The Mixtec and Coixtlahuaca Valley codices stress divine participation, whereby supernaturals either provide the materials for the founding—the staffs of rule, the fire-

drilling apparatus, the musical instruments, and the symbolic plants—or they conduct it themselves (e.g., Vienna, Zouche-Nuttall, Selden Roll [Figs. 52, 54, 99, 100]). The Aztec codices tend to omit the equipment. Stressing human agency over divine participation, they concentrate more on naming the clan leaders who are present (e.g., Mendoza, Mexicanus, Tepechpan [Figs. 134, 146, 147]).

For some histories, the founding of *altepetl* is the culminating event for which all else has been preparation. Such are the Codex Vienna, Selden Roll, the Mapa Pintado and Map of Cuauhtinchan's Founding, as well as the Mapa Sigüenza (Figs. 52, 100, 116, 118, 105). Most of the pictorials, however, continue beyond the founding to build the story of the polity from this new base. Thus the Aztec annalists, especially, present the founding of Tenochtitlan as the fulcrum of the historical narrative, both the culmination of the migration and the springboard for imperial growth. The Coixtlahuaca Valley codices also use the founding as the pictorial base from which the dynastic records grow (e.g., C. Baranda, L. of Ihuitlan, L. of Tlapiltepec [Figs. 74, 80, 90]).

The Duration of the Family, Line of Rule, or Polity

The third theme that runs through almost all the pictorial histories (those that continue beyond the foundation) is the fact or artifice that those in power when the manuscript was painted are directly linked to those who were in power at the founding. The histories stress the duration of the dynasty or the sequence of rulers, or the continuation of the corporate body, from the time of the foundation to the present. If there has been a rupture in this line, by some mishap like the death of the last heir or the conquest of the polity by another, the pictorial histories either ignore it or they show clearly that steps were taken to repair it. Thus, the Mapa Tlotzin (Fig. 122) presents an unbroken chain of successive rulers from Tlotzin to the colonial present, totally ignoring the fact that Texcoco lost its independence and was without a *tlatoani* for a time prior to and during the Tepanec war. The Mapa de Teozacoalco (Fig. 78), in contrast, admits when Tilantongo's and Teozacoalco's dynastic lines failed for lack of a direct heir, but it includes the rituals that conveyed rulership on those lords who then took up the reins of power. The point both these manuscripts are making is that rulership continued appropriately and that the present is directly tied to the past.

The Mixtec screenfolds and the Coixtlahuaca Valley pictorials trace the descent lines of families and present successive ruling couples, as do the Texcocan Codex Xolotl and Mapa Tlotzin. The Aztec annals, in contrast, omit the females almost entirely and follow only the male rulers. These Aztec annals also put greater emphasis on the duration of the *altepetl* itself, for the annals format links the polity to the year count and thereby implies that the polity will continue as long as the year count does. In these annals, the unbroken ribbon of the years speaks eloquently about the enduring nature of the *altepetl*.

Different Concerns of the Mixtec and Aztec Histories

The pictorials preserve a past that supports the political situation and social order of their creators. They tell of the *altepetl*'s nature and its tradition of rule, and they explain, in the process, who is ruling and why that is. These are *altepetl*-based histories that address the concerns of the *altepetl*'s rulers. It is natural that the Mixtec histories should be so different from the Aztec ones, because the concerns of their leaders and their paths to rule were different.

Mixtec Stories

Rulers (male or female) in the Mixteca ruled because they were understood to be descended from specific supernatural ancestors, who are regionally Mixtec, and because they were inheriting offspring of royal parents in an unbroken line of primogeniture descent from former Mixtec kings and queens. The emphasis in this system of rule is on direct descent from royals on both male and female sides, ultimate descent from supernaturals, and a local origin. The Mixtec screenfolds thus chart, often in considerable detail, the dynastic histories of the royal families.

They also stress local origins, showing how the first

ancestors emerged from specific places in the Mixteca. The pictorials present Apoala as a principal place of origin for many Mixtec families, a virtual Chicomoztoc, where the first Mixtec ancestors emerged from a great tree, as described in the Codex Vienna (Fig. 51; Jansen 1979). The pictorials often trace subsequent royal families back to these first Mixtecs.

Thereafter, the histories concentrate on the royal genealogies. The detailed ones (e.g., Bodley) concern themselves with the parentage of both marriage partners, the birth order of the offspring, and the ultimate genealogical fate of the offspring—whether they marry (and to whom) and whether they themselves have potentially inheriting offspring. In this way the Mixtec screenfolds record a complex genealogical world of many interrelated dynastic lines, within which the pictorials explain how each person is related to the others.

At the same time the pictorials identify the community kingdoms ruled by these kings and queens and note when these kingdoms change hands. They show how the kingdoms are passed down from parent to offspring, brought together when families join, and separated again when they are distributed among different siblings. When a dynastic line ultimately fails, which happens from time to time, the pictorials explain how rule often devolves to the prestigious line of Tilantongo (Borah 1983: 46), which provided so many sons and daughters as marriage partners for other royal families. Thus the Mapa de Teozacoalco succinctly reports that a son of Tilantongo established the second Teozacoalco dynasty (Fig. 78). So many Mixtec codices record the dynastic history of Tilantongo because so many Mixtec rulers were descended from Tilantongo kings and queens.

Thus at the close of the eleventh century, when the last heir to the Tilantongo throne (Lord 2 Rain, 20 Jaguar) himself died without issue, his death threw the established system of inheritance and rule into crisis. At this point, as explained in Chapter 5, Lord 8 Deer fought successfully for control of Tilantongo even though he had no genealogical right to the throne. Having previously established himself as a ruler of other polities by right of conquest, and having gained political allies, he underwent a Central Mexican nose-piercing ceremony that raised his social and future genealogical status, enabling him to rule Tilantongo itself. Then he systematically killed his genea-

logical competitors and married the surviving wid-
ows and daughters, thus rerouting the Tilantongo line
(and the lines of other polities) through him. The one
young lord he spared, Lady 6 Monkey's son 4 Wind,
eventually killed 8 Deer and just as systematically un-
did everything 8 Deer had brought together (Caso
1955; Troike 1974: 362–364, 474); Lord 4 Wind married 8 Deer's daughter and rerouted 8 Deer's royal lines
through him.

The stories of Lady 6 Monkey, Lord 8 Deer, and
Lord 4 Wind illustrate another feature of the screenfold histories. The screenfolds record the efforts of the
rulers to preserve and enlarge their holdings through
intrigue, alliance, ritual action, and conquest when
marriage alone fails to achieve this.

The subject of the Mixtec screenfolds is the Mixtec
royal families rather than the Mixtec polities. The kingdoms are manifest in the histories usually as place signs
that can appear and disappear as the genealogies progress. For example, Red and White Bundle, so prominent in the early part of the Bodley, is not often seen after 8 Deer kills its king, whereas Place of Flints makes
its presence felt during the War of Heaven and, later,
when Lord 4 Wind becomes its ruler (Byland and Pohl
1994: 71, 93). These are histories of families rather than
histories of kingdoms. This is why the genealogical histories do not mention the Spanish conquest. The Spaniards were simply not part of these dynastic stories.[2]

When records of land and territory were required,
the Mixtec and Coixtlahuaca Valley historians turned
to a cartographic format or a tira, and they focused attention on the kingdom itself. There the community
kingdom with its center, boundaries, and neighbors is
the subject of the story, which usually then tells of the
polity's sequent rulers. Sometimes Spaniards are included in the stories when they influence local affairs.
The topical difference between the Mixtec and Coixtlahuaca Valley lienzos and tiras and the Mixtec screenfolds is that the lienzos and tiras have a polity as their
subject, whereas the screenfolds give the histories of
one or more royal families.

Aztec Stories

Aztec histories have two parts and two subjects. The
first, the migration histories, have the Aztec people
(usually the Mexica) as their subject, and they follow the Aztecs as they journey from place to place,
event to event, until they found their *altepetl*. Thereafter the story settles with the people at the *altepetl* and
takes the polity itself as its subject. Marriages, progeny
statements, and genealogies—the mainstay of Mixtec
screenfolds—are not normally recorded because these
were not such important factors in Aztec rulership as
they were for the Mixtecs. Instead the Aztecs relied on
their council of elders to select its successive *tlatoque*
from a pool of qualified royals.

The Aztecs understood that their power was ultimately based on their having departed from a distant
place and migrated as a people to their present home,
where they carved out their *altepetl* by force of will and
arms. Their rulers did not present themselves as being
directly descended from the gods but as being divinely
guided by them. The process of migrating transformed
the people from rustic nomads (Chichimecs) to civilized Mesoamericans, and for the Mexica, the migration prepared them to rule the world they knew.

Thus the migration is a major feature of the Aztec
pictorial histories. The painters focus on the people's
emergence and departure from Chicomoztoc or Aztlan, the trials and tribulations along the journey, and
the founding moment. In the Mexica documents, the
historians particularly stress the Aztecs' distant origins,
the length and difficulty of their journey, their battles
against their neighbors once they enter the Valley of
Mexico, and ultimately the foundation of their capital
city. Aztlan, as the ancient Mexica homeland and point
of origin, is pictorially described in some detail because
it remains a symbolic anchor for the community (as
per Gupta and Fergerson 1992: 11) and a promise of
Tenochtitlan. When Tenochtitlan is finally reached, its
foundation is presented as the action of a group of
tribal leaders rather than a single lord. Throughout, the
histories reinforce the understanding that this is a journey of the community of people led by its prominent
members.

For the Mexica, kingship itself is established only
after the foundation, when the imperial story begins.
Once the people are finally located at Tenochtitlan,
the Aztec annals detail events pertinent to the *altepetl*,
among which is the seating of the first *tlatoani* Acamapichtli. Although we learn from the alphabetic histories that Acamapichtli is the son of a Mexica warrior
and a Culhua princess (carrying Toltec blood in her

veins), the annals are silent on this point. They almost always ignore the rulers' genealogical makeup. They do not focus, either, on the personal exploits and histories of the rulers in the same way as do the Mixtec histories. Axayacatl is somewhat of an exception to this general tendency because the painted annals consistently picture his defeat of Moquiuix of Tlatelolco and his wounding by Tlilcuetzpal during the Matlatzinca campaign. Clearly, however, these events were so important and unusual that they warranted detailed reporting. The annals include the kind of events one might find in newspaper headlines, particularly the deaths and accessions of the sequent rulers.

Given this historical range, the annals cannot fail to include the arrival of the Spaniards and the defeat of Tenochtitlan. The events European historians group together as comprising the Spanish conquest of Mexico are centered in Tenochtitlan, for which the conquest is a local phenomenon. The association of the Spanish conquest with Tenochtitlan is especially seen in two Acolhua annals: the Codex en Cruz and the Tira de Tepechpan. When the Codex en Cruz first pictures the Spaniards on horseback, it records them with Tenochtitlan's place sign as an event occurring there (Fig. 153). Likewise the Tira de Tepechpan depicts Cortés' arrival on the Tenochtitlan side of the year count (Fig. 154). These Acolhua annalists and their Mexica colleagues also present the burning of the Templo Mayor as a specific Tenochca event. The conquest of Mexico is thus manifest in the annals by this burning, by the quick succession of the Mexica *tlatoque,* and by the introduction of Spanish authorities. Since the Spanish leaders entered Mexico and joined the political scene as controlling elites, it is natural that the annals would embrace them. The annals thus stress the ongoing nature and historical resiliency of the *altepetl.*

Structuring These Stories

Whether consciously or through habit and tradition, the Mexican historians chose narrative structures that particularly suited the stories they told. The Mixtecs were masters of the *res gestae* presentation, where events follow events, whereas the Aztecs greatly preferred the time-line structure of the annals. When historians from both cultures wished to tell of the land, they turned to cartographies.

The Mixtec event-oriented history, which characterizes most of the screenfolds, considers history as one or more series of happenings, which are topically linked by pertaining to the people who rule. It is an efficient form for recording the genealogies and deeds of the rulers. As a series of events, the narrative can move around easily in time and space. The protagonist can be in one place and then another simply by changing the place signs, and the story can switch from one person to another simply by replacing the actor; events can likewise proceed forward or jump backward in time via the date signs. Place and time are not the overriding concern that the sequence of events is. Thus the account of Lady 6 Monkey in the Codex Selden moves forward and backward in time (Figs. 37–39), and the story of Lord 8 Deer told in several codices follows him around from one polity to another on his many diplomatic visits, conquests, and pilgrimages. The *res gestae* structure is well suited for this kind of flexible reporting of individual action.

For stories about the land, the cartographic format proves to be the ideal one. The map-based history systematically arranges places on the painting surface with respect to their geographic location and attaches all its events to these places. Thus it preserves, above all, the spatial relationship between events. This spatiality casts a veil of contemporaneity over the events, which tends to make time a little ambiguous. The cartographic histories tell the reader that while, before, or after one event was happening here, this other event was happening there. It is an ideal form for juxtaposing events, especially similar events, that occur in several places. Thus the Codex Xolotl and the Mapa Tlotzin readily cover Texcoco, Huexotla, and Coatlichan (Figs. 120–123), and the Lienzo of Ihuitlan can list the rulers of Ihuitlan and Coixtlahuaca (Figs. 80, 85).

Many of the lienzos, maps, and tiras from all over Mexico combine a map of territory (as a tableau) with a single line of events (as a tour) leading to the map. This line of events is virtually a *res gestae* presentation that moves through (often undefined) space, reporting a single sequential action. Usually it is a route of travel, as with the journeys in the Selden Roll, Mapa Sigüenza, and Cuauhtinchan Map 2 that bring individuals to a place and culminate in the founding of *altepetl,* the latter presented cartographically (Figs. 88, 105, 111–

112). Thus, the sequence of the tour leads up to the tableau.

In other lienzos and maps, the tableau of the map itself gives rise to individual sequences of events attached to different places. In manuscripts from Oaxaca and southern Puebla, ruler lists rise up from individual sites on the map, as in the Mapa de Teozacoalco and the Coixtlahuaca lienzos (Figs. 79, 84–86, 90). In Central Mexico it is more common that genealogies or ruler lists drop down from the places, as in the Codex Xolotl and Mapa Tlotzin (Figs. 120, 122).[3] In every case, these sequences of people add the element of temporal duration to the land. The cartographic histories are always fundamentally about land.

When the narrative is about the events that happen to or at a single polity over a long period of time, the annals form has no peer. The annals history, driven as it is by the year count, works most efficiently when it is grounded in a single location, which obviates the need for repetitious place signs. It tends to ignore events in other places unless these are accomplished by or directly relevant to the people of its *altepetl*. Its story is firmly planted in the *altepetl*, which testifies that the *altepetl* is all that matters. The annals account explains better than any other history the temporal relationship of events. It tells one that this event occurred in this year, followed by this other event that occurred this other year, and so on, so that there is never any question, as there so often is in the *res gestae* and cartographic histories, when an event occurred. The annals form carries the implication that history is composed only of the events pertaining to its *altepetl*. This feature renders it the perfect historical form for people like the Aztecs, who understood themselves to be at the center of the world and in control of those around them.

In all these Mexican pictorials, the stories told and the structures of telling are fully interdependent. The different kinds of stories, depending on their subject and the range of data they include, call for different structures. The migration stories and the accounts of foundations, for example, beg for a cartographic treatment. Likewise, the organizational structures themselves, because they make it easier for the historians to record one kind of story rather than another, yield different narratives. The annals, for example, easily record events at a single location over time, but they have difficulty accommodating many contemporaneous events at several places. A painter would find it difficult to tell the story of Lord 8 Deer or the early dynastic histories of the Valley of Mexico (as per the Codex Xolotl) in the annals format, whereas the narrative of Aztec continuity would lose its visual force if converted from an annals history to a cartographic or *res gestae* one.

Local Histories

It has often been noted (e.g., Nicholson 1971: 67–68; Smith 1983c; Lockhart 1992: 377), but not sufficiently appreciated by others, that all the Mexican pictorial histories are determinedly local documents. Nowhere do we find a broadly cast history of a cultural group or a region from beginning to end. The pictorials all view the world from the particular perspective of their own community kingdom, patron, and historian, and they all include or omit events because those individuals judge them to be relevant or not for the purpose of the history. They all tell local stories. As Mary Elizabeth Smith (1963) has pointed out, for example, the Colombino-Becker represents a Mixteca Costa perspective on the 8 Deer story, while the Bodley and Zouche-Nuttall have their own biases. The Codex Selden almost totally ignores 8 Deer (admitting him into the narrative only as a father-in-law) because it concentrates on Jaltepec's dynasty (Smith 1983c: 261). In the same spirit of historical concentration, the Mexica Codex Aubin ignores even the major events in nearby Tlatelolco and Texcoco unless the Mexica are specifically involved.

A few histories do concern themselves with more than one polity. Manuscripts like the Mixtec Codex Bodley and the Acolhua Codex Xolotl and Codex en Cruz are the broadest in their coverage, for they report histories of several polities. Other regional annals (i.e., Anales de Tula and C. Huichiapan) also include Tenochca events along with their own. One can argue, however, that their authors chose to expand their coverage because it served the local interests of their patrons and polities.

The kind of universalizing history of the Mixtecs or the Aztecs achieved by modern writers was not a goal of the ancient historians, who set their sights locally. This is one of the reasons it has been so difficult for modern scholars to correlate the dates and events recorded in different Aztec annals. A dozen manuscripts will disagree on accession and death dates of the rulers and on what constitutes the important past. Efforts to make sense of these disparities have to accommodate the understanding that each pictorial is making its own historical statement.

The Value of the Painted Record in Mexico

These historical statements usually had a colonial context as well as a pre-Columbian one. Returning to the theme that opened this chapter, I note that although the pictorials all tell of the preconquest past, almost all are colonial efforts. All the Aztec annals (even the Codex Boturini), all the Central Mexican records, perhaps all the lienzos,[4] and most of the Mixtec codices were painted after the conquest. This means, of course, that the pictorial history continued to have value as a viable documentary genre. Far from being dismissable as derivative records tainted by European painting styles, historical traditions, and purposes, the colonial pictorials are critically important for understanding both the pre-Columbian and colonial worlds. For the pre-Columbian world, the extant pictorials serve as exemplars of the indigenous tradition of manuscript painting. Their durability in the face of the conquest is evidence of the strength of this tradition and its place as a fundamental feature of the intellectual culture of indigenous elites. If the histories are continuing to be painted in the late sixteenth and early seventeenth centuries, four generations after the first great epidemic and the fall of Tenochtitlan, this tradition must have been central to indigenous life. For the colonial world, they testify that the pictorial history still mattered as a genre and that indigenous elite culture still retained traditional values, namely pictographic writing and the ancient ways of thinking about the past.

Pictographic writing continued after the conquest because visual thinking did. Even after alphabetic writing arrived in Mexico with Cortés, the Aztecs and their neighbors still relied on painted images to record their understandings of the past and the facts of their lives. Writing in the late 1570s, Fray Diego Durán (1971: 64–

65) recalls how, when he questioned a wise man from Coatepec about the deity Topiltzin Quetzalcoatl, the sage turned from his own memory to a painted record. As Durán says: "I begged him to tell me whether what was written and painted there was true, but the Indians find it difficult to give explanations unless they can consult the book of their village. So he went to his home and brought a painted manuscript. . . . Within this document was to be found in almost unintelligible signs the entire life of Quetzalcoatl and his disciples." Although Durán found the signs incomprehensible, the sage from Coatepec trusted them rather than his memory for the details of Topiltzin Quetzalcoatl's life.

Fray Toribio de Benavente, known by his Nahuatl name Motolinía, notes how the postconquest Aztecs recorded even the most mundane information visually. Motolinía recalls:

> One lenten season when I was at Cholollan, . . . the number of those who came to confess was so great that I was unable to give them the advice I should have liked to give them. I told them that I could hear confession of only those who would bring their sins written down in figures, because writing in figures is a thing they know and understand, this being their way of writing. It was not to a deaf people I said this, for immediately they began to bring so many writings with their sins that I could not attend to all of them." (Motolinía 1971: 95; translated by Robertson 1959: 54)

By this time the Aztecs had been baptized as Christians and had embraced the notions of sin, confession, and salvation, but despite this conversion, the old substrate of indigenous pictography lay beneath the new religion.

The Spanish authorities had no choice but to accept painted records if they wanted information from the Aztecs, because at first these were the only records that existed, and pictography was the only writing system the people knew. Thus in 1531, when Hernán Cortés brought suit against Nuño de Guzmán and others over tribute from Huexotzinco that they had usurped during Cortés' absence, the indigenous authorities brought forth painted records of the town's payments to Guzmán. Local witnesses interpreted the paintings for the court scribe, who recorded their testimony alphabetically. Then he signed the paintings, attested that the once-oral, now-alphabetic testimony recorded the content of the paintings accurately, and entered the paintings into the court docket along with the alphabetic texts. Still, the preconquest paintings remained the foundation of the testimony, brought forth in a suit by one Spaniard against another (Cummins 1995; Codex Huexotzinco 1995; Boone 1998: 179–181).

An Inquisition case eight years later illustrates how manuscript painting remained the preferred, or in many cases the only, means of written expression for the Aztecs. In 1539 a manuscript painter named Mateos was brought before Bishop Zumárraga to testify to the whereabouts of the idols that had been secreted away from the Templo Mayor before it burned during the conquest. Mateos' father had originally been given charge of the wrapped idol of Huitzilopochtli, and Mateos apparently knew their history after that. Mateos gave oral testimony about the idols, which was duly transcribed, but he also presented his understanding of the facts in the form of a painted deposition. His document, painted on native paper, shows which idols were taken by whom, through whose hands they passed, and who were the last living owners. The Holy Office recognized the evidentiary fact of his document and preserved it as evidence along with the alphabetic testimony that explained it, although Zumárraga never did find the idols.[5]

Early in the postconquest period the Spanish administration took an active and official interest in the existing painted records, especially those concerning tribute. The crown in particular wanted information about the geography, demography, and economy of the Aztec empire in order to set its own tribute and service requirements, and this kind of information was contained in the painted manuscripts. Thus, a royal cedula of 1530 requesting reports on Aztec tribute specifically told the district judges of New Spain to consult the indigenous tribute paintings; Cortés himself sent such a painting to the Council of the Indies in 1538 in response to a later request (Baudot 1983: 63–64; Boone 1998: 156). A short while later, about 1541, Viceroy Antonio de Mendoza had a "relation of the things of this land" painted to send to Charles V. Expanding on the original request, he ordered a master painter to record all the land of the empire, the lords who governed, and how the land was assigned, the tribute, and the battles of the conquest. This pictorial report is thought to have survived as the Codex Mendoza, which contains

a specialized annals history as its first part (see Figs. 134, 135; Nicholson 1992: 102).

At mid-century the crown even outlined how authorities in New Spain should gather information related to preconquest tribute and the structure of the native nobility. A cedula of 1553 ordered the Audiencia to consult with the elderly and experienced natives and "in addition to the information that you secure from witnesses, you will cause to be brought before you any paintings, tablets, or other records of that time that may substantiate what is said, and you will cause the religious to search and ask for such records among the Indians. You will also secure information about all these matters from such religious and all other persons who have some knowledge of them" (Zorita 1963: 191–192; see also Baudot 1983: 65).

The crown's ongoing desire for economic and geographic information translated into a broader search for information on indigenous culture. As early as 1533 the president of the second Audiencia (Sebastián Ramírez de Fuenleal) and the custodian of the Franciscan order (Martín de Valencia) charged the Franciscan friar Andrés de Olmos with compiling a book on native antiquities. Olmos was to consult the elders and gather what existing pictorials he could. He succeeded in collecting painted manuscripts from the lords of Mexico, Texcoco, Tlaxcala, Huexotzinco, Cholula, Tepeaca, and Tlalmanalco, among others (Mendieta 1971: 75–77; Baudot 1983: 141). Such other mendicant ethnographers as Motolinía, Bernardino de Sahagún, and later Diego Durán gathered manuscripts and consulted widely with the indigenous sages. In the 1570s or 1580s, the third viceroy, Martín Enríquez, also ordered that a collection of libraries on Aztec history be gathered, for which the people of Mexico, Texcoco, and Tula brought manuscripts; he turned this library over to Tovar for consultation (Kubler and Gibson 1951: 77; Boone 1998: 158). The friars drew upon and copied many of these manuscripts to compile their own cultural encyclopedias of Aztec life. In this way, pictorials like the Codex Telleriano-Remensis came into being.

At the same time that the Spanish authorities and friars were gathering pictorials, the indigenous elites were pulling them out of their archives for their own use. Efforts to exempt themselves from taxation, to reclaim ancestral lands, and to gain privileges from the crown often relied on the older pictorials. As early as the 1530s, Juan Cano, Spanish husband of Moctezuma's daughter Isabel, had several painted histories translated and brought forth to support his petition for the restoration of his wife's hereditary rights. Other pictorials came into play in disputes between *altepetl*. Viceroy Mendoza, for example, settled the dispute between rival claimants to the five kingdoms of Amaquemecan by sending a Xochimilcan nobleman to inspect the *altepetl* histories and determine each kingdom's legitimate genealogy (Schroeder 1991: 70). Thus Mendoza's departing report to his successor sums up the situation when he notes that most of the petitions and lawsuits brought forth by the native people "are settled summarily on the basis of their pictographic accounts" (Borah 1983: 67). In the Mixteca, the Codex Selden was painted in 1560, most likely to be presented in a court case against Yanhuitlan, its purpose being to advance Jaltepec's claim to the town of Zahuatlán (Smith 1994).

When the Spaniards established themselves in Mexico, they introduced alphabetic writing as the new, elite, and officially sanctioned system of recordkeeping and expression. The Colegio of Santa Cruz of Tlatelolco, since its establishment in 1536, taught native lords and their sons to read and write alphabetically in Latin, Spanish, and Nahuatl; some of these men were later to help Bernardino de Sahagún and other mendicant ethnographers. As early as the mid-1530s or early 1540s, Aztec scribes in Cuernavaca were recording census information alphabetically in Nahuatl (Cline 1993: 3). Lockhart (1992: 335), reflecting especially on such mundane alphabetic documents in Nahuatl, even asserts that "as early as the middle of the sixteenth century, alphabeticism was gaining the upper hand over pictorial treatment, and the balance continued to shift with every passing decade."

This shift to alphabetic writing came late to the indigenous histories, however. The native history manuscripts retained their pictorial nature until very late in the century. Although the Historia Tolteca-Chichimeca of 1547–1560 (Kirchhoff, Odena Güemes, and Reyes García 1976: 15) can be considered primarily a prose work that is illustrated and enhanced by paintings, almost all the indigenous prose annals were written after 1570. Most existing ones date from the end of the sixteenth century or the seventeenth, and some date from the eighteenth.

Several factors kept the histories pictorial in the face of alphabetic writing. We have seen that the tradition of history painting was old and strong, such that history itself could not be easily separated from the paintings. As the Nahuatl poem recorded alphabetically by Juan Bautista Pomar reminds its readers, the past and the present endure in the paintings: "Oh Giver of Life! . . . Later you will destroy eagles and tigers; we live only in your painting, here, on earth" (León-Portilla 1986: 68). The pictorial formats themselves structured many of the stories, so Aztec history was inseparable from annals history. Moreover, the social context of the history documents remained within the indigenous community through the colonial period. This is in contrast to records such as censuses or wills, which specifically address and are therefore tailored to Spanish administrative needs. Although many pictorial histories were, in fact, presented to the Spanish authorities as documents to support litigation or petitions, they were not as a whole created specifically for Spanish administrators. With a few exceptions, the *altepetl* histories continued to be created for indigenous readers within traditional indigenous circles.

Thus, indigenous historians in the sixteenth century consciously chose to continue painting histories in the traditional manner. The author of the Tira de Tepechpan prepared a long amate strip that would carry the annals from the thirteenth century at least to the 1590s (when the strip breaks off), because he wished to preserve the structure of an unbroken year count. When the first painter stopped work after recording events in the 1550s, another annalist brought the account up to the close of the century; he continued the annals in the same pictorial manner rather than switching to an alphabetic one (Boone 1998: 186–190).

In 1596 the author of the Codex Aubin made a similar decision to fashion a painted annals rather than a prose one. He did not recreate a preconquest annals exactly, for he worked with European paper bound as a book; he accordingly adjusted the structure of the year count to fit on rectangular pages, and he spaced the year count out to allow more room for the postconquest years. He was also attuned to European figural conventions, and he or someone else glossed the images in Nahuatl. The Aubin historian clearly intended a traditional annals account, however, one that had more in common with the pictorial past than the alphabetic present or future. After he finished his history, another annalist carried the painted year count up to 1608. At the end of the century, the Tepechpan and Aubin historians still had the knowledge, and probably the prototypes, to recreate the traditional genre of history, whether on the old paper or the new.

Sometimes when indigenous elites needed documents for specific purposes, they refashioned old ones rather than painting new ones. An example is the Codex Colombino-Becker, a preconquest screenfold from coastal Oaxaca that details the life of Lord 8 Deer; it was partially erased, broken up, and used as two land documents by different towns. Sometime before 1541, someone scratched almost all the animal imagery off the manuscript's surface—erasing especially the mammals and reptiles from headdresses, dates, name signs, and place signs throughout—to eradicate its original meaning. The mutilated document was then broken into fragments, two sets of which are now identified as the Codex Colombino and the Codex Becker I; these sets have since followed their own separate paths (Smith 1966: 165). In 1541 the Tututepec lord who owned the Colombino pieces had a scribe add Mixtec glosses to some of the pages naming the boundaries of towns under Tututepec's control (Smith 1963). His purpose was to convert the story of 8 Deer's life to a title or record of lands belonging to Tututepec. This codex remained in the hands of the Tututepec lords at least until 1717 when it was presented as evidence in a land dispute between that town and San Miguel Sola (Caso 1966: 113). It may also have been brought forth in earlier disputes (Smith 1966: 171). Elsewhere and meanwhile, the Becker I set of fragments was also annotated with boundary names and was ultimately presented as a land document in an 1852 case involving Santa María Tindu in northern Oaxaca (Saussure 1891: 5–6; Smith in Smith and Parmenter 1991: 70, 111 n. 21). In both cases, the glosses reidentified the screenfold fragments as maps for their eighteenth- and nineteenth-century owners who wanted ancient pictorials to prove their claims.

When no ancient pictorials remained, some towns in Central Mexico tried to create them. In the seventeenth century a number of indigenous polities were asked to present land titles and boundary documents to the Spanish authorities, who, via *composiciones,* were trying to consolidate and regularize village landholdings. Towns lacking such pictorials feared the loss of their lands without them; so some had new "old" documents drawn up. Such are the archaizing Techialoyan codices, which seem to have been painted and written by document makers based in Tacuba who mass-produced picture and text histories for several dozen towns.[6] The authors of these Techialoyans usually present the moment when the towns' boundaries are first established, record aspects of preconquest and colonial history, and then concentrate on describing the town and its lands. The paintings are European in style, and the physical format is as a bound book, but the alphabetic texts attempt to record archaic Nahuatl, and the paper is amate. In the seventeenth century, alphabetic texts, even in Nahuatl, would seem more suitable to Spanish administrative needs than ancient paintings, but the pictorial component of the Techialoyans was critical to their success. The Spanish authorities wanted ancient documents, and ancient meant pictorial.

These several examples of the colonial production and use of pictorial histories testify that painted histories were more valuable than alphabetic ones to the indigenous elites. The painted histories were considered the authentic ones, the ones that recorded the truth. A list of boundaries, especially an alphabetic one on European paper, could be simply invented, but an ancient pictorial carried the weight of documentary evidence. This is why the Tututepec lords and the citizens of Santa María Tintu included their old, annotated screenfolds in the evidence they presented to press their eighteenth- and nineteenth-century land claims, and this is why, in the seventeenth century, towns in the state of Mexico had "ancient" manuscripts created as titles to their lands.

The value of the painted history as a container of truth still holds. In 1892 the people of Zacatepec near the Oaxacan coast carried their two sixteenth-century lienzos to Mexico City to help settle a land suit, returning home with copies after the case was settled (Smith 1973a: 89). More recently, in the 1970s, the town authorities of Tequixtepec in the Coixtlahuaca Valley had photographs made of their lienzos for the same purpose: a dispute over lands (Parmenter 1982: 46–48); they and the courts saw the lienzos as important documentary evidence. Towns like Tequixtepec which still have their lienzos and maps guard these documents carefully in case they need them to prove how the *altepetl* came into being, who were its rulers, and what is its rightful extent.

If we return to the very beginning of this volume, and Bishop Zumárraga's efforts to find the idols secreted away from the Templo Mayor, we recall how a local manuscript painter testified against his Culhua *tlatoani* Don Baltasar. In his oral statement, the painter did not simply report that Don Baltasar had hidden the idols in a specific cave at a certain location. Instead, he reported that he had painted a history of Don Baltasar's family, one that pictured the community gods and the *tlatoani*'s ancestors emerging from a cave; it was in that cave, he said, that the idols were hidden. Almost surely this painted history is the beginning of a migration history, where the ancestors and gods emerge from Chicomoztoc. Don Baltasar admitted commissioning the painting, but he swore that he personally had nothing to do with the idols, and as a recent convert to Christianity, he helpfully mentioned other caves and sacrificial sites in the area. The painted history remained a point of truth in the case. Its veracity as a document went unquestioned, regardless of whether Don Baltasar actually helped hide the idols there, for it made no claim about the idols. It told only about the beginning of the Culhua people and Don Baltasar's royal line. Being a history, as Father Motolinía would say, it was a book untainted with idolatry because it recorded the truth. For those who created, owned, and used the pictorial, its character as a container of truth remained after the conquest as before.

Notes

1. Configuring the Past

1. See, for example, Kubler and Gibson 1951: 37–38; Robertson 1959; Smith 1973a: 9–19; Boone 1990; Smith in Smith and Parmenter 1991: 6–11; Howe 1992; Baird 1993; Quiñones Keber 1994.

2. Peter Martyr's reaction is cited and discussed by León-Portilla (1992b: 316–317, 321–322), who mentions other early reports and argues for a strong historiographic tradition in Mexico. See López de Gómara (1964: 345), Díaz del Castillo (1956: 162, 204, 257, 360), Martir de Angleria (1964, 1: 425–426).

3. García Icazbalceta (1941, 2: 204), translated and discussed by Mignolo (1992c: 325; 1992e: 313).

4. Torquemada (1975–1979, 1: 45), translated and discussed by Mignolo (1992e: 313–314; 1994a: 300; 1995b: 94–95).

5. Acosta's perspective is discussed more thoroughly in Chapter 3.

6. Mignolo has taken up the related questions of the book, alphabetic writing, and histories in Mexico in a series of articles and a book (1992a, 1992b, 1992c, 1992d, 1992e, 1994a, 1994b, 1995a, 1995b).

7. Although Thomas (1995: 774–784) does include pictorial codices in his list of major Mexican sources, he does not draw on them.

8. See esp. Mignolo (1992a, 1992c, 1994a, 1994b, 1995a).

9. See Florescano (1994), Klor de Alva (1989), Mignolo (esp. 1992a, 1992c, 1994a, 1994b).

10. See Glass (1975b: 19–28) for the history of study and publication of Mesoamerican pictorials.

11. See Aubin (esp. 1849 [Spanish trans. 1886a, 1886b], 1886c, 1893), Ramírez (1858), Chavero (1892), Ehrle (1900), Hamy (1897, 1899), Nuttall (1902), Paso y Troncoso (1886), Peñafiel (1895, 1900, 1902).

12. See Gates (Codex Abraham Castellanos 1931, Codex Ixtlan 1931, Codex Meixueiro 1931), Mengin (1942, 1952), Preus and Mengin (1937–1938), Lehmann and Smital (1929), Clark (1912, 1938), Caso (1949, 1950, 1954, 1955, 1958a, 1958b, 1959, 1960b, 1961, 1964a, 1964b, 1966, 1992), Barlow (1948, 1949a, 1949b, 1950), Dibble (1942, 1951, 1963).

13. Those that are undisputedly pre-Columbian are the Codices Becker I and Colombino (which were originally joined), Bodley, Vienna, and Zouche-Nuttall; see Glass (1975b: 12–13).

14. See discussion by Kubler (1964), who considers the modes of extinction and survival of pre-Columbian forms.

2. History and Historians

1. See also Ricoeur (1981: 167) for a similar argument.

2. See also White (1985: 83, 105).

3. Chatman (1978: 31), Ricoeur (1984–1988, 1: 65); see also Chatman (1978: esp. 9, 19, 31–32, 37, 43; 1981b: 117–119).

4. White (1981a: 22, 5); see also White (1987: 52) and the shared views of Hedeman (1985: 171) and Scholes (1981: 206).

5. White (1987: 54–56) points out the equivocation caused by this mental division of the human past.

6. *Washington Post,* Dec. 7, 1994, A20; May 12, 1995, A1, A22.

7. These views are variously articulated in B. H. Smith (1981: 214–218), White (1981a: 9–10), Bruner (1984: 5), and Florescano (1994: vii).

8. *Washington Post,* Feb. 1, 1995, A14, A18, D1, D5; Feb. 4, 1995, A18; Feb. 10, 1995, A23; Goodheart (1995); Lanouette (1995); see also Harwit (1996).

9. Sahagún's bks. 4 and 5 are devoted to divining according to the *tonalpohualli* (260-day count) and to omens; for portents of the Spaniards, see Sahagún (1959–1982, bk. 8:17–19; bk. 12:1–3).

10. E.g., C. Vienna 48b, C. Mendoza 70r, C. Telleriano-Remensis 30r, and Mapa Tlotzin (where the painter has pots of red and black paint).

11. The Nahuatl reads: "qujtqujque in tlilli, in tlapalli, in amoxtli, in tlacujlolli qujtqujque in tlamatiliztli" (translation mine; Sahagún 1959–1982, bk. 10:191). See León-Portilla (1963: 102–103) for the other metaphors.

12. This follows León-Portilla (1966: 381, 383; 1992a: 39–40); see Molina (1970: 1st pagination, 76; 2d pagination, 67, 120, 141, 157); see also Nicholson (1971: 58–59).

13. Burgoa (1989: 210), León-Portilla (1992a: 43), Díaz del Castillo (1956: 211), Alva Ixtlilxochitl (1985, 1:286), Pomar (1941: 20). For noble and *capulli* archives, see also Schroeder (1991: 17), Zorita (1963: 110).

14. See, e.g., Burland (1965: 5), Troike (1974: 52–53; 1987: 38), Smith in Smith and Parmenter (1991: 5); for the skins of ritual almanacs, see Burland (1971: 19), Anders (1972: 28, 29, op. 30), Nowotny (1976: 13).

15. Technical analyses have been performed on only a few of the Mexican codices, among them the postconquest pictorials in Berlin (Schwede 1916), the C. Selden (a Mixtec history) in the Bodleian Library (Dark and Plesters 1959), the C. Colombino (a Mixtec history) in the Museo Nacional de Antropología in Mexico (Caso 1966: 89–102, photos 1–14), and the C. Huejotzingo (an economic document) in the Library of Congress (Albro and Albro 1990). The gessos of the C. Selden and C. Colombino are a mixture of calcium sulphate and calcium carbonate, with a medium of animal glue in the Selden (Dark and Plesters 1959: 533; Caso 1966: 91–92).

16. The question of preconquest rolls is still open. Thompson (1972: 5) recalled H. B. Nicholson's observation that "a number of screenfold skins show by folds at wrong places that probably they were rolls." Smith (in Smith and Parmenter 1991: 1), however, has suggested that since all the existing rolls are postconquest, the form

"may be a later version of the preconquest screenfold format," although she does not insist on this.

17. León-Portilla (1992b: 317, 326), Boone (1994a: 71–72), Mignolo (1994b: 231, 253), Alvarado (1962: 4v, 102r, 138r), Caso in Alvarado (1962: 136), Burgoa (1989: 210).

18. A member of the mulberry family, *Ficus petiolaris* is the most commonly used for paper. For the production and uses of native paper, both bark and maguey, see von Hagen (1944), Christensen and Martí (1971), Lenz (1973), Sandstrom and Sandstrom (1986), Albro and Albro (1990).

19. For cloth maps, see Cortés (1986: 94, 192, 340, 365), López de Gómara (1964: 181, 345). For lienzos in the Chalcatongo cave, see Florescano (1994: 112–113), who cites Burgoa (1934, 1:340). Caso (1961: 239, 251) and Smith (1973a: 89) give the width of the strips for three lienzos; I have measured a few others.

20. The Lienzo of Yolotepec lacks European images and stylistic features except for a church, which Barbara Mundy (personal communication, 1998) thinks may possibly have been added later.

21. Hernández (1959, 1:118); Martínez Cortés (1974: 74–75); Dark and Plesters (1959); Nowotny and Strebinger (1959); Caso (1966: 89–99); Albro and Albro (1990). For pigments, see also Sahagún (1959–1981, bk. 11:239–245), Smith (1973a: 11 n. 20). For details of the manuscript preparation and painting, see, for example, Boone (1983: 23–28) for the C. Magliabechiano, Smith in Smith and Parmenter (1991: 1–6) for the C. Tulane, and Quiñones Keber (1995: 123–125) for the C. Telleriano-Remensis.

22. The Mixtec painter in the C. Vienna (48b) clearly uses a brush, but the Aztec painters in the C. Mendoza (70r), C. Telleriano-Remensis (30r), C. Xolotl (4, 5), and Mapa Tlotzin seem to be using reed pens.

23. Sahagún (1959–1982, bk. 8:42, 55), Motolinía (1971: 354); see also Nicholson (1971: 59) for scribes working under supervision and (59–61) for historians more generally.

24. Alva Ixtlilxochitl (1985, 1:430, 529; 2: 7, 32); see Dibble (1980: 62–64, 76, maps 4, 5). Donald Robertson (1959: 13, 62–64) interpreted the appearance of the Tlailotlaque in the Valley of Mexico (and Alva Ixtlilxochitl's comment) to depict "the introduction of the art of manuscript painting from the Mixtec region"; I feel there is insufficient evidence to support this. Although the pictography characteristic of the Post-Classic Mixteca-Puebla style may well have originated in southern Mexico rather than in the central valleys, this topic clearly needs further investigation. Meanwhile, we should keep in mind that writing was associated with the Toltecs, those highly civilized forerunners of the Aztecs to whom extraordinary achievements were attributed, and that the Mixtecs (who were said to excel in the luxury crafts)

were also called Tolteca, sons of Quetzalcoatl (Sahagún 1959–1982, bk. 10:187–188). To my mind, the C. Xolotl depicts a group of skilled artisans (the painter first among them) from the Mixteca who resettled in the central valley.

25. Sahagún (1959–1982, bk. 10:29, 190, 191). See León-Portilla (1963: 10–18) for a more literal translation of the description of a *tlamatini*, derived from the Primeros Memoriales.

26. Sahagún (1959–1982, bk. 3:51, 61, 63, 67); see also León-Portilla (1992a: 71; 1992b: 324).

27. Schroeder (1991: 183); I thank Robert Haskett for advice about this matter, and Frances Hayashida for nudging me to delve into this gender question.

28. Sahagún (1959–1982, bk. 3:13, 35, 69); for Quetzalcoatl in the Mixteca, see Nicholson (1978).

3. Writing in Images

1. Molina (1970: 2d pagination, 120), Alvarado (1962: 102r, 168r), and Caso in Alvarado (1962: 134).

2. The correspondence between Acosta and Tovar is translated and published by Kubler and Gibson (1951: 77–78). Mignolo (1992b: 186, 191; 1992c: 317, 321–322; 1992e: 313–314) cogently discusses Acosta's hierarchy of civilizations and writing systems.

3. This is discussed more thoroughly in Boone 1994b.

4. Others who define writing broadly include Hill (1967: 93–95), Harbsmeier (1988), Larsen (1988), Crump (1990: 42), Gaur (1992: 12), and Martin (1994: 484–491).

5. Gelb (1963: 11, 191, 250), Sampson (1985: 29, 32), DeFrancis (1989: 58), Hill (1967: 93).

6. Gelb (1963: 11, 190–194, 250), Sampson (1985: 29–30), Hill (1967: 94–95).

7. See Robertson (1970), who suggested it be called the "International Style of Postclassic Mesoamerica" because of its widespread distribution. See also Nicholson (1960, 1982), Nicholson and Quiñones Keber (1994), Pohl and Byland (1994), and Byland and Pohl (1994: 6), who argue that the Mixteca-Puebla style developed to serve "as a common idiom for the validating of authority among the leaders of this wide area."

8. Jansen cites Laet (1633), Kircher (1652–1654), Clavigero (1780/81), Aubin (1849), Peñafiel (1885), and Dibble (1971), to which we should add Berdan (1992a, 1992b) and Prem (1969–1970; 1992).

9. The same convention is used by other cultures as well. As Smith (personal communication, 1997) points out, it is also seen in the Narmer Pallette from ancient Egypt and in a twelfth-century Spanish painting of David conquering Goliath (Ainaud 1962: pl. 10).

10. I am following Dibble (1971: 324), León-Portilla (1992a: 44–45, 52–53), and Lockhart in using the term "ideogram" rather than "logogram" because, as Lockhart (1992: 327–328, 576–577 n. 5) says, the purpose of the image is to hold an idea or a fact rather than to yield a word.

11. Jansen (1988a: 97) distinguishes between what he calls the indexical mode and the symbolic mode.

12. See Boone (1992: 44–46), who argues that the historical section of the C. Mendoza should be seen as a victory chronicle, recording perceived and actual "victories."

13. Compare, for example, Dibble (1971: 324) and León-Portilla (1992a: 52–53), who categorize the same images differently.

14. Sometimes this pinwheel disk has been used to stand for a period of twenty days (e.g., C. Telleriano-Remensis IV, C. Mendoza 19r [although the same disks appear on Mendoza 57r as single days; see Berdan 1992b: 97]).

15. See C. Mendoza 70r, C. Telleriano-Remensis 30r, and a boulder carving near Coatlan between Yauhtepec and Cuernavaca where Cipactonal works the image (Anders and Jansen 1988: 112).

16. Dibble (1971: 324) extends the meaning of this metaphor to include pestilence and devastation. Prem (1992: 54) points out that the *tlachinolli* part of the metaphor literally refers to "burned-off land" rather than to "fire," as it is usually interpreted. For metaphors and figures of speech in the Mixtec codices, see Furst (1978c), Jansen (1988a: 98), and King (1990).

17. See also Nicholson (1973: 33), who reports on Caso's (1960b: 16–18; 1965: 951) findings of phoneticism in the pictorial naming of Yodzocoo (Coixtlahuaca) as well.

18. Although King (1990; 1994: esp. 122–125) has argued that some dates (day and year combinations) in the C. Vienna are phonetic referents that communicate verbal messages about the related scene, Jansen (1998a: 7–12) has pointed up the problems of this approach; see also Jansen (1988a: 89) for the difficulty of interpreting tone puns.

19. See Dibble (1971: 328), Berdan (1992a: 180).

20. This translation follows Dibble (1971: 330; 1973: 375). Nicholson (1973: 9) translates *tlan* as "place of," and Berdan (1992b: 97) translates it as "where there is an abundance of."

21. I draw here on Dibble (1971, 1973), Nicholson (1973), Lockhart (1992: 329–334), and Prem (1992), who discuss phoneticism before and especially after the conquest. Victoria Bricker also shared her insights with me.

22. Alvarado's "sun" name sign appears in the C. Telleriano-Remensis (46r), Lienzo de Tlaxcala (pl. 18 bis). For Zorita see Nicholson (1973: 18–19); for Francisco see Galarza (1979: pl. 2.7) and Lockhart (1992: 332–333); for

Mendoza see Diel (n.d.c), who points out that the painters of the C. Aubin (48v), C. Telleriano-Remensis (46r), C. en Cruz (in year 4 Reed, 1535), and Tira de Tepechpan (19) all pictured the name Mendoza slightly differently. For indigenous names represented pictorially, see Dibble (1973) and Nicholson (1973).

23. Mary E. Smith (Smith and Parmenter 1991: 6–11), for example, has sorted Valley of Mexico features from more typically Mixtec features in the C. Tulane.

24. Marcus (1992: 95–142) has stressed the variety that obtained in calendrical nomenclature by presenting Mesoamerica as having "many calendars not one." I am stressing the underlying structural sameness of the system, although certainly there was regional variation over time and the terms may have been voiced differently.

25. The painter of the historical section of the C. Vaticanus A/Ríos (87rv), and presumably the painter of its prototype (the C. Telleriano-Remensis, which lacks the relevant pages), did include symbols for all eighteen months in a row beneath the conquest years 1 Reed, 2 Flint, and 3 House (1519–1521), but these month symbols do not function as dates. In the Lienzo de Tlaxcala, the painter added a deity head (said to be Tezcatlipoca, but perhaps Huitzilopochtli) to his depiction of the Toxcatl massacre at the Templo Mayor (pl. 14); Kubler and Gibson (1951: 25) consider it a month glyph, but I see it instead as identifying the deity to whom the feast was dedicated. Kubler and Gibson (1951) provide a valuable checklist of sources that picture or name one or more months. Because months figure so prominently in colonial calendrical manuscripts, but not in others, Betty Brown (1978, 1982) has argued that the "months" as such were codified after the conquest from a more loosely organized series of eighteen feasts. The principal problem with this interesting argument is that it does not take into consideration the fact that the Maya had definite months.

26. Jiménez Moreno and Mateos Higuera (1940: 69) argued that month glyphs appear on the 1555 foundation stone of the Dominican church at Cuilapan, near Monte Albán. Although Kubler and Gibson (1951: 61–62) then included the stone in their checklist, they were unconvinced that month glyphs were present. Since the dates on this colonial stone are atypical in other respects (see note 36 below), I do not consider the stone to represent an otherwise lost practice of dating among the pre-Hispanic Mixtecs.

27. See Smith (1973a: 23–27), who includes a chart comparing the different vocabularies.

28. E.g., C. Azoyu I, C. Porfirio Díaz obverse.

29. An exception is the Tlapanec year count, as seen in the C. Azoyu I, which begins with 2 and runs through 14.

30. The mosaic effectively tells the reader to read *xihuitl* (turquoise and year) rather than *chalchihuitl* (jade), since turquoise was used particularly for mosaics. See, for example, C. Aubin (70r–79r), C. Tlatelolco.

31. The painter changed colors every time a new Tepechpan ruler took office.

32. Caso's (1964a: 72; 1977: 49) pioneering work on the associative meaning of dates has been followed especially by Furst (1977: 208–209; 1978c) and Jansen (1982, 1: 92, 221–222, 357, 358; 1988b), who may not agree on the metaphoric meaning of some dates but do agree that many of the dates are metaphoric. King (1994) has read some of the nonchronological dates as phonetic captions to the relevant scene.

33. Kirchhoff (1949, 1950), Jiménez Moreno (1956; 1961: 146), Davies (1973: 193–210, chart), and Edmonson (1988: 132–133) have each proposed between 9 and 13 year counts (their proposals also differing from each other). Marcus (1992: 114–118) has recently accepted Jiménez Moreno's arguments and offered a two-page table correlating eight of them. Caso (1967: 48), however, flatly rejected the possibility that there could have been significant calendrical variation in the Valley of Mexico, and Nicholson (1971: 70; 1976: 190–191) cautioned against it, at least after the conquest of Tenayuca by Azcapotzalco c. 1370 (see discussion of the problem in Boone 1992: 50–51). In comparing the reign dates for the Mexica rulers given in thirty-nine historical sources, I found no evidence of different year counts; to the contrary, the different sources agreed with surprising consistency (Boone 1992: 50–51, 152–153).

34. As Caso (1964a: 29, 76) points out, bars are used with offerings in the Codices Cospi, Fejérváry-Mayer, and Laud (divinatory manuscripts embraced in the Borgia Group). They are presumed to symbolize quantities of 5 in scenes that have been interpreted as countings of offerings (Nowotny 1961: 272–274; van der Loo 1982; 1987: 191–194; 1994: 79; Anders and Jansen 1994: 211–216; Anders, Jansen, and van der Loo 1994: 289–330; Anders, Jansen, and Pérez Jiménez 1994: 195–233).

35. Although some Oaxacan painters used the banner for quantities of 20 (e.g., C. Sierra, L. Santiago Guevea), I have not found an instance where they likewise employed the feather and incense pouch, which may be specifically Aztec conventions.

36. Smith (personal communication, 1997) points out that the dedication stone of the Dominican monastery at Cuilapan uses bars and dots with the A-O year indicator in its calendrical notations. Whether this represents a blending of Mixtec and Zapotec conventions after the conquest is unclear. Certainly the Mixtecs, living among

the Zapotecs (who used the bar and dot), knew about this convention.

37. Aztec *huipils* always have a distinctive red rectangular patch at the base of the neck slit. For Mesoamerican clothing, see Anawalt (1981: 211–212), who points out that Aztec women wear the *quechquemitl* only in ritual situations.

38. See Caso (1960b: 14), Robertson (1964: 430), who coined the term, and Smith in Smith and Parmenter (1991: 8). The pose also appears in manuscripts of mixed heritage from southern Puebla (C. Tulane), the Coixtlahuaca Valley in northwestern Oaxaca, and in the solidly Mixtec C. Zouche-Nuttall (e.g., 9b, 40–41) and C. Vienna (e.g., 35b, 34a, 33, 32, 3a).

39. As in the C. Xolotl and Mapa Tlotzin, where founding couples are seated together in caves or near their place signs, the woman cradling an infant in her arms.

40. Compare, for example, the "mature" females in the C. Nuttall (16ab, 26c) to the Coyolxauhqui relief.

41. Caso (1960b: 39; 1979: 47, 172), Pohl (1994b: 89–91); Byland and Pohl (1994: 138–148). In the C. Bodley (32d), Lord 4 Wind also wears a gold diadem not unlike the *xihuitzolli.*

42. For priests, see Caso (1964a: 74), Smith (1973a: 32), Jansen (1982: 74; 1992: 21–22); for the *yahui* in particular see Pohl (1994a: 16–19; 1994b: 42–68).

43. The victims also wear diagonally crossed fasting cords across their torsos in the C. Telleriano-Remensis (29v, 32v, 38v, 39r, 40r, 40v, 42v).

44. For the tunic or *xicolli,* see Anawalt (1981: 130–137).

45. The *cihuacoatl* title is glyphically used in several manuscripts (C. Mendoza 2v, C. Aubin 45r, C. Mexicanus 77); Berdan (1992b: 95–96) explains the glyphs for other imperial titles that appear in the Mendoza.

46. For the Stone Men, see Smith (1973b: 69–71) and Rabin (1979: 174); for the Zapotecs, see Barnes (1997), Furst (1987: 19–22), and Pohl (1994a: 21–22); for the Chochos, see Pohl (1994a: 21–22); for the Tlaxcalans, see Nicholson (1967); for Lord 4 Jaguar, see Pohl (1994b: 93–96) and Jansen (1989: 71–73).

47. For the distinction between Chichimecs and Toltec or civilized people, see Kirchhoff (1948) and most recently Spitler (n.d.a, n.d.b), who has explained the transition from barbarian to civilized in the Texcocan pictorial histories. Several of the king lists painted in Sahagún's Primeros Memoriales and C. Florentine show the transition from Chichimec to civilized (Sahagún 1993: RAH 51r–53v; 1959–1982, bk. 8: pls. 1–54). The Tira de Tepechpan shows the rulers' transition from indigenous to Spanish dress and chair (Noguez 1978: 121–122; Barnes n.d.; Diel n.d.a, n.d.b); see Chapter 8 for further discussion.

48. Exceptionally, the Tira de Tepechpan (14, 15) pictures a female ruler of Tepechpan, who died in 1520, with the calendrical name 2 Rabbit. On Map 6 of the C. Xolotl the Texcocan ruler Ixtlilxochitl also has a 2 Rabbit day name. The C. en Cruz pictures and dates the births of five lords (including Nezahualcoyotl and Nezahualpilli) and thus provides their calendrical names, but these day dates were probably put there to date the birth event rather than name the individual; the C. en Cruz uses day dates more liberally than other Aztec manuscripts.

49. An exception is the Mapa de Teozacoalco (Caso 1949), where the personal names remain and the calendrical ones have fallen away.

50. The red and yellow bands recall the way Aztec and Borgia Group painters depicted decapitated limbs, where the red band is the muscle mass and the scalloped yellow band the fatty tissue that is revealed when the skin pulls away. This suggests that the bases of hill signs might have been viewed as cuts into the earth.

51. This paragraph is drawn largely from Smith (1973a: 38–41), who has pioneered the interpretation of place signs in the Mixtec codices (see also Smith 1983a, 1983b, 1988).

52. For the Mixtec place signs in Fig. 24, see Caso (1949: 153–156; 1960b: 17–18) for Teozacoalco and Tilantongo; Smith (1963: 277–279) for Tututepec; Smith (1973a: 55–76) for Tututepec, Apoala, Tilantongo, Teozacoalco, Place of Reeds, Tataltepec, and Tlaxiaco; Smith (1983a: 250–255) for Zahuatlán and Jaltepec; Byland and Pohl (1994: 66–73, 90–98) for Red and White Bundle, Place of Flints, Cerro Sazmin, and Hill That Opens/Insect; and Jansen (1998b: 88–98, 109–115, 120–121) for Red and White Bundle and Hill That Opens/Insect. Byland and Pohl suggest (1994: 66–73; Pohl and Byland 1996) that Red and White Bundle is the place now known as Hua Chino/Juachino (House of the Deformed or House of the Wind [Lord]) and that Hill That Opens/Insect is Yucu Noco, Ndua Que's Sina, whereas Jansen (1998b: 88–98, 109–115, 120–121) argues that Red and White Bundle or Xipe Bundle may be Ñuu Nduvua (Huaxyacac) or a nearby location and that Hill That Opens/Insect is a conflation of Tiyugh, Sayultepec de Monte Albán (Hill of Insect) and Yucu Cahnu or Monte Albán (Hill That Opens). Caso (1955: 296; 1960b: 39), Smith (1966: 168–169; 1973a: 70–74), Pohl (1994b: 96–98), and Jansen (1996; 1997: 47) have suggested different identities for Place of Reeds. For a synthetic review of the Aztec place signs in Fig. 25, see Berdan (1992a).

53. An exception is in the Mapa Sigüenza, where Chicomoztoc is represented by a cave in a hill sign accompanied by seven dots.

54. Smith (1973a: 34) points out several exceptions where individuals are presented as funerary bundles, although

there is no evidence they were killed: one is 8 Deer's father in the C. Bodley (8e) and C. Vienna Reverse (7a); others are eight rulers in the last pages of the Selden (17–20; explained by Smith 1994: 123–124, 133–135 nn. 17–18).

55. Lord 10 Rain makes this speech while facing the funeral bundles of two other lords who were killed during the War of Heaven; Zouche-Nuttall 4 shows 7 Flower's death. Byland and Pohl (1994: 112) raised the possibility that the date might read phonetically, but Pohl (personal communication, 1996) later felt this is probably not the case.

56. Troike (1982a) has pioneered the interpretation of gestures by analyzing several in the Colombino-Becker. She stresses that each manuscript should be analyzed separately because different painters may have different conventional preferences. Much work remains to be done on the gestures in both Mixtec and Aztec manuscripts.

57. Smith (1973a: 33) has pointed out that this convention is reflected in the Mixtec language as reported in the Alvarado dictionary, where a person waging war is "a man who walks to the enemy."

58. This convention is also reflected in the Mixtec language as reported by Alvarado; the idiom for conquest is "to put an arrow into the lands of another" (Smith 1983b: 244–245).

59. An exception is the C. Azoyu I, where the years frame two sides of the page and thereby reinforce the page as a unit of information; see Chapter 8.

60. Hers is an expansion of Spinden's (1935: 430) earlier one.

61. In the Colombino-Becker, Troike (1974: 115–116, 125, 304) has noticed that figures will also face against the flow when they need to be positioned near a place sign that is being used for two scenes.

62. These are the Codices Bodley, Becker II, and Egerton. The Becker II (Fig. 60) and Egerton do not use a boustrophedon pattern; they have only the two registers (Smith 1973a: 10).

63. See, for example, Miller (1975: viii), Klor de Alva (1989: 154), Mignolo (1995b: 106).

4. Structures of History

1. For discussions of these historical forms, see White (1981a: esp. 5–19; 1981b), Mink (1981), Scholes (1981), Waldman (1981).

2. This definition generally agrees with those used by art historians Kessler and Simpson (1985: 8), Winter (1985: 11), and Brilliant (1984: 11).

3. See Stone (1980) for an overview of modern musical notation.

4. Farrell (1994) argues that Labanotation can be modified

and successfully used by anthropologists in the field to record movement, including Plains Sign Talk.

5. This is true for annals that are relatively free of European influence.

6. See the commentary on the Codex Mexicanus by Ernest Mengin (1952), especially pp. 455–456.

7. In an earlier discussion of this passage (Boone 1994a: 55), I interpreted the jeweled axe as the warning message being conveyed by 10 Lizard to 6 Monkey. Caso (1964a: 32, 79–80; 1979: 109–110) interpreted the jeweled axe as 10 Lizard's personal name; Jansen and Pérez Jiménez (1986: 185) said it was a name or a title, and Smith (personal communication, 1995) agrees. This appellative is later (Selden 6c, 7b) amplified by the addition of a bloody obsidian mirror, an arrow, and a ball of down from an eagle, which makes for an unusually long name or title. For the interpretation of Selden 6–8, see Spinden (1935), Caso (1964a: 32–37, 79–84; 1979: 259–262), Jansen (1982, 1: 252), and Jansen and Pérez Jiménez (1986: 177–192).

8. See Connerton (1989: 66) for the distinction between quantitative and qualitative units that compose time.

9. The graph used the Reaumur thermometric scale, on which the boiling point of water is 80 degrees above zero, and the freezing point is at zero. A temperature of −20 Reaumur would be the equivalent of −25 Celsius.

10. See Dibble (1980a: 17–29) for the interpretation of map 1.

11. The ruined Toltec site is so identified by the Toltec glyph, two pyramids surrounded by broken rubble, and curled tufts of zacate grass. Its place sign appears to be a frog or toad in a circle, although the animal might be a javelina because Alva Ixtlilxochitl (1985, 1: 294) identified the place as Cauac, perhaps derived from the Nahuatl word for javelina (Dibble 1980a: 22).

12. For the time-geographic model, see Carlstein, Parkes, and Thrift (1978: esp. 117–120 and the articles by Shapcott and Steadman, Carlstein, and Lenntorp), Parkes and Thrift (1980: xi, 243), Carlstein (1982), and Gell (1992: 191–193).

13. See Smith (1973a: 991–92, 96–110, 112–121) for the cartographic content of the lienzo and for its historical content; see also Caso (1977: 137–144).

5. Mixtec Genealogical Histories

1. Smith (1994: 121) notes that the histories painted after the conquest "characteristically present the hereditary rulers of only one community and usually only include those rulers who inherit, while omitting subsidiary offspring or any mention of actual or potential conflict

over succession," whereas the preconquest Bodley and Nuttall Obverse contain partial genealogies for several communities.

2. See Smith (1973a: 3, 32), Troike (1978: 556), Jansen (1982, 1:429), Byland and Pohl (1994: 33), Pohl (1994: iv, 3).

3. Jansen and Pérez Jiménez (1983: 93) and Jansen (1990: 103) thus argue for the scholarly use of "Lord" and "Lady" rather than the biological symbols that some other scholars prefer because the original Mixtec usage is well documented and because the dynasties stem from sacred ancestors. See also Pohl and Byland (1990: 116).

4. See also Spores (1967: 118; 1974: 306), Troike (1978: 557).

5. Caso (1959) first described the supernatural 1 Death. Smith (1973a: 30, 44) pointed out the sacred character of Skull Place and Sun Place and suggested that 9 Grass and 1 Death were deity impersonators. Jansen (1982, 1:252–254) then linked Skull Place to Chalcatongo and noted that the Tilantongo ancestors were buried in the cave there. Pohl (1994b: 69–75, 117–120; 1994a: 20; Byland and Pohl 1994: 193–199) subsequently explained the oracular nature of these individuals and equated Sun Place with Achiutla; Pohl (1994a: 20) also links 13 Flower to Mitla.

6. My explanation of the Vienna Obverse is based on (but occasionally departs from) the commentaries by Jill Furst (1978a) and Maarten Jansen (1982), who build on the earlier work of Nowotny (1948, 1961), Caso (1977, 1979), Nicholson (1978), and others. The study by Anders, Jansen, and Pérez Jiménez that accompanies the 1992 facsimile edition is less a commentary as such than a suggested verbal reading of the manuscript, a reading that largely follows Jansen (1982).

7. See Jansen (1982, 1:88–89, 125–130); although Jansen reads two of the platforms as place signs, I think they are more probably generic like the others. It is too early in the creation for place signs.

8. Lady 4 Dog and Lord 8 Crocodile are immediately followed by an unnamed ancient pair (who probably represent their titles) and their three offspring. Jansen (1982, 1:138) sees the stones as place signs.

9. Jansen (1982, 1:143–146; 1988a: 107) identifies these figures as attributes or titles, and Monaghan (1990) discusses them as couplets. My reading draws on both but differs slightly.

10. Lord 9 Wind is either separating the waters from the earth after a great flood (Nowotny 1948: 182), raising the heavens to reveal the earth (Byland and Pohl 1994: 65), or carrying heaven and water to the locales that follow (Jansen 1982, 1:150–153; 1988b: 170; 1990: 105).

11. See Caso (1979: 60–65), Nicholson (1978: 70), Jansen (1988b: 162, 168; 1990: 105).

12. See Furst (1977; 1978c: 129–139) for an overview and analysis of the tree birth tradition in the Mixteca. Jansen (1979: 164; 1982, 1:90–99), following Nowotny's (1948) original identification, has confirmed that the tree on Vienna 37 is at Apoala.

13. See Furst (1977; 1978c: 104–107, 197), Jansen (1982, 1:92, 179–198), Monaghan (1990: 138).

14. Furst (1978a: 11, 229–230; 1978c: 95–110) focuses on the deities associated with these rites, to whom she interprets the rituals as being dedicated; Jansen (1979: 161; 1982, 1:92, 208–217; 1988b: 169) calls them New Fire ceremonies whereby the primordial Mixtec lords, born from the tree at Apoala, name and take possession of the lands.

15. A number of these place signs also appear in other Mixtec codices, several oriented to the cardinal directions; see Nowotny (1948), Jansen (1979: 166; 1982, 1:245–268).

16. This sequence is poorly understood. Anders, Jansen, and Pérez Jiménez (1992: 165–173) consider pp. 36–41 to pertain to the dynasty of "White and Black Tail," but, if so, it is an aberrant presentation. The large place sign on Zouche-Nuttall 36 embeds Apoala within the broader geography of its surrounding valley (Jansen 1979; Anders and Jansen 1988: 173; Mundy 1996: 102–104).

17. Whereas Lord 5 Wind and Lady 9 Crocodile engendered a series of flora, fauna, and human attributes in the Vienna (34), only the deer and the rabbit (Vienna 34b) are clearly present in the Bodley (40c–39c) version of their continuing story.

18. Lady 3 Flint (the mother, who had descended from the sky) first visits and makes offerings to Lady 1 Vulture/Eagle (15b) and then descends into the waters to meet Lord 1 Grass (16b). In the next generation, after Lord 12 Wind has descended with the emblems of rule, he makes offerings to Lady 1 Eagle in the river of Apoala (18b); both 1 Eagle and 1 Grass later participate in the elaborate ceremony that weds him to Lady 3 Flint (the daughter).

19. He also participates in the foundation story narrated in the Selden Roll; see Chapter 6.

20. Caso's (1979) exceptionally valuable biographical dictionary of the individuals in the Mixtec codices notes the co-appearance of these deities. For 9 Grass, see also Furst (1982: 214–221) and Pohl (1994b: 69–82); for 1 Death, see also Caso (1959); for 2 Dog, see also Furst (1978a: 161–163); for 7 Deer and 9 Movement, see also Jansen (1982, 1:283–284) and Smith in Smith and Parmenter (1991: 25–28).

21. See König (1979: 38–45), Furst (1990: 129–131), Jansen (1994: 148–154), Pohl (1994b: 31–35).

22. For the interpretation of the Bodley, see especially Caso

(1960b); see also Troike (1979: esp. 186–189) for the Bodley's conventional patterns.

23. Caso (1960b: 37) points out that the year must actually be 10 Rabbit; occasionally the scribes erred in painting too many or too few disks.

24. The Zouche-Nuttall (26, 42c) and Vienna Reverse (7c) name 11 Water as the second wife and the mother of 8 Deer.

25. See Caso (1979: 445), Colombino 3a, 18c.

26. I suggest they refer to his later stature as a Raingod priest (like his father) and a sacrificer, the eagle being a sacrificer often paired with the *yahui*.

27. The exception is the Selden, which records many deaths in its concluding pages; see the explanation in Smith (1994: 123–124, 133–135 nn. 17–18).

28. Other horizontal arrangements of marriage pairs include the Codex Dehesa (Smith in Smith and Parmenter 1991: 8–9) and Codex Baranda (see Chapter 6).

29. For the Becker II and Hamburg Fragment, see Nowotny (1964, 1975), Smith (in Smith and Parmenter 1991: 90–92), Jansen (1994: 193–214).

30. The last pictured ruler, glossed Angel Francisco, was *principal* of Santos Reyes Yucuna in the Mixteca Baja in 1582 (Smith 1979: 36–37).

31. Troike, building on the earlier work of Clark (1912) and Caso (1966), has established its original reading order and discusses the later erasures (1974: esp. 48–106).

32. Lord 2 Rain was the grandson of the Tilantongo ruler 12 Lizard; his father, 5 Movement, may have predeceased 12 Lizard because the Bodley does not show 5 Movement seated on the Tilantongo place sign (Troike 1979: 189). Since 2 Rain was the first son of his father's second wife, and not the first son of the first wife, others may have felt they had a valid claim to Tilantongo. Notably the Tilantongo ruler's brother, 10 Eagle, who was 6 Monkey's father, may have felt his offspring had equal rights to the throne. See Caso (1960b: 31–32; 1964a: 80–81), Byland and Pohl (1994: 121–124), Pohl (1994b: 37).

33. Before Rabin revised Caso's chronology for the Mixtec codices (c. 1980), it used to be thought that 5 Crocodile succeeded 2 Rain as the Tilantongo ruler, founding the second dynasty. But as Jansen (1982, 1:374–380) pointed out, 5 Crocodile died fourteen years before 2 Rain did, and he was likely a high priest rather than a ruler per se. For the events in 5 Crocodile's life, see Bodley 7–8, Caso (1960b: 33–38; 1979: 24–26), Jansen (1982, 1:374–380), Byland and Pohl (1994: 132–135), Pohl (1994b: 35–37).

34. This interpretation draws upon Caso (1960b: 38–40; 1966), Jansen (1982, 1:374–393), Troike (1974), Furst (1990), and Pohl (1994a, 1994b, 1996).

35. See Caso (1960b: 38) and Troike (1974: 113–115). Smith (personal communication, 1998) points out that Lady 4 Rabbit has an extra leg or set of legs beneath her skirt, as if someone were hiding behind her skirts. If so, she suggests the legs could possibly belong to the ill-fated Lord 2 Rain, who would later die mysteriously and leave the Tilantongo throne vacant. In this scenario, 2 Rain could conceivably be taking refuge with his great aunt from Tilantongo until the future usurper 8 Deer has left for Tututepec.

36. These visits are also recorded in the Colombino 1–2c.

37. In the Colombino (1–2b), 8 Deer plays ball with, and is then assisted by, the sun god 1 Death. As celestial supernaturals, 1 Death and 1 Movement are associated with each other. In the opening scene of the Selden (Fig. 56), they descend together from the sky and shoot darts into the earth. See Caso (1959).

38. See Caso (1960b: 39, table 2) for 3 Lizard's genealogical situation. The grandson of Lord 8 Wind "Flinted Eagle," an esteemed ancestor who is featured in the early part of the Zouche-Nuttall (Furst 1978b), 3 Flint may be the last of 8 Wind's son's sons; 8 Wind's daughter 2 Serpent married a Tilantongo ruler and fathered Tilantongo's next ruler, 12 Lizard "Arrow Legs." Lord 3 Flint, then, is a cousin and rough contemporary of 12 Lizard "Arrow Legs" (the Tilantongo ruler and grandfather of 2 Rain) and his brother 10 Eagle (lord of Jaltepec and father of 6 Monkey). Lord 3 Lizard is a nephew of Lady 9 Wind (6 Monkey's mother) and of Lady 2 Serpent (6 Monkey's paternal grandmother and 8 Deer's paternal great-grandmother). We do not know why his death was important; perhaps he represented the last of one entire side of 8 Wind's progeny, the other side being represented by the Tilantongo lords and their families.

39. See Troike (1974: 130–134). The Colombino (4b) adds to this gathering the deceased bodies of Lords 10? and 4 Grass, both costumed as birds.

40. The Colombino (1–2a and 3–6) and Zouche-Nuttall (44) versions ignore 8 Deer's conquest of River of Mouth and Flames and his visit to the lords of Apoala. Instead, they record a different version of the story, one that includes 8 Deer's offerings made to the sun, a sacrifice by 8 Deer and 12 Movement of animals (deer and coyote in Zouche-Nuttall 44d) to the celestial deity 13 Reed (Colombino 1a–2a), other conquests, and offerings made by 8 Deer in a ball court, all preceding his rule of Tututepec. They both then follow his assumption of rule with more of his conquests in coastal Oaxaca (compare Zouche-Nuttall 44–49 with Colombino 7–8, 9c).

41. The significance of this event and transformation is discussed by Caso (1955: 296; 1966: 129) and Pohl (1994b: 83–93; Byland and Pohl 1994: 138–150).

42. The species and metaphoric significance of this animal

are not yet known, although Caso (1966: 124) suggests it is related to a scene in the Zouche-Nuttall (45bc) where 8 Deer, seated in a cave, receives a bearded visitor, while a rat or gopher (accompanied by deer and jaguar feet) crawls in.

43. Caso (1960b: 39) read the personal names slightly differently and tentatively identified their home as Tula; Smith (1973a: 70–75) has suggested there were multiple Places of Reeds within the Mixteca, including a Tulixtlahuaca within Jicayán where, she argues, 8 Deer has his nose pierced, as well as Tulancingo in the Coixtlahuaca Valley where 4 Wind may have had his nose pierced. Pohl (1994b: 96–98) and Byland and Pohl (1994: 138–150) argue that the Place of Reeds is Tulancingo in the Coixtlahuaca Valley of Puebla, whereas Jansen (1996, 1997) argues for Cholula. See Smith (1973a: 74) and Pohl (1994b: 83–89) for 4 Jaguar's superhuman status.

44. Although Pohl (1994: 83–84) believes this Hill of the Moon to be the same as that conquered by Lady 6 Monkey and her ambassador 3 Lizard in the Codex Selden (8a), Smith (1973a: 68–70) has argued that it is not (that the Selden Hill of the Moon was near Jaltepec). Indeed the two 3 Lizards have different personal names.

45. This nose ornament so symbolized the status and meaning of *tecuhtli* that it later figured as part of the personal name sign of Moctezuma (Angry Lord) Xocoyotzin (Fig. 22).

46. The Zouche-Nuttall begins this episode with 8 Deer sacrificing deer at Tututepec (50bc); then he travels to the Hill of Blood and makes offerings to the supernatural Lady 9 Reed and apparently asks for her help (50d–51a). He is accompanied on this journey to the Place of Reeds by his half-brother 12 Movement (51b) and younger brother 9 Flower (52b), the latter carrying his symbols of rule. Once they meet, 8 Deer and 4 Jaguar present offerings together before (52bc) and after (53a) the nose piercing (52c). The Colombino features 10 Wind as an ambassador for 8 Deer early in the quest (9ab–10bc); like the Zouche-Nuttall, it includes offerings to Lady 9 Reed (10a), but it adds that she interceded for 8 Deer by herself visiting 4 Jaguar (11a–12a). In the Colombino (but not in the Zouche-Nuttall) 8 Deer and 4 Jaguar play a ball game (11bc), after which 8 Deer conquers Hill of the Moon (where his captive is 1 Movement; 13c); see Caso (1966: 128–129), Troike (1974: 164–202). In the coastal version of this story told in the Colombino-Becker, the nose piercing occurs in Tulixtlahuaca of Jicayán (Smith 1966: 160–162; 1973a: 70–71).

47. The Colombino (17a) pictures 8 Deer drilling a new fire (Troike 1974: 204–205, 209). See also Furst (1990: 129–131), who discusses the Bodley scene.

48. The badly damaged Colombino includes only perhaps a dozen lords (15c, 17c).

49. Colombino 18c, Zouche-Nuttall 68b.

50. The day sign is attached to the end of the warband, and the year sign is below the cradle. Although it is unusual to have the day and year signs separated like this, the Zouche-Nuttall (76b) and Colombino-Becker (Becker 1c) agree that 8 Deer arrived in 1 Death's vicinity on this date. Caso (1960b: 39–40) read the dates 4 Crocodile and 1 Death as the calendrical names of Lord 4 Crocodile and Lady 1 Death, who are supernatural ancestors of the Tilantongo lords, appearing at the beginnings of the Vienna Reverse (1c) and Bodley Obverse (1e, where 1 Death is pictured born from a tree).

51. The Colombino pictures the water roaring with high waves, whirlpools, and angry arrows as the travelers struggle across in boats or swim with the aid of gourd floats; see Caso (1966: 135), Troike (1974: 253–255). This is a marked contrast to the placid scene in the Zouche-Nuttall (75), although the Zouche-Nuttall does show high waves on the homeward crossing (80a).

52. Jansen (1997), identifying 4 Jaguar with Topiltzin Quetzalcoatl of Tula, proposes that this journey to the sun god was Quetzalcoatl's incursion into the Yucatan; he sees the great body of water as the Laguna de Términos and the sun god's temple as located at Chichén Itzá. Nicholson (n.d.) refutes this argument, however.

53. It used to be thought (e.g., Caso [1966: 139], Troike [1974: 210, 215–219, 335]) that 12 Movement ruled Tilantongo (as the first son of his father, 5 Crocodile) and that when 8 Deer planted his emblems of office at Tilantongo, this act began a new era of joint rule by the two of them. With Rabin's revised chronology, however, it is clear that 5 Crocodile did not rule Tilantongo, which makes it very unlikely that his eldest son, 12 Movement, did either. Lord 12 Movement never appears sitting on Tilantongo's place sign. We now see 8 Deer as founding the second dynasty of Tilantongo.

54. The Colombino-Becker reverses the types of sacrifice for 10 Dog and 6 House.

55. Caso (1960b: 42) suggested the place is probably within the domain of Skull Frieze, 6 Eagle's hometown, which Jansen (1982, 1:249) identifies as Chalcatongo; Troike (1974: 359) has proposed that 6 Eagle's names are there because she was responsible for informing on 8 Deer's whereabouts.

56. Lord 8 Crocodile is also the husband of 8 Deer's sister, 9 Monkey (Bodley 7e–8e).

6. Lienzos and Tiras from Oaxaca and Southern Puebla

1. Only dates and ground lines span external page breaks, and only in the Zouche-Nuttall (27–28, 37–38), which is compositionally looser than the other extant screenfolds and employs a vertical boustrophedon.

2. See McAnany (1995: esp. chap. 3), who discusses the link between land tenure and ancestor veneration among the lowland Maya.

3. See Caso (1958a), Acuña (1989), who reproduces Caso's commentary, and Vazquez (1983).

4. Smith (in Smith and Parmenter 1991: 18–19) mentions vertical marriage pairs in the Codex Tulane, Genealogy of Macuilxochitl, Lienzo of Philadelphia, Mapa de Teozacoalco, and the Coixtlahuaca lienzos of Nativitas, Ihuitlan, and Tlapiltepec. To these we can add the Lienzo Seler II (Coixtlahuaca II), the Lienzo of Tequixtepec II (Parmenter 1982), the Codex of Tecomaxtlahuaca (Smith in Smith and Parmenter 1991: 92–94), and the Lienzo of Tlapa from nearby Guerrero (Vega Sousa 1986). The Lienzo of Guevea lacks the wives but presents the male rulers in vertical columns. This listing is not complete.

5. See Smith (in Smith and Parmenter 1991) for the interpretation of the Codex Tulane.

6. Such confirmation scenes, where the subsidiary lords gather to confirm a new ruler in office (perhaps because he is founding a new dynasty), are featured in the Codex Zouche-Nuttall (54–68a, where 112 lords gather to confirm 8 Deer's rule of Tilantongo), the Codex Selden (3d–4c; Smith 1994: 130 n. 9), the Lienzo of Zacatepec (upper right corner; Smith 1973a: 113–114), the Lienzo of Yolotepec (Caso 1958b), and the Mapa de Teozacoalco (discussed below).

7. Mundy (1996: 227–230) reproduces the questionnaire's text in English translation; see Mundy (1996) for an excellent survey and analysis of the Relaciones Geográficas maps.

8. This discussion is generally based on Caso's classic 1949 interpretation of the map, amplified by Caso (1977, 1979). Mundy (1995: 112–117) corrects the number of boundaries; see her also for clarifying diagrams of the map; Anders and Jansen (1988: pl. 137) include an excellent drawing of the entire sheet. Anders, Jansen, and Pérez Jiménez (1992b: 35–53) build on Caso in identifying a number of the boundaries. Acuña (1984: 129–151) describes the individuals and reproduces the glosses on the map; he publishes many color details of the map and reproduces the Relación text.

9. Leibsohn (1995: 271) has pointed out that churches often conventionally symbolize towns or *sujetos* in sixteenth-century documents, regardless of whether the place actually has a church.

10. Caso (1949: 172–173; 1977: 151–152), Acuña (1984: 232). This last Tilantongo male ruler (Jaguar Torch) had the Spanish name Don Francisco de Mendoza, and his daughter took Doña Francisca de Mendoza.

11. Caso (1949: 165–166; 1979: 24) and Acuña (1984: 136) assigned the first ceremony to 2 Rain (noting that it was an error) and the second to 5 Crocodile rather than 8 Deer.

12. Caso (1949: 160) first read the date as the year after the marriage of 2 Rain's parents, and later (1979: 275, 379) as the year of their coronation. Acuña (1984: 136) read the year (without the day) as the year of 2 Rain's birth.

13. A Spanish gloss on the map names him Don Felipe de Santiago and his son Don Francisco de Mendoza (Acuña 1984: 138); this Don Francisco is the nephew of the Don Francisco de Mendoza (the elder) who was the last listed male ruler of Tilantongo and the cousin of Doña Francisca (Francisco the elder's daughter who is Tilantongo's last listed ruler; Caso 1977: 152–153). The similarity of the names led Acuña (1984: 137, 138) to conflate Doña Francisca with Don Francisco the younger (who, according to other documents, later came to rule Tilantongo as well as Teozacoalco [Caso 1977: 153]).

14. This explanation and analysis of the lienzo draws on Caso's (1961) pioneering interpretation, as later adjusted by Parmenter (1982, 1993) and van Doesburg (n.d.); see also Fane (1996: 76–78).

15. Although Parmenter (1982: 12) proposed that the place sign of an axe and serpent was Ihuitlan's, van Doesburg (n.d.) has recently identified that site as the *sujeto* Tepoztongo (now San Antonio Abad) and Water Hill as Ihuitlan.

16. The style is worn by two warriors in the Selden (7d), Lord 4 Jaguar and companions in the Bodley (9b, 10c, 28b, 32c, 33bc, 34a), and various males in the Selden Roll, Baranda, Fernández Leal, and Porfirio Díaz, to name a few. Some priests or participants in rituals in the Mixtec screenfolds wear their hair sheared at the top to form a wide column of hair, although this seems to be a different style (see Selden 2a, 3b, 4d, 5b; Zouche-Nuttall 18b, 25c, 52b, 69ab, 70d, 81b, 82c, 84b; Vienna Reverse 1a, 6ab).

17. The single male just to the right of Teopan along the left edge has no calendrical name. The solitary pair in the upper right are also unnamed.

18. Rincon (1997: 144, 146 n. 34) follows Caso in identifying the intruder's place as Texupan and suggests he is an

19. One is Acatlan in southern Puebla (Smith in Smith and Parmenter 1991: 54–55); the other lacks an identifying place sign.

20. To the upper right the archetypal priest/shaman 2 Dog sits at a Place of Little Trees, glossed Quauhtoco. Although the Selden Roll features an important meeting between 2 Dog and four priests in sawtooth crowns (discussed below), the two parties are not clearly associated with each other in this lienzo, and the priests have different names here.

21. For Meixueiro, see Codex Meixueiro (1931), Parmenter (1970, 1997); Coixtlahuaca I, see Codex Ixtlan (1931), Glass (1964: 169–170, pls. 123–124); Seler II or Coixtlahuaca II, see König (1984); Tulancingo, see Parmenter (1993), van Doesburg (n.d.); Nativitas, see Glass (1975a: no. 232, fig. 48); Tlapiltepec, see Caso (1961), Parmenter (1982, 1993), Johnson (1994, 1997).

22. This explanation draws on Caso (1964b), Parmenter (1966), Smith (1998: 165–172), and my own study of the original.

23. Three times the numerical parts of the names change by one: Lord 9 Lizard at Red and White Platform becomes Lord 10 Lizard at 1 Reed Plain in the lower right; Lord 13 Reed becomes Lord 12 Reed at Valley; and Lord 11 Wind becomes Lady 10 Wind at Corn Plant Place.

24. To my mind, his identification with Cobweb in the Zouche-Nuttall (38, 57) is less secure.

25. This discussion builds on Caso (1954, 1961, 1977: 118–136, 231–239) and Parmenter (1982, 1993) but interprets some of the elements and episodes differently.

26. The measurements for the two Tequixtepec lienzos derive from Rincon (1997: 134).

27. This discussion draws on Caso (1954; 1958a; 1961: 249–274; 1977: 119–129), Parmenter (1982), and Johnson (1994).

28. Parmenter (1982: 67) suggests this place may be outside the Coixtlahuaca Valley, for in Lienzo Seler II it is located outside the frame of place signs; it may also be a mythical place.

29. Jansen (1982, 1: 228–248) discusses the imagery of the cardinal directions, which also appear in Vienna Obverse and Aubin No. 20.

30. These have been identified as Cholula (Luis Reyes García as reported by Johnson 1994: 123), a location in the southern Coixtlahuaca Valley (Parmenter 1982: 73), and Tenochtitlan (Caso 1977: 126–127; Parmenter 1982: 74–76).

31. Johnson (personal communication, 1998) pointed out the reappearance of these couples on the map. In the Lienzo of Ihuitlan, we saw 3 Lizard as the founder of Tequixtepec (in the lower right corner) and 11 Lizard (married to Lady 4 Rabbit) in the early ruler list of Coixtlahuaca (col. A).

32. Johnson (1994) discovered these red lines. I thank him for sharing his fine drawing of the lienzo.

33. For several dates the Lienzo of Tlapiltepec substitutes the coefficient 1 for the 6 or 8 that appears in other manuscripts; see Johnson (1994: 128).

7. Stories of Migration, Conquest, and Consolidation in the Central Valleys

1. See Michael Smith's (1984) important article on the historicity of the Aztlan migration chronicles, which synthesizes the information in both alphabetic and pictorial sources.

2. Ruler lists do appear in some histories, however: the Texcocan Mapa Tlotzin (Fig. 122), the Mexica Codex Aubin, and in Sahagún's book on the rulers, discussed below. King lists or ruler lists also appear often in colonial land documents and (of course) genealogies.

3. Gillespie (1989: 25–56), taking a structural approach, looks at the role two Culhua women played as mothers, sisters, or wives of the Mexica kings.

4. Ultimately, because of the outstanding deeds of its rulers, the *altepetl* was accepted (Schroeder 1991: 124).

5. The discussion draws on the analyses of Ramírez (1858), Chavero (c. 1887: 459–507), and especially Orozco y Berra (1960, 3: 115–135) for the identities of the places and persons; see also Stern (1998).

6. Chavero (c. 1887: 475–476), following the suggestion of Ramírez (1858), identified the blue bird's head of the male (on the left) as the glyph for Cocoxtli (Pheasant), whereas Orozco y Berra (1960, 3: 119) read it as Cuauhtli (Eagle). Chavero and Orozco y Berra both read the female's sign (on the right) as Quetzalma (Hand Holding Quetzal Feathers).

7. Orozco y Berra (1960, 3: 122–123, 125) identified the first five travelers (reading right to left) as Huitzilihuitl (Hummingbird Feather), Papalo (Butterfly), Tlalaala (he read the blue form as the herb mallow), Huitziton (he read the bird-copal-stone configuration as Little Hummingbird), and Xomomitl (Foot Arrow). He identified the second group of ten (reading from left to right) as Atletl (Water Fire), Acaçitli (Reed Hare), Ahuexotl (Water Willow), Aatzin (Water Drinker), Cuauhpan (Eagle Banner), Ocelopan (Jaguar Banner), Iczicuauh (Eagle Talon), Mimich (Fishing Net), Tenoch (Nopal Stone), and Amimitl (Water Arrow). Huitzilihuitl, Xomomitl, Acaçitli, Ahuexotl, Cuapan, Ocelopan, and Tenoch ap-

pear in other accounts of the migration (C. Mendoza 2r [Berdan and Anawalt 1992, 2:5, 7], C. Mexicanus 44).

8. Identified as Acocolco (Twisting Water; C. Boturini 19, C. Aubin 41–42, A. de Tlatelolco 1948: 36) or Atlacuihuayan (Place Where Water Is Caught; Durán 1994: 33).

9. Those killed at Chapultepec are Ahuexotla (Water Willow) and Aatzin (Water Drinker); they appear alive again at the founding of Tenochtitlan. Those who escaped to the watery place are Acaçitli (Reed Hare), Cuahpan (Eagle Banner), and Atezcatl (Water Mirror), who is not previously named; Orozco y Berra (1960, 3:132).

10. Orozco y Berra (1960, 3:133) identified the men as belonging to the families respectively of Huitzilihuitl (Hummingbird Feather), Cuahpan (Eagle Banner), Huitziton (he read the now-lost glyph as Little Hummingbird), Mimich (Fishing Net), and Tezcatetl (Lipplug), who has not been previously named.

11. They are Acaçitli (Reed Hare) and Cuahpan (Eagle Banner).

12. Acaçitli (Reed Hare), Atezcatl (Water Mirror), and Ahuexotl (Water Willow) appear on the side near the sweatbath, while Tenoch (Nopal Stone), Ocelopan (Jaguar Banner), Aatzin (Water Drinker), and Xomomitl (Foot Arrow) appear on the side near Tlatelolco (Chavero c. 1887: 507). All but Atezcatl left Aztlan; Ahuexotl and Aatzin died at Chapultepec.

13. This discussion draws from the commentary on the Historia Tolteca-Chichimeca (1976) by Kirchhoff, Odena Güemes, and Reyes García (including a Spanish translation of the Nahuatl text), Leibsohn's (1993) fine dissertation on the Historia Tolteca-Chichimeca (including an English translation of the Nahuatl text), and the analyses of the Historia and Cuauhtinchan maps by Simons (1968), Yoneda (1991), Reyes García (1988), and Leibsohn (1994; 1996: 503–508).

14. This is also in the Historia painting (16r).

15. The severed fingers and arms of women who had died in childbirth were prized as powerful talismans by Aztec warriors (Barnes 1997); this may be a similar situation. A severed leg is also held by a figure representing the Flint Knife Lord or sacrificer in Vienna 48a (Fig. 49).

16. The prose of the Historia tallies the number of Chichimecs who emerged from Chicomoztoc as 108 men and 16 women (Historia Tolteca-Chichimeca 22v; Leibsohn 1993: 338).

17. Kirchhoff (1940) has diagrammed what he proposes to be these routes.

18. The Tira de Tepechpan (p. 3) shows the sacrifice of a quail, snake, and butterfly at the founding of Tepechpan (Boone n.d.).

19. For the general geography of the area, see the extremely helpful maps by Yoneda (1991: láms. 2, 36, 41). Reyes García (1988: map 2) has mapped the boundaries of Cuauhtinchan and its neighbors according to both Cuauhtinchan Map 2 and the Historia Tolteca-Chichimeca.

20. This discussion draws especially on Reyes García (1988: 12–13) and Leibsohn (1993: 280–282; 1994; 1996: 503–505, 521).

21. They are Nopal and Aquiauatl (Kirchhoff, Odena Güemes, and Reyes García 1976: 129).

22. Tollan Calmecauacan, featured in Cuauhtinchan Map 1, is represented on the left as a hill of reeds and an adjacent school.

23. This discussion draws on the analyses of Aubin (1886a, 1886b), Radin (1920: 35–45, pls. 13–17), Barlow (1950), Dibble (1980, 1:31–42, 149–164), Offner (1982: 18–46), and Spitler (n.d.a; n.d.b).

24. This description draws on the interpretations of Dibble (1980) and Spitler (n.d.b).

25. Two fragmentary leaves seem to be the remains of other maps that probably went between maps 1 and 2 in the sequence (Dibble 1980, 1:43–46).

26. This is consistently true unless there is a more compelling reason to describe the places pictorially. On map 2 (Fig. 120), for example, Tenayuca (the large profile cave below the lake) and the two unidentified caves in the upper middle and center right above the lake are presented as caves rather than distinctly named places because they are early sites of Chichimec occupation.

27. For map 2, see Dibble (1980, 1:31–42, and his explanation of personal and place names on 149–164) and Spitler (n.d.b).

28. See Aubin (1886b), Radin (1920: 35–38), and Spitler (n.d.a, n.d.b). My summary principally follows the pictorial imagery supplemented by information in the Nahuatl glosses.

29. Usually this principal site has been identified as the Texcocan barrio of Oztoticpac (Cave Banner) because of the white banner to the upper left of the cave (Aubin 1886b; Dibble 1980; Spitler n.d.b). But since this banner is prefixed by a curved blue element (which has not yielded a translation), I suggest the composite glyph carries a different meaning. The same glyph appears two other times on the tira, above Coatlichan and in the far upper right corner.

30. The named rulers are Tlotzin (Falcon) and wife Icpacxochitl (Crown of Flowers), Quinatzin (Shouting Deer Earth) and wife Cuauhchiuatzin (Eagle Woman), Techotlalatzin (Bird Water Stone) and wife Tozquentzin (Yellow Parrot Feather Cape), Ixtlilxochitl (Eye Black Flower) and wife Matlalcihuatl (Blue Woman), Nezahualcoyotl (Fasting Coyote), Nezahualpilli (Fasting Lord), Cacamatzin (Young Corn Ear), who died during the Noche Triste, Don Pedro Coanacochtzin (Ser-

pent Ear Ornament), Don Hernando Tecocoltzin (Wizard), Don Hernando Ixtlilxochitl (Eye Black Flower), Don Jorge Yoyontzin (Ambler ?), and Don Pedro Tetlahuehuetzquitzin (Comedian; Aubin 1886b: 313–317; Siméon 1981; Dibble 1980, 1:149–159; Spitler n.d.b). See also Sahagún (1959–1982, bk. 8:9–10) for the list of Texcoco's rulers.

31. See Aubin (1886a), Barlow (1950), Offner (1982, 1983), and Spitler (n.d.b); Barlow and Offner have analyzed page 3 in detail.

32. The arrival and intermixing of these people are also covered in the Codex Xolotl (map 5; Dibble 1980, 1:79–80; Spitler n.d.b).

33. They are, reading right to left, Azcapotzalco, Tenayuca, Toltitlan, Quahtitlan, Coyoacan, Culhuacan, and Xochimilco (Barlow 1950: 115).

34. For the status of women before and after the conquest, see Kellogg (1997).

8. Aztec *Altepetl* Annals

1. Exceptions are descent statements for Acamapichtli's children in the Telleriano-Remensis (28v–30r; Quiñones Keber 1995: 212–213, 271) and two descent and two marriage statements in the Tira de Tepechpan (Noguez 1978: 75–77, 88–89, 101–103). Lockhart (1992: 380–381) has also pointed out that late in the C. Aubin, when that annals account has become more personal and almost like a private journal, it records the births of two women who may be the annalist's daughters.

2. Births are almost never recorded for the Mexica rulers, the exception being Moctezuma Ilhuicamina's birth in the year 10 Rabbit pictured in the C. Mexicanus (56). Otherwise, the rulers of the Acolhua domain are the only ones whose births are mentioned in the annals, even Mexica annals. Nezahualcoyotl's birth in 1 Rabbit is noted in the C. en Cruz (1a), C. Azcatitlan (28), and C. Mexicanus (57); Nezahualpilli's birth in 11 Flint is recorded in the C. en Cruz (2a); the births of other Acolhua lords are recorded in the C. en Cruz (1a, 2c, 2d; Dibble 1981, 1:59) and C. Azcatitlan (43).

3. The mixed picture and prose account of the Historia Tolteca-Chichimeca focuses principally on Cuauhtinchan's early history prior to and shortly after the *altepetl*'s founding.

4. My analysis of these draws on the following studies: C. Aubin and cognates (Aubin 1893; Barlow and McAfee 1989; Lehmann and Kutscher 1981; Peñafiel 1980), C. Azcatitlan (Barlow and Graulich 1995), C. Boturini (Corona Núñez 1964–1967, 2, pt. 1), C. Mendoza (Berdan

and Anawalt 1992; Boone 1992), C. Mexicanus (Mengin 1952).

5. For the C. en Cruz and Tira de Tepechpan, I draw on the commentaries by Dibble (1981) and Noguez (1978), respectively. The C. Telleriano-Remensis has suffered losses since the C. Vaticanus A/Ríos was copied from it in the late sixteenth century (Quiñones Keber 1995: 129–130); for these manuscripts I rely on the commentaries and translations by Quiñones Keber (1995), Ehrle (1900), and Corona Núñez (1964–1967, 3).

6. I rely on Caso (1992) for the C. Huichiapan and use Barlow (1949a) and van Zantwijk (1979) for the Anales de Tula.

7. See Nicholson (1971: 48–49) for a review of these and others. To these can be added several recently discovered annals recorded by Chimalpahin (1997), including his version of the Crónica Mexicayotl text.

8. This organization of the annals builds on Nicholson (1971: 45–49).

9. Although the C. Saville is aberrant in that it employs plain turquoise disks to represent the individual years (relying on the visual pun that *xihuitl* means both turquoise and year), it does add the actual year sign at thirteen-year intervals (i.e., 1 Flint, 1 House, 1 Rabbit, and 1 Reed, the quarter points of the fifty-two-year cycle).

10. The first page of its migration, missing in the C. Telleriano-Remensis but preserved in the Vaticanus A/Ríos copy (66v), originally had three years and the second page (25r) had seven.

11. Noguez (1978: 84–86), who follows the Nahuatl glosses more literally than I do, offers a slightly different reading of Cuacuauhtzin's actions.

12. In copying the C. Telleriano-Remensis, the C. Vaticanus A/Ríos author sometimes grouped two of the U-shaped frames to a page (i.e., 71r, 82v).

13. We should remember, however, that the indigenous *tonalamatl* (the divinatory book of the 260-day count) usually follows a similar organization; it organizes data on pages, where the thirteen days and associated augural information are arranged as an "L" around the panel of each trecena.

14. The Anales de Tula (Barlow 1949a; van Zantwijk 1979) is another annals account that features a broken year count.

15. This is not the end of the manuscript, which continues with a pictorial listing of the Mexica rulers and their reign lengths, from the founder Tenoch to Don Gerónimo López, who was judge and governor of Xaltocan in 1605 (70r–79r; Lehmann and Kutscher 1981: 60).

16. See Heyden (1989) for an iconographic analysis of the Aztec migration.

17. As do the cognate sources, C. Ramírez and Tovar's history.

18. See Alvarado Tezozomoc (1975: 3, 18); Anales de Tlatelolco (1948: 31); Chimalpahin (1997: 29, 69, 179); Torquemada (1975–1979, 1:114–115). Heyden (1989: 4–9, 52–53) compares the pictorial and prose sources.

19. We know the canoer is a priest by the smear of auto-sacrificial blood by his ear in the C. Azcatitlan and by the dark gray coloring and flowing hair in the C. Boturini.

20. The exception is the alphabetic Anales de Tlatelolco (1948: 31), which dates the departure from Aztlan/Chicomoztoc/Teoculhuacan to year 1 Reed day 1 Crocodile, the descent/departure date used in the Coixtlahuaca Valley histories; it immediately then gives 1 Flint as the date that the tribes actually dispersed.

21. Michael Smith (1984: 160–161, 163–164) argues that the second tribe in the C. Boturini is the Tlahuica rather than the Chichimeca and that the fifth tribe is the Acolhua rather than Cuitlahuaca; his argument is based on comparisons with alphabetic sources, almost all of which omit the Chichimeca and include the Acolhua. I disagree with him here because the painted place signs are reasonable referents to the Chichimeca and Cuitlahuaca; there is room in this genre for variations in the tribal lists. The C. Aubin, C. Azcatitlan, and C. Boturini present the same version of the migration, one that differs from the versions recorded in several alphabetic sources. Torquemada's account (1975–1979, 1:113), derived from this same version, lists these same tribes, substituting the Mizquica for the Huexotzinca (he seems to have misinterpreted the variety of tree in the place sign) and including the Mexica.

22. Reading left to right, they are the Xochimilca, [Huexo]tzinca, Acolhua, Cuitlahuaca, Tepaneca, Mizquica, and Chalca.

23. The C. Telleriano-Remensis (25r) still preserves the names, which are the Chichimeca, Nonoalca, Michuaque, Couixca, Totonaca, Huaxteca, and Olmeca Xicalanca (Quiñones Keber 1995: 202, 204).

24. See Gillespie (1989: 69–78) for an analysis of this episode, focusing on the role of Huitzilihuitl's daughters; Davies (1980: 28–34) summarizes it in a synthetic narrative.

25. No two annals include the same founders, although the C. Mendoza (Fig. 134) and C. Mexicanus (Fig. 146) tend to agree most often. Collectively, the pictorial annals mention over twenty founders; the Azcatitlan pictures fourteen of them. Some individuals appear in the pictorials more than most: Tenoch (Stone Nopal) in five sources, Acaçitli (Reed Hare) in four, Xiuhcaque (Turquoise Sandal) in four, Xomimitl (Arrow Leg) in three, Ahuexotl (Water Willow) in two and possibly three, and

Ahatzin (Water) in two and possibly three. See Mengin (1952: 437–439), Barlow and Graulich (1995: 96–100).

26. See Boone (1991) for a discussion of this similarity and a reading of the migration as a transformative rite of passage.

27. I interpret the ruler's name sign on 29v as a human hand rather than the deer's horn that named Cuacuapitzahuac, although Cuacuapitzahuac did take office in Tlatelolco about the same time Acamapichtli did in Tenochtitlan (Barlow 1944: 28; C. Azcatitlan 25, 27; C. Mexicanus 53).

28. See Quiñones Keber's (1984) comparison of the content of the imperial annals.

29. The C. en Cruz, however, only marks one in three of the three New Fire ceremonies, that for 1502.

30. See Boone (1992: 152–153) for the reign dates of the Mexica rulers reported in thirty-nine sources.

31. The lines and glosses between 13 Reed and 1 Flint were added later.

32. The prose sources give different accounts; cf. C. Mendoza 9v (Berdan and Anawalt 1992, 4:24), Chimalpahin (1997: 139), Durán (1994: 260), Torquemada (1975–1979, 1:248).

33. Accession dates of day 2 Rain and 11 Rain are reported in two prose sources (Chimalpahin 1997: 135, 215).

34. They are Red Hill with a Circle (identified by Graulich [Barlow and Graulich 1995: 116] as Malacatepec but perhaps referring to the red leather of Cuetlaxtlan), Tlatelolco (Earth Mound), Ocuillan (Place of Caterpillars), Serpent Fire Drill, Matlatzinco (Hunting Net), Tochpan (Rabbit), Michoacan (Fish), Tolocan (Inclined Head), and Xiquipilco (Incense Pouch). Barlow has suggested that the infant in the cradle is Moctezuma Xocoyotzin (Barlow and Graulich 1995: 118).

35. These are Ocuillan (Caterpillar), Icpatepec (Thread Hill [On the Top of the Hill]), and Xiquipilco (Incense Bag but represented by a house here and in the C. Mexicanus).

36. They are Michoacan (Fish) and Cuetlaxtlan (Leather) in 4 Rabbit, Xochitlan (Flower Teeth) in 6 Flint, Ocuillan (Caterpillar) in 10 Flint, Icpatepec (Thread Hill) in 11 House, and Xiquipilco (Incense Pouch) in 12 Rabbit (Mengin 1952: 452–455).

37. In this way it represents the conquests of Tlatelolco, Cuetlaxtlan, Ocuillan, and Xiquipilco.

38. The Texcocan pictorials (i.e., C. en Cruz and C. Xolotl) seem to employ more glyphic phoneticism than do others.

39. I identify her as a regent because her bundle wears the turquoise diadem of the *tlatoque,* although she has not appeared in a formal accession statement. She is an important woman, however, because the tira (in one of the

two descent statements in the manuscript) explains that she is the mother of the previous ruler of Tepechpan and the widow of the ruler before him. She may have ruled during the two gaps in succession after the deaths of her husband and of her son, perhaps also as regent for the present ruler.

40. Cuauhtemoc and other *tlatoque* were taken along as hostages on Cortés' expedition to pacify a rebellion in Guatemala, when Cuauhtemoc was accused of plotting against Cortés and was executed.

41. See Gibson (1964: 168–170) for the colonial rulers. As Barnes (n.d.) explains, several of the pictorial histories are careful to distinguish between legitimate and illegitimate *tlatoque* after the conquest.

42. For the importance of this chair as a symbol of political authority, see Diel (n.d.a, n.d.b).

43. He actually arrived in 1528.

9. Histories with a Purpose

1. The Lienzo of Yolotepec may also; see note 4 below.

2. The C. of Yanhuitlan, a Mixtec economic document rather than a genealogical one, does include the Spanish conquest, but it is the Spanish conquest of Mexico-Tenochtitlan rather than of Yanhuitlan (Smith 1998: 132, fn. 20).

3. An exception is the ruler list on the right side of the Maguey Plan, which rises upwards (Barnes n.d.).

4. Although Parmenter (1982: 2–3) has suggested that all the lienzos are colonial, the Lienzo of Yolotepec (Caso 1958b) may lack any European imagery or stylistic elements, for Barbara Mundy (personal communication, 1998) thinks the church painted near Amoltepec's place sign may have been added later.

5. For summaries of the trial and the related documents, see Greenleaf (1962: 59), Padden (1967: 253–274), Boone (1989: 26–28; 1998: 165–168).

6. This discussion relies on Robertson and Robertson (1975), Harvey (1986), and Borah (1991).

Bibliography

Acosta, José de

1979   *Historia natural y moral de las Indias.* Edited by
        Edmundo O'Gorman. Mexico City: Fondo de
        Cultura Económica. Reprint of 2d edition, 1962.

Acuña, René, ed.

1984   *Relaciones geográficas del siglo XVI: Antequera.*
        Vol. 2. Mexico City: Universidad Nacional Autó-
        noma de México.

1989   *Códice Baranda. Comentarios de Lorenzo de Bo-
        turini, Alfonso Caso, Alfredo Chavero, Patricio
        Antonio López, Francisco del Paso y Troncoso.* Mex-
        ico City: Ediciones Toledo.

Ainaud, Juan

1962   *Spanish Frescoes of the Romanesque Period.*
        Fontana UNESCO Art Books. London: Collins,
        UNESCO.

Albro, Sylvia Rodgers, and Thomas C. Albro II

1990   The Examination and Conservation Treatment of
        the Library of Congress Harkness 1531 Huejo-
        tzingo Codex. *Journal of the American Institute
        of Conservation* 29 : 97–115.

Alva Ixtlilxochil, Fernando de

1985   *Obras históricas.* Edited by Edmundo O'Gorman.
        2 vols. Mexico City: Instituto de Investigaciones
        Históricas, Universidad Nacional Autónoma de
        México.

Alvarado, Fray Francisco de

1962   *Vocabulario en lengua Mixteca.* Facsimile edition
        with a study by Wigberto Jiménez Moreno. Mex-
        ico City: Instituto Nacional Indigenista and In-
        stituto Nacional de Antropología e Historia.

Alvarado Tezozomoc, Fernando

1975   *Crónica Mexicayotl.* Translated and edited by
        Adrián León. Primera serie prehispánica 3. Mex-
        ico City: Instituto de Investigaciones Históricas,
        Universidad Nacional Autónoma de México.

Anales de Tecamachalco

1992   *Anales de Tecamachalco, 1398–1590.* Translated and
        edited by Eustaquio Celestino Solís and Luis
        Reyes García. Mexico City: Gobierno del Estado
        de Puebla, Centro de Investigaciones y Estudios
        Superiores en Antropología Social, and Fondo de
        Cultura Económica.

Anales de Tlatelolco

1948   *Anales de Tlatelolco: Unos anales históricos de la
        nación mexicana y Códice de Tlatelolco.* Translated
        and edited by Heinrich Berlin and Robert Bar-
        low. Mexico City: Antigua Librería Robredo, de
        José Porrúa e Hijos.

Anales de Tula

1979   *Anales de Tula, BNA Cod. 35-9.* Translated and
        edited by Rudolf A. M. van Zantwijk. Graz: Aka-
        demische Druck- u. Verlagsanstalt.

Anawalt, Patricia Rieff

1981   *Indian Clothing before Cortés.* Norman: Univer-
        sity of Oklahoma Press.

Anders, Ferdinand

1972   Einleitung, Summary und Resumen. In *Codex Vaticanus 3773 (Codex Vaticanus B), Biblioteca Apoltolica Vaticana*. Graz: Akademische Druck- u. Verlagsanstalt.

Anders, Ferdinand, and Maarten Jansen

1988   *Schrift und Buch im alten Mexico*. Graz: Akademische Druck- u. Verlagsanstalt.

1994   *La pintura de la muerte y de los destinos: Libro explicativo del llamado Códice Laud.* Accompanying a facsimile of the codex. Graz: Akademische Druck- u. Verlagsanstalt; Mexico City: Fondo de Cultura Económica.

Anders, Ferdinand, Maarten Jansen, and Gabina Aurora Pérez Jiménez

1992a   *Códice Vindobonensis. Origen e historia de los reyes mixtecos.* Facsimile with commentary and line drawing. Madrid: Sociedad Estatal Quinto Centenario; Graz: Akademische Druck- u. Verlagsanstalt; Mexico City: Fondo de Cultura Económica.

1992b   *Códice Zouche-Nuttall. Crónica mixteca: El rey 8 Venado, Garra de Jaguar, y la dinastía de Teozacualco-Zaachila.* Facsimile with commentary and line drawing. Madrid: Sociedad Estatal Quinto Centenario; Graz: Akademische Druck- u. Verlagsanstalt; Mexico City: Fondo de Cultura Económica.

1994   *Códice Fejérváry-Mayer. El libro de Tezcatlipoca, señor del tiempo.* Facsimile with commentary. Graz: Akademische Druck- u. Verlagsanstalt; Mexico City: Fondo de Cultura Económica.

Anders, Ferdinand, Maarten Jansen, and Peter van der Loo

1994   *Códice Cospi. Calendario de pronósticos y ofrendas.* Facsimile with commentary. Graz: Akademische Druck- u. Verlagsanstalt; Mexico City: Fondo de Cultura Económica.

Aubin, Joseph Marius Alexis

1849   *Mémoire sur la peinture didactique et l'écriture figurative des anciens Mexicains.* Paris: Paul Dupont. Reprinted in 1885 with slight revisions and color lithographs of the Mapas Quinatzin and Tlotzin.

c. 1849–   *Mappe Quinatzin. Cour Chichimeque et histoire de*
1851   *Tezcuco, pl. 2.* Paris: Desportes Lithograph. Printed to illustrate Aubin 1849.

1886a   Mapa Quinatzin, cuadro histórico de la civilización de Tetzcuco. *Anales del Museo Nacional de México,* época 1, 3:345–368, 1 folding plate.

1886b   Mapa Tlotzin. Historia de los reyes y de los estados soberanos de Acolhuacan. *Anales del Museo Nacional de México,* época 1, 3:304–320, 1 folding plate.

1886c   Mapa de Tepechpan. Historia sincrónica y señorial de Tepechpan y México. *Anales del Museo Nacional de México,* época 1, 3:368, 1 folding plate.

———, trans. and ed.

1893   *Histoire de la nation mexicaine, depuis le départ d'Aztlan jusqu'à l'arrivée des conquérants Espagnols (et au delà 1607).* Paris: Ernest Leroux.

Aveni, Anthony

1980   *Skywatchers of Ancient Mexico.* Austin: University of Texas Press.

Baird, Ellen Taylor

1993   *The Drawings of Sahagún's Primeros Memoriales: Structure and Style.* Norman: University of Oklahoma Press.

Barlow, Robert

1944   Tlatelolco en el período Tepaneca. *Tlatelolco a traves de los tiempos* 1:23–42. Offprint from *Memorias de la Academia de la Historia* 3, no. 2:219–238.

1948   El Códice de Tlatelolco. In *Anales de Tlatelolco* 1948, 105–128, folding plate.

1949a   Anales de Tula, Hidalgo, 1361–1521. *Tlalocan* 3, no. 1:2–13.

1949b   El Códice Azcatitlan. *Journal de la Société des Américanistes,* n.s., 38:101–135. Accompanied by a facsimile of the codex in a separate album.

1950   Una nueva lámina del Mapa Quinatzin. *Journal de la Société des Américanistes,* n.s., 39:111–124.

Barlow, Robert, and Byron McAfee

1989   La segunda parte del Códice Aubin [1520–1608]. In *Obras de Robert H. Barlow.* Vol. 2, *Tlatelolco: Fuentes e historia,* edited by Jesús Monjarás-Ruiz, Elena Limón, and María de la Cruz Paillés H., pp. 261–305. Mexico City: Instituto Nacional de Antropología e Historia and Universidad de las Américas. First published in 1947 in *Memorias de la Academia Mexicana de la Historia* 6, no. 2:156–182.

Barlow, Robert, and Michele Graulich, eds.

1995   *Codex Azcatitlan.* 2 vols. Facsimile, with commentary by Barlow revised by Graulich. Spanish translation by Leonardo López Luján, French translation by Dominique Michelet. Paris: Bibliothèque Nationale de France and Société des Américanistes.

Barnes, William

1997   Partitioning the Parturient: An Exploration of the Aztec Fetishized Female Body. *Athanor* 15:20–27. Tallahassee: Department of Art History, Florida State University.

n.d.   Secularizing for Survival: Changing Depictions of

Central Mexican Native Rule in the Early Colonial Period. In *Mesoamerican Manuscript Studies in Honor of Mary Elizabeth Smith,* edited by Elizabeth H. Boone. New Orleans: Middle American Research Institute, Tulane University. Forthcoming.

Basso, Keith H.

1984 "Stalking with Stories": Names, Places, and Moral Narratives among the Western Apache. In *Text, Play, and Story: The Construction and Reconstruction of Self and Society,* edited by Edward M. Bruner, pp. 19–54. Washington, D.C.: American Ethnological Society.

Baudot, Georges

1983 *Utopia e historia en México: Los primeros cronistas de la civilización mexicana (1520–1569).* Translated from the French by Vincente González Loscertales. Madrid: Espasa-Calpe.

1995 *Utopia and History in Mexico: The First Chronicles of Mexican Civilization, 1520–1569.* Translated from the Spanish by Bernard R. Ortiz de Montellano and Thelma Ortiz de Montellano. Niwot: University Press of Colorado.

Berdan, Frances F.

1992a Appendix E. The Place-Name, Personal Name, and Title Glyphs of the Codex Mendoza: Translations and Comments. In Berdan and Anawalt 1992, 1:163–238.

1992b Glyphic Conventions in the Codex Mendoza. In Berdan and Anawalt 1992, 1:93–102.

Berdan, Frances F., and Patricia Rieff Anawalt

1992 *The Codex Mendoza.* 4 vols. Berkeley: University of California Press.

Berlo, Janet C.

1983 Conceptual Categories for the Study of Texts and Images in Mesoamerica. In *Text and Image in Pre-Columbian Art: Essays on the Interrelationship of the Verbal and Visual Arts,* edited by Janet Catherine Berlo, pp. 1–39. BAR International Series 180. Oxford: BAR.

Bierhorst, John, trans. and ed.

1992 *History and Mythology of the Aztecs: The Codex Chimalpopoca.* Tucson: University of Arizona Press.

Boban, Eugène

1891 *Documentos pour servir à l'histoire de Mexique.* 2 vols. and atlas. Paris: E. Leroux.

Boone, Elizabeth Hill

1983 *The Codex Magliabechiano and the Lost Prototype of the Magliabechiano Group.* Berkeley: University of California Press.

1989 *Incarnations of the Aztec Supernatural: The Image of Huitzilopochtli in Mexico and Europe.* Transac-

tions of the American Philosophical Society 79, no. 2. Philadelphia.

1990 The Painting Styles of the Manuscripts of the Borgia Group. In *Circumpacifica: Festschrift für Thomas S. Barthel,* edited by Bruno Illius and Mathias Laubscher, 1:35–54. Frankfurt am Main: Peter Lang.

1991 Migration Histories as Ritual Performance. In *To Change Place: Aztec Ceremonial Landscapes,* edited by Davíd Carrasco, pp. 121–151. Niwot: University Press of Colorado.

1992 The Aztec Pictorial History of the Codex Mendoza. In Berdan and Anawalt 1992, 1:35–54, 152–153.

1994a Aztec Pictorial Histories: Records without Words. In Boone and Mignolo 1994, 50–76.

1994b Introduction: Writing and Recording Knowledge. In Boone and Mignolo 1994, 3–26.

1996 Manuscript Painting in Service of Imperial Ideology. In *Aztec Imperial Strategies,* by Frances F. Berdan, Richard E. Blanton, Elizabeth Hill Boone, Mary G. Hodge, Michael E. Smith, and Emily Umberger, pp. 181–206. Washington, D.C.: Dumbarton Oaks.

1997 Prominent Scenes and Pivotal Events in the Mexican Pictorial Histories. In Rueda Smithers, Vega Sosa, and Martínez Baracas 1997, 1:407–424.

1998 Pictorial Documents and Visual Thinking in Postconquest Mexico. In *Native Traditions in the Postconquest World,* edited by Elizabeth Hill Boone and Tom Cummins, pp. 149–199. Washington, D.C.: Dumbarton Oaks.

n.d. Bringing Polity to Place: Aztec and Mixtec Foundation Rituals. *Códices y documentos sobre México, tercer simposio internacional,* edited by Constanza Vega, Hanns Prem, and Stephanie Wood. Mexico City: Instituto Nacional de Antropología e Historia. Forthcoming.

Boone, Elizabeth Hill, and Walter G. Mignolo, eds.

1994 *Writing without Words: Alternative Literacies in Mesoamerica and the Andes.* Durham: Duke University Press.

Boornazian, Lori (*see also* Diel, Lori Boornazian)

1996 A Comparative Study of Personal and Place Names in the Aztec and Mayan Writing Systems. M.A. thesis, Tulane University.

Borah, Woodrow

1983 *Justice by Insurance: The General Indian Court of Colonial Mexico and the Legal Aides of the Half-Real.* Berkeley: University of California Press.

1991 Yet Another Look at the Techialoyan Codices. In *Land and Politics in the Valley of Mexico: A Two*

Thousand Year Perspective, edited by H. R. Harvey, pp. 209–221. Albuquerque: University of New Mexico Press.

Brilliant, Richard

1984   *Visual Narratives: Storytelling in Etruscan and Roman Art.* Ithaca: Cornell University Press.

Broda, Johanna, Davíd Carrasco, and Eduardo Matos Moctezuma

1987   *The Great Temple of Tenochtitlan: Center and Periphery in the Aztec World.* Berkeley: University of California Press.

Brown, Betty Ann

1978   European Influences in the Early Colonial Descriptions and Illustrations of the Mexican Monthly Calendar. Ph.D. diss., University of New Mexico.

1982   Early Colonial Representations of the Aztec Monthly Calendar. In *Pre-Columbian Art History: Selected Readings,* edited by Alana Cordy-Collins, pp. 169–191. Palo Alto, Calif.: Peck Publications.

Brown, Donald E.

1988   *Hierarchy, History, and Human Nature: The Social Origins of Historical Consciousness.* Tucson: University of Arizona Press.

Bruner, Edward M., ed.

1984   Introduction: The Opening Up of Anthropology. In *Text, Play, and Story: The Construction and Reconstruction of Self and Society,* pp. 1–16. Proceedings of the American Ethnological Society, 1983. Prospect Heights, Ill.: Waveland Press.

Burgoa, Fray Francisco de

1934   *Geográfica descripción de la parte septentrional, del polo ártico de la América, y nueva iglesia de las Indias Occidentales.* 2 vols. 2d ed. Publicaciones del Archivo General de la Nación 25–26. Mexico City: Talleres Gráficos de la Nación.

1989   *Palestra historial de virtudes y ejemplares apostólicos.* 3d ed. Mexico City: Porrúa.

Burland, Cottie A., ed.

1955   *The Selden Roll: An Ancient Mexican Picture Manuscript in the Bodleian Library at Oxford.* Berlin: Verlag Gebr. Mann.

1965   Introduction to *Codex Egerton 2895, British Museum, London.* Graz: Akademische Druck- u. Verlagsanstalt.

1971   Introduction to *Codex Fejérváry-Mayer, 12014 M, City of Liverpool Museums.* Graz: Akademische Druck- u. Verlagsanstalt.

Byland, Bruce, and John M. D. Pohl

1994   *In the Realm of 8 Deer: The Archaeology of the Mixtec Codices.* Norman: University of Oklahoma Press.

Calnek, Edward E.

1978   The Analysis of Prehispanic Central Mexican Historical Texts. *Estudios de Cultura Nahuatl* 13:239–266.

Carlstein, Tommy

1982   *Time Resources, Ecology, and Society: On the Capacity for Human Interaction in Space and Time in Preindustrial Societies.* London: George Allen and Unwin.

Carlstein, Tommy, Don Parkes, and Nigel Thrift

1978   *Timing Space and Spacing Time.* Vol. 2, *Human Activity and Time Geography.* London: Edward Arnold.

Carrasco, Pedro

1971   Social Organization of Ancient Mexico. In *Handbook of Middle American Indians,* vol. 3, edited by Robert Wauchope, Gordon F. Ekholm, and Ignacio Bernal, pp. 349–375. Austin: University of Texas Press.

Caso, Alfonso

1949   El Mapa de Teozacoalco. *Cuadernos Americanos,* año 8, 47, 5:145–181.

1950   Explicación del reverso del Codex Vindobonensis. *Memoria de El Colegio Nacional* 5, no. 5:9–46, 2 tables, 1 fold-out plate.

1954   *Interpretación del Códice Gómez de Orozco.* Mexico City: Talleres de Impresión de Estampillas y Valores.

1955   La vida y aventura de 4. Viento "Serpiente de Fuego." In *Miscelánea de estudios dedicados al Dr. Fernando Ortiz,* 1:291–298. Havana: Sociedad Económica de Amigos del País.

1958a   Comentario al Códice Baranda. In *Miscelánea Paul Rivet, Octogenario Dicata,* 1:373–393. Mexico City: Universidad Nacional Autónoma de México.

1958b   Lienzo de Yolotepec. *Memoria de El Colegio Nacional* 3 [for 1957], no. 4:41–55.

1959   El dios 1 Muerte. *Mitteilungen aus dem Museum für Völkerkunde und Vorgeschichte, Hamburg* 25:40–43.

1960a   The Historical Value of the Mixtec Codices. *Boletín de Estudios Oaxaqueños* 16:1–7.

1960b   *Interpretación del Códice Bodley 2858/Interpretation of the Codex Bodley 2858.* Accompanied by a facsimile of the codex. Mexico City: Sociedad Mexicana de Antropología.

1961   Los lienzos mixtecos de Ihuitlán y Antonio de Léon. In *Homenaje a Pablo Martínez del Río,* pp. 237–274. Mexico City: Instituto Nacional de Antropología e Historia.

1964a *Interpretación del Códice Selden 3135 (A.2)/Interpretation of the Codex Selden 3135 (A.2).* Accompanied by a facsimile of the codex. Mexico City: Sociedad Mexicana de Antropología.

1964b El Lienzo de Filadelfia. *Homenaje a Fernando Márquez-Miranda,* pp. 237–274, 12 plates. Madrid and Seville: Universidad de Sevilla, Seminario de Antropología Americana.

1965 Mixtec Writing and Calendar. In *Handbook of Middle American Indians,* vol. 3, edited by Robert Wauchope and Gordon Willey, pp. 948–961. Austin: University of Texas Press.

1966 *Interpretación del Códice Colombino/Interpretation of the Codex Colombino.* Accompanied by a facsimile of the codex. Mexico City: Sociedad Mexicana de Antropología.

1967 *Los calendarios prehispánicos.* Mexico City: Instituto de Investigaciones Históricas, Universidad Nacional Autónoma de México.

1971 Calendrical Systems of Central Mexico. In *Handbook of Middle American Indians,* vol. 10, edited by Robert Wauchope, pp. 333–348. Austin: University of Texas Press.

1977 *Reyes y reinos de la Mixteca.* Vol. 1. Mexico City: Fondo de Cultura Económica.

1979 *Reyes y reinos de la Mixteca.* Vol. 2, *Diccionario biográfico de los señores mixtecos.* Mexico City: Fondo de Cultura Económica.

1992 *El Códice de Huichapan, comentado por Alfonso Caso.* Edited by Oscar Reyes Retana M. Mexico City: Telecomunicaciones de México.

1996 *Códice Alfonso Caso: La vida de 8-Venado, Garra de Tigre (Colombino-Becker I).* Introduction by Miguel León-Portilla. Mexico City: Patronato Indígena.

Certeau, Michel de

1984 *The Practice of Everyday Life.* Berkeley: University of California Press.

Chatman, Seymour

1978 *Story and Discourse: Narrative Structure in Fiction and Film.* Ithaca: Cornell University Press.

1981a Critical Response, V. Reply to Barbara Herrnstein Smith. In Mitchell 1981, 258–265.

1981b What Novels Can Do That Films Can't (and Vice Versa). In Mitchell 1981, 117–136.

Chavero, Alfredo

c. 1887 *México a través de los siglos.* Vol. 1, *Historia antigua y de la conquista.* Edited by Vicente Riva Palacio. Barcelona: Espasa y Compañía.

1892 *Antigüedades mexicanas publicadas por la Junta*

Colombina de México en el cuarto centenario del descubrimiento de América. Mexico City: Oficina Tipográfica de la Secretaría de Fomento.

Chimalpahin [Cuauhtlehuanitzin], Francisco de San Antón Muñón

1965 *Relaciones originales de Chalco Amaquemecan.* Translated and edited by Silvia Rendón. Mexico City: Fondo de Cultura Económica.

1997 *Codex Chimalpahin.* Vol. 1, *Society and Politics in Mexico Tenochtitlan, Tlatelolco, Texcoco, Culhuacan, and Other Nahuatl Altepetl in Central Mexico.* Translated and edited by Arthur J. O. Anderson and Susan Schroeder. Norman: University of Oklahoma Press.

Christensen, Bodil, and Samuel Martí

1971 *Brujerías y papel precolombino/Witchcraft and Pre-Columbian Paper.* Mexico City: Ediciones Euroamericanas.

Clark, James Cooper

1912 *The Story of "Eight Deer" in Codex Colombino.* London: Taylor and Francis.

1938 *Codex Mendoza. The Mexican Manuscript Known as the Collection of Mendoza and Preserved in the Bodleian Library, Oxford.* 3 vols. London: Waterlow and Sons.

Clavigero, Francisco Javier

1780/81 *Storia antica del Messico.* 4 vols. Cesena: Gregorio Biasini.

Cline, Howard F.

1973 Selected Nineteenth-Century Mexican Writers on Ethnohistory. In *Handbook of Middle American Indians,* vol. 13, edited by Howard F. Cline and Robert Wauchope, pp. 370–427. Austin: University of Texas Press.

Cline, S. L., ed. and trans.

1993 *The Book of Tributes: Early Sixteenth-Century Nahuatl Censuses from Morelos.* UCLA Latin American Center Publications 81. Los Angeles: University of California.

Codex Abraham Castellanos

1931 *Codex Abraham Castellanos.* Maya Society, Publication 5. Baltimore.

Codex Aubin. *See* Aubin 1893; Dibble 1963; Lehmann and Kutscher 1981; Peñafiel 1902.

Codex Azcatitlan. *See* Barlow 1949b; Barlow and Graulich 1995.

Codex Azoyu I. *See* Vega Sosa 1991.

Codex Baranda. *See* Acuña 1989; Caso 1958a.

Codex Becker I and Codex Becker II. *See* Nowotny 1964.

Codex Bodley. *See* Caso 1960b.

Codex Colombino. *See* Caso 1966, 1996.

Codex en Cruz. *See* Dibble 1942, 1981.

Codex Gómez de Orozco. *See* Caso 1954.

Codex Huexotzingo

1995   *The Huexotzinco Codex = El Códice de Huexo-
         tzinco: A Facsimile of the 1531 Huexotzinco Codex
         in the Harkness Collection.* With essays by Xavier
         Noguez, Sylvia Rogers Albro, and Thomas C. Al-
         bro II. Washington, D.C.: Library of Congress.

Codex Huichapan. *See* Caso 1992.

Codex Ixtlan

1931   *Codex Ixtlan.* Maya Society, Publication 3.
         Baltimore.

Codex Meixueiro

1931   *Codex Meixueiro.* Maya Society, Publication 4.
         Baltimore.

Codex Mendoza. *See* Clark 1938; Berdan and Anawalt 1992.

Codex Mexicanus. *See* Mengin 1952.

Codex Selden. *See* Caso 1964a.

Codex Telleriano-Remensis. *See* Hamy 1900; Quiñones
         Keber 1995.

Codex Tlatelolco. *See* Barlow 1948.

Codex Tulane. *See* Smith and Parmenter 1991.

Codex Vaticanus A/Ríos

1900   *See* Ehrle 1900.

1979   *Codex Vaticanus 3738 ("Cod. Vat. A," "Cod. Ríos")
         der Bibliotec Apostolica Vaticana.* Graz:
         Akademische Druck- u. Verlagsanstalt.

Codex Vienna or Codex Vindobonensis Mexicanus I.

1963   *Codex Vindobonensis Mexicanus 1, Österreichische
         Nationalbibliothek Wien,* history and description
         by Otto Adelhofer. Graz: Akademische Druck- u.
         Verlagsanstalt. *See also* Lehmann and Smital 1929;
         Anders, Jansen, and Pérez Jiménez 1992a.

Codex Xolotl. *See* Dibble 1951, 1980.

Codex Zouche-Nuttall. *See* Nuttall 1902, 1975; Troike 1987;
         Anders, Jansen, and Pérez Jiménez 1992b.

Coe, Michael D.

1992   *Breaking the Maya Code.* New York: Thames and
         Hudson.

Colección de documentos inéditos

1870   *Colección de documentos inéditos relativos al des-
         cubrimiento, conquista y organización de las an-
         tiguas posesiones españoles en América y Oceanía,*
         vol. 13. Madrid: José María Pérez.

Connerton, Paul

1989   *How Societies Remember.* Cambridge: Cambridge
         University Press.

Conway, Martin A.

1996   Autobiographical Knowledge and Autobiographi-
         cal Memories. In *Remembering Our Past,* edited
         by David C. Rubin, pp. 67–93. Cambridge: Cam-
         bridge University Press.

Corona Núñez, José

1964–   *Antigüedades de México, basadas en la recopilación*
1967   *de Lord Kingsborough.* 4 vols. Mexico City: Secre-
         taría de Hacienda y Crédito Público.

Cortés, Hernán

1986   *Hernan Cortes: Letters from Mexico.* Translated
         and edited by Anthony Pagden. New Haven: Yale
         University Press.

Crónica Mexicayotl. *See* Alvarado Tezozomoc 1975.

Crump, Thomas

1990   *The Anthropology of Numbers.* Cambridge: Cam-
         bridge University Press.

Cuevas, Mariano

1929   The Codex Saville: America's Oldest Book. *His-
         torical Records and Studies* 19:7–20, and folding
         plate facing p. 4. New York: United States Catho-
         lic Historical Society.

Cummins, Tom

1995   The Madonna and the Horse. In *Native Artists
         and Patrons in Colonial Latin America,* edited
         by Emily Umberger and Tom Cummins, pp. 52–
         83. Special issue of *Phoebus—A Journal of Art
         History* 7.

Dark, Philip, and Joyce Plesters

1959   The Palimpsests of Codex Selden: Recent At-
         tempts to Reveal the Covered Pictographs. *Pro-
         ceedings of the 33rd International Congress of
         Americanists* 2:530–539. San José, Costa Rica.

Davies, Claude Nigel

1973   *Los mexicas: Primeros pasos hacia el imperio.* Mex-
         ico City: Instituto de Investigaciones Históricos,
         Universidad Nacional Autónoma de México.

1980   *The Aztecs: A History.* 2d ed. Norman: University
         of Oklahoma Press.

DeFrancis, John

1989   *Visible Speech: The Diverse Oneness of Writing Sys-
         tems.* Honolulu: University of Hawaii Press.

Díaz del Castillo, Bernal

1956   *The Discovery and Conquest of Mexico, 1517–1521.*
         Translated by Irving A. Leonard, edited by Genaro
         García. New York: Farrar, Straus and Cudahy.

Dibble, Charles E.

1955   The Aztec Writing System. In *Readings in An-
         thropology,* edited by E. Adamson Hoebel, Jesse
         D. Jennings, and Elmer Smith, pp. 296–302.
         New York: McGraw-Hill.

1971   Writing in Central Mexico. In *Handbook of
         Middle American Indians,* vol. 10, *The Archaeol-
         ogy of North America,* pt. 1, edited by Gordon F.
         Ekholm and Ignacio Bernal, pp. 322–332. Austin:
         University of Texas Press.

1973   The syllabic-alphabetic trend in Mexican codices.

40th International Congress of Americanists, Roma-Genova, 1972 1:373–378. Rome.

———, ed.

1942 *Códice en Cruz.* 1 vol. and portfolio. Mexico City: Talleres Linotipográficos Numancia.

1951 *Códice Xolotl.* Mexico City: Universidad Nacional de México and the University of Utah.

1963 *Historia de la nación mexicana. Reproducción a todo color del Códice de 1576 (Códice Aubin).* Madrid: Ediciones José Porrúa Turanzas.

1980 *Códice Xolotl.* 2 vols. Mexico City: Universidad Nacional Autónoma de México.

1981 *Codex en Cruz.* 2 vols. Salt Lake City: University of Utah Press.

Diel, Lori Boornazian

n.d.a Painting Colonial Mexico: The Appropriation of European Iconography in Mexican Manuscript Painting. In *Mesoamerican Manuscript Studies in Honor of Mary Elizabeth Smith,* edited by Elizabeth H. Boone. New Orleans: Middle American Research Institute, Tulane University. Forthcoming.

n.d.b Seats of Power in Colonial Mexico: Indigenous Paintings of a Spanish Icon of Rule. Paper presented at the College Art Association meeting, Los Angeles, February 1999.

n.d.c Spanish Names through Aztec Eyes: An Examination of the Hieroglyphic Depictions of Spanish Names within Colonial Aztec Codices. Paper written for seminar "Mesoamerican Manuscript Painting," Tulane University, spring 1996.

Diringer, David

1962 *Writing.* London: Thames and Hudson.

Durán, Diego

1971 *Book of the Gods and Rites and the Ancient Calendar.* Translated and edited by Fernando Horcasitas and Doris Heyden. Norman: University of Oklahoma Press.

1994 *The History of the Indies of New Spain.* Translated and edited by Doris Heyden. Norman: University of Oklahoma Press.

Edmonson, Munro S.

1988 *The Book of the Year: Middle American Calendrical Systems.* Salt Lake City: University of Utah Press.

Ehrle, Franz

1900 *Il manoscritto messicano vaticano 3738, detto il Codice Rios, riprodotto in fotocromografia a spese di sua eccellenza il duca de Loubat per cura della Biblioteca Vaticana.* Rome: Danesi.

Fane, Diana, ed.

1996 *Converging Cultures: Art and Identity in Spanish America.* New York: Brooklyn Museum in association with Harry N. Abrams.

Farrell, Brenda

1994 Ethno-graphics and the Moving Body. *Man* 29, no. 4:929–974.

Flannery, Kent, and Joyce Marcus, eds.

1983 *The Cloud People: Divergent Evolution of the Zapotec and Mixtec Civilizations.* New York: Academic Press.

Florescano, Enrique

1994 *Memory, Myth, and Time in Mexico: From the Aztecs to Independence.* Translated from the Spanish by Albert G. Bork with Kathryn R. Bork. Austin: University of Texas Press.

Furst, Jill

1977 The Tree Birth Tradition in the Mixteca, Mexico. *Journal of Latin American Lore* 3, no. 2:183–226.

1978a *Codex Vindobonensis Mexicanus I: A Commentary.* Albany: Institute for Mesoamerican Studies, State University of New York at Albany.

1978b The Life and Times of 8 Wind "Flinted Eagle." *Alcheringa* 4, no. 1:2–37.

1978c The Year 1 Reed, Day 1 Alligator: A Mixtec Metaphor. *Journal of Latin American Lore* 4, no. 1:93–128.

1982 Skeletonization in Mixtec Art: A Re-evaluation. In *Art and Iconography of Late Post-Classic Central Mexico,* edited by Elizabeth H. Boone, pp. 207–225. Washington, D.C.: Dumbarton Oaks.

1986 The Lords of "Place of the Ascending Serpent": Dynastic Succession on the Nuttall Obverse. In *Symbol and Meaning beyond the Closed Community: Essays in Mesoamerican Ideas,* edited by Gary H. Gossen, pp. 57–68. Albany: Institute of Mesoamerican Studies, State University of New York at Albany.

1987 Mixtec Narrative Conventions and Variations: Problems in Defining Codex Nuttall as Mixtec. *Latin American Indian Literatures Journal* 3, no. 1:9–26.

1990 Rulership and Ritual: Myth and the Origin of Political Authority in Mixtec Pictorial Manuscripts. In *Circumpacifica: Festschrift für Thomas S. Barthel,* edited by Bruno Illius and Matthias Laubscher, 1:123–141. Frankfurt am Main: Peter Lang.

Freedberg, David

1989 *The Power of Images: Studies in the History and Theory of Response.* Chicago: University of Chicago Press.

Galarza, Joaquín

1966 Glyphes et attributs chrétiens dans les manuscrits pictographiques mexicains du XVIe siècle: Le

Codex Mexicains 23–24. *Journal de la Société des Américanistes* 55, no. 1:7–42.

1979   *Estudios de escritura indígena tradicional (Azteca-Nahuatl).* Mexico City: Archivo General de la Nación.

Gaur, Albertine

1992   *A History of Writing.* Rev. ed. New York: Cross River Press.

García Icazbalceta, Joaquín, ed.

1941   *Nueva colección de documentos para la historia de México.* 3 vols. Mexico City: Salvador Chávez Hayhoe.

Garibay K., Angel Ma.

1979   *Teogonía e historia de los mexicanos: Tres opúsculos del siglo XVI.* Mexico City: Editorial Porrúa.

Gelb, I. J.

1963   *A Study of Writing.* 2d ed. Chicago: University of Chicago Press.

Gell, Alfred

1992   *The Anthropology of Time: Cultural Constructions of Temporal Maps and Images.* Oxford: Berg.

Gibson, Charles

1964   *Aztecs under Spanish Rule.* Stanford: Stanford University Press.

1971   Structure of the Aztec Empire. In *Handbook of Middle American Indians,* vol. 10, edited by Robert Wauchope, Gordon F. Ekholm and Ignacio Bernal, pp. 376–394. Austin: University of Texas Press.

Gibson, Charles, and John B. Glass

1975   A Census of Middle American Prose Manuscripts in the Native Historical Tradition. In *Handbook of Middle American Indians,* vol. 15, edited by Robert Wauchope and Howard F. Cline, pp. 322–400. Austin: University of Texas Press.

Gillespie, Susan D.

1989   *The Aztec Kings: The Construction of Rulership in Mexica History.* Tucson: University of Arizona Press.

Glass, John B.

1964   *Catálogo de la colección de códices.* Mexico City: Museo Nacional de Antropología, *Instituto Nacional de Antropología e Historia.*

1974   *Aztec Chronology in the Codex of La Magdalena Mixiuca.* Contributions to the Ethnohistory of Mexico 1. Lincoln, Mass.: Conemex.

1975a   (in collaboration with Donald Robertson) A Census of Native Middle American Pictorial Manuscripts. In *Handbook of Middle American Indians,* vol. 14, edited by Robert Wauchope and Howard F. Cline, pp. 81–252. Austin: University of Texas Press.

1975b   A Survey of Native Middle American Pictorial Manuscripts. In *Handbook of Middle American Indians,* vol. 14, edited by Robert Wauchope and Howard F. Cline, pp. 3–80. Austin: University of Texas Press.

Goodheart, Adam

1995   The Invasion That Never Was. *Civilization: The Magazine of the Library of Congress* 2, no. 1:40–43.

Goody, Jack

1982   Alternative Paths in Knowledge in Oral and Written Cultures. In *Spoken and Written Language: Exploring Orality and Literacy,* edited by Deborah Tannen, pp. 201–215. New Jersey: Ablex.

1986   *The Logic of Writing and the Organization of Society.* Cambridge: Cambridge University Press.

1987   *The Interface between the Written and the Oral.* Cambridge: Cambridge University Press.

Greenleaf, Richard E.

1962   *Zumárraga and the Mexican Inquisition, 1536–1543.* Washington, D.C.: Academy of American Franciscan History.

Guest, Ann Hutchinson

1984   *Dance Notation: The Process of Recording Movement on Paper.* New York: Dance Horizons.

Gupta, Akhil, and James Fergerson

1992   Beyond "Culture": Space, Identity, and the Politics of Difference. *Cultural Anthropology* 7, no. 1:6–23.

Hamy, Ernest Theodore

1897   Le Codex Becker no. 1 et le Manuscrit du Cacique récemment publié par M. H. de Saussure. *Journal de la Société des Américanistes de Paris,* o.s., 1:171–174.

———, ed.

1899   *Codex Telleriano-Remensis. Manuscrit mexicain du Cabinet de Ch. M. Le Tellier, Archevêque de Reims, à la Bibliothèque Nationale (MS Mexicain no. 385).* Paris: Bibliothèque Nationale.

Hanke, Lewis

1974   *All Mankind Is One; A Study of the Disputation between Bartolomé de Las Casas and Juan Gines de Sepulveda in 1550 on the Intellectual and Religious Capacity of the American Indians.* DeKalb: Northern Illinois University Press.

Harbsmeier, Michael

1988   Inventions of Writing. In *State and Society: The Emergence and Development of Social Hierarchy and Political Centralization,* edited by John Gledhill and Barbara Bender, pp. 253–276. London: Unwin Hyman.

Harvey, H. R.

1986   Techialoyan Codices: Seventeenth-Century In-
        dian Land Titles in Central Mexico. In *Handbook
        of Middle American Indians, Supplement 4,* edited
        by Victoria Bricker and Ronald Spores, pp. 153–
        164. Austin: University of Texas Press.

Harwit, Martin

1996   *An Exhibit Denied: Lobbying the History of ENOLA
        GAY.* New York: Copernicus.

Hedeman, Anne D.

1985   Restructuring the Narrative: The Function of
        Ceremonial in Charles V's *Grandes chroniques de
        France.* In *Pictorial Narrative in Antiquity and
        the Middle Ages,* edited by Herbert L. Kessler and
        Marianna Shreve Simpson, pp. 171–181. Center
        for Advanced Studies in the Visual Arts Sympo-
        sium Series 4, Studies in the History of Art 16.
        Washington, D.C.: National Gallery of Art.

Hermann Lejarazu, Manuel A.

1997   El *Códice Muro* y los señores mixtecos de Ñunaha.
        In Rueda Smithers, Vega Sosa, and Martínez Ba-
        racas 1997, 1:319–332.

1998   Estudio e interpretación de un manuscrito mix-
        teco denominado: Códice Muro. M.A. thesis,
        Universidad Nacional Autónoma de México.

Hernández, Francisco

1959   *Historia natural de Nueva España.* 2 vols. (vols. 2
        and 3 of his *Obras completas*). Mexico City: Uni-
        versidad Nacional Autónoma de México.

Heyden, Doris

1989   *The Eagle, the Cactus, the Rock: The Roots of Mex-
        ico-Tenochtitlan's Foundation Myth and Symbol.*
        BAR International Series 484. Oxford: BAR.

Hill, Archibald A.

1967   The Typology of Writing Systems. In *Papers in
        Linguistics in Honor of Leon Dostert,* edited by
        William M. Austin, pp. 92–99. The Hague:
        Mouton.

Historia de los Mexicanos por Sus Pinturas

1941   *See* García Icazbalceta 1941, 3:209–240.

1979   *See* Garibay 1979, 23–66.

Historia Tolteca-Chichimeca

1976   *See* Kirchhoff, Odena Güemes, and Reyes García
        1976.

Howe, Kathleen Stewart

1992   The Relationship of Indigenous and European
        Styles in the *Codex Mendoza:* An Analysis of Pic-
        torial Style. In Berdan and Anawalt 1992, 1:25–33.

Hutchinson, Ann

1966   *Labanotation.* New York: Theatre Arts Books.

Jansen, Maarten

1979   Apoala y su importancia para la interpretación de
        los códices Vindobonensis y Nuttall. *42nd Inter-
        national Congress of Americanists, Paris, 1976*
        7:161–171.

1982   *Huisi tacu: Estudio interpretativo de un libro mix-
        teco antiguo: Codex Vindobonensis Mexicanus I.*
        2 vols. Amsterdam: Centro de Estudios y Docu-
        mentación Latinoamericanos.

1988a   The Art of Writing in Ancient Mexico: An Ethno-
        iconological Perspective. In *Visible Religion: An-
        nual for Religious Iconography,* vol. 6, *The Image
        in Writing,* pp. 86–113. Leiden: E. J. Brill.

1988b   Dates, Deities, and Dynasties: Non-durational
        Time in Mixtec Historiography. In *Continuity
        and Identity in Native America,* edited by Maar-
        ten Jansen, Peter van der Loo, and Roswitha
        Manning, pp. 156–192. Leiden: E. J. Brill.

1989   Nombres históricos e identidad étnica en los
        códices mixtecos. *Revista Europea de Estudios
        Latinoamericanos y del Caribe* 47:65–87.

1990   The Search for History in Mixtec Codices. *An-
        cient Mesoamerica* 1, no. 1:99–112.

1992   Mixtec Pictography: Conventions and Contents.
        In *Handbook of Middle American Indians,
        Supplement 5, Epigraphy,* edited by Victoria R.
        Bricker, pp. 20–33. Austin: University of Texas
        Press.

1994   *La gran familia de los reyes mixtecos. Libro expli-
        cativo de los códices llamados Egerton y Becker II.*
        Facsimile with commentary. Graz: Akademische
        Druck- u. Verlagsanstalt; Mexico City: Fondo de
        Cultura Económica.

1996   Lord 8 Deer and Nacxitl Topiltzin. *Mexicon* 18,
        no. 2:25–29.

1997   Un viaje a la Casa del Sol. *Arqueología Mexicana*
        4, no. 23:44–49.

1998a   Introduction to *The Shadow of Monte Alban: Poli-
        tics and Historiography in Postclassic Oaxaca, Mex-
        ico,* edited by Maarten Jansen, Peter Kröfges, and
        Michel R. Oudijk, pp. 1–12. CNWS Publications
        64. Leiden: Research School CNWS, Leiden
        University.

1998b   Monte Albán y Zaachila en los códices mixtecos.
        In *The Shadow of Monte Alban: Politics and His-
        toriography in Postclassic Oaxaca, Mexico,* edited
        by Maarten Jansen, Peter Kröfges, and Michel R.
        Oudijk, pp. 67–122. CNWS Publications 64. Lei-
        den: Research School CNWS, Leiden University.

Jansen, Maarten, and Margarita Gaxiola

1978   Primera Mesa Redonda de Estudios Mixtecos:
        Síntesis de las ponencias. *Estudios de Antropología*

e Historia 15. Mexico City: Centro Regional de Oaxaca, Instituto Nacional de Antropología e Historia.

Jansen, Maarten, and Gabina Aurora Pérez Jiménez

1983   The Ancient Mexican Astronomical Apparatus: An Iconographical Criticism. *Archaeoastronomy* 6:89–95.

1986   Iyadzehe Añute: Valor literario de los códices mixtecos. In *Etnicidad y pluralismo cultural: La dinámica étnica en Oaxaca,* edited by Alicia M. Barabas and Miguel A. Bartolomé, pp. 173–211. Mexico City: Instituto Nacional de Antropología e Historia.

Jiménez Moreno, Wigberto

1956   *Notas sobre historia antigua de México.* Mexico City: Sociedad de Alumnos de la Escuela Nacional de Antropología e Historia.

1961   Diferente principio del año entre diversos pueblos y sus consecuencias para la cronología prehispánica. *El México Antiguo* 9:137–152.

Jiménez Moreno, Wigberto, and Salvador Mateos Higuera, eds.

1940   *Códice Yanhuitlán.* Mexico City: Instituto Nacional de Antropología e Historia.

Johnson, Nicholas

1994   Las líneas rojas desvanecidas en el Lienzo de Tlapiltepec: Una red de pruebas. In *Códices y documentos sobre México, primer simposio,* edited by Constanza Vega Sosa, pp. 117–144. Mexico City: Instituto Nacional de Antropología e Historia.

1997   The Route from the Mixteca Alta into Southern Puebla on the *Lienzo of Tlapiltepec.* In Rueda Smithers, Vega Sosa, and Martínez Baracas 1997, 1:233–268.

Keen, Benjamin

1971   *The Aztec Image in Western Thought.* New Brunswick, N.J.: Rutgers University Press.

Kellogg, Susan

1997   From Parallel and Equivalent to Separate but Unequal: Tenochca Mexica Women, 1500–1700. In *Indian Women of Early Mexico,* edited by Susan Schroeder, Stephanie Wood, and Robert Haskett, pp. 123–143. Norman: University of Oklahoma Press.

Kessler, Herb, and Marianna Shreve Simpson, eds.

1985   *Pictorial Narrative in Antiquity and the Middle Ages.* Center for Advanced Studies in the Visual Arts Symposium Series 4, Studies in the History of Art 16. Washington, D.C.: National Gallery of Art.

King, Mark

1990   Poetics and Metaphor in Mixtec Writing. *Ancient Mesoamerica* 1, no. 1:141–151.

1994   Hearing the Echoes of Verbal Art in Mixtec Writing. In Boone and Mignolo 1994, 103–136.

Kingsborough, Lord

1831–   *Antiquities of Mexico, Comprising Facsimiles of*
1848   *Ancient Mexican Paintings and Hieroglyphs.* 9 vols. London: A. Aglio.

Kircher, Athanasius

1652–   *Oedipus Aegyptiacus.* 3 vols. in 2. Rome: Ex Typo-
1654   graphia V. Mascardi.

Kirchhoff, Paul

1940   Los pueblos de la Historia Tolteca-Chichimeca: Sus migraciones y parentesco. *Revista Mexicana de Estudios Antropológicos* 4:77–104.

1948   Civilizing the Chichimecs: A Chapter in the Culture History of Ancient Mexico. *Latin American Studies,* no. 5. Austin: University of Texas. Reprinted in *Ancient Mesoamerica: Selected Readings,* edited by John A. Graham, pp. 273–278. Palo Alto, Calif.: Peek Publications, 1966.

1949   A New Analysis of Native Mexican Chronologies. Paper presented at the 19th International Congress of Americanists, New York.

1950   *The Mexican Calendar and the Founding of Tenochtitlan-Tlatelolco.* Transactions of the American Philosophical Society, ser. 1, vol. 12, no. 4. Philadelphia.

Kirchhoff, Paul, Lina Odena Güemes, and Luis Reyes García

1976   *Historia Tolteca-Chichimeca.* Mexico City: Instituto Nacional de Antropología e Historia.

Klor de Alva, Jorge

1989   Language, Politics, and Translation: Colonial Discourse and Classical Nahuatl in New Spain. In *The Art of Translation: Voices from the Field,* edited by Rosanna Warren, pp. 143–162. Boston: Northeastern University Press.

König, Viola

1979   *Inhaltliche Analyse und Interpretation von Codex Egerton.* Beiträg zur mittelamerikanischen Völkerkunde 15, Hamburgischen Museum für Völkerkunde. Munich: Klaus Renner.

1984   Der Lienzo Seler II und seine Stellung Innerhalb der Coixtlahuaca-Gruppe. *Baessler-Archiv,* n.s., 32, no. 2:229–320.

Kubler, George

1964   On the Colonial Extinction of the Motifs of Pre-Columbian Art. In *Essays in Pre-Columbian Art and Archaeology,* by S. K. Lothrop et al., pp. 14–34. Cambridge: Harvard University Press.

Kubler, George, and Charles Gibson
1951   *The Tovar Calendar: An Illustrated Mexican Manuscript ca. 1585.* Memoirs of the Connecticut Academy of Arts and Sciences, vol. 11. New Haven.

Laban, Rudolf
1974   *The Language of Movement: A Guidebook of Choreutics.* Annotated and edited by Lisa Ullmann. Boston: Plays.

Laet, Joannes de
1633   *Novus orbis, seu Descriptionis Indiae Occidentalis, libri XVIII.* Batavia: Elzevirios.

Lanouette, William
1995   Why We Dropped the Bomb. *Civilization: The Magazine of the Library of Congress* 2, no. 1: 28–39.

Larsen, Mogens Trolle
1988   The Role of Writing and Literacy in the Development of Social and Political Power. In *State and Society: The Emergence and Development of Social Hierarchy and Political Centralization,* edited by John Gledhill and Barbara Bender, pp. 173–191. London: Unwin Hyman.

Las Casas, Bartolomé de
1967   *Apologética historia sumaria.* 2 vols. Edited by Edmundo O'Gorman. Mexico City: Instituto de Investigaciones Históricas, Universidad Nacional Autónoma de México.

Lehmann, Walter, and Gerdt Kutscher, trans. and eds.
1981   *Geschichte der Azteken: Codex Aubin und verwandte Dokumente.* Berlin: Gebr. Mann.

Lehmann, Walter, and Ottokar Smital
1929   *Codex Vindobonensis Mexic, 1. Faksimileausgabe der Mexikanischen Bilderhandschrift der Nationalbibliothek in Wien.* 2 vols. Vienna: Kunstanstalt Max Jaffe.

Leibsohn, Dana
1993   The Historia Tolteca-Chichimeca: Recollecting Identity in a Nahua Manuscript. Ph.D. diss., University of California at Los Angeles.
1994   Primers for Memory: Cartographic Histories and Nahua Identity. In Boone and Mignolo 1994, 161–187.
1995   Colony and Cartography: Shifting Signs on Indigenous Maps of New Spain. In *Reframing the Renaissance: Visual Culture in Europe and Latin America, 1450–1650,* edited by Claire Farago, pp. 264–281. New Haven: Yale University Press.
1996   Mapping Metaphors: Figuring the Ground of Sixteenth-Century New Spain. *Journal of Medieval and Early Modern Studies* 26, no. 3: 497–523.

Lenz, Hans
1973   *El papel indígena mexicano.* Mexico City: Secretaría de Educación Pública.

León-Portilla, Miguel
1963   *Aztec Thought and Culture: A Study of the Ancient Nahuatl Mind.* Civilization of the American Indian Series 67. Norman: University of Oklahoma Press.
1966   *The Broken Spears: The Aztec Account of the Conquest of Mexico.* Boston: Beacon Press.
1975   *Trece poetas del mundo azteca.* Mexico City: Universidad Nacional Autónoma de México.
1986   *Pre-Columbian Literatures of Mexico.* Translated from the Spanish by Grace Lobanov and the author. Norman: University of Oklahoma Press.
1992a   *The Aztec Image of Self and Society: An Introduction to Nahua Culture.* Introduction by J. Jorge Klor de Alva. Salt Lake City: University of Utah Press.
1992b   Have We Really Translated the Mesoamerican "Ancient Word"? In *On the Translation of Native American Literatures,* edited by Brian Swann, pp. 313–338. Washington, D.C.: Smithsonian Institution Press.

Lockhart, James
1992   *The Nahuas after the Conquest: A Social and Cultural History of the Indians of Central Mexico, Sixteenth through Eighteenth Centuries.* Stanford: Stanford University Press.

López de Gómara, Francisco
1964   *Cortés: The Life of the Conqueror by His Secretary.* Translated and edited by Lesley Byrd Simpson. Berkeley: University of California Press.

Lounsbury, Floyd
1989   The Ancient Writing of Middle America. In *The Origins of Writing,* edited by Wayne M. Senner, pp. 203–237. Lincoln: University of Nebraska Press.

Mapa Tlotzin
1849   *Mappe Tlotzin: Histoire du royaume d'Acolhuacan ou de Texcuco (peinture non chronologique).* Paris: Lith. de Jules Desportes.

Marcus, Joyce
1992   *Mesoamerican Writing Systems.* Princeton: Princeton University Press.

Martin, Henri-Jean
1994   *The History and Power of Writing.* Translated by Lydia G. Cochrane. Chicago: University of Chicago Press.

Martínez Cortés, Fernando
1974   *Pegamentos, gomas y resinas en el México prehis-*

pánico. Mexico City: Secretaría de Educación Pública.

Martir de Angleria, Pedro [Martyr d'Anghiera, Peter]

1964   *Décadas del Nuevo Mundo.* 2 vols. Edited by Edmundo O'Gorman, translated by Agustín Millares Carlo. Mexico City: José Porrúa e Hijos.

McAnany, Patricia A.

1995   *Living with the Ancestors: Kinship and Kingship in Ancient Maya Society.* Austin: University of Texas Press.

Mendieta, Gerónimo de

1971   *Historia eclesiástica indiana.* Edited by Joaquín García Icazbalceta. Facsimile of the 1870 edition. Mexico City: Editorial Porrúa.

Mengin, Ernst

1942   *Historia Tolteca-Chichimeca.* Corpus Codicum Americanorum Medii Aevi 1. Copenhagen: Einar Munksgaard.

1952   Commentaire du Codex Mexicanus Nos. 23–24 de la Bibliothèque Nationale de Paris. *Journal de la Société des Américanistes* 41, no. 2:387–498. Facsimile of the codex published as a supplement to the *Journal.*

Mignolo, Walter

1992a   The Darker Side of the Renaissance: Colonization and the Discontinuity of the Classical Tradition. *Renaissance Quarterly* 45, no. 4:808–828.

1992b   Nebrija in the New World: The Question of the Letter, the Colonization of Amerindian Languages, and the Discontinuity of the Classical Tradition. *L'Homme, Revue Française d'Anthropologie* 32, nos. 122–124:185–207.

1992c   On the Colonization of Amerindian Languages and Memories: Renaissance Theories of Writing and the Discontinuity of the Classical Tradition. *Comparative Studies in Society and History* 34, no. 2:301–330.

1992d   Putting the Americas on the Map (Geography and the Colonization of Space). *Colonial Latin American Review* 1, nos. 1–2:25–63.

1992e   When Speaking Was Not Good Enough: Illiterates, Barbarians, Savages, and Cannibals. In *Amerindian Images and the Legacy of Columbus,* edited by René Jara and Nicholas Spadaccini, pp. 312–345. Minneapolis: University of Minnesota Press.

1994a   Afterword: Writing and Recorded Knowledge in Colonial and Postcolonial Situations. In Boone and Mignolo 1994, 292–313.

1994b   Signs and Their Transmission: The Question of the Book in the New World. In Boone and Mignolo 1994, 220–270.

1995a   *The Darker Side of the Renaissance: Literacy, Territoriality, and Colonization.* Ann Arbor: University of Michigan Press.

1995b   Literacy and the Colonization of Memory: Writing Histories of People without History. In *Literacy: Interdisciplinary Conversations,* edited by Deborah Keller-Cohen, pp. 91–113. Creskill, N.J.: Hampton Press.

Miller, Arthur G.

1975   Introduction to the Dover Edition. *The Codex Nuttall: A Picture Manuscript from Ancient Mexico.* Peabody Museum facsimile. Edited by Zelia Nuttall, pp. vii–xviii. New York: Dover Publications.

Mink, Louis

1981   Critical Response, I. "Everyman Is His or Her Own Analyst": A Reply to Hayden White. In Mitchell 1981, 233–239.

Mitchell, W. J. T., ed.

1981   *On Narrative.* Chicago: University of Chicago Press.

Molina, Alonso de

1970   *Vocabulario en lengua castellana y mexicana y mexicana y castellana.* 4th ed. Edited by Miguel León-Portilla. Mexico City: Editorial Porrúa.

Monaghan, John

1990   Performance and the Structure of the Mixtec Codices. *Ancient Mesoamerica* 1, no. 1:113–140.

Motolinía [Toribio de Benvente]

1951   *Motolinía's History of the Indians of New Spain.* Translated and edited by Francis Borgia Steck. Washington, D.C.: Academy of American Franciscan History.

1971   *Memoriales o libro de las cosas de Nueva España y de los naturales de ella.* Edited by Edmundo O'Gorman. Mexico City: Universidad Nacional Autónoma de México, Instituto de Investigaciones Históricas.

Mundy, Barbara E.

1996   *The Mapping of New Spain: Indigenous Cartography and the Maps of the Relaciones Geográficas.* Chicago: University of Chicago Press.

Nicholson, H. B.

1960   The Mixteca-Puebla Concept in Mesoamerican Archaeology: A Re-Examination. In *Men and Cultures: Selected Papers from the Fifth International Congress of Anthropological and Ethnological Sciences, Philadelphia, September 1–9, 1956,* edited by Anthony F. C. Wallace, pp. 612–617. Philadelphia: University of Pennsylvania.

1967   The Royal Headband of the Tlaxcalteca. *Revista Mexicana de Estudios Antropológicos* 21:71–106.

1971　Pre-Hispanic Central Mexican Historiography. In *Investigaciones contemporáneas sobre historia de México: Memorias de la Tercera Reunión de historiadores mexicanos y norteamericanos, Oaxtepec, Morelos, 4–7 de noviembre de 1969*, pp. 38–81. Mexico City: Universidad Nacional Autónoma de México, El Colegio de México; Austin: University of Texas.

1973　Phoneticism in the Late Pre-Hispanic Central Mexican Writing System. *Mesoamerican Writing Systems: A Conference at Dumbarton Oaks, October 30th and 31st, 1971*, edited by Elizabeth P. Benson, pp. 1–46. Washington, D.C.: Dumbarton Oaks.

1976　Correlating Mesoamerican Historical Traditions with Archaeological Sequence: Some Methodological Considerations. In *Actes du XLII Congrès International des Américanistes, Paris, 1–9 septembre 1976*, 9B:187–198.

1978　The Deity 9 Wind "Ehecatl-Quetzalcoatl" in the Mixtec Pictorials. *Journal of Latin American Lore* 4, no. 1:61–92.

1982　The Mixteca-Puebla Concept Revisited. In *The Art and Iconography of Late Post-Classic Central Mexico*, edited by Elizabeth Hill Boone, pp. 227–254. Washington, D.C.: Dumbarton Oaks.

1992　The History of the Codex Mendoza. In Berdan and Anawalt 1992, 1:1–11.

n.d.　Ce Acatl Nacxitl Topiltzin Quetzalcoatl of Tollan = 4 Jaguar of "Cattail Frieze" and Military Ally of 8 Deer "Jaguar Claw"? In *Mesoamerican Manuscript Studies in Honor of Mary Elizabeth Smith*, edited by Elizabeth H. Boone. Forthcoming.

Nicholson, H. B., and Eloise Quiñones Keber
1994　Introduction to *Mixteca-Puebla: Discoveries and Research in Mesoamerican Art and Archaeology*, edited by H. B. Nicholson and Eloise Quiñones Keber, pp. vii–xv. Culver City, Calif.: Labyrinthos.

Noguez, Xavier, ed.
1978　*Tira de Tepechpan: Códice colonial procedente del valle de México*. 2 vols. Mexico City: Biblioteca Enciclopédica del Estado de México.

Nowotny, Karl Anton
1948　Erläuterungen zum Codex Vindobonensis (Vorderseite). *Archiv für Völkerkunde* 3:156–200.

1961　*Tlacuilolli: Die mexicanischen Bilderhandschriften, Stil und Inhalt, mit einem Katalog der codex-Borgia-Gruppe*. Berlin: Verlag Begr. Mann.

1964　*Codices Becker I/II. Comentario, descripción y corrección*. Translated by Baron W. v. Humboldt. Graz: Akademische Druck- u. Verlagsanstalt;

Mexico City: Instituto Nacional de Antropología e Historia.

1975　*El fragmento de Nochistlan*. Beiträg zur mittelamerikanischen Völkerkunde 13. Hamburg: Hamburgisches Museum für Völkerkunde; Munich: Klaus Renner Verlag.

1976　Kommentar. In *Codex Borgia, Biblioteca Apostolica Vaticana (Messicano Riserva 28)*. Graz: Akademische Druck- u. Verlagsanstalt.

Nowotny, Karl Anton, and Robert Strebinger
1959　Der Codex Becker I (Le Manuscrit du Cacique). Technische Beschreibung und mikroanalytische Untersuchung der Farbstoffe. *Archiv für Völkerkunde* 13:222–226.

Nuttall, Zelia, ed.
1902　*Codex Nuttall. Facsimile of an Ancient Mexican Codex Belonging to Lord Zouche of Harynworth, England*. Cambridge: Peabody Museum of American Archaeology and Ethnology, Harvard University.

1975　*The Codex Nuttall: A Picture Manuscript from Ancient Mexico*. New York: Dover Publications.

Offner, Jerome A.
1982　Aztec Legal Process: The Case of Texcoco. In *The Art and Iconography of Late Post-Classic Central Mexico*, edited by Elizabeth H. Boone, pp. 141–157. Washington, D.C.: Dumbarton Oaks.

1983　*Law and Politics in Aztec Texcoco*. Cambridge: Cambridge University Press.

Ong, Walter J.
1967　*The Presence of the Word*. New Haven: Yale University Press.

1982　*Orality and Literacy: The Technologizing of the Word*. London: Methuen.

Orozco y Berra, Manuel
1960　*Historia antigua y de la conquista de México*. 3 vols. Mexico City: Editorial Porrúa. First published in 1880.

Padden, R. C.
1967　*The Hummingbird and the Hawk: Conquest and Sovereignty in the Valley of Mexico, 1503–1541*. Columbus: Ohio State University Press.

Pandya, Vishvajit
1990　Movement and Space: Anamanese Cartography. *American Ethnologist* 17, no. 4:775–797.

Parkes, Don, and Nigel Thrift
1980　*Times, Spaces, and Places: A Chronogeographic Perspective*. Chichester: John Wiley and Sons.

Parmenter, Ross
1966　Break-through on the "Lienzo de Filadelfia." *Expedition* 8, no. 2:14–23.

1970　The Identification of Lienzo A: A Tracing in the

Latin American Library of Tulane University. Preprint from *Middle American Research Institute, Publication 12, Philological and Documentary Studies* 2, no. 5:181–195.

1982   *Four Lienzos of the Coixtlahuaca Valley.* Studies in Pre-Columbian Art and Archaeology 26. Washington, D.C.: Dumbarton Oaks.

1993   *The Lienzo of Tulancingo, Oaxaca.* Transactions of the American Philosophical Society, vol. 83, pt. 7. Philadelphia.

1997   A Nativitas Ruler List on *Lienzo A.* In Rueda Smithers, Vega Sosa, and Martínez Baracas 1997, 1:269–303.

Paso y Troncoso, Francisco del

1886   Códice indiano del Sr. Sánchez Solís. *Anales del Museo Nacional de México,* época 1, 3:121–123.

Peñafiel, Antonio

1885   *Nombres geográficos de México. Catálogo alfabético \de los nombres de lugar pertenecientes al idioma "Nahuatl."* Mexico City: Secretaría de Fomento.

1895   *Códice Fernández Leal.* Mexico City: Secretaría de Fomento.

1900   *Códice Mixteco: Lienzo de Zacatepec.* Mexico City: Secretaría de Fomento.

1902   *Códice Aubin. Manuscrito azteca de la Biblioteca Real de Berlin.* Mexico. Reprinted 1980 by Editorial Innovación, Mexico.

Pohl, John

1994a   *Notebook for the Mixtec Pictographic Writing Workshop at Texas: Codex Zouche Nuttall.* Third Mixtec Codex Studies Group, Austin, Texas, March 14–19, 1994.

1994b   *The Politics of Symbolism in the Mixtec Codices.* Vanderbilt University Publications in Anthropology 46. Nashville: Department of Anthropology, Vanderbilt University.

1996   *Codex Bodley: Notebook for the Mixtec Pictographic Writing Workshop, no. 3.* Fifth Mixtec Codex Studies Group, Austin, Texas, March 11–16, 1996.

Pohl, John M. D., and Bruce E. Byland

1990   Mixtec Landscape Perception and Archaeological Settlement Patterns. *Ancient Mesoamerica* 1, no. 1:113–131.

1994   The Mixteca Puebla Style and Early Post Classic Socio-Political Integration. In *Mixteca-Puebla: Discoveries and Research in Mesoamerican Art and Archaeology,* edited by H. B. Nicholson and Eloise Quiñones Keber, pp. 189–199. Culver City, Calif.: Labyrinthos.

1996   The Identification of the Xipe Bundle–Red and White Bundle Place Sign in the Mixtec Codices. *Journal of Latin American Lore* 19:3–29.

Pomar, Juan Bautista

1941   Relación de Texcoco. *See* García Icazbalceta 1941, 3:1–64.

Prem, Hanns J.

1969–   Aztec Hieroglyphic Writing System—Possibilities
1970   and Limits. *38th International Congress of Americanists, Stuttgart-München,* 2:159–165. Munich: Klaus Rener.

1992   Aztec Writing. In *Handbook of Middle American Indians, Supplement 5, Epigraphy,* edited by Victoria R. Bricker, pp. 53–69. Austin: University of Texas Press.

Prem, Hanns J., and Berthold Riese

1983   Autochthonous American Writing Systems: The Aztec and Maya Examples. In *Writing in Focus,* edited by Florian Coulmas and Konrad Ehlich, pp. 167–186. Berlin: Mouton.

Preus, Konrad Theodor, and Ernst Mengin, trans. and eds.

1937–   Die mexikanische Bilderhandschrift Historia
1938   Tolteca-Chichimeca. Part 1, Die Bilderhandschrift nebst Übersetzung, *Baessler Archiv,* Supplement 9 (1937). Part 2, Der Kommentar, *Baessler Archiv* 21 (1938): 1–66.

Procesos

1912   *Procesos de indios idólatras y hechiceros.* Publicaciones del Archivo General de la Nación 3. Mexico City.

Quiñones Keber, Eloise

1984   Art as History: The Illustrated Chronicle of the Codex Telleriano-Remensis as a Historical Source. In *The Native Sources and the History of the Valley of Mexico,* edited by Jacqueline de Durand-Forest, pp. 95–116. Proceedings of the 44th International Congress of Americanists, Manchester, 1982, general editor, Norman Hammond. BAR International Series 204. Oxford: BAR.

1994   The Codex Style: Which Codex? Which Style? In *Mixteca-Puebla: Discoveries and Research in Mesoamerican Art and Archaeology,* edited by H. B. Nicholson and Eloise Quiñones Keber, pp. 143–152. Culver City, Calif.: Labyrinthos.

———, ed.

1995   *Codex Telleriano-Remensis: Ritual, Divination, and History in a Pictorial Aztec Manuscript.* Austin: University of Texas Press.

Rabin, Emily

1979   The War of Heaven in Codices Zouche-Nuttall and Bodley: A Preliminary Study. *Actas del XLII Congreso Internacional de Americanistas* (Paris) 7:173–182.

Radin, Paul

1920   The Sources and Authenticity of the History of

the Ancient Mexicans. *University of California Publications in American Archaeology and Ethnology* 17, no. 1 : 1–150, 17 pls.

Ramírez, José Fernando

1858   Cuadro histórico-geroglífico de la peregrinación de las tribus aztecas que poblaron el Valle de México, num. 1 (and num. 2). Acompañado de algunas explicaciones para sus inteligencia por José Fernando Ramírez. In *Atlas geográfico, estadístico e histórico de la República Mexicana,* edited by Antonio García y Cubas. Mexico City: Imprenta de José Mariano Fernández de Lara. Not paginated.

Reyes García, Luis

1988   *Cuauhtinchan del siglo XII al XVI.* 2d ed. Mexico City: Fondo de Cultura Económica. First edition published in 1977 by Franz Steiner Verlag, Weisbaden.

Ricoeur, Paul

1981   Narrative Time. In Mitchell 1981, 165–186.

1984–   *Time and Narrative.* 3 vols. Translated from the

1988   French by Kathleen McLaughlin and David Pellaver (vols. 1 and 2) and Kathleen Blamey and David Pellaver (vol. 3). Chicago: University of Chicago Press.

Rincon Mautner, Carlos

1997   Reading the History of Place-Becoming in the Codices from the Coixtlahuaca Basin. In *Latin American Indian Literatures: Messages and Meanings,* edited by Mary H. Preuss, pp. 129–148. Papers from the Twelfth Annual Symposium, Latin American Indian Literatures Association. Lancaster, Calif.: Labyrinthos.

Robertson, Donald

1959   *Mexican Manuscript Painting of the Early Colonial Period: The Metropolitan Schools.* New Haven: Yale University Press.

1964   Los manuscritos religiosos mixtecos. *Proceedings of the 35th International Congress of Americanists* (Mexico 1962) 1 : 425–435.

1970   The Tulum Murals: The International Style of the Late Postclassic. *Verhandlungen des 88th Internationalen Amerikanisten-Kongresses, Stuttgart-München, 1968* 2 : 77–88.

1971   Commentary. In *Investigaciones contemporáneas sobre historia de México: Memorias de la Tercera Reunión de historiadores mexicanos y norteamericanos, Oaxtepec, Morelos, 4–7 de noviembre de 1969,* pp. 91–95. Mexico City: Universidad Nacional Autónoma de México, El Colegio de México; Austin: University of Texas.

1982   A Preliminary Note on the Codex Tulane. In *Coloquio internacional: Los indígenas de México en la época prehispánica y en la actualidad,* edited by Maarten Jansen and Ted Leyenaar, pp. 223–231. Leiden: Rijksmuseum voor Volkenkunde.

1983   Comments on the Earliest Mixtec Dynastic Records. Topic 68 in Flannery and Marcus 1983, 213–214.

Robertson, Donald, and Martha Robertson

1975   Techialoyan Manuscripts and Paintings, with a Catalog. In *Handbook of Middle American Indians,* vol. 14, edited by Howard Cline and Robert Wauchope, pp. 253–280. Austin: University of Texas Press.

Rodman, Margaret

1992   Empowering Place: Multilocality and Multivocality. *American Anthropologist* 94 : 640–656.

Root, Deborah

1988   The Imperial Signifier: Todorov and the Conquest of Mexico. *Cultural Critique* 9 : 197–219.

Rueda Smithers, Salvador, Costanza Vega Sosa, and Rodrigo Martínez Baracas, eds.

1997   *Códices y documentos sobre México, segundo simposio internacional.* Mexico City: Instituto Nacional de Antropología e Historia and Consejo Nacional para la Cultura y las Artes.

Sahagún, Bernardino de

1959–   *Florentine Codex: General History of the Things of*

1982   *New Spain.* Translated and edited by Charles E. Dibble and Arthur J. O. Anderson. 12 books in 13 vols. Santa Fe: School of American Research and the University of Utah.

1993   *Primeros Memoriales: Facsimile Edition.* Photographed by Ferdinand Anders. Norman: University of Oklahoma Press.

1997   *Primeros Memoriales by Bernardino de Sahagún: Paleography of Nahuatl Text and English Translation,* edited by Thelma D. Sullivan, revised by H. B. Nicholson et al. Norman: University of Oklahoma Press.

Sampson, Geoffrey

1985   *Writing Systems: A Linguistic Introduction.* Stanford: Stanford University Press.

Sandstrom, Alan R., and Pamela E. Sandstrom

1986   *Traditional Papermaking and Paper Cult Figures of Mexico.* Norman: University of Oklahoma Press.

Saussure, Henri Louis Frederic de

1891   *Antiquités mexicaines: Le manuscrit du Cacique.* Geneva: Aubert-Schuchardt.

Schacter, Daniel L.

1996   *Searching for Memory: The Brain, the Mind, and the Past.* New York: Harper Collins.

Scholes, Robert

1981   Afterthoughts on Narrative, II: Language, Narrative, and Anti-Narrative. In Mitchell 1981, 200–208.

Schroeder, Susan

1991   *Chimalpahin and the Kingdoms of Chalco*. Tucson: University of Arizona Press.

Schwede, Rudolf

1916   Ein weiterer Beitrag zur Geschichte des altmexikanischen Papiers. *Jahresbericht der Vereinigung für angewandte Botanik* 13 : 35–55. Berlin.

Seler, Eduard

1902–   *Gesammelte Abhandlungen zur amerikanischen*

1923   *Sprach- und Alterthumskunde*. 5 vols. and index. Berlin. Reprinted 1960–1961, Graz: Akademische Druck- u. Verlagsanstalt.

Senner, Wayne M., ed.

1989   *The Origins of Writing*. Lincoln: University of Nebraska Press.

Siméon, Rémi

1981   *Diccionario de la lengua nahuatl o mexicana*. Translated from the French by Josefina Oliva de Coll. Mexico City: Siglo Veintiuno.

Simons, Bente Bittmann

1968   *Los mapas de Cuauhtinchan y la "Historia tolteca-chichimeca."* Investigaciones 15. Mexico City: Instituto Nacional de Antropología e Historia.

Smith, Barbara Herrnstein

1981   Narrative Versions, Narrative Theories. In Mitchell 1981, 209–232.

Smith, Mary Elizabeth

1963   The Codex Colombino: A Document of the South Coast of Oaxaca. *Tlalocan* 4, no. 3 : 276–288.

1966   *Las glosas del Códice Colombino/The Glosses of Codex Colombino*. Bound with Caso 1966.

1973a   *Picture Writing from Ancient Southern Mexico: Mixtec Place Signs and Maps*. Norman: University of Oklahoma Press.

1973b   The Relationship between Mixtec Manuscript Painting and the Mixtec Language: A Study of Some Personal Names in Codices Muro and Sánchez Solís. In *Mesoamerican Writing Systems*, edited by Elizabeth P. Benson, pp. 47–98. Washington, D.C.: Dumbarton Oaks.

1979   Codex Becker II: A Manuscript from the Mixteca Baja? *Archiv für Völkerkunde* 33 : 29–43.

1983a   Codex Selden: A Manuscript from the Valley of Nochixtlán? Topic 20 in Flannery and Marcus 1983, 248–255.

1983b   The Mixtec Writing System. Topic 71 in Flannery and Marcus, 1983, 238–245.

1983c   Regional Points of View in the Mixtec Codices. Topic 76 in Flannery and Marcus, 1983, 260–266.

1988   It Doesn't Amount to a Hill of Beans: The Frijol Motif in Mixtec Place Signs. In *Smoke and Mist: Mesoamerican Studies in Memory of Thelma D. Sullivan*, edited by J. Kathryn Josserand and Karin Dakin, pp. 696–710. BAR International Series 402. Oxford: BAR.

1994   Why the Second Codex Selden Was Painted. In *The Caciques and Their People: A Volume in Honor of Ronald Spores*, edited by Joyce Marcus and Judith Francis Zeitlin, pp. 111–141. Ann Arbor: Museum of Anthropology, University of Michigan.

1998   *The Codex López Ruiz: A Lost Mixtec Pictorial Manuscript*. Vanderbilt University Publications in Anthropology 51. Nashville: Department of Anthropology, Vanderbilt University.

n.d.a   The Codex Muro as a Land Document. In *Mesoamerican Manuscript Studies in Honor of Mary Elizabeth Smith*, edited by Elizabeth H. Boone. New Orleans: Middle American Research Institute, Tulane University. Forthcoming.

n.d.b   The Hometown of the Rulers of the Codex Muro. In *Homenaje to Doris Heyden*, edited by Eloise Quiñones Keber. Culver City, Calif.: Labyrinthos. Forthcoming.

Smith, Mary Elizabeth, and Ross Parmenter

1991   *The Codex Tulane*. New Orleans: Middle American Research Institute, Tulane University.

Smith, Michael

1984   The Aztlan Migrations of the Nahuatl Chronicles: Myth or History? *Ethnohistory* 31, no. 3 : 153–186.

Spinden, Herbert J.

1935   Indian Manuscripts of Southern Mexico. *Smithsonian Institution Annual Reports of the Board of Regents*, June 1933, pp. 429–451, 3 pls. Washington, D.C.

Spitler, Susan

n.d.a   The Mapa Tlotzin: Preconquest History in Colonial Texcoco. *Journal de la Société des Américanistes*. Forthcoming.

n.d.b   *The Painted Histories of Texcoco: History as Legitimation of the Rule of Nezahualcoyotl*. Washington, D.C.: Dumbarton Oaks, Studies in Pre-Columbian Art and Archaeology. Forthcoming.

Spores, Ronald

1967   *The Mixtec Kings and Their People*. Civilization of the American Indian Series 85. Norman: University of Oklahoma Press.

1974   Marital Alliance in the Political Integration of Mixtec Kingdoms. *American Anthropologist* 76 : 287–311.

1984   *The Mixtecs in Ancient and Colonial Times.* Norman: University of Oklahoma Press.

Stern, Alison Meg

1998   The *Mapa Sigüenza:* A Mexica Migration Story. M.A. thesis, Tulane University.

Stone, Kurt

1980   *Musical Notation in the Twentieth Century: A Practical Guidebook.* New York: W. W. Norton.

Taylor, Isaac

1899   *The History of the Alphabet.* 2 vols. New York: Scribner's.

Tedlock, Dennis, trans. and ed.

1985   *Popol Vuh: The Mayan Book of the Dawn of Life.* New York: Simon and Schuster.

Thomas, Hugh

1995   *Conquest: Montezuma, Cortés, and the Fall of Old Mexico.* New York: Simon and Schuster.

Thompson, John Eric S.

1972   *A Commentary on the Dresden Codex: A Maya Hieroglyphic Book.* Philadelphia: American Philosophical Society.

Tira de Tepechpan. *See* Noguez 1978.

Todorov, Tzvetan

1984   *The Conquest of America.* Translated from the French by Richard Howard. New York: Harper and Row.

Torquemada, Juan de

1975–   *Monarquía indiana: De los veinte y un libros ri-*
1979   *tuales y monarquía indiana, con el origen y guerras de los indios occidentales, de sus poblazones, descubrimiento, conquista, conversión y otras cosas maravillosas de la mesma tierra.* 6 vols. Edited by Miguel León-Portilla. Mexico City: Universidad Nacional Autónoma de México.

Troike, Nancy P.

1974   The Codex Colombino-Becker. Ph.D. diss., University of London.

1978   Fundamental Changes in the Interpretation of the Mixtec Codices. *American Antiquity* 43, no. 4:553–568.

1979   Preliminary Notes on Stylistic Patterns in the Codex Bodley. *Actas del XLII Congreso Internacional de Americanistas, Mexico* 7:183–192.

1980   The identification of individuals in the Codex Colombino-Becker. *Tlalocan* 8:397–418.

1982a   The Interpretation of Postures and Gestures in the Mixtec Codices. In *The Art and Iconography of Late Post-Classic Central Mexico,* edited by Elizabeth H. Boone, pp. 175–206. Washington, D.C.: Dumbarton Oaks.

1982b   Studying Style in the Mixtec Codices: An Analysis of Variations in the Codex Colombino-Becker.

    In *Pre-Columbian Art History: Selected Readings,* edited by Alana Cordy-Collins, pp. 119–151. Palo Alto, Calif.: Peek Publications.

1987   Notes on the Codex Zouche-Nuttall. In *Codex Zouche-Nuttall, British Museum, London (Add. MS. 39671).* Graz: Akademische Druck- u. Verlagsanstalt.

n.d.   Notes on the Possible Source of the Codex Zouche-Nuttall and the Codex Colombino-Becker. Paper presented at the 41st International Congress of Americanists, Mexico City, 1974.

Tuan, Yi-fu

1990   *Topophilia: A Study of Environmental Perception, Attitudes, and Values.* 2d ed. New York: Columbia University Press.

Tufte, Edward

1983   *The Visual Display of Quantitative Information.* Cheshire, Conn.: Graphics Press.

van der Loo, Peter

1982   Rituales con manojos contados en el grupo Borgia y entre los tlapanecos de hoy día. In *Los indígenas de México en la época pre-hispánica y en la actualidad,* edited by Maarten Jansen and Ted Leyenaar, pp. 232–243. Leiden: Rijksmuseum voor Volkenkunde.

1987   *Códices, costumbres, continuidad: Un estudio de la religión mesoamericana.* Indiaanse Studies 2. Leiden: Archeologische Centrum R. U. Leiden.

1994   Voicing the Painted Image: A Suggestion for Reading the Reverse of the Codex Cospi. In Boone and Mignolo 1994, 77–86.

van Doesburg, Bas

n.d.   The Origin of the "Lienzo de Tulancingo": New Facts about a Pictographic Document from the Coixtlahuaca Region. *Ancient Mesoamerica.* Forthcoming.

van Zantwijk, Rudolf A. M.

1979   *Anales de Tula, Museo Nacional de Antropología, Mexico City (Cod. 35-9): Kommentar/Comentario.* Graz: Akademische Druck- u. Verlagsanstalt.

Vazquez, Juan A.

1983   The Cosmic Serpent in the Codex Baranda. *Journal of Latin American Lore* 9, no. 1:3–15.

Vega Sosa, Constanza

1986   El Códice Azoyú 1 y el Lienzo de Tlapa: Relaciones temáticas. In *Arqueología y etnohistoria del estado de Guerrero,* pp. 295–308. Mexico City: Instituto Nacional de Antropología e Historia and Gobierno del Estado de Guerrero.

———, ed.

1991   *Códice Azoyú: El reino de Tlachinollan.* 2 vols., including a facsimile. Mexico City: Fondo de Cultura Económica.

Veyne, Paul

1988   *Did the Greeks Believe in Their Myths? An Essay on Constitutive Imagination.* Translated by Paula Wissing. Chicago: University of Chicago Press.

Vogt, Evon Z.

1981   Some Aspects of Sacred Geography of Highland Chiapas. In *Mesoamerican Sites and World-Views,* edited by Elizabeth P. Benson, pp. 119–142. Washington, D.C.: Dumbarton Oaks.

von Hagen, Victor Wolfgang

1944   *The Aztec and Maya Papermakers.* New York: J. J. Augustin.

Waldman, Marilyn Robinson

1981   Critical Response, II. "The Otherwise Unnoteworthy Year 711": A Reply to Hayden White. In Mitchell 1981, 240–248.

White, Hayden

1973   *Metahistory: The Historical Imagination in Nineteenth-Century Europe.* Baltimore: Johns Hopkins University Press.

1981a   The Value of Narrativity in the Representation of Reality. In Mitchell 1981, 1–23.

1981b   Critical Response, III. The Narrativization of Real Events. In Mitchell 1981, 249–254.

1985   *Tropics of Discourse: Essays in Cultural Criticism.* Baltimore: Johns Hopkins University Press.

1987   *The Content of Form: Narrative Discourse and Historical Representation.* Baltimore: Johns Hopkins University Press.

Whitecotton, Joseph W.

1990   *Zapotec Elite Ethnohistory: Pictorial Genealogies from Eastern Oaxaca.* Vanderbilt University Publications in Anthropology 39. Nashville: Department of Anthropology, Vanderbilt University.

Whitrow, G. J.

1961   *The Natural Philosophy of Time.* London: Thomas Nelson & Sons.

Winter, Irene

1985   After the Battle Is Over: The *Stele of the Vultures* and the Beginning of Historical Narrative in the Art of the Ancient Near East. In *Pictorial Narrative in Antiquity and the Middle Ages,* edited by Herbert L. Kessler and Marianna Shreve Simpson, pp. 11–32. Center for Advanced Study in the Visual Arts Symposium Series 4, Studies in the History of Art 16. Washington, D.C.: National Gallery of Art.

Wolf, Eric R.

1982   *Europe and the People without History.* Berkeley: University of California.

Yoneda, Keiko

1991   *Los mapas de Cuauhtinchan y la historia cartográfica prehispánica.* 2d ed. Mexico City: Archivo General de la Nación.

Zorita, Alonso

1963   *Life and Labor in Ancient Mexico: The Brief and Summary Relation of the Lords of New Spain.* Edited and translated by Benjamin Keen. New Brunswick, N.J.: Rutgers University Press.

Index